Life Course Perspectives on Adulthood and Old Age

Edited by

Marsha Mailick Seltzer
University of Wisconsin–Madison

Marty Wyngaarden Krauss
Brandeis University

Matthew P. Janicki
New York State Office of Mental Retardation
and Developmental Disabilities

AAMR Special Publications
Michael J. Begab, Editor

American Association on Mental Retardation
Washington, DC
1994

Published by
American Association on Mental Retardation
444 North Capitol Street, NW
Washington, DC 20001 U.S.A.

. The points of view expressed herein are those of the authors and do not
necessarily represent the official policy or opinion of the American Association on
Mental Retardation. Publication does not imply endorsement by the Editors, the
Association, or its individual members.

Library of Congress Cataloging-in-Publication Data
Life course perspectives on adulthood and old age/edited by Marsha Mailick
Seltzer, Marty Wyngaarden Krauss, Matthew P. Janicki.
      p.   cm.
    Includes bibliographical references.
    ISBN 0-940898-31-4 (pbk.)
    1. Mentally handicapped aged—United States. 2. Developmentally disabled
aged—United States. 3. Mentally handicapped aged—Services for—United States.
4. Developmentally disabled aged—Services for—United States. I. Seltzer, Marsha
Mailick. II. Krauss, Marty Wyngaarden. III.
HV3009.5.A35L54 1994   93-41155
362.4'084'6 — dc20   CIP

Printed in the United States of America.

Contents

Foreword

Sharon Landesman Ramey
Craig T. Ramey
University of Alabama at Birmingham

What an exciting time to be part of the community of scholars, social scientists, practitioners, and advocates who are discovering the value of a life-span perspective. This volume is a tribute to the breadth, vigor, and sensitivity of the inquiry on adulthood and aging in developmental disabilities. The findings presented include those that are comforting and reassuring about how families adapt to continued decades of careproviding, as well as others that are provocative and counterintuitive. There are lessons to be learned from the grace and dignity shown by many individuals with mental retardation as they become older and wiser, as well as from families who prove that caring is a two-way, mutually interdependent system from which aging parents derive benefits as well. At the same time, this volume does not treat lightly the complexity of the health and clinical service issues or the need to address systems issues in future scientific inquiry.

There are two refreshing and delightful facts about this book. The first is that the excitement of the original Roundtable convened in Boston by Matthew Janicki, and Marsha Seltzer is captured in the chapters. We had the privilege of being part of that historic gathering and we have been changed as a result. We hope that, as you read these thoughtful contributions, you too will benefit and be encouraged in your own work. The second special dimension of this work is that it is undeniably interdisciplinary but does not bother to say much about this. We herald this as a sign of the success that accompanies effective interdisciplinary endeavors—that is, that the participants themselves forget to notice who comes from what disciplines, but jump into the issues and discussions of ideas directly. This is not a volume about health versus social well-being, family versus community responsibility, psychological versus sociological theories, gerontology versus developmental disabilities, participant observations techniques versus psychometrically robust instruments. Rather, it is about what is known today, what the key unanswered questions are, and where we might dream of being in a decade or two. The dreams are big ones. They encompass both a better world of service provision, one that is truly integrated yet retains special sensitivity to the needs of those with a lifelong history of developmental disabilities, and advances in the methods used in conducting longitudinal inquiry into people's everyday and very remarkable lives.

Historically, the field of mental retardation and developmental disabilities has received strong support for children especially young children. The hope and promise of a young life and the possibility of making a long lasting difference through early intervention are undeniable. Yet the specialty interest in adulthood and aging has added to the field an enlightened realization of why childhood is so important as the foundation for a personally rewarding and healthy later life. The revolution in the quality of support services and the value our society places on individuals with disabilities is reflected in the dramatically changing demography as well as the passage of the landmark legislation, the Americans with Disabilities Act of 1990. As we continue to educate ourselves and the next generation of practitioners and scientists, we will do well to remember that each age period may be enhanced by those that precede it and, in turn, influences those that follow.

To understand human development and to maximize opportunities for quality of life, a life-span perspective underscores the fact that we are never too old to learn, to benefit, to contribute, and to be valued members of our communities. With eagerness, we look forward to learning what results can be achieved when high quality, intensive interventions are interwoven with natural helpers and community supports to improve the later years for those who once were children and young families facing major developmental challenges. The new knowledge and innovative service delivery strategies contribute to the emotional assurance—that sense of security about the future—that families and individuals so understandably want. Above all, in our pluralistic society, the answers themselves will be multifaceted and adapted to the cultural and individual preferences and needs of those involved.

Preface

Interest in understanding the full life course of persons with mental retardation has quickened over the last two decades. Fueled by the recognition that children with mental retardation grow up to be adults, and even elders, the need to describe "typical" and "atypical" life course patterns of development became obvious. Studies have proliferated on three fronts: on the flexibility and responsiveness of human services, on the consequences to families of extended caregiving, and on differences in various domains of human development among aging persons with mental retardation.

One product of these early studies was evidence that called into question the assumption that development during the adult years is *quiescent*. Indeed, evidence has confirmed patterns of *continued* development and growth. The steady increase in quantity and quality of research on life-span development of persons with mental retardation and their families, and on the service system that supports them, illustrates how variable human development can be and how much there is still to learn about and from the life course of persons with mental retardation.

This volume takes stock of our current state of knowledge about aging and mental retardation. Its contributors articulate the implications of our knowledge for service delivery issues and policy development and chart directions for future research. We have invited leading researchers in the field to present the results of their work, many of whom participated in the Boston Roundtable on Research and Applications in Aging and Developmental Disabilities, held in Boston in November 1990. The impetus for this publication is linked to the effectiveness of the Roundtable meeting, held in conjunction with the Annual Meeting of the Gerontological Society of America, in exposing the dynamic range of research currently being conducted and reported.

The volume is composed of four sections. The first section addresses the family context of care for adults and elders with mental retardation. Although there is undisputed recognition of the primacy of families in the development of *young* children, belated attention has been paid to the role of families in the lives of *adults and elders* with mental retardation. These days, persons with lifelong disabilities are more likely to live with or under the supervision of their families than in any other "setting." Thus the chapters in this section examine three critical issues that are particularly relevant: living with one's family into adulthood (M. Seltzer & Krauss), the interaction between the family and the formal service system (Smith, Fullmer, & Tobin), and transitioning from family to nonfamily living (Heller & Factor).

The second section examines individual development of persons with mental retardation during adulthood and old age. It is now well accepted that, as with all people, distinct stages of life are experienced by persons with mental retardation and other disabilities. Although this may sound obvious, as recently as a decade ago most researchers, policy analysts, and service providers in the field of mental retardation viewed the period past childhood as a relatively undifferentiated (and thus, uninteresting) stage of life. It is now understood, however, that development continues throughout the life course and that old age brings to persons with mental retardation—as it does to all of us—continued opportunities for development. This section begins with an examination of the quality of life of older persons with mental retardation (Edgerton), presents a review of the behavioral and mental health changes that accompany the aging process in this population (Zigman, Silverman, & G. Seltzer), and identifies factors that might limit their length of life (Eyman & Borthwick-Duffy).

The third section focuses on the provision of services to older persons with mental retardation and their families. As attitudes have changed regarding aging in persons with mental retardation, there is a new recognition of the need for a durable, yet flexible, infrastructure of programs and supports for this population. The fledgling infrastructure that exists today has emerged from the confluence of two well-developed service systems: the developmental disabilities service system and the aging network. Collaboration between these two systems has begun on the federal, state, and local levels, and steps have been taken toward enabling the integration of older persons with mental retardation with other seniors who do not have a lifelong disability. Beginning with a discussion of clinical services for adults and elders with mental retardation (G. Seltzer & Luchterhand), this section addresses the structure of the community-based service system (Janicki) and the special legal and financial considerations that should be addressed by families and service providers (R. Freedman & D. Freedman).

The final section addresses methodological challenges facing researchers who study aging in persons with mental retardation and their families (Widaman, Borthwick-Duffy, & Powers). These challenges can daunt or inspire researchers who seek to unravel the mysteries of human development in the later decades of life. They are also important for consumers of research to appreciate in their attempts to distinguish between common assumptions and empirically based findings. Concluding this section is an integration of the various themes regarding research, policy development, and service provision that each chapter highlighted (Krauss & Seltzer). It is our hope that accomplishments in policy and service provision will facilitate continued scientific investigation of the various issues that converge in the study of life-span development among persons with mental retardation and that the research findings presented in this volume will continue to have an impact on our nation's evolving policy agenda and support structures for persons with mental retardation.

We wish to acknowledge the very important contribution to the preparation of this volume made by Dr. Michael J. Begab, Editor of AAMR Special Publications and the AAMR Monograph Series. Throughout the process, he was an extremely active editor, bringing his unusually broad and deep knowledge about mental retardation to the review of each chapter, and always providing a constructively critical perspective. We are fortunate to have had the opportunity to prepare this volume under his Editorship. We are also extremely grateful to Susan Yoder for her work in the copy editing and production of the volume. Her careful eye for detail and language has made this a more polished collection of papers. Finally, we thank the Starr Center on Mental Retardation at Brandeis University and the Waisman Center on Mental Retardation and Human Development at the University of Wisconsin Madison for administrative support for the preparation of this volume.

> Marsha Mailick Seltzer
> Marty Wyngaarden Krauss
> Matthew P. Janicki

Families in Later Life

Chapter 1

Aging Parents With Coresident Adult Children: The Impact of Lifelong Caregiving

Marsha Mailick Seltzer, University of Wisconsin-Madison
Marty Wyngaarden Krauss, Brandeis University

This chapter examines family caregiving for persons with mental retardation using a life course perspective. This perspective is based on the recognition that, in most families, parenting is a commitment that lasts for the rest of one's life (Lancaster, Altmann, Rossi, & Sherrod, 1987) and that the roles of parent and child continue even after the child has become an adult. The life course perspective investigates both the continuities and changes that characterize family functions, composition, and relationships. Because there are changes over time in these dimensions, patterns of individual and family interaction that occur during the first decade of a child's life may not be predictive of how a parent or a family functions when the "child" is in his or her 30s or 40s and the parents are in their 60s or 70s. As little is known about the course of intrafamilial change and development over the full life course for families with a child with mental retardation, there is a need to extend the focus of research on the family impact of such a child through the adulthood and old age of both the parents and the son or daughter with retardation.

Family care is the dominant residential arrangement for persons with mental retardation. According to Fujiura and Braddock (1992), fully 85% of persons with mental retardation live with their families, many for their entire lives. Although the probability of family living decreases with advancing age (Meyers, Borthwick, & Eyman, 1985), nonfamily placement does not predominate until the parent is disabled or deceased. There is considerable debate among professionals about whether it is most appropriate for adults with retardation to live at home. However, family care is the single most common residential arrangement and, therefore, it warrants the attention of researchers, policy analysts, and service providers.

Three substantive issues are addressed in this chapter. First, we note some of the major demographic and social changes that will affect family caregiving in the latter part of this century and into the next. Second, we review the literature about the impacts on individuals of having a family member with mental retardation. We focus primarily on mothers (about whom most research on "parents" is conducted) and siblings. Third, we examine the literature about impacts on the family as a social unit of having a member with retardation. Drawing upon family life course theory, we concentrate on the effects of retardation on a specific stage, the launching stage, and discuss factors associated with launching when the individual with retardation is still in childhood as compared with launching in adulthood or old age. The chapter concludes with a discussion of implications for research, policy, and service provision.

The research reviewed in this chapter examines changes across the life course in family caregiving at both the family and at the individual level. This dual focus is necessary because some changes are experienced by the family as a whole (such as changes in family cohesion), whereas other changes affect the individuals who comprise the family unit (such as changes in the caregiving responsibilities of family members).

Demographic and Social Trends Affecting Family Caregiving

Most research on the consequences of family based care for persons with mental retardation has focused on young children and their parents (Blacher, 1984; Gallagher & Vietze, 1986). There are, indeed, very little data about several important issues, including the prevalence of family based care throughout the life span, the characteristics of families whose child remains at home in adulthood, and the characteristics of those adults who reside with family members throughout their lives.

However, changes in the life expectancy of persons with mental retardation and the aging of the "baby boom" generation have sparked interest in knowing where these adults will live. As described by Eyman & Borthwick-Duffy in chapter 6 of this volume, until the last two decades, the life expectancy of most persons with mental retardation typically has been shorter than that of the general population. Although persons with more severe retardation still have a shorter life expectancy than the general population (Eyman, Grossman, Chaney, & Call, 1990; Eyman, Grossman, Tarjan, & Miller, 1987), the majority of persons with mild retardation can be expected to live about as long as the non-cognitively impaired population. Therefore, it is now common for a child with retardation to outlive his or her parents (Janicki & Wisniewski, 1985).

In addition, changes in the age structure of American society are having an effect on the context of family based care. In the United States and other industrialized countries, there are now many more older persons than in the past. In 1900, about 44% of Americans were younger than 19 years of age and only 4% were older than age 65. By 1980, the younger group had decreased to 32% and the elderly group had increased to 11%. By 2050, these two groups are expected to be about equal in size (23% and 22%, respectively) (U.S. Senate Special Committee on Aging, 1985–1986). In fact, by the middle of the next century, the number of deaths per year is expected to exceed the number of births (Rossi, 1987).

These demographic trends affect families with a member with retardation in several ways. First, the period of family responsibility for a relative with retardation is now prolonged as a result of the increases in life expectancy. Parents can anticipate having primary responsibility for caregiving throughout their own adult and elder years, and siblings and other extended family members may inherit important caretaking roles during their middle adult years.

Second, the dependency ratio is becoming less favorable. This means that there are fewer potential caregivers and more potential care recipients than in the past. Thus, a mother of a child with retardation today—like other women her age—is more likely to have caregiving responsibilities for her own parents than did mothers in previous generations because her parents live longer and because she has fewer brothers and sisters with whom to share the tasks of parent care.

Third, in the future, there will be more older caregiving families and fewer younger caregiving families. As a result, there will have to be changes in the types of services provided to families. In a society in which most caregiving families are young, the greatest needs for family support are directed to the education and socialization of children. However, in a society in which older families outnumber younger families, family support priorities are more likely to be in the areas of health maintenance and long-term care.

Fourth, U.S. society currently includes a larger proportion of primarily female-headed, single-parent families than in past generations (Masnick & Bane, 1980). This trend is the result of high rates of divorce and the increasing likelihood for women to outlive their husbands (Rossi, 1987). As a result, fewer persons with retardation live in two-parent households than in the past. Although research has not been focused on this issue, the special demands and stresses facing single-parent families may reduce the potential for such families to provide long-term family care to their son or daughter with retardation.

Another demographic trend that has received recent attention is the prevalence in the general population of coresidence of adult (nondisabled) children with their aging parents. In 1980, one third (35%) of ever-married mothers who were 55 years of age and almost one fifth (18%) of mothers who were 65 years of age had a child living at home (Sweet & Bumpass, 1987). Data from the 1988 National Survey of Families and Households, a representative national sample of U.S. households, indicated that nearly three quarters of adults between the ages of 19 and 25 had resided with parents for at least some time after age 19. Among parents between the ages of 45 and 54 who had an adult child, nearly half (45%) had an adult child at home (Aquilino, 1990).

Researchers have also investigated the precipitants of coresidence in the general population and found that adult child-aging parent coresidence was not, in most instances, attributable to parental dependency. At all ages, parents were much more likely to provide a home for adult children than adult children for their parents, and no evidence was found that adult children lived in their parents' household in order to care for them (Aquilino, 1989). Indeed, coresidence is more likely to be based on the needs of the adult child rather than those of their parents. For example, parents of unmarried adult children have a much higher likelihood of coresidence than parents of married adult children.

These demographic trends suggest that, for aging and elderly parents, having an adult child live at home is increasingly normative. Although this trend may not conform to traditional expectations about the launching of adult children from the family home, studies suggest that the consequences of postponed launching are not necessarily deleterious for parents. Aquilino (1991) reported that parental satisfaction with the presence of unlaunched adult children is closely linked to the quality of the parent-child relationship. Parent-child relationships that are characterized by infrequent and noninflamed disagreements and by the enjoyment of shared leisure time were associated with positive experiences for parents in the coresident living arrangement. Thus, for many parents, continued involvement with their adult children is a source of important emotional and psychological benefits.

These findings have important implications for the study of lifelong family based caregiving when one member has mental retardation. First, given the increasing prevalence of coresidence between adult children and their aging parents, the phenomenon of lifelong caregiving by parents of adults with retardation can be viewed as less atypical in relation to the general population. Second, the enumeration of positive effects of coresidence within the general population suggests an important elasticity in the parental role. According to Aquilino (1991), the inability to "retire" from active parenting roles may result in surprisingly pleasurable family experiences and enhanced well-being for older women, emanating from shared activities and companionship. Third, the predictive power of the quality of the parent-child relationship in understanding variations in the adaptation by parents to the continued coresidence of adult children may be particularly important for families of adult children with retardation. For example, further research is needed to understand whether and under what conditions the characteristic dependency of adult children with retardation on their parents contributes to or detracts from parental satisfaction with their caregiving roles.

In summary, it is now common for caregiving family members to have lifelong rather than time-limited responsibility for a relative with retardation, for caregivers to have more than one family member dependent on them at the same time, and for caregivers to have less marital support. It is also recognized that it is increasingly common among older parents to have an adult child reside in the parents' home and for this coresidence to be perceived positively by both the parents and the adult children. Thus, although the specific parenting requirements of parents with an adult child with retardation may be atypical, the fact that they continue to have an adult child in their home is now less unusual. The impact of these demographic changes in U.S. society on families with a child with retardation is not fully understood. Clearly, an expanded research agenda is warranted to unravel the complexity of family relationships across the life course and to identify the factors that contribute to positive adaptation by parents to lifelong caregiving roles.

The Impacts on Family Members

Impacts on Parents

Family members constitute the most enduring support network for persons with mental retardation across the life course. However, the ability of family members to maintain a supportive and involved role with their relative with retardation depends, in part, on the "costs" and "benefits" to them. Most research on family caregiving has examined the perceived costs, such as the psychological, social, and economic impacts on parents (primarily mothers). More recently, many studies have described the range of coping and adaptive strategies utilized by caregivers to minimize deleterious impacts of sustained caregiving and, indeed, to benefit from their unique experiences. The benefits may be realized in all of the domains in which the costs are manifested: economic, social, and psychological. The issue of positive and negative effects of family caregiving, and the balance between the two, is particularly salient for older parents of adults with mental retardation as they adapt to the consequences of their own aging in the context of ongoing parental responsibilities.

This section describes what is known, and what may be inferred, about the life course impacts on families of having a member with mental retardation. As will be evident, the literature on this subject is not comprehensive. As Hagestad (1987) points out, it is the norm for an individual to be a child (i.e., to have a living parent) for 50 years or longer. However, research on parents and children has focused either on the first decade of the *child's life* (child development research) or on the last decade of the *parent's life* (gerontological research), leaving a 30-year

gap in our understanding of the parent-child relationship. Recently, however, there has been increasing interest in family life across the full life span, and, in this context, researchers have begun to examine the continuing impact of early life experiences on adult development (e.g., Ainsworth, 1989; Richardson, Koller, & Katz, 1985), the earlier life antecedents of adaptation to old age (e.g., Labouvie-Vief, DeVoe, & Bulka, 1989; Ryff, 1989a, 1989b), and the continuity in family relationships across the life span (Kreppner & Lerner, 1989).

There has been a great deal of research on the impacts on parents of having a young child with mental retardation (for reviews, see Blacher, 1984; Byrne & Cunningham, 1985; Crnic, Friedrich, & Greenberg, 1983). It is now widely recognized that most parents cope effectively and positively with the additional demands experienced in parenting a child with mental retardation (Bristol, 1987; Noh, Dumas, Wolf, & Fisman, 1989; Shonkoff, Hauser-Cram, Krauss, & Upshur, 1992; Singer & Farkas, 1989). Recent studies suggest that families of young children with mental retardation exhibit variability comparable to the general population with respect to important outcomes such as parenting stress (Gowen, Johnson-Martin, Goldman, & Appelbaum, 1989; Krauss, 1993), family functioning (Frey, Greenberg, & Fewell, 1989), and marital satisfaction (Kazak & Marvin, 1984). Studies of the relationships between older parents and their adult children with mental retardation are rare (an exception is Winik, Zetlin, & Kaufman, 1985).

In general, less is known about the stability or volatility of parental impacts or about the cumulative effects of decades of caregiving on aging mothers and fathers. Given the absence of longitudinal studies on families across the life span and the small number of cross-sectional studies of older families, we have little empirical information about the consequences to parents (or other family members) of lifelong caregiving (Seltzer & Ryff, in press). Studies from the gerontological literature, however, provide both theoretical models and empirical findings that may be instructive for the study of parental impacts over time.

Research on adult caregivers of older relatives suggests that long-term caregiving can result in considerable personal stress and burden for the caregiver (Zarit, Reever, & Bach-Peterson, 1980). In a study of caregivers of impaired elders, emotional strain was found to be significantly greater than either financial or physical strain. Further, the closer the emotional bond between the caregiver and the care-receiver, the greater the amount of emotional strain (Cantor, 1983). George and Gwyther (1986) reported that caregivers of older, memory-impaired adults exhibited three times as many stress symptoms as age-peer noncaregivers and had significantly lower levels of participation in social activities. Thus, the impacts on caregivers of impaired elderly relatives appear to place caregivers at considerable emotional and social risk. One explanation for these findings is the "wear and tear" hypothesis, which posits that prolonged exposure to stress (such as generated by daily caregiving) can result in a depletion of either physical or psychological resources (Johnson & Catalano, 1983; Pearlin, Lieberman, Menaghan, & Mullan, 1981). This hypothesis may have applicability to older parents of adults with mental retardation due to the very long duration of their caregiving responsibility, the cognitive and physical characteristics of their adult child, and the intimacy of the familial relationship.

Alternatively, Townsend, Noelker, Deimling, and Bass (1989) proposed an adaptational model of long-term caregiving. They found that many adult children who provided interhousehold care to an impaired elderly parent exhibited stability or improvements, rather than decrements, in their mental health over time. Interestingly, they also reported that the duration of caregiving was unrelated to the caregiver's subjective stress, perceived personal effectiveness, or mental health. Rather, the caregivers' subjective appraisals of their immediate circumstances were much more predictive of these outcomes. They concluded that, "This ability of some family members to provide extended community care without significant distress has been largely overlooked by gerontology's emphasis on caregivers experiencing strain" (Townsend et al., p. 399).

Quantitative and qualitative data from a longitudinal study of 462 older mothers (mean age = 66 years) providing in-home care for an adult with retardation (mean age = 33 years) provide preliminary support for the adaptational hypothesis (Seltzer & Krauss, 1989). It was found that despite the long duration of their caretaking roles, many of the mothers seemed to be resilient, optimistic, and able to function well in multiple roles. Specifically, the women were substantially healthier than other, noncaregiving women their age, had better morale than caregivers of elderly persons, and reported no more burden than family caregivers for elderly residents and less stress than parents of young children with retardation (Krauss & Seltzer, 1993).

Several explanations for these unexpectedly positive findings can be advanced. First, there are selection factors regarding which families continue to rear their child at home into adulthood. Parents with the poorest health and well-being may be more likely to have placed their child out of the home. Second, it is possible that the stresses associated with having a child with retardation were greater during the earlier years, particularly following the initial diagnosis and while the child was attending school. The disappointments of those years may have been replaced by an accommodation to the adult child's limitations and an appreciation of his or her strengths at a time in life when intellectual achievement is less of an issue. Third, many of the mothers described the unexpected benefits they have enjoyed from their atypical parenting experiences in later life—a sense of feeling needed, the opportunity to advocate for services and "make a difference" as a result of their efforts, and the development of a different set of personal and familial values. The majority described the gratifications as well as the frustrations experienced in rearing a child with retardation to adulthood, as in these examples:

"This child has taught me an appreciation for the little things in life that we all take for granted. My other children learned about love and caring for others from Cindy. I don't ask, 'Why me?' I ask, 'Why not me?'"

"It took me five years to accept Bob's limitations and come to value who he is. Our other seven children are better people because of Bob's presence in our lives. I had to grow, too. My advice to other parents is to value who he is, not who he isn't. Forgive yourself. Keep special time for yourself, and the other members of the family. Martyrs are hard to live with."

Although most mothers had positive—as well as negative—comments about their experiences, certain characteristics of their social and familial environments were associated with more favorable maternal well-being. For example, having an adult child in poor physical health was predictive of poorer maternal health, lower life satisfaction, increased sense of burden, and greater maternal stress. Aspects of the social environment, such as the level of conflict in the family and the mother's sense of satisfaction with social support, were also related to maternal well-being (Seltzer & Krauss, 1989). Having a child with Down syndrome was associated with lower levels of stress and burden in the mothers than having a child with other types of mental retardation (Seltzer, Krauss, & Tsunematsu, 1993). The results of this study attest to the enduring importance of the social environment in which caregiving is provided and the critical impacts on the mother of the characteristics of the son or daughter with mental retardation. These conclusions have been reached in studies on families of young children with mental retardation, and their applicability to families at later stages in the life course has only recently begun to be investigated.

Impacts on Siblings

As in studies of the impacts on parents reviewed above, most studies of the dynamics of relationships between siblings have focused on the early childhood period. Viewed from a life course perspective, the gaps in our current knowledge about how sibling relationships change over time are quite glaring. Although the literature is sparse, there is increasing evidence that during middle age and the elder years, sibling relationships retain an intensity and importance that mirrors that experienced in early childhood (Cicirelli, 1982; Lamb, 1982).

Four specific qualities of most sibling relationships have important implications for researchers, professionals, and siblings. First, sibling relationships endure over one's entire life span and thus constitute one of the more durable relationships between people (Cicirelli, 1982). Second, one does not shed the identity of being a sibling. Indeed, the status of "brother" or "sister" remains with an individual throughout one's life and, regardless of differences between siblings, cannot be lost. Third, siblings have a common or shared base of experience. The family environment in which siblings were reared provides a set of experiences, values, and traditions that establishes a frame of reference for siblings throughout their lives. Ross and Dalton (1981) refer to this as a "family life space." Fourth, siblings tend to be peers to each other, with relationships that are likely to be egalitarian with respect to their power structures. In contrast, parent-child relationships are more typically characterized as hierarchical, with parents enjoying more power in the relationship than children. Because of these four important qualities, research on the continuities and changes in sibling relationships has revealed age-specific patterns of emotional intensity and reciprocal influences among siblings over the life course (Allan, 1977; Cicirelli, 1982; Goetting, 1986).

Some aspects of sibling relationships are likely to be affected by mental retardation, whereas in other areas, the effects may be less pronounced. Mental retardation in one sibling will not alter the ascribed nature of the relationship. It may well affect, however, the duration of the relationship (if the sibling with mental retardation is at risk for a shorter than expected life span), the degree to which both individuals in a sibling dyad experience the "same" family environment (as a result of cognitive and social adaptation differences between the siblings and differences in how the parents interact with each), or the degree to which the relationship is perceived as egalitarian (as a result of the different roles assumed by the siblings with and without mental retardation).

Most of the extant research has focused on the psychological effects of having a brother or sister with mental retardation, chronic illness, or other type of handicaps (Breslau, 1982; Drotar & Crawford, 1985; Lobato, 1983; McHale & Gamble, 1989; Wilson, Blacher, & Baker, 1989). The most common theme from these studies is that siblings of children with mental retardation, particularly during adolescence, are vulnerable for emotional morbidity. This vulnerability may result from a host of factors. For example, because parents may spend proportionately larger amounts of time meeting the needs of the child with mental retardation, the other children may feel resentful, neglected, or less valued. Further, parents may look to their other children (particularly older girls) to provide unusual amounts of assistance in meeting the needs of the child with retardation, thereby instilling expectations and responsibilities for caretaking that are atypical and nonnormative for children. Less visibly, siblings may experience considerable anxiety regarding the cause of their brother's or sister's retardation and may worry about their own risk for bearing children with similar disabilities (Begun, 1989). The vulnerability of any individual sibling to these issues is highly variable. Indeed, Lobato (1983) notes that there are many protective factors for siblings that may reduce the probability of emotional morbidity, and, in fact, transform what may appear to be a high-risk environment into one which promotes positive growth and development among the children.

To date, there has been no life-span developmental research on the long-term impact of disability on sibling relationships. The few studies that are available, however, suggest that in adulthood, siblings are emotionally and instrumentally involved with their brother or sister with retardation. In one of the only studies on the postinstitutionalization relationship among siblings, Cleveland and

Miller (1977) reported that nondisabled siblings expressed positive perceptions about their early childhood experiences with their brother or sister with retardation. These siblings also reported that a critical factor in their experiences was whether their parents encouraged open communication and positive behaviors towards their sibling with severe or profound retardation.

Zetlin (1986) conducted an 18-month participation observation study of sibling relationships among 35 adults with mild mental retardation. The dimensions on which she categorized sibling relationships were their affective quality, frequency of contact, and level of involvement. Five types of relationships were identified; they ranged from surrogate parents (e.g., almost daily contact and oversight of both major and minor daily events) to acrimonious relationships (e.g., almost no contact and strong feelings of hostility and emotional disconnectedness). In general, sibling relationships were described as hierarchical rather than egalitarian, insofar as the adult with retardation was emotionally dependent upon the nondisabled sibling. Zetlin also noted that the quality of the sibling relationship was influenced strongly by parental expectations and influences.

Similarly, in a study of adult females and their brothers or sisters with mental retardation, relationships were characterized as positive, but not intimate (Begun, 1989). It was also found that living arrangements affected the quality of the sibling relationship; siblings who coresided had higher levels of conflict than those who lived apart.

Seltzer, Begun, Seltzer, and Krauss (1991) studied the roles of adult siblings for their brothers and sisters with retardation who coresided with their parents. They found that having a nondisabled sibling was a very common event, with nearly all the members of their sample having a least one living sibling. They also found that having a nondisabled sibling who provided instrumental assistance (e.g., help with daily activities) was a relatively *uncommon* event. In contrast, the provision of affective support by the sibling was the norm. Having a sibling who was involved with the brother or sister with mental retardation was found to be a protective factor for the mother's well-being. Specifically, social interaction between at least one nondisabled sibling and the brother or sister with retardation was correlated with lower levels of maternal stress and reduced subjective burden. The potential role of siblings as the "next generation" of careproviders was also noted. Most mothers said that one of their other children was likely to become the primary careprovider for the child with retardation when they are no longer able to continue in this role (Krauss & Seltzer, 1993).

These studies suggest that siblings of persons with mental retardation are, or can be, an integral component of the family's capacities and resources devoted to the care of a member with retardation. The finding that, in many sibling pairs, strong expressions of affective support prevail in adulthood, despite the disability of one sibling and the unequal patterns of give and take, confirms that sibling relationships have a durability and extensiveness that is somewhat unique in human relationships. The maintenance of an emotionally based relationship may prove important if siblings "inherit" the responsibility for the care or supervision of their brother or sister with mental retardation.

The Impacts on the Family As A Social Unit

Most theorists of family life (e.g., Duvall, 1962; Olson, McCubbin & Associates, 1983) note that families, like individuals, follow a fairly predictable life course that governs their growth, development, and functioning. The identification of stages in family development, proposed initially by Duvall (1962), has generated descriptions of the developmental careers of families and the consequences of failure to pass through the expected sequence of stages (Farber, 1959; Haley, 1973). Although family development theorists differ in the division of stages that constitute the family life course, all stage theories include the salient events of marriage, the birth and rearing of children, the launching or departure of family members from the household,

and changes in the status of the primary wage earner (Carter & McGoldrick, 1980). At each stage, family members have different developmental tasks to accomplish. For example, the primary family functions during a family's early years are establishing a household and childbearing. As the children age, socialization and education take over as primary family functions. As the family matures, a major family function is the enhancement of the parents' social roles, including their careers, social networks, and community relationships. In old age, family functions include maintaining the extended family and providing support and care to members who have limitations in their independent functioning.

The extent to which these functions are performed differently by families with a child with retardation—or the extent to which they experience a different set of stages—has been the subject of very little research, especially with respect to the later stages of the family life course (Krauss & Giele, 1987; Turnbull, Summers, & Brotherson, 1986). However, a great deal has been written about family and individual factors that are implicated in what is often termed the "launching" stage. This stage is normatively identified as beginning with the departure of the first child from his or her family of origin and ending with the departure of the last child. This stage brings with it a variety of changes in family roles and relationships among members, including renegotiation of the marital system as a dyad, development of adult to adult relationships between grown children and their parents, realignment of relationships to include in-laws and grandchildren, and dealing with the disabilities and death of elder members of the family (Carter & McGoldrick, 1980).

In families with a child with retardation, the onset of the launching stage may occur prematurely (i.e., placement of the child prior to adulthood) or it may be postponed (i.e., delayed until well into the adult years of the child with retardation or not accomplished during the parents' lifetime). The consequences to the family unit of premature or postponed launching of a child with retardation with respect to the anticipated changes in family roles and relationships have not been studied. Rather, studies have focused on the factors associated with the *event* of premature or postponed launching, and are reviewed below.

Research on "Premature" Launching

Studies of the factors associated with out-of-home placement for children with mental retardation note the salience of a small number of factors: age, severity of retardation, presence of behavior and physical problems, and the inability of the parents to meet the chronic daily needs of the child (Blacher, Hanneman, & Rousey, 1992; Seltzer & Krauss, 1984). Suelzle and Keenan (1981) examined age-related placement patterns and found that the risk of out-of-home placement is highest when the child is between 6 and 12 years of age and again between 19 and 21 years of age. The authors relate these findings to the higher level of family stress during transition points in the child's life, particularly beginning and completing school.

Cole (1986) provided a theoretical framework for understanding the roles of family stressors and resources in influencing the decision to place a child with developmental disabilities out of the home. When stressors related to the child combine with other family stressors to produce a crisis, the family may cope by removing the stressors, including placing the child out of the home. Internal and external family resources and positive perceptions of life circumstances can buffer the impact of these stressors, allowing the family to cope by assimilating and accommodating the handicapped member within the home.

Several studies have examined the influence of the factors articulated in Cole's model on families' placement decisions. As summarized by Heller and Factor (chapter 3 this volume) families are most likely to seek out-of-home placements when their child has more severe retardation and more serious maladaptive behaviors, when the parents are older and in worse health, when the family is larger and has few informal and formal community supports. However, although these overall trends seem to be strong predictors

of placement, they are mediated by the stage of life of the family. Tausig (1985) is one of the few researchers to examine differences in the factors associated with "premature" launching and launching during adulthood. He examined the factors associated with placement requests among families whose child was under age 21 and among families whose child was over age 21. For families of children under the age of 21, placement requests were associated with the child's poor social behavior, rather than with characteristics of the family. For children over the age of 21, placement requests were associated most strongly with disruptions of family relations, rather than with any characteristics of the child. Additional research is needed to determine the extent to which factors predicting placement are differentially applicable at different life stages.

Research on Continued Coresidence in Adulthood

The phenomenon of lifelong family care for a member with retardation raises important questions about the reasons why some families "postpone" launching or never plan to have their child live away from family. Interestingly, our research has revealed that many older mothers report a strong and unyielding preference to continue in the caregiving role until death or physical infirmity (Seltzer & Krauss, 1992). The resolution to retain the parental role may reflect a realistic appraisal of the lack of acceptable residential options and the continued need of the adult for care or supervision. It is also possible that the resolution may provide insight into the functionality of durable and concrete nurturing roles for older women.

The available research, summarized by Heller and Factor (chapter 3 this volume), indicates that predictors of placement after the person with retardation has reached adulthood include parental health problems, parental subjective burden, and high levels of dependent and maladaptive behaviors in the adults with retardation. Additionally, greater use of formal services has been found to be associated with an increased probability that caregivers would prefer a residential program placement. It may be that use of family support services decreases family apprehensiveness towards the community residential service system and is a first step toward placement for families who need to arrange for these nonfamily living arrangements within their lifetime.

Continued coresidence of an adult with retardation with his or her parent reflects different reasons in different types of families. For some, this living arrangement emanates from a deep commitment to the idea of the family taking care of its own. These families do not intend to place the member with retardation in a nonfamily setting, even after the parents' death. For others, the "option" of placement may be seen as highly problematic. For example, alternative settings may be judged as unavailable, unsatisfactory, too expensive, or having too long a waiting list. For these families, the opportunity to place might be taken if parental concerns were assuaged. Yet other families continue coresidence because of an interdependence between parent and child that increases with parental age. There may, in fact, be disincentives to launch an adult with retardation who provides care or support to a frail or infirm elderly parent. Importantly, advice from service providers to place "because it is the normative living arrangement in adulthood" may alter any of these family perspectives. At the present time, we have very little scientific knowledge about the dynamics of launching versus continued coresidence of persons with mental retardation during adulthood, a process warranting research in future studies.

Implications for Research, Policy, and Service Provision

This chapter has reviewed the reasons for embracing a life course perspective on family caregiving, a theoretical perspective that is now being informed by the results of empirical research. Although this perspective is increasingly accepted by researchers, policy analysts, and service providers in the field of mental retardation, a great deal remains to be learned about the specific course of intraindividual and intrafamilial change and stability, and the adaptability and well-being of families of children with mental retardation across the life course. A number of implications emanate from the current knowledge base for future research, policy development, and service provision.

Implications for Research

The study of family caregiving over the life course is in its infancy. While the plea for "more studies" is often sounded, there is a compelling need for a stronger descriptive base of information about how families adjust to the challenges of mental retardation, not just initially or in the early years of parenting, but also "over the long haul." Further, studies need to take a multidimensional perspective, investigating the biological, psychological, and social dimensions of long-term family based care. Both descriptive and theoretically grounded studies that provide naturalistic information on the context and patterns of family based care are required in order to generate and test specific hypotheses about the determinants of family based care that is successfully experienced by both the family care provider and the person with retardation.

Developmental studies are also needed that examine patterns of constancy and change in the experience of parents as long-term caregivers. Most family research has focused on the effects of parental attributes, parenting styles, and family resources on the child's development. These are important issues, but studies must also take note of how the experience of mental retardation alters *who these parents are*—how they cope, what their life goals are, how they manage the aging process. Too great an emphasis has been placed in past research on *what these parents do* for their sons and daughters with retardation, and too little investigation has been devoted to *who these parents become* as a result of the experience.

The common assumption that a single event or feature within a family—such as the experience of mental retardation—is experienced similarly by all families needs to be avoided. Comparative studies are needed that examine the differences in the impacts of family based care for different populations. For example, more research is needed to examine whether there are unique or common aspects of family based care depending on the family's religious, cultural, or ethnic background, type of disability of the family member, the characteristics of the primary care provider, the duration of caregiving, or the generational cohort of the parents (to name but a few of the potentially relevant dimensions). For example, younger cohorts of families have experienced a vastly different educational, medical, and social service system than was available to older cohorts of families, potentially resulting in important differences in family functioning, parental adaptation, and sibling development. Focused and sensitive family support services require far more information than is currently available on the salient differences within the potential pool of service recipients.

It is also important to acknowledge that families differ in their levels of involvement with members with disabilities over time. Studies are needed that compare families who have not remained actively involved in the direct care of their son or daughter with mental retardation, as well as those who have remained actively involved. It is possible that the families who experience the "wear and tear" of caregiving reduce their involvement, and those who derive gratification from this role or develop new coping mechanisms remain active caregivers. By studying only the "involved families," our conclusions may be positively biased. Similarly, parents differ in their use of supportive services (e.g., respite care, parent support groups, etc.), and the effects of service use on family functioning warrants continued research.

Further, many important questions can only be answered by longitudinal studies that can disaggregate individual-level change from family-level change over the life course. Understanding the mutual influences of these "units" on each other and on the family member receiving care is critical for the design of effective interventions. This type of research will likely yield a greater understanding of the importance of structural and functional changes (such as may be witnessed in the family as a unit) and of changes in personal coping strategies (as an example of individual level changes) that may be implicated in the desirability of continued family based care.

In this regard, it will be important for future research to take into account the views of all family members, including mothers, fathers, siblings, and in particular, the adults with mental retardation. The multidimensional and interactive nature of family well-being cannot be validly assessed from one perspective only. However, the challenges in assessing family well-being from the perspective of adults with more severe cognitive or language impairments are significant, as are the challenges inherent in collecting data from those very elderly parents who have sensory or memory limitations.

Implications for Policy Development

There have been numerous indictments of current federal and state policies that are seen as supplanting, rather than supporting, the natural family (Dunst, Trivette, & Deal, 1988; Moroney, 1981; Skarnulis, 1979). The disparity in public resources devoted to individuals with mental retardation who live in licensed, residential settings, in contrast to those who live with family members, has been often criticized (Fujiura & Braddock, 1992). Although proposals for greater support of family caregiving have resulted in a larger array of supportive services, most notably respite care and cash subsidies, there is a need for comprehensive, family-oriented public policies that encourage and support family based care and that provide support to continued family involvement following placement out of the home.

From a life course perspective, it is important that family support policies be flexible. For example, both younger and older families with a member with mental retardation have significant unmet needs for support and services. However, family needs differ at different points of the family life course. A major challenge to policymakers is to balance the needs of older and younger caregiving families in the distribution of increasingly scarce resources.

Relatedly, despite the predominance of lifelong family living for most persons with mental retardation, there is a crucial need to expand the placement opportunities for families. The long waiting lists prolong family living in some situations beyond the time it is desirable for parents or for the adult with retardation. It is also necessary to develop viable alternatives to the dominant community-based system of group homes, supervised apartments, and foster homes. Many family members want to create options that mirror conditions in which their adult children have lived most of their lives. Continued supported living in the parents' home after the parents die is a strongly voiced goal of many older families.

There is also a need to assign priority status to services for older families who have provided lifelong care. Access to respite, counseling, and social activities for their son or daughter should be enhanced with the goal of supporting continued family living as long as desirable and possible. Timely access to supportive services for parents that may be available from the aging network of services needs to be enhanced. Policymakers who base their thinking solely on their understanding of the needs of families of younger children may unwittingly undermine the resolve of families of adults with retardation to provide in-home care and avoid costly out-of-home placement. It is also important for policymakers to recognize that many older families had negative experiences with the mental retardation service system during their children's early childhood—most frequently hearing the recommendation to institutionalize their child—and harbor long-standing distrust of professionals from this system. These families may be more receptive to support services sponsored by the aging network of services and thus, outreach efforts should be launched from both service systems.

Implications for Service Provision

Service providers, such as case managers, counselors, and therapists, occupy a critical position in the human service system. Because of their direct contact with service recipients and the individuals who support them, they can provide guidance and advice about a range of issues that may affect the quality of life for families as well as persons with retardation. The ability of service providers to assist families to marshal the full range of resources potentially available to them may prove critical over the life course of family caregiving. Although the most "visible" family support system may be the parents of adults with mental retardation, it is extremely important that service providers view the family more broadly. Specifically, the research reviewed in this chapter suggests that siblings of persons with mental retardation constitute a population of potential or actual care providers. Developing outreach programs that encourage siblings to become involved in the development of long-term care plans for adults with mental retardation is needed, particularly for families in which the parents are no longer able to provide leadership or direction in long-term care planning. The vital, though often unacknowledged, role that siblings play in the well-being of their parents should be acknowledged, as well as their future role as the next generation of caregivers.

Service providers should also recognize that the life course of many older families of adults with retardation may be different from that of the "idealized" or "typical" family whose children have assumed independent, adult roles outside of the family home. Whereas in the general society, the launching of children is assumed to be an event that is welcomed by parents, for many parents of persons with mental retardation, launching may constitute a loss of a valued role or a life of increased danger for their adult with retardation. The endurance of an active parenting role for mothers and fathers who are elderly may be a critical component to their well-being, rather than a burden to which they have accommodated. Further, as Aquilino's research attests (1990), the fact that launching has not occurred is increasingly normative and should be treated as a viable and valued contemporary alteration of the family life course.

Families need support in their attempts to use the formal service system. Many older parents are justifiably afraid of the consequences of receiving services—they may feel threatened or judged with respect to how much they have done for their son or daughter or criticized for keeping him or her at home for so many years. The transition away from parental care should be a gradual rather than an abrupt process, facilitated by service utilization.

In conclusion, the "baby boom" generation with retardation is a very large cohort whose parents have reached old age or will reach this stage of life shortly. Therefore, there are compelling demographic pressures on the service system to be responsive to the needs of these older families, who have been the mainstay of the informal care system in which so many persons with mental retardation reside. This is not a simple task, as no clear linear relationship has ever been demonstrated between service utilization and family well-being. Nevertheless, the challenge is to determine how best to respond to the needs of what Fujiura and Braddock (1992) have termed "the nation's largest alternative 'system' of care" (p. 336) for persons with mental retardation—the family.

References

Ainsworth, M.D.S. (1989). Attachments beyond infancy. *American Psychologist, 44,* 709–716.

Allan, G. (1977). Sibling solidarity. *Journal of Marriage and the Family, 39,* 177–184.

Aquilino, W. S. (1989). *Antecedents of parent-adult child coresidence.* Madison: University of Wisconsin, Center for Demography and Ecology.

Aquilino, W. S. (1990). The likelihood of parent-adult child coresidence: Effects of family structure and parental characteristics. *Journal of Marriage and the Family, 52,* 405–419.

Aquilino, W. S. (1991). Parent-child relations and parent's satisfaction with living arrangements when adult children live at home. *Journal of Marriage and the Family, 53,* 13–27.

Begun, A. L. (1989). Sibling relationships involving developmentally disabled people. *American Journal on Mental Retardation, 93,* 566–574.

Blacher, J. (Ed.). (1984). *Severely handicapped children and their families: Research in review.* New York: Academic Press.

Blacher, J., Hanneman, R. A., & Rousey, A. B. (1992). Out-of-home placement of children with severe handicaps: A comparison of approaches. *American Journal on Mental Retardation, 96,* 607–616.

Breslau, N. (1982). Siblings of disabled children: Birth order and age-spacing effects. *Journal of Abnormal Child Psychology, 10,* 85–96.

Bristol, M. M. (1987). Mothers of children with autism or communication disorders: Successful adaptation and the double ABCX model. *Journal of Autism and Developmental Disabilities, 17,* 469–486.

Byrne, E. A., & Cunningham, C. C. (1985). The effects of mentally handicapped children on families: A conceptual review. *Journal of Child Psychiatry, 26,* 847–864.

Cantor, M. H. (1983). Strain among caregivers: A study of experience in the United States. *The Gerontologist, 23,* 597–604.

Carter, E. A., & McGoldrick, M. (1980). The family life cycle and family therapy: An overview. In E. A. Carter and M. McGoldrick (Eds.), *The family life cycle: A framework for family therapy* (pp. 3–20). New York: Gardner Press.

Cicirelli, V. C. (1982). Sibling influence throughout the lifespan. In M. E. Lamb & B. Sutton-Smith (Eds.), *Sibling relationships: Their nature and significance across the lifespan* (pp. 267–284). Hillsdale, NJ: Erlbaum.

Cleveland, D. W., & Miller, N. (1977). Attitudes and life commitments of older siblings of mentally retarded adults: An exploratory study. *Mental Retardation, 15,* 38–41.

Cole, D. A. (1986). Out-of-home child placement and family adaptation: A theoretical framework. *American Journal of Mental Deficiency, 91,* 226–236.

Crnic, K. A., Friedrich, W. N., & Greenberg, M. T. (1983). Adaptation of families with mentally retarded children: A model of stress, coping, and family ecology. *American Journal of Mental Deficiency, 88,* 125–138.

Drotar, D., & Crawford, P. (1985). Psychological adaptation of siblings of chronically ill children: Research and practice implications. *Developmental and Behavioral Pediatrics, 6,* 355–362.

Dunst, C., Trivette, C., & Deal, A. (1988). *Enabling and empowering families: Principles and guidelines for practice.* Cambridge, MA: Brookline Press.

Duvall, E. (1962). *Family development.* Philadelphia: Lippincott.

Eyman, R., Grossman, H., Chaney, R. H., & Call, T. L. (1990). The life expectancy of profoundly handicapped people with mental retardation. *The New England Journal of Medicine, 323,* 584–589.

Eyman, R., Grossman, H., Tarjan, G., & Miller, C. R. (1987). *Life expectancy and mental retardation* (Monograph No. 7). Washington, DC: American Association on Mental Deficiency.

Eyman, R. K., & Borthwick-Duffy, S. A. (1994). Trends in mortality and predictors of mortality. In M. M. Seltzer, M. W. Krauss, & M. P. Janicki (Eds.), *Life course perspectives on adulthood and old age* (pp. 93–105). Washington, DC: American Association on Mental Retardation.

Farber, B. (1959). Effects of a severely mentally retarded child on family integration. *Monographs of the Society for Research in Child Development, 24* (2, Serial No. 71).

Frey, K. S., Greenberg, M. T., & Fewell, R. R. (1989). Stress and coping among parents of handicapped children: A multidimensional approach. *American Journal on Mental Retardation, 94,* 240–249.

Fujiura, G. T., & Braddock, D. (1992). Fiscal and demographic trends in mental retardation services: The emergence of the family. In L. Rowitz (Ed.), *Mental retardation in the year 2000* (316–338). New York: Springer.

Gallagher, J. J., & Vietze, P. M. (Eds.). (1986). *Families of handicapped persons: Research, programs, and policy issues.* Baltimore, MD: Brookes.

George, L. K., & Gwyther, L. P. (1986). Caregiver well-being: A multidimensional examination of family caregivers of demented adults. *The Gerontologist, 26,* 253–259.

Goetting, A. (1986). The developmental tasks of siblingship over the life cycle. *Journal of Marriage and the Family, 48,* 703–714.

Gowen, J. W., Johnson-Martin, N., Goldman, B. D., & Appelbaum, M. (1989). Feelings of depression and parenting competence of mothers of handicapped and non-handicapped infants: A longitudinal study. *American Journal on Mental Retardation, 94,* 259–271.

Hagestad, G. O. (1987). Parent-child relations in later life: Trends and gaps in past research. In J. B. Lancaster, J. Altman, A. S. Rossi, & L. R. Sherrod (Eds.), *Parenting across the life span: Biosocial dimensions* (pp. 405–434). New York: Aldine de Gruyter.

Haley, J. (1973). *Uncommon therapy.* New York: Norton.

Heller, T., & Factor, A. (1994). Facilitating future planning and transitions out of the home. In M. M. Seltzer, M. W. Krauss, & M. P. Janicki (Eds.), *Life course perspectives on adulthood and old age* (pp. 39–50). Washington, DC: American Association on Mental Retardation.

Janicki, M. P., & Wisniewski, H. M. (Eds.) (1985). *Aging and developmental disabilities: Issues and approaches.* Baltimore, MD: Brookes.

Johnson, C., & Catalano, D. (1983). A longitudinal study of family supports to impaired elderly. *The Gerontologist, 23,* 612–618.

Kazak, A., & Marvin, R. (1984). Differences, difficulties, and adaptation: Stress and social networks in families with a handicapped child. *Family Relations, 33,* 67–77.

Krauss, M. W. (1993). Child-related and parenting stress: Differences and similarities between mothers and fathers of children with disabilities. *American Journal on Mental Retardation, 97,* 393–404.

Krauss, M. W., & Giele, J. Z. (1987). Services to families during three stages of a handicapped person's life. In M. Ferri & M. B. Sussman (Eds.), *Childhood disability and family systems* (pp. 213–230). New York: Haworth Press.

Krauss, M. W., & Seltzer, M. M. (1993). Current well-being and future plans for older caregiving mothers. *The Irish Journal of Psychology, 14,* 47–64.

Kreppner, K., & Lerner, R. M. (Eds.). (1989). *Family systems and life-span development.* Hillsdale, NJ: Erlbaum.

Labouvie-Vief, G., DeVoe, M., & Bulka, D. (1989). Speaking about feelings: Conceptions of emotion across the life span. *Psychology and Aging, 4,* 425–437.

Lamb, M. E. (1982). Sibling relationships across the lifespan: An overview and introduction. In M. E. Lamb & B. Sutton-Smith (Eds.), *Sibling relationships: Their nature and significance across the lifespan* (pp. 1–12). Hillsdale, NJ: Erlbaum.

Lancaster, J. B., Altman, J., Rossi, A. S., & Sherrod, L. T. (Eds.). (1987). *Parenting across the life span: Biosocial dimensions.* New York: Aldine de Gruyter.

Lobato, D. (1983). Siblings of handicapped children: A review. *Journal of Autism and Developmental Disorders, 13,* 347–364.

Masnick, G., & Bane, M. J. (1980). *The nation's families: 1960 to 1990.* Cambridge, MA: Joint Center for Urban Studies.

McHale, S. M., & Gamble, W. C. (1989). Sibling relationships of children with disabled and nondisabled brothers and sisters. *Developmental Psychology, 25,* 421–429.

Meyers, C. E., Borthwick, S. A., & Eyman, R. (1985). Place of residence by age, ethnicity, and level of retardation of the mentally retarded/developmentally disabled population of California. *American Journal of Mental Deficiency, 90,* 266–270.

Moroney, R. M. (1981). Mental disability: The role of the family. In J. J. Bevilacqua (Ed.), *Changing government policies for the mentally disabled* (pp. 209–238). Cambridge, MA: Ballinger Press.

Noh, S., Dumas, J. E., Wolf, L. C., & Fisman, S. N. (1989). Delineating sources of stress in parents of exceptional children. *Family Relations, 38,* 456–461.

Olson, D. H., McCubbin, H. I., & Associates. (1983). *Families: What makes them work.* Beverly Hills: Sage.

Pearlin, L., Lieberman, M., Menaghan, E., & Mullan, J. (1981). The stress process. *Journal of Health and Social Behavior, 22,* 337–356.

Richardson, S. A., Koller, H., & Katz, M. (1985). Relationship of upbringing to later behavior disturbance of mildly retarded young people. *American Journal of Mental Deficiency, 90,* 1–8.

Ross, H. G., & Dalton, M. J. (1981). *Perceived determinants of closeness in adult sibling relationships.* Paper presented at 89th Annual Conference of the American Psychological Association Convention, Los Angeles, CA.

Rossi, A. S. (1987). Parenthood in transition: From lineage to child to self-orientation. In J. B. Lancaster, J. Altmann, A. S. Rossi, & L. R. Sherrod (Eds.), *Parenting across the life span: Biosocial dimensions* (pp. 31–81). New York: Aldine de Gruyter.

Ryff, C. D. (1989a). In the eye of the beholder: Views of psychological well-being among middle-aged and older adults. *Psychology and Aging, 4,* 195–210.

Ryff, C. D. (1989b). *Getting better, getting worse with time: Beliefs about personal change from young adulthood through old age.* Paper presented at the meeting of the International Society for the Study of Behavioral Development, Finland.

Seltzer, G., Begun, A. L., Seltzer, M. M., & Krauss, M. W. (1991). Adults with mental retardation and their aging mothers: Impacts of siblings. *Family Relations, 40,* 310–317.

Seltzer, M. M., & Krauss, M. W. (1984). Placement alternatives for mentally retarded children and their families. In J. Blacher (Ed.), *Severely handicapped children and their families: Research in review* (pp.143–175). New York: Academic Press.

Seltzer, M. M., & Krauss, M. W. (1989). Aging parents with mentally retarded children: Family risk factors and sources of support. *American Journal on Mental Retardation, 94,* 303–312.

Seltzer, M. M., & Krauss, M. W. (1992). *Aging families of children with mental retardation: The impact of lifelong caregiving.* Madison:

University of Wisconsin, Waisman Center.

Seltzer, M. M., & Krauss, M. W., & Tsunematsu, N. (1993). Adults with Down syndrome and their aging families: Diagnostic group differences. *American Journal on Mental Retardation, 97,* 496–508.

Seltzer, M. M., & Ryff, C. D. (in press). Parenting across the lifespan: The normative and nonnormative cases. In D. L. Featherman, R. Lerner, & M. Perlmutter (Eds.), *Life-span development and behavior, Vol. 12.* Hillsdale, NJ: Erlbaum.

Shonkoff, J. P., Hauser-Cram, P., Krauss, M. W., & Upshur, C. C. (1992). Development of infants with disabilities and their families: Implications for theory and service delivery. *Monographs of the Society for Research in Child Development, 57,* (Serial No. 230).

Singer, L., & Farkas, K. J. (1989). The impact of infant disability on maternal perception of stress. *Family Relations, 38,* 444–449.

Skarnulis, E. (1979). Support, not supplant, the natural home: Serving handicapped children and adults. In S. Maybanks & M. Bryce (Eds.), *Home-based services for children and families* (pp. 64–76). Springfield, IL: Charles C Thomas.

Suelzle, M., & Keenan, V. (1981). Changes in family support networks over the life cycle of mentally retarded persons. *American Journal of Mental Deficiency, 86,* 267–274.

Sweet, J. A., & Bumpass, L. (1987). *American families and households.* New York: Russell Sage Foundation.

Tausig, M. (1985). Factors in family decision-making about placement for developmentally disabled individuals. *American Journal of Mental Deficiency, 89,* 352–361.

Townsend, A., Noelker, L., Deimling, G., & Bass, D. (1989). Longitudinal impact of interhousehold caregiving on adult children's mental health. *Psychology and Aging, 4,* 393–401.

Turnbull, A. P., Summers, J. A., & Brotherson, M. J. (1986). Family life cycle: Theoretical and empirical implications and future directions for families with mentally retarded members. In J. J. Gallagher & P. M. Vietze (Eds.), *Families of handicapped persons: Research,* *programs, and policy issues* (pp. 45–66). Baltimore, MD: Brookes.

U.S. Senate Special Committee on Aging. (1985–86). *Aging America: Trends and projections.* Washington, DC: U.S. Government Printing Office.

Wilson, J., Blacher, J., & Baker, B. L. (1989). Siblings of children with severe handicaps. *Mental Retardation, 27,* 167–174.

Winik, L., Zetlin, A. G., & Kaufman, S. Z. (1985). Adult mildly retarded persons and their parents: The relationship between involvement and adjustment. *Applied Research in Mental Retardation, 6,* 409–419.

Zarit, S., Reever, K., & Bach-Peterson, J. (1980). Relatives of the impaired elderly: Correlates of feelings of burden. *The Gerontologist, 20,* 649–655.

Zetlin, A. (1986). Mentally retarded adults and their siblings. *American Journal of Mental Deficiency, 91,* 217–225.

An earlier version of this paper was presented at the 1990 Boston Roundtable on Research Issues and Applications in Aging and Developmental Disabilities. The authors gratefully acknowledge the contributions of Tamar Heller, Ph.D., to this paper. We also acknowledge the generous support provided by grants from the National Institute on Aging (AG08768), the Retirement Research Foundation (12-225), the Andrus Foundation, the March of Dimes Birth Defects Foundation, and the Joseph P. Kennedy, Jr., Foundation for the preparation of this chapter and the research on which it is based.

Chapter 2

Living Outside the System: An Exploration of Older Families Who Do Not Use Day Programs

Gregory C. Smith, University of Maryland, College Park
Elise M. Fullmer, University of North Carolina, Charlotte
Sheldon S. Tobin, State University of New York at Albany

There is long-standing recognition that significant numbers of adults with mental retardation who reside in the community with their families are either inadequately involved with the service network for this population or they live entirely outside of it (Justice, O'Connor, & Warren, 1971; Rose & Ansello, 1987; Smith & Tobin, 1989). Over 15 years ago, for example, Segal (1977) noted a wide gap in services needed for older persons with mental retardation in the community. This gap occurred because these individuals were not easily identified, inadequate effort was made to uncover them, available programs were typically directed toward children rather than adults, and most professionals had little knowledge about the needs of aging clients.

Later, Jacobson, Sutton, and Janicki (1985) estimated from 1980 census data that perhaps only one quarter of persons age 55 and older with mental retardation in the United States were being served by the formal service system. The most common explanation for the lack of service utilization among those not residing in institutions has been that community services were unavailable throughout most of the lifetime of the present cohort of older adults with mental retardation.

More recently, Seltzer, Krauss, and Heller (1991) noted that the majority of individuals with mental retardation live with their families and that increased attention has been directed toward patterns of service needs and use among aging families. They further observed, however, that the available research is based on samples of families that are known to providers within the mental retardation service system. Indeed, the only published attempt to identify older adults with mental retardation outside the service system was conducted by Horne (1989) in the United Kingdom, who labeled them "the hidden." Because so many aging families of persons with mental retardation in the United States are believed not to be benefiting from the service system, the generalizability of findings based on only the served population is limited (Seltzer et al., 1991).

It is imperative then to learn more about aging families who are not fully utilizing the service network established for persons with mental retardation and their families. Toward the end of the family life cycle, both offspring with mental retardation and their parents are likely to experience increasing age-related difficulties that will require assistance from formal service providers if family stability is to be maintained. Older parents, however, are usually more reluctant than younger parents to seek assistance from professionals (Brubaker, Engelhardt, Brubaker, & Lutzer, 1989; Grant, 1986). Until this reluctance is better understood, the needs of many older families will continue to go unmet.

Knowledge about older families of adults with mental retardation that are not adequately using relevant services is also necessary because planners must anticipate the residential service needs that will occur when aging caregivers can no longer continue in this role (Seltzer et al., 1991; Seltzer & Janicki, 1991; Smith & Tobin, 1989). Many older parents wait until a crisis precipitates placement decisions, and then the offspring with mental retardation is confronted with the emotional trauma of sudden relocations (Heller & Factor, 1988; Kaufman, Adams, & Campbell, 1991). Possibly, use of formal services decreases caregivers' apprehensiveness towards community residential services (Heller & Factor, 1991) which, in turn, facilitates their ability to engage in permanency planning (Seltzer et al., 1991; Smith & Tobin, 1993; Wood & Skiles, 1992).

How is it determined, however, whether or not older families are well-integrated with the service system? Or, asked differently: Are some services more pivotal than others in promoting the overall well-being of these families? In the next section, it will be argued that day program services are preeminent in the lives of adults with mental retardation and their elderly parents. Moreover, in states where day program services are readily available, nonuse of such services may reflect purposeful avoidance and a desire to live in isolation from the formal service system.

The Importance of Day Services

Day services for adults with developmental disabilities may be defined as "any focused and purposive activity of a full day duration that involves work or habilitative tasks, or sociorecreational, avocational, and stimulatory activities" (Janicki, Otis, Puccio, Rettig, & Jacobson, 1985, p. 295). For individuals with minimal functional impairments, day services encompass such activities as competitive employment and sheltered workshops. For more severely disabled persons, day programs involve a combination of clinical services and habilitation activities (Janicki et al., 1985). These services benefit disabled adults by promoting skill development (personal, interpersonal, and vocational), socialization, recreation, creativity, self-esteem, educational enrichment, and ancillary support from the community (Barbero, 1989). Moreover, when the individual's parental caregivers are elderly, day programs can assist aging parents in coping with the care and supervision of their

disabled offspring, especially when coupled with various ancillary support services (Janicki et al., 1985).

It is important to distinguish between older families who do use day program services and those who do not for a variety of reasons. With such programs as day treatment, sheltered workshops, or even competitive employment, parents of adults with mental retardation permit someone outside the family to act as their surrogate on a consistent basis. Day services also provide socialization opportunities for the offspring outside the realm of the immediate family environment. Day services may thus help to abate the kind of parent-offspring interdependence thought to hinder permanency planning by older parents (Grant, 1986). Furthermore, as already noted, day programming may encourage the use of supplemental services that are frequently needed by older parents to remain in the caregiver role.

In this chapter, findings will be presented from a study in which we interviewed 235 mothers, 58 to 96 years of age, who were caring at home for adult offspring with mental retardation. Although the majority (176) of the respondents were caring at home for an offspring who attended some form of day programming service (day treatment, $n = 46$; sheltered workshops, $n = 99$; or competitive employment, $n = 31$), the remaining 59 cared for offspring who were not involved with any type of day programming service. Those in competitive employment were considered day program users because they obtained their jobs with the assistance of formal service providers.

This sample is clearly unique because past studies of this population have chiefly involved older parents whose offspring were enrolled in some sort of day service activity (e.g., Gold, Dobrof, & Torian, 1987; Grant, 1986; Heller & Factor, 1991; Kaufman et al., 1991; Roberto, 1988; Seltzer & Krauss, 1989). Also, because the study occurred in New York State, where there are no waiting lists for day programming services, the nonusers in our sample represented families who were not benefiting from a readily available service.

Given the uniqueness of the study sample, then, we are able to address the following questions in this chapter: What methodological issues should be considered in locating underserved adults with mental retardation and their families? Do older families who use day program services differ significantly from those do not use on sociodemographic characteristics, utilization of additional family supports, extent of permanency planning, or maternal well-being? What reasons might exist for the underutilization of formal services by older families? What implications do all of the above have for practice, policy, and research?

Methodological Issues in Locating Families Outside the Service System

Before contrasting the older families in our sample that either used or did not use day programming services, it is instructive to describe the difficulty associated with locating families who are outside of the formal service system. In this section, we consider four methods that have been used to locate families that are not linked to formal services. These strategies varied in important ways and yielded different results. The first three are service-oriented attempts, whereas the fourth involves methods that we used to obtain our sample of day program nonusers.

A service-oriented project sponsored by the Rehabilitation Research and Training Center (RRTC) Consortium on Aging and Developmental Disabilities in Akron, Ohio, presented workshops on permanency planning that attracted many older parents of adults with mental retardation who were previously unknown to service providers (Becker, 1991). Only 12 families attended the first workshop, but attendance rose to 60 at a second workshop, and then to over 100 at the third. The majority of attendees were previously unknown to formal services for mentally retarded individuals and their families. Apparently, these older parents attended the workshops because they perceived them to be both useful and nonthreatening. The workshops were advertised in newsletters associated with ag-

ing network programs and were conducted under the auspices of a generic social service agency, the Jewish Community Center, rather than a provider from the mental retardation service system. Thus, parents' apprehension of mental retardation professionals was deliberately circumvented.

Another effort to locate older underserved families was carried out in a five-county area in rural Virginia with a population of approximately 100,000 people. This outreach was conducted by the Rappahannock-Rapidan Community Service Board, an organization that combines aging, mental health, developmental disability, and substance abuse agencies under one administrative umbrella. Using a federal grant, the Board established an outreach program that identified 84 caregivers, who ranged in age from 53 to 100 years, during a one and a half year period. The majority (64) had previously been unknown to formal service providers (Rappahannock-Rapidan Community Services Board, unpublished manuscript).

At least three reasons may explain why this outreach effort was productive. First, funded by a federal grant, it supported a full-time outreach worker. Second, this effort was also facilitated by having one community organization administering the diverse agencies within this rural environment. Because professionals from the agency on aging were already a part of the lead umbrella organization, they were readily trained to identify and refer aging families with developmentally disabled members. Before this training, they had tended to focus solely on their elderly clients without probing the needs of other family members. Third, the program targeted many nontraditional sources for referrals, such as postmasters, rescue squads, pharmacists, churches, business people, and members of consumer organizations. The congenial social climate within the rural setting apparently facilitated communication between outreach staff and these referral sources.

Another method used to locate unserved individuals and their families was a collaborative effort by the New York State Office of Mental Retardation and Developmental Disabilities (NYSOMRDD), the New York State Office for Aging (SOFA), and a utility company servicing 37 counties in New York State. The utility company inserted a brief message in its monthly utility bill requesting recipients to call the SOFA toll-free hotline if they were aware of an older person with a developmental disability "who may need assistance with daily living." Despite the large population base covered by the 37 counties involved in this effort, only three previously unknown adults with a developmental disability were identified and referred to the NYSOMRDD system. A drawback of this approach was that the insert was placed into only one bill and might easily have been overlooked among the other materials included by the utility company. Another limitation was the phrasing of the announcement. Because no specific benefits or services were offered, the request to refer older persons with developmental disabilities may have been too vague to stimulate a higher response rate.

A fourth approach was undertaken by the authors in the research reported here. Because we were engaged in a research project, as opposed to a service outreach program, our goals and efforts were different than those reported above. We attempted to locate families who were not using day programs, recognizing that some of these families might be using other services provided by the mental retardation service system. To reach such families, we used a "snowball sampling" strategy (i.e., referrals coming from other respondents), mass media appeals, and referrals from sources apart from the mental retardation service system. These particular methods were selected because pilot investigations revealed that an informal social support network existed among families outside the formal service system, and media appeals were found to be useful in previous attempts to recruit family caregivers of elderly parents as research participants.

Of the 59 nonuser families identified, 22 had previously used some sort of day program but had withdrawn from this service within one year prior to the study. The remaining 37 nonuser families were far more difficult to locate because, as will be demonstrated later in this chapter, their use of other family support services was quite scarce.

Snowball sampling yielded only 8 of these 37 families, and mass media appeals only an additional 9. Contacts with sources including churches and clergy, Visiting Nurse Associations, hospital social work departments, senior citizen centers, and community mental health centers yielded a total of 11 families. Referrals from chapters of The Arc yielded 6 additional families, and another 3 were brought to our attention by the Developmental Disability Services Offices of New York State; in both agencies, workers had learned about the nonuser families through friends and other informal contacts rather than as a result of professional outreach activities.

Given that our efforts to locate older families outside the service system extended into nearly one half of the population base of New York State (including parts of New York City), it was surprising that only 37 families who had never used day services were identified. These meager results were most likely due to two factors. First, the time line of the research project allowed for only a limited period of time to be devoted to sample recruitment. Thus, both referral sources and potential respondents might not have had sufficient time to ponder their involvement with the study. Second, in contrast to the workshops in Ohio and the outreach conducted in Virginia, our project offered no concrete information or services to participating families. As a result, there was little incentive for underserved families to reveal themselves.

It was also impossible to determine how many potential families refused to participate when approached by our referral sources. Conversations with potential respondents, parent advocates, and others who identified these families for us, however, said that mothers who declined to participate did so because they feared the study was sponsored by service providers who would bring about unwanted intrusion into their lives.

Comparisons of Day Program Users and Nonusers

It is evident from the previous section that knowledge of outreach with older families of adults with mental retardation who are outside the service system is in its infancy. Even less information exists, however, regarding how these families differ from those that are well-integrated with formal service providers. In response to this concern, we have compared day program user and nonuser groups along several important dimensions.

Sociodemographic Characteristics

Sociodemographic differences, as shown in Table 1, were found between the two groups. These differences not only suggest that older families not using day programs may be at greater risk for potential disequilibria, but also that mothers in these families may have fewer of the resources that facilitate the understanding and accessing of needed services.

Mothers and offspring alike from the nonuser group were significantly older than their counterparts among the day program users. Mothers in the nonuser group were significantly more likely to be of lower socioeconomic status, to live in a rural environment, and to have more functional impairment. The nonuser mothers were also more likely to be without a spouse and to have less education than the users, although not significantly so.

Besides being older, offspring not using day programs were significantly more likely to be female and more functionally disabled than those who were day program users. The percentages of users (39.8%) and nonusers (32.2%) with Down syndrome, however, were similar.

Whereas less than one third (31.8%) of the offspring using day programs were age 40 or older, more than two thirds (67.9%) of the nonuser offspring were in this age category. This difference reflects how older cohorts of adults with mental retardation entered young adulthood at a time when community services were undeveloped (Jacobson et al., 1985; Segal, 1977). It also supports the assertion by Seltzer and Seltzer (1985) that access to services often becomes more difficult as adults with mental retardation age.

Two thirds (66.1%) of the nonuser offspring were female as compared to less than one half (42.6%) of user offspring. It could be that nonuser parents, especially the oldest cohort, were more likely to have sheltered their daughters at home. It is also possible that mother-daughter dyads use day programs less because females attract more informal social supports than do their male counterparts (Krauss, Seltzer, & Goodman, 1992). Another plausible explanation for the prevalence of female offspring among nonuser families is that this group was older, and the mortality rate among males is higher as individuals with mental retardation age (Jacobson et al., 1985).

It should be noted, however, that the differences observed between the two groups were actually quite modest, and there was considerable heterogeneity within each group. For example, although nonuser mothers were somewhat older, less educated, and had less functional ability, it should not be overlooked that 39% were in the youngest age category, nearly 30% had a college education or better, and over 35% reported having no functional problems. Thus, like the families that used day programs, our nonuser families were remarkably diverse, a fact that must be addressed in any attempt to more fully involve these families in the service system.

Service Utilization Variables

The extent to which the older mothers from the day program user and nonuser groups used, knew about, and perceived a need for 17 family support services commonly available to persons with mental retardation and their families (Heller & Factor, 1988) is summarized in Table 2.

Use of Family Support Services. Overall service utilization on the part of the nonusers of day programming was low, confirming that they have minimal interactions with professionals who serve persons with mental retardation and their families. Of the 17 services surveyed, only benefits was reported as being used by any more than 20% of the nonusers.

Table 1. Sociodemographic comparisons.

Variable	Users (n = 176)	Nonusers (n = 59)	Test Statistic
Mother's age (years)			
Mean	69.34	73.07	$t = 3.48^{***}$
SD	6.43	8.89	
Mother's marital status			
Without spouse	51.1%	64.4%	$\chi^2 = 3.14$
With spouse	48.9%	35.6%	
Mother's education			
Graduate education	6.8%	1.7%	$\chi^2 = 11.05$
College graduate	7.4%	13.6%	
Partial college	17.0%	13.6%	
High school	44.3%	33.9%	
Partial high school	15.9%	16.9%	
Junior high school	6.3%	13.6%	
Less than 7 years	2.3%	6.8%	
Mother's disability[a]			
Mean score	7.37	8.49	$t = 3.08^{**}$
SD	2.27	2.83	
Socioeconomic status[b]			
Mean score	3.41	3.09	$t = 2.18^{*}$
SD	1.01	.99	
Geographic locale			
New York City	2.8%	8.5%	$\chi^2 = 11.17^{*}$
Large-Moderate city	11.9%	11.9%	
Suburb	31.8%	16.9%	
Small city	31.3%	25.4%	
Rural	22.2%	37.3%	
Offspring's age (years)			
Mean	36.69	42.86	$t = 4.65^{***}$
SD	8.48	9.80	
Offspring's level of functioning[c]			
High ability	40.3%	28.8%	$\chi^2 = 21.64^{***}$
Competent in self-care	36.4%	27.1%	
Needs assistance	17.0%	15.3%	
Low ability	6.3%	28.8%	
Offspring's gender			
Female	42.6%	66.1%	$\chi^2 = 9.76^{**}$
Male	57.4%	33.9%	

[a] Mothers reported their Activities of Daily Living on the Shanas (1962) scale for 6 items (e.g., "Do you have trouble walking stairs?") as either (0) *No difficulty whatsoever,* (1) *Some difficulty but manageable,* or (2) *Cannot manage alone.*

[b] Hollingshead's Two-Factor Index of Social Position based on occupation and education (Miller, 1983). For 8 respondents who did not have husbands as primary breadwinners during most of the offspring's adulthood, SES was based on the mothers' status.

[c] McConkey and Walsh (1982) Index of Social Competence with mothers informing on 3 subscales: Communication Skills; Self-Care Skills (e.g., eating, use of hands, mobility); Community Skills (reading, writing, time, money). Low Ability = low rank on all three subscales; Needs Assistance = low rank on Self-Care and 1 other subscale; Competent in Self-Care = high rank on Self-Care and low rank on 1 other subscale; High Ability = high rank on all 3 subscales.

$^{*}p < .05.$ $^{**}p < .01.$ $^{***}p < .001.$

These benefits included Supplemental Security Income and Medicaid for the offspring with mental retardation. There were nine services (in addition to day programs) for which there was statistically significant higher usage among users than nonusers.

Five services (special equipment, in-home nursing, in-home respite, home services, and benefits) were reported to be used by higher percentages of nonuser than user families, yet the only statistically significant difference was that regarding home services. Nonetheless, except for benefits, each of these are direct in-home services that meet the kinds of needs associated with the advancing age of both mothers and their offspring. These services also do not require appreciable interaction with professionals from the mental retardation service system.

It is conceivable that nonuser mothers, when confronted with age-associated declines, avail themselves of support services that are necessary to maintain family stability, but only if they perceive these services to be nonintrusive.

Knowledge of Services. Higher percentages of nonusers than users reported not knowing about services. As shown in Table 2, for 10 of these services, statistically significant higher percentages of day program users than nonusers reported knowledge. Furthermore, there were 14 services about which 40% or more of the nonusers indicated no knowledge. In contrast, there were only 5 services for which the same result was observed among the users. Thus, the possibility exists that use of family support services is lower among nonusers, at least in part, because they know less about them.

On the other hand, it is conceivable that nonuse of day programs among the families in our sample reflects a deliberate choice not to use a known service. Although by definition the nonusers were not involved with day programs, 81.4% did know about their existence. Still, as noted by Krout (1983), "Hearing of a program does not indicate knowledge of what the program is or does, where it is located, or how one gets involved with it" (p. 155).

Perceived Need for Services. For 13 of the 17 services listed in Table 2, smaller percentages of nonusers than users perceived a need. There were, however, only 5 services (day programs, involvement with other families, transportation, recreational and social programs, and case management) for which these disparities were statistically significant. Thus, the differences observed between day program users and nonusers regarding perceived need for family support services were not nearly as salient as those found regarding use and knowledge of services.

Inspection of Table 2 further reveals that perceived need for most of the 17 services was surprisingly low for day program users and nonusers alike. Indeed, there were 12 services for which over 50% of the respondents from both groups perceived no need at all. Yet, there were some noteworthy exceptions, such as benefits, a service for which nearly 80% of our entire sample felt a need. Also, some services were reported to be highly needed by the user group in particular, including day programs, transportation services, and recreational activities.

Substantiating the conclusion that nonusers deliberately do not use day programs was the finding that slightly over 70% did not feel a need for them. Nevertheless, one fourth of this group did recognize a need for day programs even though they were not using them at the time of the study.

Differences in Permanency Planning

Despite speculation that use of formal services may lessen caregivers' apprehensiveness towards community residential services, and thereby facilitate long range planning for the future of their offspring (Seltzer et al., 1991; Smith & Tobin, 1993; Wood & Skiles, 1992), empirical evidence has been limited. Thus, a major goal of our study was to contrast mothers from nonuser and user families regarding the extent of their residential, financial, and legal planning.

Residential arrangements were categorized according to five ascending stages of planning: (1) No discussion of future residence had taken place; (2) early discussions

Table 2. Comparison of nonusers ($n = 59$) and users ($n = 176$) on service utilization variables.

Service	Use	Knowledge	Perceived Need		
			Not at all	Somewhat	Very much
Direct Out-of-Home Services					
Day programs					
Nonusers	0.0%	81.4%	71.2%	13.6%	11.9%
Users	100.0%	97.2%	11.9%	9.1%	79.0%
χ^2	158.57***	17.39***		95.59***	
Out-of-home respite					
Nonusers	1.7%	49.2%	72.9%	11.9%	10.2%
Users	12.5%	77.3%	67.6%	18.2%	12.5%
χ^2	5.84*	16.71***		1.73	
Specialized therapies					
Nonusers	5.1%	59.3%	64.4%	11.9%	18.6%
Users	36.4%	83.0%	55.1%	15.3%	29.5%
χ^2	21.21***	13.94***		3.88	
Transportation					
Nonusers	6.8%	61.0 %	57.6%	18.6%	18.6%
Users	73.9%	91.5 %	19.3%	4.5%	75.6%
χ^2	81.14***	30.25***		60.68***	
Recreational activities					
Nonusers	13.6%	61.0%	57.6%	15.3%	22.0%
Users	60.8%	84.7%	21.0%	20.5%	58.0%
χ^2	39.46***	14.75***		35.69***	
Direct In-Home Services					
Special equipment					
Nonusers	10.2%	44.1%	88.1%	5.1%	5.1%
Users	5.1%	46.6%	88.6%	4.5%	6.3%
χ^2	1.89	0.11		0.13	
In-home nursing					
Nonusers	10.2%	52.5%	86.4%	6.8%	3.4%
Users	5.7%	59.1%	90.9%	2.8%	4.5%
χ^2	1.40	0.78		1.97	
In-home respite					
Nonusers	11.9%	44.1%	72.9%	13.6%	10.2%
Users	5.1%	65.9%	79.5%	11.9%	8.5%
χ^2	3.17	8.82**		0.29	
Home services					
Nonusers	18.6%	52.5%	76.3%	3.4%	20.3%
Users	8.0%	59.1%	87.5%	2.3%	9.1%
χ^2	5.31*	0.78		5.70	

Table 2. (continued)

Service	Use	Knowledge	Perceived Need		
			Not at all	Somewhat	Very much

Indirect Services

Benefits

	Use	Knowledge	Not at all	Somewhat	Very much
Nonusers	84.7%	94.9%	20.3%	13.6%	66.1%
Users	81.3%	94.3%	17.0%	10.2%	72.7%
χ^2	0.37	0.03	0.98		

Case management

	Use	Knowledge	Not at all	Somewhat	Very much
Nonusers	15.3%	55.9%	52.5%	15.3%	25.4%
Users	39.2%	68.2%	42.0%	33.5%	22.7%
χ^2	11.43***	2.92	7.48*		

Parent training

	Use	Knowledge	Not at all	Somewhat	Very much
Nonusers	1.7%	39.0%	78.0%	8.5%	10.2%
Users	13.6%	57.4%	75.0%	12.5%	10.2%
χ^2	6.63**	6.00**	0.72		

Family counseling

	Use	Knowledge	Not at all	Somewhat	Very much
Nonusers	5.1%	57.6%	84.7%	10.2%	5.1%
Users	10.2%	64.2%	81.3%	11.9%	6.3%
χ^2	1.44	0.82	0.27		

Other families

	Use	Knowledge	Not at all	Somewhat	Very much
Nonusers	6.8%	55.9%	84.7%	6.8%	3.4%
Users	26.1%	71.0%	64.2%	23.3%	12.5%
χ^2	9.88**	4.57*	13.99***		

Permanency Planning Services

Residential planning information

	Use	Knowledge	Not at all	Somewhat	Very much
Nonusers	15.3%	72.9%	55.9%	20.3%	23.7%
Users	30.7%	85.8%	53.4%	18.8%	27.8%
χ^2	5.36*	5.12*	0.39		

Guardianship information

	Use	Knowledge	Not at all	Somewhat	Very much
Nonusers	5.1%	61.0%	72.9%	6.8%	20.3%
Users	17.6%	77.8%	63.6%	14.8%	21.0%
χ^2	5.61*	6.44**	2.72		

Financial planning information

	Use	Knowledge	Not at all	Somewhat	Very much
Nonusers	10.2%	45.8%	78.0%	5.1%	16.9%
Users	18.2%	44.3%	68.2%	17.0%	14.2%
χ^2	2.09	1.75	5.25		

Note. Percentages do not equal 100% due to missing data.
*$p < .05$. **$p < .01$. ***$p < .001$.

Table 3. Permanency planning activities reported by users and nonusers.

Planning Activities	Users (n = 176)		Nonusers (n = 59)	
	n	%	n	%
Level of residential planning				
No discussion	27	15.3	20	33.9
Early discussion	21	11.9	9	15.3
Serious consideration	22	12.5	6	10.2
Provisional plans	21	11.9	3	5.1
Definite plans	85	48.3	21	35.6
Existing financial plans				
No arrangements	60	34.1	19	32.2
Money/Property willed to other person	52	29.5	15	25.4
Money/Property willed to offspring with mental retardation	23	13.1	10	16.9
Trust	22	12.5	7	11.9
Other	19	10.8	8	13.6
Guardianship plans made				
Yes	99	56.3	19	32.2
No	77	43.8	40	67.8

had occurred, but they were not serious in nature; (3) alternatives had been seriously considered without any resolution of choices; (4) provisional plans had been made that were somewhat indefinite or tenuous; and (5) definite residential plans had been established. This hierarchy of planning stages is conceptually similar to the measure of placement tendency recently developed by Blacher (1990) for use with parents of severely handicapped children.

Significant differences were found between the two groups regarding the five stages of residential planning (χ^2 = 11.80, df = 4, p < .02). As shown in Table 3, a greater proportion of nonuser mothers indicated that they had not yet discussed the future residence of their offspring. In contrast, a higher percentage of the user mothers reported that they had made definite plans. Still, over half (51.6) of the mothers from families using day programs had not made definite plans for where their offspring would eventually live.

Similar findings were obtained for guardianship plans. A significantly higher proportion of nonusers than day program

users reported having made no plans for who will eventually become guardian for their mentally retarded son or daughter (χ^2 = 10.22, df = 1, p < .001). Over two fifths (43.8%) of the mothers in user families, however, said that they had not yet made guardianship plans.

No significant differences were found between the two groups concerning future plans for their offsprings' financial well-being. About one third of the mothers from both groups reported that they had not established any financial plans.

Given that the sociodemographic differences described earlier between the user and nonuser groups may have confounded the results regarding residential and guardianship planning, two regression analyses were carried out to explore this possibility. First, a multiple regression analysis was conducted in which group status (day program use vs. nonuse) and 8 sociodemographic variables were entered into the regression equation simultaneously as predictors of residential planning. As shown in Table 4, group status remained significantly related to residential planning when the sociodemographic variables were controlled, and none of the 8 was found to be significantly associated with residential planning.

Next, a logit regression analysis was similarly performed with guardianship plans as the dependent variable. This analytic method was selected because future guardianship arrangements were scored dichotomously as having been made or not. As shown also in Table 4, the results of this analysis were parallel to those obtained for the multiple regression analysis for residential planning. Specifically, group status was the only variable found to be significantly related to having made future guardianship plans.

These findings support the speculation that use of day services fosters long-range planning. Nevertheless, with respect to all three forms of permanency planning, a large number of families had left the future of their offspring unresolved, regardless of whether or not they were using day programs. Indeed, it seemed that some parents would probably never make plans. For example, a 96-year-old mother told her interviewer that it was not yet "due time" to make any plans. Another mother said that she hoped that Armageddon would come soon so that she would not have to worry any more about her daughter's future.

Planning for the eventuality of relinquishing the care of a loved one to another is not a simple act that occurs at a single point in time. Instead, it is a painstakingly difficult process that may require support from others. This was evidenced by the finding that use of formal services was associated with greater planning, as well as by comments from mothers that the interview itself had encouraged them to begin planning. Moreover, similar conclusions have recently been reached in studies of caregivers from different populations. Blacher (1990), for example, asserted that counselors can best assist par-

Table 4. Regression results for residential planning and guardianship plans ($N = 235$).

Variables	Residential Planning Stage (Multiple Regression)	Guardianship Plans (Logit Regression)		
	Betas	B	SE	Wald
Group status				
Users vs. nonusers	.16*	-1.04	.35	8.77**
Offspring characteristics				
Gender	-.07	.13	.28	.21
Functional ability	.01	-.28	.15	3.57
Mother characteristics				
Age (years)	-.12	.02	.02	.89
Marital status	.07	-.43	.29	2.23
Education	.06	-.05	.12	.16
Disability level	-.05	.02	.06	.13
Family characteristics				
Socioeconomic level	-.13	-.19	.16	1.40
Geographic location	-.03	-.06	.12	.32

Note. Offspring age was not entered into the regression equations due to multicollinearity with mother age.
*$p < .05$. **$p < .005$.

ents of severely handicapped children with permanency planning concerns by first determining the stage parents have reached in the process of deciding whether or not to place their child outside the home. Similarly, Pruchno, Michaels, and Potashnik (1990), in their research on elderly persons caring for a demented spouse, suggested that the institutionalization of a spouse should be viewed by practitioners as a process rather than an event.

Differences in Maternal Well-Being

Presently, a dearth of knowledge exists regarding factors associated with the well-being of older parents who care for a mentally retarded son or daughter living at home. Seltzer and Krauss (1989) found that use of formal services (including day programs) was unrelated to four conceptually different indices of well-being among a sample of 203 mothers age 55 and older. They also noted, however, that "the generalizability of these findings to families who are either not well integrated or more integrated into their state's service network is unknown" (p. 310).

We, therefore, compared day program user and nonuser mothers on four separate indices of emotional well-being: Caregiver satisfaction, subjective caregiving burden, current mood state, and an interviewer rating of emotional well-being. Caregiver satisfaction was measured by a four-item Likert-type scale which assessed affect directly linked to caregiving (e.g., "I take care of more because I want to than out of a sense of duty"). The Zarit Burden Interview (Zarit & Zarit, 1983) was used to measure the extent of burden perceived regarding caregiving. Current mood state was assessed using the Bradburn Affect Balance Scale (Bradburn, 1969), which reflects the ratio between the respondent's experience of positive and negative affect. To assess more persistent qualities of emotional well-being, our clinical interviewers were asked to rate mothers on the Life Satisfaction Rating Scale (Neugarten, Havighurst, & Tobin, 1961).

Multivariate analysis of variance was used to compare the mean scores for the two groups

on all four measures, and a statistically significant overall group effect emerged, $F(4, 218) = 2.48$, $p < .05$. Subsequent univariate tests revealed that mothers in the day program user group had significantly more favorable mean scores on the interviewer rating of overall well-being, $F(1, 221) = 8.21$, $p < .005$. No statistically significant differences were found between the groups, however, on caregiver satisfaction, subjective burden, or mood state.

Given the possibility that differences on the interviewer rating of emotional well-being might have been affected by knowledge of the previously reported sociodemographic differences between day program users and nonusers or of the greater permanency planning achieved by the user mothers, a multiple regression analysis was performed to determine if use of day programs would remain associated with emotional well-being when these other potential influences were controlled. As shown in Table 5, the interviewer rating of emotional well-being was primarily attributable to differences in the functional ability of the mothers in the two groups. That is, it appears that the lower level of emotional well-being among nonuser mothers was most likely due to their greater disability. This finding also diminishes any concern that the interviewers' ratings of emotional well-being were biased by their knowledge of the mothers' group status. In summary, these results are consistent with those of Seltzer and Krauss (1989) who found no relationship between service utilization and four distinct indices of maternal well-being, only one of which (i.e., subjective burden) overlapped those reported here. Across the two studies, then, service utilization *per se* was found to be unrelated to such conceptually distinct dimensions of caregiver well-being as current mood state, physical health, caregiving satisfaction, parenting stress, life satisfaction, and perceived burden. These findings clearly contradict the assumption by policymakers in both mental retardation and gerontology that "formal services enable families to continue to care for a dependent member because services improve the well-being of caregiving families" (Seltzer & Krauss, 1989, p. 310).

Table 5. Multiple regression results for interviewer rating of emotional well-being.

Variables	Beta Coefficients
Group status	
Users vs. nonusers	.09
Permanency planning	
Guardianship plans	-.05
Residential plans	.01
Offspring characteristics	
Gender	-.04
Functional ability	-.06
Mother characteristics	
Age (years)	.04
Marital status	-.09
Education	.14
Disability level	-.21*
Family characteristics	
Socioeconomic level	-.01
Geographic location	.07

$R^2 = .13$

Note. Variables were introduced into the equation simultaneously, and offspring age was not entered due to multicollinearity with mother age.

*$p < .005$.

Why Do Families Not Use Services?

Although the reasons for lower levels of service utilization among some older families are not known, our findings are consistent with explanations in both the aging and mental retardation literature regarding lack of service use. The finding that the nonuser offspring with mental retardation, as well as their mothers, were older suggests the possibility of a cohort effect on utilization of mental retardation services.

There are several ways in which belonging to older cohorts might affect service use. One is that older cohorts of parents may use less mental retardation services because of historical factors concerning their availability to families. As noted earlier, the majority of community services were unavailable throughout most of the lifetime of the existing cohort of older adults with mental retardation. Prior to the deinstitutionalization of the 1960s and the development of family support programs during the 1970s, options for persons with mental retardation and their families were at the extremes of either institutionalization or sole reliance on informal support from relatives, neighbors, and friends (Lippman & Loberg, 1985; Tymchuk, 1983).

Despite the later development of community service alternatives, many parents grew older with the erroneous belief that contact with the service system would quickly lead to institutionalization of their son or daughter with mental retardation. A 90-year-old mother in our nonuser group, for example, recalled the recommendation of her family physician to place her mentally retarded daughter in an institution, advice that led this mother to believe "that they wanted to throw her away like an old dish rag." As a result, this belief has persisted for more than one half century. It is also possible that, without the availability of formal assistance in their youth, many parents from older cohorts were compelled to develop coping skills enabling them to handle problems on their own with great self-assurance. Thus, in their later years, they may regard professional help as being superfluous, even when objective circumstances suggest otherwise (Engelhardt, Brubaker, & Lutzer, 1988). As one of our respondents said, "My son's daily needs are taken care of by me, we don't need help from anyone." For many older parents, it is inconceivable that the young professionals in mental retardation agencies could possess the same level of patience, understanding, and competence that took them so many years to achieve with their son or daughter with mental retardation.

It is also possible that older cohorts of parents use few mental retardation services due to painful interactions with professionals that occurred when they were younger. These unfavorable interactions could have resulted in a lack of confidence and trust in professionals that, in turn, prompted avoidance or withdrawal from professional help in later stages of the family life cycle. One of our respondents calmly stated, "Many of the people connected to the services that we have used have not been dependable in fulfilling their responsibilities." Another mother more angrily blurted, "I'm frustrated with service providers, and they have not been very helpful." Such attitudes may be reinforced by the prevailing focus of today's mental retardation services on children and young adults (Seltzer et al., 1991; Sison & Cotten, 1989), which may act as a further disincentive for parents of aging offspring to make use of formal services.

Recall also that today's older parents conceived their child with mental retardation during a historical period when people with mental retardation were predominantly viewed as worthless and inferior (Tymchuk, 1983). This stigmatization often produced feelings of shame, low self-worth, and even nonacceptance of the disability among parents that may have inhibited them from seeking professional assistance (Nadler, Lewinstein, & Rahav, 1991). Now, in their later years, these older parents' feelings of low self-worth are likely to be exacerbated by the ageism that has been reported to exist within the mental retardation service system (Janicki, 1988; Seltzer & Seltzer, 1985; Smith & Tobin, 1993). Case managers have reported to us (Smith & Tobin, 1993) that older mothers are often anxious because they believe that they will be perceived as inadequate by younger and better educated female professionals in the mental retardation field. Thus, older parents may be reluctant to seek help from a service system which they feel stigmatizes both their offspring with mental retardation and themselves (Paul & Beckman-Bell, 1981).

Another possible cohort effect on the use of mental retardation services is reflected in our finding that older mothers from nonuser families tend to be more disabled and less educated than user mothers. These two characteristics, which are more typical of today's oldest cohorts, are likely to affect the ability of older parents to understand and access needed services for both themselves and their mentally retarded offspring. Seltzer (1992) has commented that "contemporary aging and disability service networks are highly complex, and family members may therefore be insufficiently aware of community entitlements and resources" (pp. 66–67). Likewise, case managers from the mental retardation service system have noted that the oldest parents require more assistance to deal with the system's bureaucracy (Smith & Tobin, 1993). Thus, parents from the older cohorts (i.e., those likely to have less energy due to increased frailties and fewer cognitive skills because of less education) may opt to avoid these complexities by remaining distant from the mental retardation service system.

Finally, research on service utilization within the aging network suggests that negligible participation characterizes all but a small minority of the elderly in the United States, and this holds true even for those elderly persons who have knowledge of services and physical access to them. Krout (1983) concluded, "Many elderly do not hold positive attitudes towards services, utilization rates are extremely low, and the correlates of service use are not well understood" (p. 153). Thus, the failure of many older families to utilize mental retardation services may simply reflect a bias against service utilization that is present among older cohorts in general.

Implications for Practice, Policy, and Research

Practice Implications

Although our findings suggest that older families who are not well-integrated in the mental retardation service system differ in a number of ways from those older families who are well-integrated, there is also a considerable amount of heterogeneity observed among the nonuser families. Thus, practitioners must realize that there is no such thing as a typical nonuser family, that each family may have its own reasons for their limited use formal services, and that use of services "exists at many different levels of frequency, duration, and intensity" (Krout, 1983, p. 162).

It should also be recognized that engaging older nonuser families, especially those who have never used day programming services, in permanency planning may be even more difficult than locating them. This was evidenced by the finding that nonuse was associated with less planning, particularly for future residence and guardianship, the two aspects of permanency planning foreshadow separation from an offspring with mental retardation.

On the other hand, the permanency planning workshops conducted in Ohio revealed that some older families who do not avail themselves of formal services do welcome assistance with the planning process, that is, apparently when help is perceived as coming from outside the realm of the mental retardation service system. Thus, while input from mental retardation professionals is essential for developing outreach programs, maybe such activities should not be promoted under the auspices of mental retardation providers, but rather by family service agencies or organizations within the aging network.

Another practice implication is that, to be successful, outreach efforts directed towards older families outside the service system must be truly resolute and comprehensive in nature. These efforts must be resolute because experience has shown that it can take as long as 6 to 12 months for outreach appeals to be effective.

Resoluteness is also necessary because administrators must be willing to commit extensive staff time to outreach. Agencies that expect clinicians to divide their time between their caseloads and outreach may compromise both endeavors. As noted by Stuen (1985), "The hiring of qualified staff and their training is the first phase of outreach" (p. 89).

Outreach efforts to identify older families of adults with mental retardation who are outside of the mental retardation service system must also be comprehensive in nature. These efforts must not only involve professionals from the mental retardation and aging networks, but they must also include clergy, lawyers, elected officials, physicians, nurses, and a wide variety of other nontraditional

contacts (see, for discussion, Stuen, 1985). Furthermore, to insure their interest and cooperation, it is sensible to invite representatives from these diverse potential referral sources to participate in an advisory committee.

The involvement of individuals from diverse professional and nonprofessional backgrounds may rest on raising their consciousness to be heedful of a mentally retarded offspring within older families. After a referral is made, an experienced mental retardation professional can provide a personalized follow-up (Stuen, 1985).

Outreach efforts to identify families of adults with mental retardation outside the system must also encompass complexity in the sense that they must address ethnic and cultural factors. To be effective, outreach must be sensitive to the differing values, customs, and preferences that exist among special populations. It is especially important not to violate or offend cultural tradition (Stuen, 1985). Unfortunately, however, little information is available about nonuser families of differing race, ethnicity, or culture.

Finally, the mental retardation service system must become more responsive and meaningful to older families. It is important to provide services on the families' terms rather than according to standard professional guidelines. For example, many clinicians find that chatting with parents over coffee is an effective way of establishing trust and rapport. Some older parents may prefer to talk extensively to professionals on the phone, but refuse to allow them to meet the offspring with mental retardation.

Professional time spent in these informal interchanges may be effective in enabling clinicians to secure information that may eventually facilitate assistance to older parents or their offspring with mental retardation.

Although patience and tolerance are required in serving older parents, the mental retardation service system does not typically reward these behaviors. One case manager that we interviewed provided the following perspective: "In this job you're judged successful if you give services that result in outcome. So, the feeling is why work with older parents who will die. Your job tenure is threatened if you work too much with older parents" (Smith & Tobin, 1993).

The mental retardation service system can also become more meaningful to all older families by recognizing that their most pressing needs are different from those of younger families. Whereas the greatest family support needs of younger families center on the education and socialization of children, health maintenance and long-term care become the predominant focus of services to support older family caregivers (Seltzer & Krauss, chapter 1 this volume). Indeed, our data suggest that health related issues are especially salient among older nonuser families. Thus, mental retardation professionals need to know more about aging issues to understand the age-related changes and transitions that confront these families. They must also know how to make appropriate referrals to professionals and programs within the aging services network (Smith & Tobin, 1993). Another possibility worth considering is the cultivation of geriatric specialists within the mental retardation service system (Sutton, Sterns, Schwartz, & Roberts, 1992).

Policy Implications

One major impediment to service delivery to older families has been a lack of coordination between the aging and mental retardation networks (Sison & Cotten, 1989). Given the complexity and bureaucracy that is present within each of these networks, it is not surprising that so many older families do not use the services provided by both. In order to be successful, attempts to identify and serve older families that are outside the system will require closer collaboration between the two service networks.

There also is a strong tendency within the mental retardation service system to regard family members as merely resources for the disabled member, rather than recognizing that the family itself has needs that must be met (Slater & Wikler, 1986). This was exemplified recently by the Legislative and Social Policy Document of the American Association on Mental Retardation (1992), which invoked the integration of elderly persons with mental retardation into mainstream aging services, but failed to address specifically the concerns of their family caregivers. In contrast, the 1992 amendments to the Older Americans Act of 1965 called directly for the provision of services to "older individuals who provide uncompensated care to their adult children with disabilities, or counseling to assist such older individuals with permanency planning for such children" (U.S. House of Representatives, 1992, p. 2606).

Further, outreach to older parents of adults with mental retardation will necessitate additional resources and expenditures by the mental retardation service system. It was noted earlier that outreach will not be productive unless extensive staff time is devoted to it. As increasing numbers of families become identified, a parallel increase in available services may be required (Stuen, 1985). Moreover, additional community residences will be needed to insure placement options for the offspring with mental retardation following parental death (Seltzer et al., 1991).

Research Implications

Future research is needed to establish typologies of older families of adults with mental retardation who are outside the service system. As the composition of our sample suggests, nonuse of services is best regarded as a continuum rather than as a simple dichotomy (see also Krout, 1983). Some older families have never used any services; others have used services in the past, but have since withdrawn from them; whereas still others are using available services to a minimal degree. However, potential sociodemographic and psychological characteristics that differentiate these family types remain unknown.

The finding that nonuser families contained higher proportions of female offspring with mental retardation than did user families suggests that the impact of offspring's gender on service use warrants further consideration. It remains to be determined, for example, if this finding is attributable to a sampling artifact or due to such factors as greater interdependence within mother-daughter dyads, or superior informal supports evoked by female offspring that preclude the need for formal services.

Although there are important findings regarding perceived need for various family support services among nonuser families in our study, these data are self-report and subjective in nature. Thus, studies are needed in which self-report data is triangulated with more objective techniques such as detailed clinical assessments, input from key informants, and sociodemographic profiles.

Research is also needed to replicate the findings regarding service utilization and permanency planning. Why do nonusers engage in less residential and legal planning than users? Does service utilization reduce parents' apprehensiveness towards future caregivers for their offspring with mental retardation, or are both nonuse of mental retardation services and lack of permanency planning indicative of generalized avoidance coping on the part of nonusers?

To date no studies have been reported regarding clinical interventions with older families of adults with mental retardation who do not use formal services. One obvious direction for future research is to examine the impact of outreach efforts directed at this target population. Are some outreach techniques more effective than others in motivating nonusers to intensify their involvement with formal services? Do those families who are identified through outreach eventually develop increased acceptance of formal services, or do they remain resistant? And, would older parents from nonuser families be more receptive to services for their offspring with mental retardation if they were provided by the aging network?

Another direction for intervention research with older families that do not use mental retardation services is to examine the efficacy of workshops and support groups that are designed to assist them with permanency planning. As noted earlier in this chapter, many nonuser families may be attracted to such programs when they are presented under the auspices of providers outside the mental retardation system. Whether or not these families actually benefit from or use the information provided by interventions like these, however, remains unknown.

This list of prospective studies suggests the kinds of research that need to be undertaken in order to better understand and more adequately serve older families of persons with mental retardation who are presently outside the formal service system.

References

American Association on Mental Retardation. (1992). *Legislative and social policy document: Final text draft for 1993 edition.* Washington, DC: Author.

Barbero, S. L. (1989). Community-based, day treatments for mentally retarded adults. *Social Work,* November, 545–548.

Becker, P. (1991). *Report of the Committee for Future Planning.* Jewish Community Center, Canton, Ohio.

Blacher, J. (1990). Assessing placement tendency in families with children who have severe handicaps. *Research in Developmental Disabilities, 11,* 349–359.

Bradburn, N. (1969). *The structure of psychological well-being.* Chicago: Aldine.

Brubaker, T. H., Engelhardt, J. L., Brubaker, E., & Lutzer, V. D. (1989). Gender differences of older caregivers of adults with mental retardation. *The Journal of Applied Gerontology, 8,* 183–191.

Engelhardt, J., Brubaker, T. H., & Lutzer, V. (1988). Older caregivers of adults with mental retardation: Service utilization. *Mental Retardation, 26,* 191–195.

Gold, M., Dobrof, R., Torian, L. (1987). *Parents of the adult developmentally disabled* (Final report presented to the United Hospital Trust Fund). New York: Brookdale Center on Aging.

Grant, G. (1986). Older carers, interdependence and care of mentally handicapped adults. *Ageing and Society, 6,* 333–351.

Heller, T., & Factor, A. (1988). Permanency planning among black and white family caregivers of older adults with mental retardation. *Mental Retardation, 26,* 203–208.

Heller, T., & Factor, A. (1991). Permanency planning for adults with mental retardation living with family caregivers. *American Journal on Mental Retardation, 96,* 163–1976.

Horne, M. (1989). Identifying a "hidden" population of older adults with mental handicap: Outreach in the U.K. *Australia and New Zealand Journal of Developmental Disabilities, 15,* 207–218.

Jacobson, J. W., Sutton, M. S., & Janicki, M. P. (1985). Demography and characteristics of aging and aged mentally retarded persons. In M. P. Janicki & H. M. Wisniewski (Eds.), *Aging and developmental disabilities: Issues and approaches* (pp. 115–142). Baltimore, MD: Brookes.

Janicki, M. P. (1988). Symposium overview — The new challenge. *Mental Retardation, 26,* 177–180.

Janicki, M. P., Otis, J. P., Puccio, P. S., Rettig, J. H., & Jacobson, J. W. (1985). Service needs among older developmentally disabled persons. In M. P. Janicki & H. M. Wisniewski (Eds.), *Aging and developmental disabilities: Issues and approaches* (pp. 289–304). Baltimore, MD: Brookes.

Justice, R. S., O'Connor, G., & Warren, N. (1971). Problems reported by parents of mentally retarded children – who helps? *American Journal of Mental Deficiency, 75,* 685–691.

Kaufman, A. V., Adams, J. P., & Campbell, V. A. (1991). Permanency planning by older parents who care for adult children with mental retardation. *Mental Retardation, 5,* 293–300.

Kaufman, A. V., DeWeaver, K., & Glicken, M. (1989). The mentally retarded aged: Implications for social work practice. *Journal of Gerontological Social Work, 14,* 93–110.

Krauss, M. W., Seltzer, M. M., & Goodman, S. J. (1992). Social support networks of adults with mental retardation at home. *American Journal on Mental Retardation, 96,* 432–441.

Krout, J. A. (1983). Knowledge and use of services: A critical review of the literature. *International Journal of Aging and Human Development, 17,* 153–167.

Lippman, L., & Loberg, D. E. (1985). An overview of developmental disabilities. In M. P. Janicki & H. M. Wisniewski (Eds.), *Aging and developmental disabilities: Issues and approaches* (pp. 41–58). Baltimore, MD: Brookes.

McConkey, R., & Walsh, J. (1982). An index of social competence for use in determining the service needs of mentally handicapped adults. *Developmental Deficiency Research, 26,* 47–61.

Miller, D.C. (1983). *Handbook of research design and social measurement.* New York: Longman.

Nadler, A., Lewinstein, E., & Rahav, G. (1991). Acceptance of mental retardation and help-seeking by mothers and fathers of children with mental retardation. *Mental Retardation, 29,* 17–23.

Neugarten, B. L., Havighurst, R. J., & Tobin, S. S. (1961). The measurement of life satisfaction. *Journal of Gerontology, 16,* 134–143.

Paul, J. L., & Beckman-Bell, P. (1981). *Understanding and working with parents of children with special needs.* New York: Holt, Rinehart & Winston.

Pruchno, R. A., Michaels, J. E., & Potashnik, S. L. (1990). Predictors of institutionalization among Alzheimer Disease victims with caregiving spouses. *Journal of Gerontology, 45,* S259–266.

Rappahannock Rapidan Community Services Board (unpublished manuscript). Project evaluation report.

Roberto, K. A. (1988). *Caring for aging developmentally disabled adults: Perspectives and needs of older parents* (Final report presented to the Colorado Developmental Disabilities Planning Council). Greeley: University of Northern Colorado, Department of Human Services.

Rose, T., & Ansello, E. F. (1987). *Aging and developmental disabilities: Research and planning.* College Park, MD: University of Maryland, Center on Aging.

Segal, R. (1977). Trends in services for the aged mentally retarded. *Mental Retardation, 15,* 25–27.

Seltzer, M. M. (1992). Training families to be case managers for elders with developmental disabilities. *Generations, 16,* 65–70.

Seltzer, M. M., & Janicki, M. P. (Eds.) (1991). *Aging and developmental disabilities: Challenges for the 1990s* (Proceedings of the Boston Roundtable on Research Issues and Applications in Aging and Developmental Disabilities). Washington, DC: American Association on Mental Retardation, Special Interest Group on Aging.

Seltzer, M. M., & Krauss, M. W. (1989). Aging parents with mentally retarded children: Family risk factors and sources of support. *American Journal on Mental Retardation, 94,* 303–312.

Seltzer, M. M., & Krauss, M. W. (1994). Aging parents with coresident adult children: The impact of lifelong caregiving. In M. M. Seltzer, M. W. Krauss, & M. P. Janicki (Eds.), *Life course perspectives on adulthood and old age* (pp. 3–18). Washington, DC: American Association on Mental Retardation.

Seltzer, M. M., Krauss, M. W., & Heller, T. (1991). Family caregiving over the life course. In M. P. Janicki & M. M. Seltzer (Eds.), *Aging and developmental disabilities: Challenges for the 1990s.* (Proceedings of the Boston Roundtable on Research Issues and Applications in Aging and Developmental Disabilities) (pp. 3–24). Washington, DC: American Association on Mental Retardation, Special Interest Group on Aging.

Seltzer, M. M., & Seltzer, G. B. (1985). The elderly mentally retarded. A group in need of service. *Journal of Gerontological Social Work, 8,* 99–119.

Shanas, E. (1962). *The health of older people: A social survey.* Cambridge: Harvard University Press.

Sison, G. F. P., & Cotten, P. D. (1989). The elderly mentally retarded person: Current perspectives and future directions. *The Journal of Applied Gerontology, 8,* 151–167.

Slater, M. A., & Wikler, L. (1986). "Normalized" family resources for families with a developmentally disabled child. *Social Work, 31,* 385–389.

Smith, G. C., & Tobin, S. S. (1989). Permanency planning among older parents of adults with lifelong disabilities. *Journal of Gerontological Social Work, 14,* 35–59.

Smith, G. C., & Tobin, S. S. (1993). Case managers' perceptions of practice with older parents of developmentally disabled adults. In K. A. Roberto (Ed.), *The elderly caregiver: Caring for adults with developmental disabilities* (pp. 146–169). Beverly Hills, CA: Sage.

Stuen, C. (1985). Outreach to the elderly: Community based services. *Journal of Gerontological Social Work, 8,* 85–96.

Sutton, E., Sterns, H. L., Schwartz, L., & Roberts, R. (1992). The training of a specialist in developmental disabilities and aging. *Generations, 16,* 71–74.

Tymchuk, A. J. (1983). Interventions with parents of the mentally retarded. In J. L. Matson & J. A. Mulick (Eds.), *Handbook of mental retardation* (pp. 369–380). New York: Pergamon Press.

U.S. House of Representatives. (1992). *Congressional Record,* April 9, H 2606.

Wood, J. B., & Skiles, L. L. (1992). Planning for the transfer of care. *Generations, 16,* 61–62.

Zarit, S. H., & Zarit, J. M. (1983). *The burden interview.* University Park: Pennsylvania State University.

Funded by a grant from the National Institute on Aging (AG09198) and by support to the first author from the General Research Board of the University of Maryland, College Park (Summer 1992).

Chapter 3

Facilitating Future Planning and Transitions Out of the Home

Tamar Heller, University of Illinois at Chicago
Alan Factor, University of Illinois at Chicago

Most families of persons with developmental disabilities provide lifelong care for them. Although out-of-home placement increases as parents age, it is not the predominant residential arrangement for these persons until parental death or disability occurs (Meyers, Borthwick, & Eyman, 1985). Two major concerns are faced by these families: Can they continue providing care in their homes? What plans are in place for their relative's future when they can no longer provide care?

Long-term care planning for the future of adults with lifelong mental retardation is a major task faced by their families and by service providers. As family caregivers of these adults age, they face the dual strain of their own aging process and the aging of their relative. Hence, they need to plan not only for their own aging, but also for that of their relative who may outlive them. In particular, older caregivers need to consider arrangements for the time when they can no longer care for their relative due to age-related incapacities or death. Until recently researchers and policymakers in the fields of both mental retardation and gerontology have paid scant attention to the planning needs of these caregivers.

In this chapter, we review the literature on future planning among families of adults with mental retardation and discusses the implications for future research, public policy, and service provision. First, we describe plans families have made in regard to residential, legal, and financial arrangements. Second, we review findings on the factors associated with planning and out-of-home placements and the implications of long-term care planning on

family functioning. Next, we review family support needs and interventions, and, in the last section, we suggest guidelines for facilitating transitions and long-term planning and address future research needs.

Content and Context of Planning

Long-term planning includes making future residential, legal, and financial arrangements and planning for the future quality of life of the adult with mental retardation. Despite the importance of these areas, there has been little research on family decision-making regarding these issues and on the preferences of caregivers and adults with retardation regarding available and desired options. It has long been noted that older caregivers often neglect to plan for their relative's long-term care, put it off for years, or give up in frustration (Carswell & Hartig, 1979; Gold, Dobrof, & Torian, 1987; Goodman, 1978; Heller & Factor, 1991; Kriger, 1975; Roberto, 1988; Turnbull, Brotherson, & Summers, 1985). Yet a major concern voiced by caregivers in these studies is planning for the future when they will no longer be able to provide care. Examples of the concern expressed by families are illustrated by caregivers interviewed in our studies of future planning:

"I worry about if I should lose my health, what will it be like for her?"

"She has been our main concern in life in taking care of her—but our years of life are fast coming to the end; for this and other arrangements will have to he made. I have not been able to do this as yet. If one or the

other should die, the decision would have to be made, because as a team we can manage but one alone will not be able to carry the load."

Residential Planning

Although all these studies note the high ambivalence, anxiety, and difficulty families experience in discussing these issues and in making plans, several recent studies conducted in three different states have noted considerable variation in the percentage of families who do engage in planning. In regard to living arrangements, Heller and Factor's (1991) study in Illinois found that only one quarter of the 100 caregivers interviewed (mean age of 63) had made concrete plans (defined as placement on a waiting list or making arrangements for long-term care with another family member). Roberto's (1988) study in Colorado found that less than one quarter of the 61 caregivers (mean age of 69) had toured any residential facilities and only 43% had begun to make any future care arrangements with relatives. In a study of 235 caregivers in New York state (mean age of 70 years), Smith (1992) found that 45% had established definite residential plans and another 10% had made provisional residential plans for their relative. Gold et al. (1987) reported that in their New York study of 42 caregivers (mean age of 72) at least two thirds of the families had applied for their relative's placement in a residential program. However, most had made applications years ago that were no longer kept on current waiting lists.

Although concrete planning may be limited, a sizable number of respondents in the above studies expressed their desire for placement. For example, Gold et al. (1987) reported that over 60% of the caregivers wanted placement for their relative while the caregiver was still alive and well. In contrast, only 30% of the caregivers in the Heller and Factor (1991) study indicated that they wanted these placements to occur in their lifetime. Some of the discrepancy in findings could be due to demographic differences in these studies. For example, the Gold et al. sample was somewhat older and urban, and

the Heller and Factor sample was younger and from both urban and rural areas. Also, the sample in Heller and Factor's study included more African-American caregivers than did the Roberto study (25% versus 17%). (The Gold et al. study did not include data on race.) As indicated later in this review, socioeconomic status and race are likely to influence the degree to which families seek out-of-home placement plans for their relative with mental retardation. Another demographic difference among the studies was in numbers of sibling caregivers, which were higher in the Heller and Factor (15%) and Roberto (21%) studies than in the Gold et al. study (4%). The Smith study included only mother primary caregivers. One would expect less concrete planning in families where the caregiver is a sibling.

Generally, families who want residential placements have preferred placements in community residences, with a minority opting for nursing homes or institutions (Baker & Blacher, 1988; Goodman, 1978; Heller & Factor, 1991; Schatz, 1983). In considering residential placements, families desire continuous and caring staff and a family-like social climate (Gold et al., 1987). Their greatest fears center around resident abuse, uncaring staff, uncleanliness of the home, sexual permissiveness, poor quality of meals, not enough supervision, neighborhood safety, future home closure, and negative attitudes of neighbors (Heller & Factor, 1988). The negative attitudes of older caregivers toward the residential service system are not surprising given that this age cohort of parents raised their children in a time when the primary out-of-home residential option for persons with retardation was large institutions.

Estimates of the percentage of families preferring continued home placement with a family member when they can no longer care for their relative with retardation have ranged from one third to one half of caregivers (Goodman, 1978; Heller & Factor, 1991; Roberto, 1988). Typically, a sibling is expected to take over the family responsibility (Heller & Factor, 1988; Krauss, 1990). Surprisingly, many families do not discuss future arrangements with these siblings or other relatives

(Heller & Factor, 1991; Kriger, 1975). Hence, when siblings do take on the caregiving responsibility, which is likely to be during a family crisis, such as when their parents die or become ill, the siblings are often unprepared.

Similarly, family caregivers frequently refrain from discussing future care preferences and options with their relative with disabilities (Gold et. al, 1987; Goodman, 1978; Heller & Factor, 1988; Heller, Smith, Kopnick, & Braddock, 1992; Roberto, 1988; Smith & Tobin, 1989). Smith and Tobin's (1989) pilot study suggested that even when preferences of dependent offsprings are well understood, parents tend to disregard these preferences if they are incompatible with their own attitudes and fears. Often families comment that their relative with disabilities is not able to comprehend these issues or that the topic would upset their relative. In the Heller, Smith, Kopnick, and Braddock (1992) study of participants in a family support program for adults with developmental disabilities, over 61% of the family caregivers never discussed the service plan with their relative.

Researchers also have also paid scant attention to the future living arrangement preferences of persons with retardation. One study, which interviewed 37 adults with retardation age 30 and over living in their natural homes, indicated that the majority (63%) wanted to currently continue living in their parent's home (Heller & Factor, 1990). The major reason was that they enjoyed the stability and care provided in the home by their parents. Of those who wanted to move, the preferred setting was a group home, and the main reasons given for wanting to move were the greater independence, activity involvement, and friendship opportunities offered in residences out of the family home.

The extent to which persons with mental retardation can make future plans that are in their best interest is an area warranting further research. What is unknown is to what extent training in later life planning can increase the capacity to make these choices and whether such training is only effective for those persons with higher functioning levels.

Legal and Financial Planning

Long-term planning also involves legal and financial matters. Caregivers face the tasks of providing financially for their relative without jeopardizing current government benefits and providing for legal guardianship when the relative is determined to be incompetent. As with residential planning, the few studies examining this issue have discrepant findings.

In the Gold et al. (1987) study, most of the caregivers did not plan for their relative's financial future, with only a few willing money to another relative for the disabled relative's behalf and none establishing a trust for their relative. Less than 20% of the caregivers in Roberto's (1988) study had contacted a lawyer regarding estate planning. In contrast, Heller and Factor (1991) found that about two thirds of the families had made some financial arrangements. Of those who had made plans, options included willing money and property in the name of another relative (48%), willing money or property directly to the relative with disabilities (21%), and establishing a trust so that government benefits would not be affected (31%).

In summary, studies of long-term care planning show considerable discrepancies in estimates of families' degree of planning for future residential, legal, and financial arrangements. However, across studies there is a clear indication that a sizable number of families have not made concrete plans and that many express a high need for future residential placements outside of the family home.

Factors Associated With Planning

Extent of Planning

The finding that many families of adults with retardation do not make concrete plans for their relative is consistent with the fact that most elderly persons do not plan for themselves in the areas of health, living arrangements, or finances (Heyman & Jeffers, 1965; James, 1964; Kulys & Tobin, 1980). Most elderly persons express little concern for the future, particularly if there is no immediate crisis to be resolved (Heyman & Jeffers, 1965; Shanas et al., 1968). Heyman and Jeffers (1965) found that among a sample of 180 persons 65 and older, two thirds had made some financial plans and only 8% had made any specific plans for housing or nursing care in the event of a long-term illness. Similarly, in Kulys and Tobin's study of 60 persons over age 70 years who were not in an acute crisis, less than 20% had made any medical, living arrangements, or financial plans in the event of a serious illness. The research on family caregivers of elderly persons has indicated that these caregivers also tend to postpone or avoid making long-term care plans. In Cox, Parsons, and Kimboko's (1988) study, nearly half of caregiver respondents indicated that, previous to taking their elderly relative into their home, they had no plans or expectations for assuming their care in their family homes. Families have great difficulty in making decisions regarding placing a relative in a nursing home (Townsend, 1988).

Research on families of persons with mental retardation has consistently found a pervasive worry about the future throughout the life span (Birenbaum, 1971; Bristol & Schopler, 1984; Turnbull et al., 1985). Nevertheless, as noted with the general elderly population, the most common coping strategy has been to maintain a strong present rather than a future orientation by taking one day at a time (Turnbull, Summers, & Brotherson, 1986). Goodman's (1978) study of 23 families of adults with mental retardation indicated that over two thirds of the parents reported facing each day as it came rather than planning ahead for their offspring's future.

In Heller and Factor's (1991) study, characteristics of the family, rather than of the person with disabilities, were primarily related to the extent that families engaged in long-term residential or financial planning for their relative with mental retardation. Older caregivers of higher socioeconomic levels were more likely to make financial plans for their relative. Other research also has indicated that age and socioeconomic status differences are associated with the extent to

which people make retirement financial plans (Kilty & Behling, 1986). For example, Heller and Factor (1988) found that African-American families were less likely than white families to make residential or financial plans for their relative. Both economic and sociocultural factors could explain the lower degree of planning among the African-American caregivers. Generally, the African-American caregivers in their sample were of lower socioeconomic level, were younger, and were more likely to be sibling caregivers. Also, they were much more likely to prefer that any future placement of their relative with a disability be with another relative. Others have noted the tendency of African-American families to care for family members within the extended family and the reluctance to place their older relatives in a nursing home (Agree, 1985).

Smith and Tobin (1989) suggested that coping characteristics and parent-child relationship factors, such as parental overprotectiveness, caregiving satisfaction and benefits, and feelings of guilt, discriminate between families who engage in long-term planning from those who do not. In an analysis of mothers' plans for their offsprings' residential placements, Smith (1992) indicated that mothers who made residential plans were likely to have (a) perceived themselves as adversely affected by their aging, (b) refrained from using avoidance coping, (c) used formal services, and (d) received help from other offspring. Grant (1986) noted that frail older parents who received instrumental assistance from their offspring were less likely to make long-term plans for their dependent child. Heller and Factor (1990) found that high morale and greater caregiving satisfaction among parents were associated with their tendency to defer placement of their child with retardation.

In their study of correlates of personal future planning among nonretarded aging persons, Kulys and Tobin (1980) found that persons who did plan for their future were more anxious, more submissive, and less trusting of their responsible others. They theorized that planning for long-term care reflects maladaptive coping, as it indicates a preoccupation with possible, but not certain, crises. Although there are no empirical studies on the personal characteristics associated with future planning for relatives with mental retardation, it can be speculated that, for these caregivers, planning for their dependent relative's future care represents positive anticipatory coping.

In summary, the predictors of families' degree of planning are complex, entailing family demographics, support resources, and coping mechanisms. Further research is needed to understand the differential role of these factors in determining families' planning efforts in various aspects of planning for their relative's future.

Out-of-Home Placements

Very few studies have focused exclusively on determinants of long-term planning or of residential placement desire among these older families, but research on younger families of persons with developmental disabilities and on family caregivers of elderly persons can shed light on key factors influencing such planning.

Families are most likely to seek out-of-home placements when their child with disabilities has more severe retardation and displays more maladaptive behaviors (Blacher, Hanneman, & Rousey, 1992; Cole & Meyer, 1989; Sherman, 1988; Sherman & Cocozza, 1984). Internal family resources, supports external to the family, and perceived burden also shape the placement decision. Placements also are more likely when the caregivers are older and in worse health and when the family is larger, has few informal and formal community supports, and perceives the person with retardation as disruptive of family life (Cole & Meyer, 1989; McCubbin, 1979; Sherman, 1988; Tausig, 1985).

Only a handful of studies have examined predictors of future placement preferences and plans specifically with adults. Black, Cohn, Smull, and Crites (1985) studied families of adults with mental retardation who had requested an out-of-home placement in 1982. They found these families characterized by a high rate of serious health problems

and caregiver strain among the parents, low levels of service utilization, and high levels of dependent and maladaptive behavior among the adults with mental retardation. Heller and Factor's (1991) study of families' future placement preferences for their adult relative with retardation indicated that having a relative with greater maladaptive behaviors, having lower levels of extended family support, and greater perceived burden of care were associated with preferences for out-of-home placement. Greater use of formal services, particularly respite, case management, and future planning information, increased the probability that caregivers would prefer a residential program placement.

It may be that use of family support service in later years decreases family apprehensiveness towards the community residential service system and facilitates adaptive coping for families who need to arrange for these placements within their lifetime. The unexpected relationship between the use of formal services and placement has been reported in studies of young families with a child with retardation as well (Blacher, 1990). The effects of other ecological factors, such as the availability and quality of local residential services on aging families' placement preferences, have not yet been empirically studied.

In a two-year, longitudinal follow-up of Heller and Factor's sample (Heller & Factor, 1993), the key variable affecting perceived caregiving burden and desire for future out-of-home placement was the degree to which service needs were not met rather than the actual degree of service utilization. A second study by Heller and Factor (1992) of parents of adults 30 years and over in three states (Ohio, Indiana, and Illinois) investigated both predictors of out-of-home placement preference and of actual placements over a two-year period. A key variable associated with both initial placement urgency and with actual placement was parents' perceptions of high unmet needs for formal services. Whereas a high degree of maladaptive behavior of the child related to placement urgency, a low level of adaptive behavior related to actual placements made, suggesting greater difficulty in making placements for those with challenging behaviors. Placements also were more likely to occur when fathers rather than mothers were the primary caregivers. This finding warrants further study to elucidate whether this is due to differential desires or perceived capabilities of fathers or whether the service system is more likely to facilitate placements in circumstances where fathers are primary caregivers.

The most powerful predictor of placement in the Heller and Factor (1992) study was the perceived urgency of placement two years earlier. Blacher (1986) has noted that placement is a process and not a single act. Once steps are taken towards placement, the probability of placement is high.

In summary, the sparse literature on adult placements indicates that caregivers of relatives with maladaptive behaviors who perceive high unmet formal service needs and high subjective caregiving burden are more likely to desire out-of-home placements. However, only through longitudinal studies of larger samples can we differentiate between factors predictive of actual placements, rather than merely of placement desire. Such studies also can better elucidate the impact of the changing informal and formal support systems on families' tendencies to seek out-of-home placements.

Impact of Planning on Family Functioning

Achieving a sense of integrity and continuity is a major task faced by aging persons. Most older persons are able to face their future death knowing that their child rearing tasks are over and that they can transcend death through their children (Ryckman & Henderson, 1965). Parent caregivers of offspring with retardation are often denied the comfort of knowing that child rearing is over (Gold et al., 1987). Hence, they may have greater conflict around their loss of immortality (Ryckman & Henderson, 1965). It would seem that making adequate long-term plans for their offspring would enable them to face death with greater equanimity (Smith & Tobin, 1989). Heller and Factor (1991, 1992) have

noted that, among older family caregivers of persons with mental retardation, the major reason given for making plans for out-of-home placement or for making actual placements is the belief that their relative's adjustment to placement would be easier if it occurred while their family caregivers were still alive. Planning prior to crisis situations or prior to becoming frail may enable caregivers to advocate more strongly for their relative and to make well thought out decisions regarding their housing and financial support. Such planning also can more adequately address the preferences of all key family members. Without such planning, families frequently approach the service system for emergency residential placements after the primary caregiver is ill or has died (Janicki, Otis, Puccio, Rettig, & Jacobson, 1985). In such circumstances, families face long waiting lists and few acceptable options. The adults with disabilities may be quickly placed in inappropriate institutional settings and may face "transfer trauma" as there is little time for psychological preparation (Heller, 1988).

In summary, the literature on long-term care planning among families of an adult with mental retardation is of relatively recent origin and has been conducted with small samples of unknown generalizability. However, studies reveal a disturbing amount of family ambivalence towards the creation of formal plans to govern the care of their dependent family member. Indeed, for many parents, the expectation that other family members will assume responsibility upon the parents' death or infirmity seems widespread. Yet, families appear to have difficulty discussing long-term care with their relatives, particularly with their relative with mental retardation. Thus, developing a more explicit approach to balancing private and public responsibilities for the long-term care of adults with retardation is critical. In particular, the role that siblings are explicitly or implicitly assumed to play warrants study in the creation of responsive public policies in this area.

Family Support

Need for Family Support Programs

There is a need for both family support programs serving families of adults with mental retardation living at home and residential options for those needing out-of-home placements when families can no longer provide care in the home. For families that continue providing home care to an adult member with mental retardation, support programs designed to enhance their caregiving capacities are needed. Several studies have documented high unmet needs of these families for financial assistance (Fujiura & Roccoforte, 1990), information and referral regarding future planning (Louro & Miller, 1988), and case management and respite (Heller & Factor, 1991). Fujiura and Roccoforte (1990) have noted that families of adults with developmental disabilities spend an average of 20% of their pre-tax annual income on unreimbursed expenses for their relative. In Heller and Factor's (1993) longitudinal study the highest unmet service needs were for case management that provided information regarding residential programs, financial plans, and guardianship; family counseling; and respite.

A study of family support programs nationwide indicated that as of fiscal year 1988, 42 states had discrete developmental disabilities agency-based family support initiatives, either cash subsidy, respite, or other family support (Fujiura & Braddock, 1992). However, at least 8 of these states limited their family support initiatives to families of children, and 4 other states limited only their financial assistance programs to families of children. No state was offering cash stipends to older families of persons with developmental disabilities.

Although all families who provide care to a child with developmental disabilities need family support, when resources are scarce, family support services should be targeted to the families at greatest risk of caregiving burden and stress. These are families of persons with maladaptive behavior and families experiencing the poor health of either the adult with retardation or the caregiver. There is also a need to target services to families who are unstable and who may abuse or neglect their family member with disabilities. The support needs of sibling caregivers, who often assume responsibility during crises, have rarely been addressed and warrant further study. They often are not included in family decision-making, planning efforts, and family training initiatives.

For many families who can no longer provide care within the family home, other alternatives are needed. Families face long waiting lists and few acceptable options. In view of the critical shortage of residential placements, family support programs can play a critical role in bolstering family caregiving efforts. A recent Arc study in 45 states indicated that over 63,000 persons were estimated to be waiting for mental retardation/developmental disabilities residential services (Davis, 1987). Furthermore, there are over 135,000 residents of large public and private mental retardation/developmental disabilities facilities and 50,000 nursing home residents with mental retardation, many of whom are slated to move into family-scale residential alternatives (Fujiura & Braddock, 1992). Hence, the service system and families need to plan for the residential service needs of the growing population of older adults with mental retardation.

Effectiveness of Family Support Interventions

There have been very few evaluations of family support interventions for this population. Most of the family support programs reported in the literature have provided support to families of children (rather than adults) with developmental disabilities. Cash subsidies to families have been shown to reduce the amount of stress experienced by families and to improve their life satisfaction and ability to cope (Herman, 1991; Meyers & Marcenko, 1989; Zimmerman, 1984). In addition, in the first two studies, the availability of a cash subsidy reduced the number of families who anticipated placing their children out-of-home.

In Illinois a recent evaluation study (Heller, Smith, Kopnick, & Braddock, 1992) is underway evaluating the impact of the Home-Based Support Services Program for adults with severe developmental and mental disabilities. This program provides a flexible array of services to families at a cost of up to about $1,200 per month. A six-month, follow-up study comparing participants in the program with nonparticipants (chosen randomly from eligible applicants through a lottery) indicated that participants were more likely to have increased service use and satisfaction, decreased unmet formal service needs, and greater community integration of their relative with disabilities. Comparisons of older and younger families (Heller, Smith, & Kopnick, 1992) indicated that the older family caregivers (age 55 and over) were more likely than younger participants to benefit from the program in each of the above outcomes. Among the older group only, the program resulted in a decreased need for out-of-home placement and an increase in establishing guardianship. Older caregivers participating in the program also had greater decreases in caregiving burden than younger families. An example of the tremendous benefits for older caregivers is depicted in the following statements made by an 80-year-old mother:

"This program helped me keep my daughter at home. I'm so happy I can keep her; she is my life; she makes me want to live to be with her. I don't know what I would do without it as I could not afford the services—as age gets up on us we change in strength."

In examining implementation issues, Heller, Smith, Kopnick and Braddock (1992) found that characteristics of the case coordinators played a key role in the extent to which families benefited from the program. Families with case coordinators that whom they described as more knowledgeable were more likely to use more of their service allotment.

Implications for Research, Policy Development, and Service Provision

Guidelines for Facilitating Transitions
Our review of the research suggests several areas that need to be addressed in facilitating successful transitions out of the family home. Preparatory planning and participative decision-making among family members, including the adult with retardation, are critical. Preparatory planning entails family discussions, visits to sites, and discussions with other families who have already made the transition. Families need sufficient information on available and potential services in their communities. In many cases families would benefit from counseling to alleviate the heightened stress that can be associated with making an out-of-home placement in later life (Heller & Factor, 1992). After placement, it is important for residential staff to encourage continued family contact and involvement (Baker & Blacher, 1988). Meaningful family involvement can include participating in developing short- and long-term goals for the resident's programs, monitoring activities in which parents can make suggestions for changes, and participating on advocacy boards.

Recommendations for Family Support Programs
Both the mental retardation and aging service networks need to address the issue of long-term planning among older caregivers. The 1992 amendments to the Older American Act of 1965, in recognition of this important issue, call for the provision of services to "older individuals who provide uncompensated care to their adult children with disabilities, or counseling to assist such older individuals with permanency planning for such children." The amendments also recommend demonstration projects that provide "supportive services relating to such care, including respite services; and legal advice, information, and referral services to assist such older individuals with permanency planning" (U.S. House of Representatives, 1992, p. 2606).

The service network can assist families in developing future plans that encompass the multiple domains of residential, financial, legal, and support services and that integrally involve persons with mental retardation and key family members in decision-making. To assist families in making these plans, "front-line" professionals (i.e., social workers, case managers, counselors) need information and training regarding aging families with a son or daughter with retardation. More comprehensive training programs also are needed that provide information and training to caregivers and to adults with mental retardation concerning aging and later life planning. One such effort is being developed by the Rehabilitation Research and Training Center Consortium on Aging and Developmental Disabilities. As part of this effort, researchers at the University of Illinois and at the University of Akron have developed a later life planning curriculum and assessment package for adults with mental retardation and for staff and family caregivers (Heller, Factor, Sterns, Sutton, & Heck, 1993).

In addition to training efforts, a concerted effort is needed to expand and improve upon current family support programs. Our evaluation of the Illinois family support project (Heller, Smith, Kopnick, & Braddock, 1992) suggested the following recommendations for family support programs serving this population:

1. Family support programs need to invest in significant case coordination to help families develop short- and long-term plans, to help with the eligibility criteria, and to help link families to services and providers.

2. Training and technical assistance is needed to transmit the program's philosophy and to help case coordinators and families access needed services. Development of resource guides and involvement of families who have already participated in the program can help facilitate this process effectively.

3. Decision-making power in regard to the use of cash subsidies or the design of a service plan should rest primarily with the families themselves.

4. More family support programs geared to families of adults with disabilities are needed to serve more families. For example, in Illinois, there were over 1,200 applicants, of whom only 330 received services.

Research Agenda

Evaluation studies are needed to identify aspects of family support programs that are particularly effective in helping families maintain care in the home. Studies of the impact of long-term care planning initiatives are particularly needed in order to develop appropriate models that can confront effectively the pronounced propensity of older caregivers to delay forming concrete residential, legal, and financial plans. Further, research in this area needs to elucidate the impact of long-term care planning on parental well-being and family functioning. Developing strategies that minimize the distress of planning, however transitory, represents an important arena for program developers. Such programmatic innovations need to be linked to well-designed research efforts that evaluate the effectiveness of different approaches and document the effects of planning on families.

It is important that these studies evaluate the impact of family support programs on persons with retardation, their families, and the service network from each of their perspectives. The multidimensional and interactive nature of family well-being cannot be validly assessed from one perspective only. However, the challenges in assessing family well-being from the perspective of adults with more severe cognitive or language impairments are significant, as are challenges inherent in collecting data from those very elderly parents who have sensory or memory limitations.

Future research needs to examine the effect of long-term care planning intervention on the families themselves. Although planning may result in short-term stress, it may lead to long-term comfort and smooth transitions. However, long-term plans made by families cannot assure smooth transitions given the gaps in available services.

References

Agree, E. (1985). *A portrait of older minorities*. Washington, DC: American Association of Retired Persons.

Baker, B., & Blacher, J. (1988). Family involvement with community residential programs. In M. Janicki, M.W. Krauss, & M.M. Seltzer (Eds.), *Community residences for persons with developmental disabilities: Here to stay* (pp. 172–188). Baltimore, MD: Brookes.

Birenbaum, A. (1971). The mentally retarded child in the home and the family life cycle. *Journal of Health and Social Behavior, 12,* 55–65.

Blacher, J. (1986). *Placement of severely handicapped children: Correlates and consequences (Grant No. HD21324)*. Washington, DC: National Institute of Child Health and Human Development.

Blacher, J., Hanneman, R. A., & Rousey, A. B. (1992). Out-of-home placement of children with severe handicaps: A comparison of approaches. *American Journal on Mental Retardation, 96,* 607–616.

Black, M., Cohn, J., Smull, M., & Crites, L. (1985). Individual and family factors associated with risk of institutionalization of mentally retarded adults. *American Journal of Mental Deficiency, 90,* 271–276.

Bristol, M. M., & Schopler, E. (1984). A developmental perspective on stress and coping in families of autistic children. In J. Blacher (Ed.), *Severely handicapped children and their families: Research in review* (pp. 91–141). New York: Academic Press.

Carswell, A. T., & Hartig, S. A. (1979). *Older developmentally disabled persons: An investigation of needs and social services*. Athens: University of Georgia, Georgia Retardation Center, Athens Unit.

Cole, D. A. (1986). Out-of-home child placement and family adaptation: A theoretical framework. *American Journal of Mental Deficiency, 91,* 226–236.

Cole, D. A., & Meyer, L. H. (1989). Impact of needs and resources on family plans to seek out-of-home placement. *American Journal on Mental Retardation, 93,* 380–387.

Cox, E. O., Parsons, R. J., & Kimboko, P. J. (1988). Social services and intergenerational caregivers: Issues for social work. *Social Work, 33,* 430–434.

Davis, S. (1987). *A national status report on waiting lists of people with mental retardation for community services*. Arlington, TX: Association for Retarded Citizens.

Fujiura, G. T., & Braddock, D. (1992). Fiscal and demographic trends in mental retardation services: The emergence of the family. In L. Rowitz (Ed.), *Mental retardation in the year 2000* (pp.316–338). New York: Springer.

Fujiura, G. T., & Roccoforte, J. R. (1990). *Cost of disability to the American family*. Public Policy Forum, American Association on Mental Retardation, Washington, DC.

Gold, M., Dobrof, R., & Torian, L. (1987). *Parents of the adult developmentally disabled* (Final report presented to the United Hospital Trust Fund). New York: Brookdale Center on Aging.

Goodman, D. M. (1978). Parenting an adult mentally retarded offspring. *Smith College Studies in Social Work, 48,* 209–234.

Grant, G. (1986). Older carers, interdependence and care of mentally handicapped adults. *Aging and Society, 6,* 333–351.

Heller, T. (1988). Transitioning: Coming in and going out. In M. Janicki, M. Krauss, & M. Seltzer (Eds.), *Community residences for developmentally disabled persons: Here to stay* (pp. 149–158). Baltimore, MD: Brookes.

Heller, T., & Factor, A. (1988). Permanency planning among black and white family caregivers of older adults with mental retardation. *Mental Retardation, 26,* 203–208.

Heller, T., & Factor, A. (1990). *Quality of life of older adults with developmental disabilities living with their parents*. Paper presented at the 114th Annual Meeting of the American Association on Mental Retardation, Atlanta, GA.

Heller, T., & Factor, A. (1991). Permanency planning for adults with mental retardation living with family caregivers. *American Journal on Mental Retardation, 96,* 163–176.

Heller, T., & Factor, A. (1992). *Adaptation of older parents to out-of-home placement*. Paper presented at the Annual Meeting of the American Association on Mental Retardation, New Orleans, LA.

Heller, T., & Factor, A. (1993). Aging family caregivers: Support resources and changes in burden and placement desire. *American Journal on Mental Retardation, 98,* 417–426.

Heller, T., Factor, A., Sterns, H., Sutton, E., & Heck, K. (1993). *Pre-retirement training for older persons with developmental disabilities*. Paper presented at the Annual Meeting of the American Society on Aging, Chicago, IL.

Heller, T., Smith, B., & Kopnick, N. (1992). *The impact of a state-wide family support program on aging parents of adult children with mental retardation or mental illness*. Paper presented at the Annual Meeting of the Gerontological Society of America, Washington, DC.

Heller, T., Smith, B., Kopnick, N., & Braddock, D. (1992). *The Illinois Home-Based Support Service Program Evaluation Report*. Chicago: University of Illinois at Chicago, Illinois University Affiliated Program in Developmental Disabilities.

Herman, S.E. (1991). Use and impact of a cash subsidy program. *Mental Retardation, 29,* 253–258.

Heyman, D., & Jeffers, F. (1965). Observations on the extent of concern and planning by the aged, for possible chronic illness. *Journal of the American Geriatric Society, 13,* 152–159.

James, R. L. (1964). *Edmonton senior resident's survey report*. Edmonton, Alberta: Edmonton Welfare Council.

Janicki, M. P., Otis, J. P., Puccio, P. S., Rettig, J. S., & Jacobson, J. W. (1985). Service needs among older developmentally disabled persons. In M. P. Janicki & H. M. Wisniewski (Eds.), *Aging and developmental disabilities: Issues and approaches* (pp. 289–304). Baltimore, MD: Brookes.

Kilty, K. M., & Behling, J. H. (1986). Retirement financial planning among professional workers. *The Gerontologist, 26,* 525–530.

Krauss, M. W. (1990). *Later life placements: Precipitating factors and family profiles*. Paper presented at the 114th Annual Meeting of the American Association on Mental Retardation, Atlanta, GA.

Kriger, S. (1975). *Lifestyles of aging retardates living in community settings in Ohio*. Columbus, OH: Psychologia Metrika.

Kulys, R. K., & Tobin, S. S. (1980). Interpreting the lack of future concerns among the elderly. *International Journal of Aging and Human Development, 11,* 111–125.

Louro, C., & Miller, L. S. (1988). *Illinois family support study*. Springfield, IL: Governor's Planning Council on Developmental Disabilities.

McCubbin, H. L. (1979). Integrating coping behavior in family stress theory. *Journal of Marriage and the Family, 41,* 237–244.

Meyers, C. E., Borthwick, S. A., & Eyman, R. (1985). Place of residence by age, ethnicity, and level of retardation of the mentally retarded/developmentally disabled population of California. *American Journal of Mental Deficiency, 90,* 266–270.

Meyers, J. C., & Marcenko, M. O. (1989). Impact of a cash subsidy program for families of children with severe developmental disabilities. *Mental Retardation, 27,* 383–386.

Roberto, K. A. (1988). *Caring for aging developmentally disabled adults: Perspectives and needs of older parents* (Final report presented to the Colorado Developmental Disabilities Planning Council). Greeley, CO: University of Northern Colorado, Department of Human Services.

Ryckman, D. B., & Henderson, R. A. (1965). The meaning of a retarded child for his parents: A focus for counselors. *Mental Retardation, 3,* 4–7.

Schatz, G. (1983). The problem of preparing mentally retarded people adequately for the future. *International Journal of Rehabilitation Medicine, 6,* 197–199.

Shanas, E., Townsend, P., Wedderburn, D., Friis, H., Milhoj, P., & Stehouwer, M. (1968). *Older people in three industrial societies*. New York: Atherton Press.

Sherman, B. (1988). Predictors of the decision to place developmentally disabled family members in residential care. *American Journal on Mental Deficiency, 92,* 344–351.

Sherman, B. R., & Cocozza, J. J. (1984). Stress in families of the developmentally disabled: A literature review of factors affecting the decision to seek placements. *Family Relations, 33,* 95–103.

Smith, G. (1992). *Elderly mothers caring at home for offspring with mental retardation: A model of permanency planning.* Paper presented at the Annual Meeting of the Gerontological Society of America, Washington, DC.

Smith, G. C., & Tobin, S. S. (1989). Permanency planning among older parents of adults with lifelong disabilities. *Journal of Gerontological Social Work, 14,* 35–59.

Tausig, M. (1985). Factors in family decision-making about placement for developmentally disabled individuals. *American Journal of Mental Deficiency, 89,* 352–361.

Townsend, A. L. (1988). *Family caregivers' perspectives on institutionalization decisions.* Ann Arbor, MI: The University of Michigan. (ERIC/CAPS Accession No. CG020923)

Turnbull, A. P., Brotherson, M. J., & Summers, J. A. (1985). The impact of deinstitutionalization on families: A family systems approach. In R. H. Bruininks & K. C. Lakin (Eds.), *Living and learning in the least restrictive environment* (pp. 115–140). Baltimore, MD: Brookes.

Turnbull, A. P., Summers, J. A., & Brotherson, M. J. (1986). Family life cycle: Theoretical and empirical implications and future directions for families with mentally retarded members. In J. J. Gallagher & P. M. Vietze (Eds.), *Families of handicapped persons: Research, programs, and policy issues* (pp. 45–65). Baltimore, MD: Brookes.

U.S. House of Representatives. (1992). *The Congressional Record,* April 9, H 2606.

Zimmerman, S. (1984). The mental retardation family subsidy program: Its effect on families with a mentally handicapped child. *Family Relations, 33,* 105–118.

This research was supported in part by Grant No. 2-5-37074 from the National Institute on Disability and Rehabilitation Research and Training Center Consortium on Aging and Developmental Disabilities. The authors gratefully acknowledge the valuable contributions of Marty Wyngaarden Krauss and Marsha Mailick Seltzer to this chapter.

Individual Development in
Adulthood and Old Age

Chapter 4

Quality of Life Issues:
Some People Know How to Be Old

Robert B. Edgerton, University of California at Los Angeles

As parents of persons with mental retardation grow older, they often worry about the well-being of their children, and when these parents become elderly, their fears mount. They wonder what will become of their now middle-aged children after they die, and a good many are greatly distressed about it. Personnel in human service agencies also worry as they try to plan for the delivery of needed services to mentally retarded people who are living longer and can reasonably be expected to need more and more services as they become elderly and infirm. These concerns are anything but exaggerated. A 55-year-old man who has lived his entire life with his parents is very likely to face a traumatic transition to alternative residential care after his parents die. And growing numbers of older mentally retarded people may require expensive residential, medical, and psychological services (Seltzer & Krauss, 1987). These are issues that need to be addressed, but there is another, more positive, side to growing old for people with mental retardation, and it is that phenomenon I would like to discuss first.

In one of his better-known maxims, La Rochefoucauld observed that "Few people know how to be old." Many of the mildly mentally retarded people whose lives I have tried to document for over 30 years put the lie to this maxim. They are very good at being old, better, in fact, than they were at being young. As most of these people have grown old, their social competence has increased and so has their satisfaction with life. Moreover, their dependence on others has lessened at the same time that their ability to give meaningful support to others has grown. Hence the title for this chapter. Not everyone has grown older so gracefully, and there may be dark days ahead for all of these older people (as there may be for any aging person), but there are many positive aspects to aging that need to be considered along with the potentially negative ones.

The Populations and Procedures

The findings I would like to explore here are based on research carried out with several different populations. First, and in some respects most intriguing, is the longitudinal ethnographic research I began in 1960 with 48 mildly retarded men and women recently released from what was then Pacific State Hospital (now Lanterman State Hospital) in Southern California. After the initial period of research in 1960–61, many of these people were studied again during 1972–73 and others in 1982. Between these periods of intensive study, we have had sporadic but frequent contact by telephone along with occasional personal contact. Sixteen of these people have been studied continuously since 1985. As this is written in 1992, the mean age of these 16 people is 65 (with a range from 57 to 70) and their average IQ is 62. With the exception of a few who receive Supplemental Security Income (SSI), these people have not received services from the mental retardation service delivery system, and as yet not one has received residential services from any source. It is impossible to assert that these 16 individuals are representative of the original cohort, but there is nothing about the IQ scores, pre-institutional history, earlier social competence, or relative degree of independence when first studied to distinguish them from the 32 people with whom contact has been lost. Of course they may differ in various less tangible ways.

Beginning in 1987, another sample of older persons (matched on age, sex and IQ with the 16 persons studied since 1960), who lived with their parents or in a community residential facility and received various services based on their status as people with mental retardation, was studied using the same ethnographic methods as before. Also, throughout much of the 1960s, various residents of Pacific State Hospital were studied, and during the 1970s, two major ethnographic studies of younger persons with mental retardation living in community settings were conducted. One of these concentrated on a Euro-American sample of men and women in their twenties and thirties living in middle-class residential areas (Edgerton, 1981); another focused on the lives of young adult African-Americans with mental retardation in an economically deprived, inner-city environment (Koegel & Edgerton, 1982). Finally, since 1970, research has been conducted in a variety of community residential facilities, including nursing homes, that have older persons with mental retardation as residents (Bercovici, 1983; Edgerton, 1975).

These studies have employed various methods of data collection, but they have all relied primarily on the naturalistic use of participant-observation over considerable periods of time. In essence, this means that my various research associates and I have as unobtrusively as possible spent considerable periods of time with the people in our samples, as well as their families, friends, and acquaintances. We have usually avoided the use of direct questioning because we believe that in longitudinal research an "interview" format can damage rapport as well as lead to evasive or socially desirable answers. Instead, we have relied on "natural" conversations, discussing whatever seemed interesting and appropriate to the sample member at the time. Occasionally, we have asked questions for clarification but we have seldom probed further if anyone seemed reluctant to pursue the topic. We have also carefully observed interactions among sample members, ourselves, and others in a variety of settings including their residences, places of employ-

ment, and public places. Most important for an understanding of the generalizations that will follow, we have made these contacts frequently (typically every two weeks with phone calls in between), and we have continued them for long periods.

Materials from these studies, along with gleanings from smaller research activities over the years, provide the basis for the discussion that follows. It is not my purpose to present quantitative data bearing on the points I will make, nor will I attempt to test any formal hypotheses. Instead, I will describe some general patterns of behavioral change that I believe are characteristic of the life span among persons with mild mental retardation. Where appropriate, I will refer to publications that discuss these matters in more detail.

The Indeterminacy of the Life Course

Variables capable of predicting the life course of people with mental retardation have proven to be every bit as elusive as the Holy Grail. One investigator after another has concluded that neither IQ, personality attributes, demographic characteristics, nor life events predict the life course of these people with any great accuracy (Cobb, 1972; Edgerton, 1983; McCarver & Craig, 1974). But with all due respect to the hazards of prognostic research, these findings are counterintuitive because it would seem to be self-evident that human lives are influenced and constrained in many more or less predictable ways. For example, the values and expectations of family members, friends, and employers often have predictable effects on the course of life, as does the general subculture in which we live. So too do our physical, emotional, and intellectual gifts and limitations. The major decisions we make in life can have predictably lasting consequences, as is so often seen in the aftermath of a decision not to finish high school, to prepare for one particular career rather than another, or to become a single mother rather than have an abortion or relinquish one's infant to adoption. So it is when a person decides to leave one job for another, to marry one person rather than another, or have yet another child. Lives may not be definitively determined by personal decisions or life events such as these, but on a probabilistic basis many of our decisions do have great consequences. Like our own, the lives of people with mental retardation are influenced by the expectations of others, by their race and gender, and by their own physical, emotional, and intellectual abilities. But there is reason to believe that many of them make fewer truly consequential decisions than people who do not have mental retardation and, moreover, that many of the decisions that they do make are less likely to shape the remainder of their lives. As some people with mental retardation who live in community settings grow old, it is apparent that their lives have not followed a predictable path, while the lives of other, more regimented, individuals are all too predictable.

These latter people with mental retardation usually make fewer important decisions than the rest of us because they are typically given fewer opportunities to do so by parents and careproviders who make decisions for them. On the other hand, those individuals who live independently enough to make their own decisions would seem in principle to be as constrained by the consequences of life events and their decisions as anyone else, but there is some evidence to suggest that this often is not the case. For example, before I carried out the first restudy of the 48 individuals released from Pacific State Hospital to live independently, I carefully made predictions about the ways their lives would prove to have changed over the period of a decade. I was right only about half the time and then usually for the wrong reasons (Edgerton & Bercovici, 1976).

The reasons for my inability to predict accurately (in addition to my obtuseness) usually had to do with the fact that, at least during their younger years, these people's lives fluctuated dramatically for reasons over which they usually had little control. They lived on the margin, with few resources in money, skills, and social or occupational supports to stabilize them when crises occurred.

The loss of a job or a place to live could easily spiral them down into desperation, but because it took so little to restore them to their previous level of adaptation, or a better one, the intervention of a concerned acquaintance often readily provided them with a place to stay or a job as good as the one they lost. A few of these people lived in ways that were as stable as anyone could imagine, but most were up one month and down the next for reasons that were usually difficult to identify. There was little evidence that either their problems or their subsequent good fortune was a result of their own decision-making. They did not overtly decide to change jobs or apartments or to find a new benefactor. To all appearances, these things simply happened, more or less unbidden.

But one thing about them *was* predictable. The lives of these and other younger people with mental retardation were characteristically nothing less than chaotic, with dramatic changes following one after the other for no discernible reasons other than emotional turmoil and social immaturity. To take but one example among many, during a period of 30 months beginning in 1976, another 48 middle-class, Euro-American persons with mild mental retardation but no physical handicaps were studied ethnographically. The mean age of the sample in 1976 was 27 and the mean IQ was in the mid-60s. Approximately one third of these people lived reasonably stable, trouble-free lives although even most of these individuals had significant interpersonal problems. The remaining two thirds of these people were emotionally highly unstable. For one thing, they were frequently victimized by other people. In addition, they made various kinds of trouble for themselves, and they made trouble for others as well. For example, 15 of these 48 persons assaulted someone physically, and 6 of these assaults involved the use of a deadly weapon. Only 3 of the assaults were reported to the police, and they resulted in 2 convictions with probated sentences. Knives were possessed and sometimes carried by 5 persons, and guns by 2, although, to my knowledge, these were never fired. Of the sample, 19 members engaged in one or another form of sexual deviance or crime. Thefts were committed by 5 persons, and 4 stole repeatedly. Of the 13 members of the sample who drove motor vehicles at least occasionally, 3 drove without any known trouble, but the remaining 10 drivers admitted to many traffic offenses. In addition to innumerable instances of undetected speeding, recklessness and driving while intoxicated, these 10 persons received 10 citations for moving violations, 2 for drunk driving, and 3 for driving without a valid license. They also were involved in 5 accidents, 4 of which involved injuries. Serious suicide attempts were made by 4 members of the sample (all women), and 8 experienced severe episodes of mental illness, 4 of which resulted in brief periods of hospitalization.

To look at one of these troubled—and troubling—people more closely, consider a young man who had 12 known arrests, 4 of which occurred during the period of this study. Most were for petty theft or for breaking and entering homes or cars. In addition to the robberies for which he was arrested, he admitted to stealing from the manager's office of a movie theater, from a parked car, and from friends. He also had several fights including one with inmates while he was in jail awaiting trial. He often carried a knife that he kept under his pillow at night, and he sometimes carried a realistic toy gun. On some occasions he carried both a switchblade knife in his pocket and a 6-inch hunting knife in a scabbard on his belt. He sometimes smoked marijuana, often drank excessively, and he was accused of masturbating publicly on at least one occasion. His last conviction for robbery led to a sentence of 18-months' probation under the supervision of the caregiver of his group home. He freely admitted that his thefts were planned in advance and said that he has been stealing since he was 8 years old (Edgerton,1981). Although no one in a comparable sample of African-American, inner-city people with mental retardation engaged in as much antisocial or self-injurious behavior as this, most of those young adults also have lived turbulent lives (Koegel & Edgerton, 1984).

Recently, initial follow-up contacts have been made with nearly half of these people,

now 15 years older. Data collection is in its early stages but, consistent with the findings of previous research indicating that community adaptation stabilizes over time, it is already apparent that the lives of most of these people are far less changeable and troubled now than they were earlier. It is a common finding of many investigators that with the passage of years, the quality of community living generally stabilizes and improves (Cobb, 1972). However, whether one looks at younger people or older ones with many years of experience in community living, the impression one comes away with is not one of linear improvement but instead, that of lives evolving, repeating themselves and oscillating. That the lives of mentally retarded people who live largely on their own resources are less predictable than those of the rest of us may be an illusion (and is impossible to prove in any event), but I am convinced that this is so.

On the other hand, it is quite clear that the lives of mentally retarded people who live with their parents or residential careproviders are overdetermined, one might say, because not only is their present day organized, arranged, and regimented by other people, so is tomorrow and the future. What is more, there is very little that mentally retarded people can do in most of these living arrangements that can make a significant difference in their lives. As our years of research in community residential facilities have made only too clear, the lives of people like these are depressingly predictable.

Some people more than others, then, have the course of their lives determined by other people through their power to constrain or control. Those mentally retarded people I have studied who live beyond the reach of relatives or human service delivery system personnel are largely free of such constraint. Quite literally, they can be said to have shaped the course of their own destiny, albeit a meandering, largely unpredictable one. What they become when they reach their 50s and 60s seems to be far more a product of their own internal resources as these have been nurtured and expressed over time than of the influence of major life events, other people, or their own decisions. What seems to matter most in shaping the course of their lives are personal attributes such as perseverance, optimism, self-esteem, sociability, and emotional equanimity. Qualities such as these allow them to master adversity, to form relationships with others, and to think positively about themselves and the future.

This is not to say that environmental factors play no role in determining the life course of older people with mental retardation. People who are institutionalized or held in other restricted living arrangements can have their lives dominated by factors quite independent of their personal attributes. But for those who live independently or semi-independently, their personal attributes are all-important. "Positive" attributes like those mentioned earlier have enormous adaptive value no matter how difficult environmental conditions may be. And negative attributes such as dysphoric mood, low self-esteem, pessimism, and abrasive interpersonal skills are likely to be maladaptive no matter what the environment may be. What makes prediction of the life course so difficult is the reality that relatively few people possess only adaptive or only maladaptive personal attributes.

Beyond Dependency

That dependent people have relatively little control over their lives is surely a banal observation, but what I would like to illustrate here are some of the ways in which aging mentally retarded people have been heavily dependent as well as ways that others have been able to move beyond dependency and take their lives into their own hands. To be sure, some aging mentally retarded people never escape from the control of others. Many older people who live in group homes or nursing homes not only have virtually no control over the daily course of their lives, they have no control over the long-term direction of their futures. They may react, rebel, and manipulate in small ways, but these are minor victories in a lost war against dependency. Now, of course, dependency can have its rewards, such as a comfortable routine of life with few demands, worries, or failures, but it

has its frustrations, too. For example, we have found that when one of these dependent people is taken away from the immediate supervision of a parent or careprovider for a few hours on an excursion, he or she is quick to complain about some form of parental or careprovider control. What is more, their behavior changes. Away from supervision, these people typically speak more confidently, are more assertive in making decisions, such as in which restaurant they would like to have lunch, and exhibit greater social competence in, for example, how they dress, express opinions, or ask questions.

Thus far, we have had only one opportunity to observe such a dependent person move to a more independent residential living arrangement. (That this has not happened more often is, no doubt, strong testimony to the strength of their dependency.) This person has displayed surprising social competence and independence. However, we have several times witnessed an analogous transition away from dependency, namely the transition mentally retarded wives make when their intellectually dominant husbands die. Earlier, I mentioned my inability to predict how the lives of persons released from Pacific State Hospital would change over time. One of the reasons for my failure to predict accurately was my assumption that mentally retarded women who were married to older men of average intelligence who controlled almost every aspect of their wives' lives would have difficulty adapting after their husbands' deaths. To put this in perspective, it is important to emphasize that the women's dependency was almost childlike in its extreme. Their husbands did everything for them—made the money, paid the bills, did the shopping and the cooking, protected against inquiring or critical neighbors, and even cleaned the house. I frankly did not believe that any of the women would be able to live independently without their husbands. I acknowledged that these women might succeed in finding another man who would look after them, but it was not credible to me that they could take over their own lives without help.

None of the women could read, write, or use money. They lacked many ordinary housekeeping skills, too, and they had few of the abilities needed to cope with life on the streets or in the workplace. Nevertheless, we have now had occasion to observe how seven highly dependent wives like these responded after the deaths of their husbands. Each woman made a dramatic shift from dependency to social competence and independence. They did not do so overnight or without stress, but were strikingly different people. They did not accuse their deceased spouses of mistreating them or of being inappropriately domineering. They did not speak resentfully of their previous dependency either. Instead, they found hitherto unused—and unneeded—skills as well as the determination to remake their lives, and they did so with a degree of success that continues to surprise as much as it pleases me.

For example, consider the experience of Mary, who had been married to her intellectually average husband, Bill, for 30 years when he died a few years ago. Mary, whose IQ was 56, was very attractive as a young woman, a competent conversationalist, an adequate housekeeper, and a passable cook. But she could neither read nor write and did not understand money well enough to go shopping. For 30 years, Mary was a thoroughly isolated housewife who rarely left home without Bill's company. Bill chose their friends, made their living, did all the shopping and benevolently dominated every aspect of Mary's life. Although some of my research associates and I often spent time with Mary while she was home alone during the day (usually ironing and always watching television) while Bill was away at work, we never sensed that she resented Bill's dominance. Quite the contrary, she gave every indication that she was happy with her life and very fond of Bill.

When Bill died of emphysema, Mary felt his loss keenly, but she was not devastated. On the contrary, her passively dependent role vanished. She quickly decided to move to Oklahoma to be near her stepmother, partly because she was fond of her but also because she correctly foresaw the possibility of relying on her for help. This woman did help Mary, in no small measure by urging her to convert to Catholicism and attend her parish church. As a result, fellow parishioners agreed to help Mary with shopping and managing her money (from Bill's pensions and her own Social Security payments). But Mary did not simply trade one benefactor for others. She became far more independent than she had been before. She soon learned how to shop, and, indeed, to enjoy doing so. She also began to explore her new community on her own, to make friends, and to develop new interests. She enjoys her new freedom to "get into mischief," saying that "I'm on my own now, and I like it that way."

Life Satisfaction

A large and robust set of research findings indicates that major environmental changes or life events, as they are often called—major illness, the loss of a job, residence, or loved one—may bring about changes in persons' expressions of satisfaction with their lives, but these changes are short-lived. Several longitudinal surveys in the United States and Europe have found that the best predictor of how satisfied people say they are with their lives is not stressors or major environmental changes but how people answered a similar question years earlier (Edgerton, 1990). It seems that internal dispositions, one's attitudes and temperament, predict life satisfaction better than environmental variables do, and there is evidence from my own longitudinal studies to support this assertion. The people with mental retardation whose lives I have tried to document sometimes react to misfortune with dysphoria, even despondency, and they can become euphoric when their fortunes improve, but these changes in mood are temporary. With rare exceptions, they quickly return to their previous mood.

I first reported this pattern of stability in affect in 1975 before I was aware that it was a common phenomenon (Edgerton, 1975). I remain impressed by the temperamental stability of these people, who can be optimistic no matter how difficult life becomes or pessimistic and dour no matter how well life smiles on them, but I am also impressed by a long-term pattern of positive adaptation in their lives. Those older people who have lived largely on their own resources without assistance from parents or the mental retardation service delivery systems have grown more satisfied with themselves and their lives as they have grown older (Edgerton, 1993). They complain less, make fewer self-disparaging remarks, and sometimes volunteer that they are happier than they were in earlier years. From everything they say and do, those of us who have known them over the years agree that most of them are indeed happier and more satisfied now than they were when they were younger. To a lesser extent, this is also true of the people with mental retardation who lived with their parents or in a community residential facility. These people still complain about many things and seldom volunteer that they are happier now than they were earlier, but they seem to us to be much more content with themselves and their lives than they used to be. Perhaps they are simply resigned to their lives, but that too can bring a kind of contentment.

We cannot be certain why this improvement in outlook has occurred but there are several likely reasons. For one thing, as we have seen, with very few exceptions their young lives were quite unhappy. The passage of time lessened the pain and the stigma of placement in special education classes or a residential institution, just as it reduced much of the turbulence of youthful confusion and frustration. Also, years of growing success in adapting to the demands of community or institutional living have given them justifiable confidence and pride. Finally, and in some respects most importantly, I think, when these people were young they compared themselves to other young people who had better education, jobs, cars, and affluence; now that they are in their 60s they compare themselves to their closest reference group—low-income retired people living on pensions or Social Security who are often in worse health and lower spirits than the older people with mental retardation. At their age, it is quite "normal" to live modestly, not to work, to receive welfare or Social Security payments, and to have a limited circle of friends and activities. A sense of relative deprivation and relative inferiority tormented

most of these people when they were young; it is much less likely to do so now that they have grown older.

Increase in Social Competence

Since the late 1960s, some scholars have proposed that the cognitive limitations commonly referred to as mental retardation in the United States or mental handicap in the United Kingdom are products of environmental factors and may therefore be remediable. It has been argued that as people labeled "mentally retarded" gain experience in community living, their cognitive limitations should diminish (Bogdan & Taylor, 1982; Gerber, 1990). Now, there is no doubt that mild mental retardation is strongly associated with poverty, and we infer therefore that environmental factors play a major etiological role, but my research suggests that the cognitive limitations that handicap mildly retarded people are usually *not* remediable. These limitations most often have to do with literacy, quantification, and abstract reasoning, abilities that become particularly problematic when children attend school. In its report entitled *The Six-Hour Retarded Child,* published in 1970, the President's Committee on Mental Retardation addressed itself to the "racism, poverty, alienation and unrest" that it concluded beset the country. The Committee wrote that "We now have what may be called a 6-hour retarded child—retarded from 9 to 3, five days a week, solely on the basis of an IQ score, without regard to his adaptive behavior, which may be exceptionally adaptive to the situation and community in which he lives."

The Committee's dramatic conclusion exaggerated the adaptive ability of children with IQs below 70, but there is no doubt that children from educationally deprived families are at a disadvantage when they enter school and may sometimes, as a result, fail to become literate, to master arithmetic, or to think abstractly. But this does not mean that young people with mental retardation are simply victims of their culturally deprived childhoods. Whenever evidence was available, almost all of the persons in my research samples were identified as developmentally "slow" by their parents and siblings *before* they entered school. Other children in these same families were considered to be developmentally normal and entered regular classes in school, whereas the "slow" children found their way into special classes (Koegel & Edgerton, 1982). The same cognitive limitations that handicapped these people as children persisted into adulthood, indeed into old age. When they were retested, these individuals did not have appreciably higher IQ test scores, and they did not learn to read and write, increase their arithmetic skills, or utilize abstract concepts.

However, their *social* competence has improved as they have aged. All of the research samples I have studied have demonstrated increased social competence as the individuals in them have aged. With the passage of time, communicative and interpersonal skills improve, and so do the skills necessary for success in the workplace and appropriateness in public places. These people learn how to control their emotions, use public transportation, shop more efficiently, better cope with health professionals and bureaucracies, and find the help of others when they need it. Some of these skills are evident when people with mild mental retardation are in their 30s and 40s, but as these people grow still older they tend to become even more competent in social interactions. In fact, when they are in their 60s, these people are not only more competent in absolute terms than they have ever been before, they also seem to be relatively more competent than at any prior period in their lives. No doubt this is the result of the continuing accumulation of experience and confidence, but it also appears to occur because at this age, others expect less of them. A person in their mid-60s may walk and talk more slowly, appear fuddled at times, make mistakes in a market, dress shabbily, and forget things without attracting attention. In a very real sense, when these people reach their 60s, they enter a niche in which their age normalizes their behavior.

Increased Social Integration

Unlike the young-adult African-Americans we studied who often were very much involved in the everyday activities of their community, the young-adult, middle-class Euro-Americans in our research samples have tended to have relationships only with other persons with mental retardation and to be isolated from community activities. Those aging persons who live with their parents or in community residential facilities are even more isolated. Many never meet anyone who is not a family member, a caretaker, or fellow resident. Those who once attended sheltered workshops used to have many friends, but most workshops now "retire" their older workers, especially since the introduction of competitive contracts that call for more productive workers. As a result, most of these people are quite lonely. However, those aging people with mental retardation who have continued to live independently have become more and more involved in the life of their communities. Despite their advanced age, they walk around their neighborhoods where they chat with merchants, waitresses, and acquaintances. They ride buses and some use them to travel extensively. All have acquaintances and friends (and some have lovers or spouses) who are not persons with mental retardation. And all help other people with small gifts, loans of money, useful chores, or volunteer work through churches or social agencies. All in all, their lives are as varied and full as one would expect of low-income people their age.

A few brief illustrations may be helpful. An illiterate man who is now aged 64 has lived on his own resources in the same deteriorated and dangerous area of downtown Los Angeles since his release from Pacific State Hospital over 30 years ago. He knows this area intimately, has many friends (including girlfriends), and is fully involved in the life of this neighborhood. His cognitive limitations are apparent to those who know him well (his IQ is 52, he can neither read nor write, has trouble calculating money, and has difficulty with complex concepts), but his charm and social skills are so great that the people with whom he interacts like him, and most of them do not suspect that he is a person with mental retardation. To take another example, a 63-year-old woman with an IQ of 56 and clearly limited intellectual abilities was for years wholly dependent on her intellectually average but physically handicapped husband until he died. Despite her plain, overweight appearance and rather irascible personality, she quickly married another intellectually average man and moved into his large house in a middle-class neighborhood. She was not always treated as an equal by his relatives and friends, and he had to do all the shopping, but she went many places on her own, chatted endlessly on her CB radio, and had a large circle of intellectually average acquaintances. Her husband knew that she was cognitively limited (but not that she was mentally retarded). Others seem to have accepted her as an ordinary, if a bit eccentric, housewife.

"Bobby" is a gay, Mexican-American man (aged 65, IQ 69) whose early years of community living were troubled by drunkenness, poverty, sexual profligacy, violence, vagrancy, and short jail terms. For years he survived by selling his own blood as often as twice a week for $5 a pint and by collecting aluminum cans. With the help of a woman who provided him with a place to stay (sometimes without charging him rent), he eventually became less troubled and less troubling, curbing his more promiscuous sexual encounters and drinking less. Although Bobby readily admits that he is gay and calls himself a "slow learner" who did not get enough schooling (which is certainly true), he denies that he is mentally retarded, pointing out that he can read a little as proof. In fact, there is little about him except his illiteracy and some difficulty with money and numbers to suggest that he is intellectually limited. He now lives a happy, if quieter, life. He no longer drinks, and his sexual life is muted in comparison to earlier times, but he loves to use his bus pass to ride all over Los Angeles, "looking at the sights." He is still involved in the local gay community where he is thought of as a man without a disability, but he usually lives quietly, watching television and listening to music at night. He is very pleased with his current life.

"Midge" (aged 69, IQ 67) has lived a truly volatile life that did not begin to stabilize until 1982, when she moved into a house with her mother and brother. Midge now fits quite well into her current lifestyle in a quiet lower middle-class neighborhood. Even before her mother's final illness, Midge took care of the household chores, including cleaning and grocery shopping. She especially enjoys her walks to the market, which allow her to chat with neighbors and fellow shoppers. Always something of a busybody, she knows many of her neighbors and greets them by name, along with bus drivers, police officers, salespeople, and regular customers like herself. She is devoted to her infirm brother (although she bridles when he is "bossy"), and, in addition to caring for his needs, paying the bills, and shopping, she spends evenings discussing current events with him or suggesting (usually incorrectly) ways to complete one of the jigsaw puzzles on which he is constantly working. She is interested in politics and votes for Democrats, complaining that she is always surrounded by Republicans, by which she means her brother. Midge is a fully involved member of her neighborhood who has no intention of becoming isolated. Her feelings are well summarized by her frequent and heated declaration that whatever may happen "'I'm not going to stay home and feel sorry for myself 'cause I'm getting up in years like a lot of them do'" (Gaston, 1991, p. 69).

"Martha" (aged 70, IQ 67) is the most isolated person among the independently living persons with whom we have retained contact. Yet she is fully independent, relying on no one to help her meet her needs. Indeed, much of her time is devoted to helping others. For more than 15 years, she has devoted four days a week to volunteer service in a Senior Meals program run by her church. Martha arrives before any of the other workers to organize the meal preparation and delivery activities which involve seven or eight other older women from the church. Because of her excellent memory for numbers, which allows her to recall how many ingredients will be necessary for the preparation of the day's meals, she has taken on a leadership role in the group. Unfortunately, her frequent irritability and domineering ways often alienate other workers, and she has made no real friends in the group. Indeed, she is almost totally isolated from other people except for a few casual acquaintances she knows from the church. In 1992, at the age of 70, she has still had no intimate relationship of any kind with a man or a woman, and apparently she has never wanted one. Each night before dark, she locks herself in her apartment, where she watches television or reads magazines until it is time to go to bed. She is a painfully lonely woman who must devote herself to finding things to do with her time until she is tired enough to sleep.

Of all the former patients, she has the least appropriate interpersonal skills, but what she lacks in this domain of life, she makes up for by her sheer determination and her intelligence. She is the hardest working and perhaps the most competent of the Senior Meals volunteers. She has made herself entirely self-sufficient, doing all her shopping, food preparation, and household tasks quite well without any need for assistance. She knows her way around her neighborhood and can take the bus to wherever she needs to visit. She maintains lively interest in the world, and while her tastes tend to run to tabloid sensationalism, she is very much aware of what is taking place in the world around her. Except for an occasional bout of painful facial neuralgia, her health is excellent. Martha's IQ has been tested between 67 and 72, but scores of this magnitude appear to greatly underestimate her cognitive abilities. Her memory is remarkable, and her numerical skills are adequate for any everyday task including banking and dealing with bureaucracies. Despite her limited education, she reads and writes adequately, and her problem-solving ability, too, suggests that her IQ scores underrepresent her intellectual ability. Indeed, she is unique among the former patients in possessing better cognitive than social skills. Perhaps she is in reality a casualty of her orphaned childhood and

hospitalized young adult years. Martha will probably always be lonely and fearful, but at the age of 70 she is self-reliant and seems to feel better about herself than she ever did before.

Implications for Research, Policy Development, and Service Provision

Despite the various indications that many people with mental retardation can experience striking improvement in their life satisfaction, social competence, and quality of life as they grow older, the process of aging is Janus-faced. With age come the experience, confidence, and self-esteem that help to transform troubled youths into satisfied "seniors," but aging can also bring ill health that endangers all that has been gained. One outcome can be premature death. For two independently-living older men in my sample, sudden heart attacks brought an end to their lives. One 68-year-old man with moderate mental retardation had worked every day for over 30 years selling newspapers at a street-corner stand. Happily married and otherwise in good health, the quality of his life had improved steadily over the years. Although he had slowed down somewhat, he still had "an eye for the ladies," as his wife sourly put it, and was talking optimistically about the future the day before he died. Another 68-year-old man also died of a heart attack. He too lived independently and was happy. Despite repeated warnings from doctors that his stupendous consumption of candy, eggs, meat, milk, and other fats would kill him, he continued to eat what he wished and live as he pleased until his heart, too, suddenly failed.

Preventive health care is a major issue for research, service provision, and policy development. For otherwise healthy and happy men to die at the age of 68 from coronary disease is sad, of course, but chronic illness that leads to years of suffering and dependency may be sadder still. Several of the people whose lives we have been following have suffered serious illness and physical debility. Those who live in community residential facilities typically have ready access to medical care, and unless their condition requires that they be moved to a nursing home, the quality of their lives may be little affected by ill health. Even many who are moved from board and care facilities to nursing homes may find that their lives are largely unchanged. But for those more independent people, serious illness can endanger everything they have striven so long to achieve. Consider Al, a man who since leaving Pacific State Hospital had worked hard at a foundry until a few years ago when an economic downturn led to his layoff and serious phlebitis in his legs threatened to leave him helpless. Thanks to a concerned physician who treated his phlebitis and arranged for him to receive SSI for his physical disability, Al was able to maintain his independence, and the quality of his life actually improved in succeeding years. Yet he is now 70 and the next medical problem may be more difficult to surmount. Or consider Ted, an independent man in his mid-60s who recently had a heart attack and had to be hospitalized. Luckily, angioplasty was successful, and bypass surgery that would have greatly affected his independent life style was avoided for the time being. But he continues to experience episodes of chest pain, and the future is uncertain.

Unfortunately, many of these more competent and independent individuals like Al and Ted have serious difficulty obtaining appropriate medical care. As a result, their independence is in jeopardy, and some may suffer needlessly, become infirm, or die. The following problems appear to be commonplace: recognizing that a threat to health exists, locating adequate and affordable medical care, communicating their complaints effectively with health care personnel, understanding the health care professional's explanations and instructions, and complying with instructions concerning medication or at-home therapy.

Many of these older persons with mental retardation are acutely aware of the health hazards of smoking cigarettes and using alcohol or drugs, but some are not. Others are unaware of the dangers of overmedicating themselves with vitamins, Valium, aspirin, or various over-the-counter preparations. Some engage in high-risk sexual activity but do not understand the dangers posed by AIDS, and few of them adequately understand the relationship between diet and health. Similarly, the symptoms of cardiovascular disease are not understood, nor is the need to have regular physical examinations for the early detection of life-threatening conditions. As a result, older persons with mental retardation are probably even less likely than their counterparts in the general population to seek preventive health care or to recognize early warning signs of potentially serious health problems.

Most older persons with mental retardation lack the financial resources for any health care not covered by Medicare or Medi-Cal (California's Medicaid program). For those under 65 who are dependent solely on Medi-Cal, finding adequate health care can be extremely difficult because almost all of California's Medi-Cal patients are treated by less than 4% of the state's physicians. As a result, it may be difficult for them to find a nearby clinic at all or to determine whether the clinic accepts Medi-Cal. If an appropriate clinic is located, finding transportation (especially in a city like Los Angeles where public transportation is inadequate) can also be a difficult problem. Many of the available clinics that accept Medi-Cal for low-income patients see so many patients that histories and examinations are perfunctory, and perhaps because many of these clinics operate their own pharmacies, routine treatment often consists of the prescription of large numbers of medications.

Even more than most lay people, older people with mental retardation have difficulties communicating with health care personnel, and such difficulties may begin even before they see a health care provider. Because many lack an adequate vocabulary of medical terms for their symptoms, they may have difficulty explaining the nature of their complaint or understanding questions posed by a receptionist or nurse. Most older individuals with mental retardation are functionally illiterate, so filling out medical history forms without help is a virtual impossibility. Confronted by such difficult and embarrassing problems, they are likely to act as if they understand something when in fact they do not or to agree with whatever may be said to avoid the embarrassment of asking for clarification. In fact, some are so intimidated by these challenges of communication that they avoid seeking medical care altogether.

If a patient actually succeeds in being seen by a physician, the same problems of comprehension continue and may, in fact, become even more troublesome. Questions about the nature or duration of the patient's condition often elicit confusing responses which the physician often interprets for the patient in the form of a statement, such as, "So you have these headaches every morning but they go away after a few hours." The patient is likely to agree, even if this statement is incorrect. When the physician's questions concern antecedent or correlative events such as exercise, diet, or stress, the confusion mounts. Confronted by a patient whose comprehension and verbal skills seem to be limited, some physicians try valiantly to reach a correct diagnosis, but others visibly lose interest in pursuing such an outcome and settle for prescribing a variety of medications.

Patients typically leave the physician's office with a number of prescriptions, instructions for their use, and various directions involving bed rest, diet, exercise, and the like. With a few exceptions, these instructions are either forgotten or misconstrued, and when the prescriptions are filled, the pharmacist is seldom helpful. A few pharmacies recognize that their customers may be cognitively limited or illiterate, and some take pains to explain how the medications should be taken, but most merely hand out the prescription. We have seen older persons with mental retardation leave a pharmacy with as many as five new prescriptions and no comprehension of when or how they should be taken. The efficacy of medications that are dispensed in this manner is obviously suspect, and the risk of unintentional overdoses or harmful drug interactions cannot be discounted.

That adequate health care is a problem for older persons with mental retardation is obvious. That there is a solution for this problem is a good deal less clear. I believe it was Ambrose Bierce who once said that for every complex problem there is a simple solution...and it is wrong! Providing adequate health care for older Americans with mental retardation is a complex problem by any criterion, and any simple solution to it would assuredly prove to be wrong. One reason for this (aside from Bierce's axiom) is the heterogeneity of the population. If funds were available, it would be a relatively uncomplicated matter to provide better health care for those older persons with mental retardation who live in community residential facilities. But the majority of older people with mental retardation do not live in easily identified group facilities like these (Seltzer, 1985). Like many of the older people whose lives I have tried to document, they live in places that are difficult to identify and their needs for health care are far more difficult to ascertain, much less meet. Actually, I should say that it must be *assumed* that the majority of older people with mental retardation live like this, because in reality it is not known how many older people with mental retardation there are in this country nor where they live. Without adequate epidemiological data we can make only the crudest of estimates about the numbers of such people and their medical needs.

Because only charter members of the Flat Earth Society believe that large-scale epidemiological research of the sort needed to identify the hidden majority of people with mental retardation will take place any time soon, we are obliged to make policy recommendations based on the limited information we have at hand. One place we might begin is with information. If lists could be compiled of health care providers within specific neighborhoods who were willing to accept Medicare patients, and if these lists could be made available in places where older people with mental retardation might run across them (bus stops, markets, pharmacies), some might be encouraged to call. If the receptionists who received their phone calls were sympathetic and trained to give good directions to the office or clinic, more older people might have access to health care. Of course, health care providers would have to learn to speak more plainly and effectively, especially concerning the importance of complying with their instructions (a problem that is hardly confined to older persons with mental retardation). A visiting nurse or mobile neighborhood health van can be of great help for people like these.

Even if this admittedly optimistic scenario were played out, many older people, particularly those who did not read, would not benefit. For them, the best, and perhaps only, solution would be the creation of a national network of neighborhood-based clinics ("seniors' health clinics" might be an acceptable gloss) that would be or soon become visible centers where older persons knew that they and people like them could receive low-cost sympathetic care. There is a long-established precedent in this country for local, state, and federal funding of free clinics when there is a clear threat to public health. The polio vaccination campaign is one example; the current effort to control drug-resistant tuberculosis among new immigrants to the U.S. is another.

Whatever the future may hold with regard to improved health care for older people with mental retardation, it is evident that their good health, like life's quality in general, depends in large measure on the availability of other people who take an interest in them, monitor their well-being, and help them in times of ill health. Older people who have such friends, or "benefactors" as I once called them, are much more likely to have their health needs met than those who do not.

Many other research and policy issues concerning older people with mental retardation need to be addressed. Better housing, social integration, and social support are a few of these. But because health is a concern of such overriding importance, I have chosen to concentrate on it. As for all older Americans and, indeed, for Americans of all ages, better health care is a priority for older persons with mental retardation. It is a bitter irony that people with mental retardation often achieve their greatest sense of well-being late in life when they are most vulnerable to ill health that can deprive them of the happiness it has taken them so long to attain.

As a final comment, I would like to encourage a research agenda that would examine the various ways in which older persons with mental retardation not known to human service agencies maintain their health and find satisfaction in their lives. The goal would be development of national policies that heighten concern for the well-being of older persons with mental retardation and that prevent as many as possible from becoming infirm and dependent. A vision of "golden years" for all older people is chimerical, of course, but our nation can ill afford not to expend the modest cost of providing better preventive health services given the clear reality that our failure to do so will prove to be far more costly.

References

Bercovici, S. M. (1983). *Barriers to normalization: The restrictive management of retarded persons*. Baltimore, MD: University Park Press.

Bogdan, R., & Taylor, S. J. (1982). *Inside Out: Two first-person accounts of what it means to be labeled mentally retarded*. Toronto: University of Toronto Press.

Cobb, H. V. (1972). *The forecast of fulfillment: A review of research on predictive assessment of adult retarded for social and vocational adjustment*. New York: Teachers College Press.

Edgerton, R. B. (1975). Issues relating to the quality of life among mentally retarded persons. In M. Begab & S. Richardson (Eds.), *The mentally retarded and society: A social science perspective* (pp. 127–140). Baltimore, MD: University Park Press.

Edgerton, R. B. (1981). Crime, deviance and normalization: Reconsidered. In R. H. Bruininks et al. (Eds.), *Deinstitutionalization* and community adjustment of mentally retarded people (Monograph No. 4) (pp. 145–166). Washington, DC: American Association on Mental Deficiency.

Edgerton, R. B. (1983). Failure in community adaptation: The relativity of assessment. In K. Kernan, M. Begab, & R. B. Edgerton (Eds.), *Environments and behavior: The adaptation of mentally retarded persons* (pp. 123–143). Baltimore, MD: University Park Press.

Edgerton, R. B. (1990). Quality of life from a longitudinal perspective. In R. L. Schalock (Ed.), *Quality of life: Perspectives and issues* (pp. 149–160). Washington, DC: American Association on Mental Retardation.

Edgerton, R. B. (1993). *The cloak of competence* (rev. ed.). Berkeley: University of California Press.

Edgerton, R. B., & Bercovici, S. M. (1976). The cloak of competence: Years later. *American Journal of Mental Deficiency, 80,* 485–497.

Gaston, M. A. (1991). "I'll manage these things as they come up." In R. B. Edgerton & M. A. Gaston (Eds.), *"I've seen it all!" Lives of older persons with mental retardation in the community* (pp. 45–69). Baltimore, MD: Brookes.

Gerber, D. A. (1990). Listening to disabled people: The problem of voice and authority in Robert B. Edgerton's *The Cloak of Competence. Disability, Handicap & Society, 5,* 3–23.

Koegel, P., & Edgerton, R. B. (1982). Labeling and perception of handicap among black mildly retarded adults. *American Journal of Mental Deficiency,* 87, 266–276.

Koegel, P., & Edgerton, R. B. (1984). Black "six-hour retarded children" as young adults. In R. B. Edgerton (Ed.), *Lives in process: Mildly retarded adults in a large city* (Monograph No. 6) (pp. 145–171). Washington DC: American Association on Mental Deficiency.

McCarver, R. B., & Craig, E. M. (1974). Placement of the retarded in the community: Prognosis and outcome. In N. R. Ellis (Ed.), *International review of research in mental retardation* (Vol. 7). New York: Academic Press.

President's Committee on Mental Retardation. (1970). *The Six-Hour Retarded Child.* Washington, DC: U.S. Government Printing Office.

Seltzer, M. M. (1985). Research in social aspects of aging and developmental disabilities. In M. P. Janicki & H. M. Wisniewski (Eds.), *Aging and developmental disabilities: Issues and approaches* (pp. 161–173). Baltimore, MD: Brookes.

Seltzer, M. M., & Krauss, M. W. (1987). *Aging and mental retardation: Extending the continuum* (Monograph No. 9). Washington, DC: American Association on Mental Retardation.

I gratefully acknowledge support from the National Institute of Child Health and Human Development: Grant No. HD04612 to the Mental Retardation Research Center, UCLA, and Grant No. HD11944-02, The Community Adaptation of Mildly Retarded Persons.

Chapter 5

Behavioral and Mental Health Changes Associated With Aging in Adults With Mental Retardation

Warren B. Zigman, New York State Institute for Basic Research in Developmental Disabilities
Gary B. Seltzer, University of Wisconsin–Madison
Wayne P. Silverman, New York State Institute for Basic Research in Developmental Disabilities

During the past 100 years, dramatic advances have occurred in medical technologies and services, as well as in public health practices, resulting in reductions in early mortality rates and significant extension of life expectancy. In 1900, approximately 4% of the United States population, or 3.1 million adults, were age 65 and over, but by the turn of the century, projections indicate that over 12% of the population will be age 65 and over (Butler, 1980). Similar trends have been occurring among individuals with mental retardation (Carter & Jancar, 1983). For example, in 1931–1935, the average age at death for institutionalized mentally retarded males was 14.9 years and for females, 22.0 years. These figures had increased to 58.3 years and 59.8 years, respectively, in 1976–1980 (Carter & Jancar, 1983).

Elderly adults with mental retardation may have special needs because of age-associated changes in their adaptive and cognitive capacities, as well as their emotional well-being, perhaps paralleling those seen in the elderly population without mental retardation, However, without supporting data it would be inappropriate to assume that age-associated changes will be present to similar degrees or manifest themselves in qualitatively similar patterns for all adults with mental retardation. Indeed, there are many different causes of mental retardation, both genetic and nongenetic (Abuelo, 1983; Lott, 1983), which are known to express themselves developmentally in a wide variety of symptomology, and there is little reason to expect that individuals with mental retardation attributed to different biological or social factors should age in a similar manner. For example, many studies have demonstrated that adults with Down syndrome represent a group with a known genetic predisposition to premature aging.

Many issues that are relevant to aging among adults with mental retardation only can be clarified by the results of empirical studies. One overriding definitional issue that needs to be addressed is the chronological age at which an adult should be considered to be aged. For example, Janicki and Hogg (1989) found that the operational definition of "aged" varies greatly across research studies. This lack of uniformity in the operational definition of "aged" will invariably cause some problems in comparing research findings from different investigations, but more importantly, a consensus needs to be developed for determining eligibility for "senior" benefits and programs. In the general population, 65 is commonly accepted as the criterion for defining senior citizen status, but a lower age may be more appropriate for adults with mental retardation.

Another overriding issue is related to the differences among persons with mental retardation attributable to etiology. To the extent possible we have reviewed research on specific subpopulations of adults with mental retardation. Unfortunately, the existing research in this area has tended to examine groups that are not well defined with regard to etiology, except when premature aging among adults with Down syndrome is a central issue. Unfortunate also is the paucity of literature on other conditions considered to be developmental disabilities; thus the chapter will focus almost solely on mental retardation.

The remainder of this chapter provides a review of recent research on behavioral (i.e., adaptive and cognitive) and mental health characteristics that have been examined with respect to variation in aging among adults with mental retardation. Specifically, we will examine (a) research that links adaptive behavior changes with age, (b) research that links cognitive changes with age, and (c) research relating age and mental health among older adults with mental retardation. Of course there are conceptual overlaps among these three areas, in that deficits in one area may be related to significant deficits in other areas (e.g., observed cognitive or adaptive deficits may cause anxiety or depression). However, differences in the design of studies and in the types of dependent variables used to measure these areas necessitate reviewing each area separately.

Adaptive Behavior

Adaptive behavior refers to "everyday performance in coping with environmental demands," and to "what people do to take care of themselves and to relate to others in daily living" (Grossman, 1983, p. 42). Subareas of adaptive behavior usually identified explicitly include eating, toileting, dressing, grooming, and communication skills, as well as simple cognitive skills necessary for an independent lifestyle (Meyers, Nihira, & Zetlin, 1979). Mobility is also commonly considered an adaptive behavior because the ability to ambulate freely is closely related to achieving independence in daily life.

The review that follows is separated into two sections. The first section is concerned with studies of age-related adaptive decline (or deficits) in adults with Down syndrome. The second section includes studies of adults with mental retardation with no specific focus on etiology or diagnosis. This distinction is made because the studies of aging and Down syndrome tend to focus on ages typically considered middle rather than old age. These studies suggest a very different pattern of age-associated changes than do those studies focusing on more classically defined geriatric age groups.

Adults With Mental Retardation With Down Syndrome

Aging among adults with Down syndrome has drawn the interest of researchers for many years because of the elevated risk of Alzheimer disease in this population. One of the first papers addressing this issue was written by Fraser and Mitchell (1876), who noted that in many instances, mortality in this population was due to a "general decay—a sort of precipitated senility." Subsequent work has shown that virtually all adults with Down syndrome over the age of 35 develop Alzheimer neuropathology (Ball & Nuttall, 1980; Jervis, 1948; Malamud, 1972; Solitaire & LaMarche, 1966; Wisniewski, Wisniewski, & Wen, 1985), indicating that Alzheimer disease, the most prevalent cause of dementia among elderly adults in the general population (Terry & Katzman, 1983), may occur precociously in adults with Down syndrome. (For a full review of this topic see Zigman, Schupf, Zigman and Silverman, 1993.)

Recent molecular biological studies support this notion because key sites on chromosome 21, present in triplicate in people with Down syndrome, are involved in Alzheimer disease. Several investigators have reported that the occurrence of early-onset Alzheimer disease (i.e., < 65 years of age) in families is linked to specific markers located on chromosome 21 (Goate et al., 1989; St. George-Hyslop et al., 1987), as is the gene coding for beta amyloid precursor protein, a key substance involved in Alzheimer disease neuropathology (e.g., Robakis et al., 1987).

Early investigations of Alzheimer disease in adults with Down syndrome focused on identifying and describing the pathological and clinical syndrome of the disease (e.g., Jervis, 1948). More recently, research has focused on determining the age-specific prevalence of dementia in this population (e.g., Lai & Williams, 1989), as well as determining the specific behavioral, neurological, and biological changes associated with the neuropathology of Alzheimer disease.

Before reviewing specific research relating to adaptive, cognitive, or mental health changes in adults with Down syndrome that may or may not be due to the presence of Alzheimer disease, an issue of major significance must be discussed. The majority of the extant research on the relationship between the development of Alzheimer disease and dementia among adults with Down syndrome 30 years of age and older has noted a large discrepancy between the hypothesized prevalence of neuropathology (i.e., 100%) and the estimated prevalence of dementia (i.e., ranging from 6% to 75%; Wisniewski & Rabe, 1986). This discrepancy has precipitated considerable debate. Some investigators have suggested that early manifestations of dementia may go undetected, while others have hypothesized that something inherent in the Down syndrome genotype results in an extended prodromal phase of Alzheimer disease (Haxby & Shapiro, 1992), perhaps associated with some underlying biological mechanism that compensates for the progressive Alzheimer neuropathology (Wisniewski, Rabe, & Wisniewski, 1987). However, recent data have indicated that within both the general population (e.g., Ulrich, 1985) and the population of adults with mental retardation due to causes other than Down syndrome (e.g., Popovitch et al., 1990), neuropathology consistent with Alzheimer disease can be present without a clinical history of frank dementia. These findings suggest that the lack of a strong correlation between the manifestation of neuropathology consistent with a diagnosis of Alzheimer disease and observed indications of clinical dementia may not be unique to adults with Down syndrome.

Nevertheless, for the purposes of the current presentation, specification of the etiology of the decline is less important than objective confirmation of its existence. If adults with Down syndrome do indeed show age-related behavioral regression, it is of immense practical value to know at what age functional decline can be expected. Further, if dementia is a prevalent characteristic of older adults with Down syndrome, careful longitudinal research is needed to determine whether the pattern of decline varies within this population and whether the pattern(s) exhibited are similar to those that may be seen later in life among adults with mental retardation without Down syndrome.

In a series of reports, Silverstein and his colleagues (Silverstein et al., 1988; Silverstein, Herbs, Nasuta, & White, 1986) noted the results of several cross-sectional studies that examined the relationship between age (ranging between 2 and 69 years of age) and adaptive behavior of hundreds of people with mental retardation with or without Down syndrome. Silverstein et al. (1986), for example, analyzed 62 separate items pertaining to adaptive functioning in six areas of behavioral skills. These included items measuring behavioral competence in the following domains: motor, independent living, social, emotional, cognitive and communication. Silverstein et al. found only weak evidence that adults with Down syndrome exhibited age-related deficits compared to their peers without Down syndrome and suggested that the relatively low level of functioning of their participants, all of whom were institutionalized, may have made it difficult to detect group differences.

Silverstein et al. (1988) subsequently reported a more comprehensive investigation that included noninstitutionalized subjects. Adults with Down syndrome in this study who were over the age of 60 exhibited age-related deficits in motor functioning (a factor that includes items related to ambulation, arm-hand use, eating, and toileting).

In another study, Zigman, Schupf, Lubin, and Silverman (1987) examined adaptive behavior of adults with mental retardation with and without Down syndrome. Their sample included 6,316 adults with and without Down syndrome who were 20 to 69 years of age. They found that among adults over 50 years of age, those with Down syndrome exhibited lower levels of adaptive skills than matched controls, but below 50 years of age, skill levels were comparable in the two subpopulations. Adults with Down syndrome over the age of 60 exhibited the poorest performance of any group, with the largest difference between etiologically defined groups seen in a factor measuring adaptive as opposed to cognitive skills. In a subsequent report, Zigman, Schupf, Silverman, and Sterling (1989) noted a pattern of similar results as a function of age and etiology when they reanalyzed these data on the basis of individual domain scores reflecting gross motor functioning, toileting, dressing/grooming, eating, independent living, language, reading/writing, and quantitative skills. Specifically, the findings were more persuasive in domains measuring adaptive skills (e.g., toileting, dressing/grooming, eating) as opposed to cognitive skills.

Young and Kramer (1991) found age-related deficits with advancing age in a study investigating the language and self-care skills of 60 adults with Down syndrome (22 to 67 years of age), although there were no observed deficits in expressive language. These findings, if replicated, would suggest that changes in adaptive skills within specific functional areas may be more sensitive indices of age-associated changes compared to more global domain type scores.

Adaptive functioning skills among adults with Down syndrome were also described by Fenner, Hewitt, and Torpy (1987). They found no evidence of age-associated deficits in feeding, toileting, washing, and dressing skills in 39 adults, 19 to 49 years of age, using selected items from the American Association on Mental Retardation's Adaptive Behavior Scale (AAMR-ABS) (Nihira, Foster, Shellhaas, & Leland, 1974). These data are not inconsistent with Silverstein et al. (1986; 1988) and Zigman et al. (1987), who found that marked age-associated deficits were only manifested after the age of *50* in adults with Down syndrome.

Recent studies by Collacott (1992; 1993) provide further evidence of an age-associated pattern of adaptive regression in adults with Down syndrome. In two cross-sectional studies, Collacott presented the results of the AAMR-ABS completed on 308 adults, aged 18 to 60+, with Down syndrome. Generally, these studies indicated that adults with Down syndrome over age 50 display the patterns of age-associated deficits in adaptive behavior found by other researchers. Collacott also presented data indicating that the general pattern of skill loss does not differ as a function of whether the individual under study was ever institutionalized, indicating that the obtained results probably were not due to cohort effects. Finally, Collacott found that the late development of a seizure disorder (i.e., over age 35) in adults with Down syndrome was associated with lower AAMR-ABS scores, suggesting that seizures may be a manifestation of Alzheimer-type dementia.

All previously reviewed studies, with the exception of Silverstein et al. (1988), have employed cross-sectional designs. There were only 15 subjects over 40 years of age, with the oldest 63, in the study conducted by Silverstein et al.; therefore, the results are not generalizable. Cross-sectional analysis is not as reliable as longitudinal analysis for determining changes over time and age because the differences among groups described by cross-sectional analyses are potentially confounded by "cohort" and "healthy survivor" effects.

Especially relevant for studies of aging among groups of adults with mental retardation receiving state services are the different life experiences, exposures, and treatment histories of adults who develop during different historical periods, otherwise called "cohort effects." It is obvious when one looks at the many historical changes in service philosophy, design, and practice, that different cohorts of disabled individuals within service systems were likely to have been subject to widely disparate treatment. In fact, as a function of the current philosophy of service provision for individuals with disabling conditions (i.e., which decries institutionalization), many current elderly service consumers might never have entered the service system if they had been born later, and some of our more seriously disabled current service consumers may not survive to reach their 65th birthday.

Healthy survivor effects refer to the fact that, as a group, older surviving subjects clearly are healthier than were their peers who died at an earlier age, an artifact that would tend to reduce aging effects in cross-sectional studies. Accordingly, an investigation into the development of age-related disorders in an aging population may result in the fewest cases being found among the oldest subjects. This is because the group at greatest risk (i.e., the group who did have the disorder) may not have survived long enough to be included in the study sample.

Six recent studies have presented data on various aspects of longitudinal changes in adaptive functioning in adults with Down syndrome (Burt, Loveland, & Lewis, 1992; Devenny, Hill, Patxot, Silverman, & Wisniewski, 1992; Evenhuis, 1990; Lai & Williams, 1989; Schupf, Silverman, Sterling, & Zigman, 1989; Zigman et al., 1990). Schupf et al. (1989) and Zigman et al. (1990) utilized retrospectively collected data, whereas Lai & Williams (1989), Burt et al. (1992), Evenhuis (1990), and Devenny et al. (1992) utilized prospective designs.

Zigman et al. (1990) investigated whether the prevalence of dementia, measured by utilizing increasingly stringent objective criteria of adaptive skill loss, differed as a function of disability etiology (i.e., Down syndrome versus other) and level of intellectual functioning. On the basis of descriptive analyses, adults with Down syndrome over 50 years of age generally exhibited higher levels of adaptive skill loss than did adults with mental retardation due to other causes.

Burt et al. (1992) presented the baseline data for a prospective study of depression, dementia, and adaptive skill loss in a group of adults (20 to 60 years of age) with Down syndrome (n = 61) and adults with mental retardation without Down syndrome (n = 43). They diagnosed dementia in sample members using modified DSM III-R (American Psychiatric Association, 1987) criteria and either (a) objective evidence of loss of previously attained skills or (b) questioning informants about individuals' changes in functioning. Burt et al. found that 8 of 61 adults

with Down syndrome had symptoms of dementia (including declines in adaptive behavior), whereas none of the comparison subjects had any diagnosable dementia.

The findings of a prospective study of a group of 46 adults with mental retardation, 28 of whom had Down syndrome, have been presented by Devenny et al. (1992). The longitudinal assessment data, covering a 3–5 year period, included evaluation of mental status (including questions relating to adaptive functioning) and auditory and visual memory. Subjects (27 to 55 years of age) were chosen for inclusion in the study if they (a) had mild or moderate mental retardation and (b) had no history of functional regression, seizures, or severe sensory impairments. Over the course of the study, no person with Down syndrome showed signs of regression or dementia, a result that is at odds with much of the previously presented data. However, this group may not be representative of the broader population of adults with Down syndrome at similar ages because participants were chosen to exclude any individuals with previous signs or symptoms of Alzheimer disease. Additionally, there were few participants within the age range at which the risk for dementia would be the highest (i.e., over 50). Finally, all participants had mild or moderate mental retardation, and it may be that this group, which has the least severe phenotypic expression of the Down syndrome genotype, is at lower age-specific risk for dementia of the Alzheimer type.

With few exceptions, extant studies have consistently found that fewer than 50% of adults with Down syndrome displayed significant signs and symptoms of dementia. Two exceptions include studies conducted by Evenhuis (1990) and Lai and Williams (1989). Evenhuis prospectively followed 17 people with Down syndrome from initial institutionalization until death. A clinically diagnosable dementia syndrome was found in 15 of the 17 adults (i.e., 88%). Neuropathological examination of brain tissue found pathology of the Alzheimer-type in all individuals. Explanations for the extraordinarily high prevalence rate of clinical dementia found by

Evenhuis may include small sample size and the fact that subjective ratings of deterioration were sometimes utilized. Also, because these 17 people were terminally ill during the course of data collection (i.e, they had to have died to be included within the study), declines in functioning may have been due to "terminal drop," that is, the regression in ability associated with the presence of a terminal illness. Lai and Williams (1989), utilizing a broad design that included the collection of data regarding neurological signs and symptoms, tests of orientation, memory, verbal skills, and adaptive behavior, evaluated the entire population of individuals with Down syndrome over 35 years of age in an institution for mentally retarded individuals (N = 73). Over a period of eight years, 53 adults survived to complete the entire cycle of assessments, and 55% of those 50–59 years old and 75% of those 60 and older had diagnosable dementia. Dementia was also observed in 100% of the 20 adults who died during the course of the study. Included among the clinical features described by Lai and Williams are the loss of self-help skills, such as dressing, toileting, and eating skills.

Results of these studies, as well as the studies presented earlier, clearly support the proposition that adults with Down syndrome are especially prone to loss in adaptive skills with advancing age. However, as mentioned previously, studies demonstrating decline in adaptive competence for adults with Down syndrome also may have been influenced by acute conditions associated with differential patterns of mortality in subjects with Down syndrome. Specifically, with increasing age a greater proportion of study participants may become terminally ill and die. Therefore, adaptive skill loss apparently associated with aging may be due to differential "terminal drop," the loss of function due to any terminal disease state. To control for this potential confound, Schupf et al. (1989) examined data from 99 deceased individuals with Down syndrome and 99 matched deceased controls in a historical cohort study of adaptive behavior during the three years immediately prior to death. Analyses verified that the adults with Down syndrome age 50

and older showed greater regression in overall adaptive competence compared both to younger individuals with Down syndrome and to their age-matched controls. Unfortunately, Schupf et al. were unable to estimate the age-specific prevalence of dementia in any formal way from the data available for analysis.

In summary, there is a substantial body of research supporting the hypothesis that adults with Down syndrome older than 50 years of age are at increased risk for losses in adaptive skills. This pattern remains evident regardless of where the individual resides. One issue in need of further clarification is whether observed age-related declines in adaptive skills are manifested in similar ways among adults with Down syndrome at different levels of mental retardation. It also remains to be determined whether these losses are due to precocious but otherwise "normal" aging or to an increased age-specific susceptibility to Alzheimer disease. These declines, whatever their underlying cause, must be considered in planning and providing programs and services for adults with Down syndrome.

Adults With Mental Retardation With Undifferentiated Etiologies

Research reviewed within this section includes (a) studies excluding subjects with Down syndrome, (b) large scale studies of unselected adults with mental retardation that do not classify subjects on the basis of etiology, and (c) studies that have subjects without Down syndrome as a distinct group. Because participants without Down syndrome in type C studies are not age-matched to participants with Down syndrome, observed findings are more generalizable to the larger population of adults with mental retardation. For example, in a series of reports, Haveman and his colleagues noted the results of their examination of a number of older residents of group living arrangements in the Netherlands. In one cross-sectional study, including some 509 adults with mental retardation who resided both in institutions and group homes, they found that, among adults without Down syndrome, people over 50 years of age had a small but nonsignificant increase in motor problems compared to younger adults (Haveman, Maaskant, & Sturmans, 1989). No other age-related changes in adaptive skills were noted. In contrast, individuals with Down syndrome over age 50 displayed skill loss. In other studies, these investigators examined these data in greater detail and in relation to residential placement (Haveman & Maaskant, 1989). Adults over 50 years of age who lived in institutional settings displayed a higher prevalence of problems with motor functioning than did younger residents, but residents of group homes did not exhibit a similar pattern until after the age of 60. Linguistic skills increased across all age groups, however, making interpretation of deficits difficult (Haveman & Maaskant, 1989). Maaskant and Haveman (1989), in another study of 416 group home residents, found that mobility and motor functioning were related to age, with adults over age 60 exhibiting the poorest performance. Results regarding age-associated deficits in other areas were less obvious. Analysis of scale scores reflecting social functioning (i.e., personal skills and linguistic skills) exhibited no significant age-associated patterns, although analyses of the data on an item-by-item basis indicated that older adults may develop some specific adaptive problems (e.g., dressing, making their beds). Unfortunately, neither of these studies considered Down syndrome status in their analyses, and effects suggesting age-related declines may have been even smaller if only persons without Down syndrome were considered.

Lund (1988) analyzed age-related differences on the Vineland Social Maturity Scale in a sample of 302 adults with mental retardation (age 20 years and older) from the Danish National Register for the Mentally Retarded and noted a negative linear trend with age for adults with Down syndrome (n = 44). Adults without Down syndrome did not seem to exhibit this trend. However, the age groups utilized by Lund (i.e., the oldest group was 45 and older) may have included too many younger subjects to be able to find significant age-associated effects in individuals without Down syndrome. Day (1987)

studied all 99 adults with mental retardation over the age of 65 who lived in one institution. None of the subjects had an etiological diagnosis of Down syndrome. He found a significant increase in the proportion of individuals with problems in mobility in persons over age 74 as compared with the late 60s. Continence, the only other activity of daily living for which there was information, showed no difference as a function of age.

A series of large scale investigations, including national studies conducted by Hauber, Rotegard, and Bruininks (1985), as well as state-specific studies conducted by Janicki and his colleagues in New York (Janicki, 1989; Janicki & Jacobson, 1986; Janicki & MacEachron, 1984) and Krauss and Seltzer (1986) in Massachusetts, reported cross-sectional data regarding the characteristics of large numbers of older adults with mental retardation. These studies included adults with many different etiologic diagnoses and are presented together because they employed similar large scale approaches.

Hauber et al. (1985) utilized an index measuring level of dependence/independence in adaptive skills and found that older adults (over 62 years of age) were less dependent in the activities of daily living measured by this index than were younger adults (40–62 years of age). As expected, residents in public facilities (i.e., primarily institutional facilities) were more dependent than residents of community facilities, but similar age effects were found. Although these findings may initially seem counterintuitive and at odds with previously presented data, further examination of the data reveals that a greater proportion of the younger adults, in comparison with the older adults, had severe or profound mental retardation. This pattern was consistent for adults in both community and public facilities. Janicki and MacEachron (1984) conducted a large cross-sectional study investigating the characteristics of 7,823 adults with mental retardation age 53 and older. This study included all individuals listed on a statewide information system who fit into three age groups (i.e., 53 to 62, 63 to 72, and 73 and older). Overall age-related differences in the proportion of adults who were independent in mobility, toileting, eating, and dressing/grooming were found, with major deficits found in the cohort aged 73 and older. When the data were presented as a function of intellectual ability, older adults with mild or moderate mental retardation showed generalized patterns of deficit, whereas adults with severe or profound mental retardation only exhibited deficits in mobility and, to a lesser extent, in toileting skills. The finding of greater stability in self-care skills for people with severe or profound mental retardation apparently is not a function of floor effects (i.e., that the scores are so low that the scale cannot measure any further decline), as a sizeable proportion of the adults with severe or profound mental retardation was independent in the self-care skills described. An alternative explanation may be that there are differential survivor effects. Specifically, surviving adults with severe or profound mental retardation may be the most functionally capable of their cohort; in the cohort of adults with mild or moderate mental retardation, the relationship between survival and functional capability may be weaker.

Janicki and Jacobson (1986) conducted additional analyses of data from an extended sample of 10,532 adults with mental retardation 45 years of age and older. Adaptive functioning was analyzed both in terms of eight separate domains and two aggregate scores, representing activities of daily living (gross motor, toileting, dressing/grooming and eating) and cognitive skills (language, read/write, quantitative, and independent living). Data were presented separately for adults with mild/moderate and severe/profound mental retardation. Adults with mild/moderate mental retardation exhibited lower skill levels in gross motor and independent living skills after the age of 50; functional differences in the other domains were not evident until after age 70. A similar deficit at age 50 in gross motor skills was found for adults with severe/profound mental retardation; performance in other areas did not decrease until after age 70. Concerning the two aggregate scores, adults with mild/moderate mental retardation declined in activities

of daily living skills after age 50 but maintained their abilities in cognitive skills until their late 70s. Adults with severe/profound mental retardation maintained integrity in both aggregate scores into their 70s and declined thereafter. When these data were presented as a function of residential setting, similar patterns appeared, although on the whole older adults who resided in institutions exhibited greater age-associated differences and scored lower than did older adults residing in community settings. Generally, results of these analyses mirrored those of Janicki and MacEachron (1984); similarly, these findings may reflect differential mortality and healthy survivor effects.

Krauss and Seltzer (1986) compared cognitive, medical, functional, and service need characteristics of 1,085 adults with mental retardation in two age groups (22 to 54 and 55 to 91 years of age). People in this sample resided in community or institutional settings. Consistent with the Hauber et al. (1985) study, older adults with mental retardation were found to be less functionally impaired in adaptive skills than were younger adults, regardless of residential placement. Older adults, however, also were found to be less impaired in terms of level of mental retardation (again, consistent with the Hauber et al. study), which may have been the cause of the observed effect. These results differ from those presented by Seltzer, Seltzer, and Sherwood (1982), which indicated that older adults with mental retardation were more limited in their adaptive skills. Differences in the residential placement between the younger and older groups in these studies, however, may account for the discrepant findings. Specifically, the older group examined by Seltzer et al. resided in more restrictive settings, and placement decisions were likely to have been related to adaptive skills.

In one of the few studies that examined aging in adults with mental retardation with a specific disability in addition to mental retardation, Janicki (1989) examined the characteristics of 883 older adults with cerebral palsy. Age-related changes in mobility, toileting skills, eating skills, and dressing/grooming skills were found, with the age group 75 and older containing the lowest proportion of individuals who were independent in terms of functioning in these areas.

The studies presented above have employed cross-sectional designs. As stated earlier, cross-sectional analyses are sensitive to confounding by "cohort" and "healthy survivor" effects, and, as is the case with studies focusing on aging in adults with Down syndrome, few studies present data focusing on changes over time within individuals. One such study is a retrospective examination of 148 adults with mental retardation (without Down syndrome) aged 64 and older who lived in four institutions in Bristol, England (Hewitt, Fenner, & Torpy, 1986). Staff were questioned using a structured interview regarding (a) the current status of the individual's abilities in dressing, toileting, washing, and feeding and (b) whether the current status reflected a deterioration from previously obtained levels of behavioral functioning. Approximately 10% of these adults experienced a deterioration in self-care skills, with this decline related to a significant drop in intellectual ability (measured by the Stanford Binet Intelligence Scale).

Another retrospective study examined records of 70 deceased adults with mental retardation without Down syndrome, all over the age of 65 at time of death (Barcikowska et al., 1989). The objective of this study was to understand the relationship between specific measures of Alzheimer pathology and signs of dementia. Data on changes in adaptive functioning were derived from a comprehensive review of existing medical records. Between 5% and 10% of the subjects had significant declines in reading/writing, speech/language, and eating skills. Activity of daily living skills were more affected, with between 20% and 30% of the subjects showing significant declines in dressing skills, motor ability, social skills, or toileting skills. Finally, 64% of the adults were unable to continue in the day program in which they had been enrolled, reflecting declines in production or employee skills that could be indicative of dementia in the general population. However, as Barcikowska et al. noted, many of these elderly adults developed physical conditions that accounted for their declines in adaptive competence (e.g., cataracts, hip fractures), and it was therefore impossible to draw firm conclusions regarding the significance of these retrospective measures as indicators of Alzheimer disease in many cases.

In a comprehensive cross-sequential study, Eyman and Widaman (1987) examined life-span development of adaptive skills in 30,749 individuals with mental retardation between the ages of 4 and 90. Etiological diagnoses were not specified. Six factors derived from the statewide information system utilized in California (Widaman, Gibbs, & Geary, 1987) were used as the dependent measures. These factors included data describing adaptive skills in the following areas: motor control, independent living, cognition, social competence, social maladaption, and personal maladaption. Each dependent variable was related to age group, level of retardation, residential placement, and assessment period (there were four assessments). Eyman and Widaman (1987) graphically presented some interesting findings regarding changes over time in various adaptive areas, with the major results of this study indicating that there are specific differences in longitudinal patterns of adaptive change associated with age, level of functioning, and residential setting. Therefore, future studies must be sensitive to the influence of these variables. Additionally, Eyman and Widaman noted the importance of investigating longitudinal patterns of adaptive change over an extended period.

In summary, contrary to the wealth of evidence pointing to the existence of age-related adaptive declines in adults with Down syndrome, data regarding similar declines in mentally retarded adults without Down syndrome are less conclusive. The data presented by Janicki and his colleagues (Janicki, 1989; Janicki & Jacobson, 1986; Janicki & MacEachron, 1984) and Eyman and Widaman (1987) seem to indicate the existence of some patterns of age-related declines in adaptive functioning occurring later in life. (The specific ages differ as a function of various demographic variables.) All these large scale studies presumably included subjects with Down syndrome, however, which may have influenced the obtained pattern of results. In the future, studies of aging in populations of adults with mental retardation should subdivide samples into distinct groups based upon etiological diagnoses whenever possible.

Cognitive Changes With Age

The studies of adaptive behavior reviewed in the previous section emphasize functional relationships between chronological age and specific competencies and relate these relationships to various population characteristics (e.g., etiology, severity of mental retardation). Typically, these reports do not consider how aging affects the cognitive processes underlying performance of the tasks included in the behavior inventories. Indeed, because the tasks themselves are not selected for the purpose of clarifying the nature of the underlying processes, results from studies of adaptive behavior can provide only limited insights into the nature of the underlying processes determining performance. For example, all items on behavioral inventories minimally require (a) analysis of ill-defined stimulus conditions, (b) retrieval of information from memory regarding previous experience with stimulus situations and appropriate responses, (c) selection of an appropriate response, (d) execution of the selected response, (e) evaluation of the consequences of the action, and (f) storage of new/updated information in memory. Although the relative demands on these separate processes vary across behavioral items, performance effectiveness for any of the overt behaviors included in the inventories necessarily depends upon the efficiency of the entire processing system.

Rather than describing the functional relationships between chronological age and specific objective indicators of behavioral competence, studies of cognitive functioning are designed to infer the nature of age-associated changes in the mental processes underlying overt performance. These studies usually employ standard neuropsychological assessment instruments or experimental protocols that provide controls on task demands sufficient to permit inferences about specific cognitive processes. Thus, while the same processing system always determines performance, whether measured by a behavioral inventory or a neuro-psychological/cognitive task, only the latter category of measurement provides insights into the specific operations of the processing system. Therefore, studies focusing on the effects of aging on the cognition of adults with mental retardation are reviewed separately from studies of adaptive functioning. The review that follows will be limited to those studies including at least one identifiable group of nondemented participants 40 years of age or older.

Relevant studies can be segregated into several broad categories. Some were designed to investigate aging of all adults with mental retardation; others have as their primary interest the subpopulation with Down syndrome. Some studies focus explicitly on changes in IQ or mental age across the adult life span; others emphasize measures of more specific cognitive processes. This latter distinction is of major conceptual significance because studies employing IQ as their primary measure, like studies of adaptive behavior, can be used to infer age-associated changes only in nonspecific cognitive functioning because variation in IQ test performance can be associated with the efficiency of many underlying processes.

IQ Changes Associated With Aging Among Adults

The review that follows is limited to those studies that have employed essentially cross-sequential designs to examine change over time within individuals varying in age. Of historical significance is the work of Kaplan (1943) and Bell and Zubek (1960). Kaplan (1943) examined 66 adults with mild mental retardation over 45 years of age and reported a modest mean decline in mental age (6.65 months) as measured by the Stanford-Binet over a period of from 7 to 21 years (mean intertest interval was around 14 years). No information was reported regarding etiology, and this drop in mental age was not associated with the chronological age of individuals (under or over 55).

Bell and Zubek (1960) examined Wechsler-Bellevue IQ changes over a 5-year period in a group of 100 adults with mild retardation, none of whom had Down syndrome. Ages ranged from 15 years to 64 years at the time of initial assessment. Results indicated that individual IQs changed from -5 to +33 points, with no participant over 45 years of age showing any decline (0 < IQ change < 16). Thus, the overall pattern of results indicated that IQ remained stable throughout the age range sampled.

IQ changes among a diverse group of 1,159 adults with mental retardation, 102 (8.8%) of whom were described as having Down syndrome, were examined by Fisher and Zeaman (1970). The study sample was divided roughly equally among people with mild, moderate, severe, and profound mental retardation and included an additional 75 people with borderline mental retardation. Analyses indicated that mental ages were stable throughout the adult age range until around 60, with slight declines thereafter. This pattern was similar for all levels of mental retardation.

Fisher and Zeaman specifically compared severely and profoundly retarded people with Down syndrome (n = 97) to adults with comparable levels of mental retardation due to other causes. Results indicated that age trends in test performance of the two etiologically defined groups were parallel up to approximately age 48. Unfortunately, there were too few older adults for whom data were available to determine if patterns of IQ change for adults with and without Down syndrome diverged after they reached 50 years of age.

Hewitt et al. (1986) described the relationship between mental age and chronological age throughout the adult life span (ages 20 to over 90) among a group of 148 mentally retarded people, none of whom had Down syndrome or profound retardation. According to this cross-sectional analysis, mental age remained stable until roughly 65 years of age, and then declined slightly thereafter. For those individuals who

exhibited a decline in mental age during the course of the study, mean age of onset of decline was 65.8 years. Harper and Wadsworth (1990) studied 90 adults with mental retardation (6 of whom had Down syndrome), ranging in age from 35 years to 79 years. Overall, individual change in IQ was unrelated to chronological age.

Demaine and Silverstein (1978) compared 189 people with Down syndrome (mean initial IQ = 29.4) to a group of peers without Down syndrome matched at initial testing based upon IQ and age. Their results provided a description of changes in mental age for chronological ages ranging from under 10 to 50 years. Throughout the adult age range assessed, mental age remained stable, with no interaction observed between chronological age and etiology (Down syndrome versus non-Down syndrome).

Fenner et al. (1987) and Hewitt, Carter, and Jancar (1985) examined changes in mental age among adults with Down syndrome ranging in age from 19 to 64 years (N = 62) using the Stanford-Binet. Of 30 adults with Down syndrome over 45 years of age, 20 showed a decrement in mental age (mean = 15 months); only 7 of the 32 adults under age 45 showed a decline.

In summary, these findings suggest that for the population of adults with mental retardation without Down syndrome, overall intellectual capability remains stable until approximately the age of 65 years (Fisher & Zeaman, 1970; Walz, Harper, & Wilson, 1986). Thereafter, declines in mental age (or IQ) appear to be gradual. Similar stability in mental age (or IQ) is evident for individuals with Down syndrome until the age of 45 to 50, with some evidence of decline thereafter.

Among adults with Down syndrome over the age of 45 to 50, as well as adults without Down syndrome over the age of 65, gradual age-associated declines in mean sample performance can be due to two, quite distinct patterns of performance within individuals. One possibility is that uniform but gradual changes with aging occur for the vast majority of individuals. The other possibility is that the majority of older adults maintain their earlier intellectual capabilities, but with advancing age an increasing minority may be affected by a dementing disorder (e.g., Alzheimer disease), a significant sensory impairment that interferes with test performance (Cooke, 1988), or other age-associated impairments. It is not yet possible to determine which of these alternative patterns accounts for the relationship between age and IQ test performance, and individual performance profiles need to be examined in detail in order to address this issue.

Neuropsychological and Experimental Measures of Aging

Studies of age-associated changes in specific aspects of cognitive processes have employed a wide variety of tasks. Such studies have universally focused on adults with Down syndrome, because of both their precocious development of neuropathology characteristic of Alzheimer disease and reports of a dementia syndrome affecting a significant proportion of this population. Dalton and Wisniewski (1990), in a review of longitudinal studies focusing on the association between Down syndrome and Alzheimer disease, noted wide individual differences in the expression of signs of dementia, age of onset of symptoms, and duration. Dalton and Wisniewski emphasized that Alzheimer disease is difficult to recognize in adults with Down syndrome except in advanced cases, and that there is a current need to develop improved methods for diagnosis of the earlier clinical expressions of dementia in adults with mental retardation.

Thase and his colleagues (Thase, Liss, Smeltzer, & Maloon, 1982) employed a battery of neuropsychological tests to compare 40 adults with Down syndrome ranging in age from 25 years to 64 years (mean IQ = 30, range 15 to 62) to a group of adults without Down syndrome matched on the basis of age and IQ. Each subject was assessed once. The test battery included measures of orientation, attention span, delayed matching-to-sample, digit span, and object identification. The Down syndrome group exhibited negative age-associated trends in measures of orientation, attention, digit span,

object identification and delayed matching-to-sample. These cross-sectional results suggest that, as a group, adults with Down syndrome exhibit deterioration in their cognitive processing efficiency well before they reach the age of 60. Further, the specific effects described by Thase et al. (1982) suggest that progressive declines in the efficiency of memory and attention mechanisms in particular may be associated with increasing age. However, because these investigators found evidence of similar age-associated differences among adults with Down syndrome in all their measures, these findings are unable to differentiate specific from nonspecific effects of aging.

Among adults without Down syndrome studied by Thase et al. (1982), no differences across individuals were associated with increasing age. These findings are consistent with the studies focusing on less specific measures of cognition (IQ or mental age) showing virtually no variation due to age until these people reach at least 60 to 65 years of age. (Thase, Tigner, Smeltzer, and Liss [1984] reported an extension of the Thase et al. [1982] study that included 165 adults with Down syndrome and 163 age and IQ matched adults without Down syndrome. The neuropsychological test battery appeared to be identical to that used earlier in all critical respects, and results largely confirmed their previous report.)

Dalton and his colleagues have reported studies focusing on Alzheimer dementia among adults with Down syndrome and severe/profound mental retardation (Dalton, Crapper, & Schlotterer, 1974; Dalton & Crapper-McLachlan, 1984; 1986). Participants ranged from under 20 to 59 years of age. These investigators included in their assessment battery a delayed matching-to-sample task to assess changes in memory processes, and they evaluated study participants both cross-sectionally and longitudinally. The task required participants to match a visually presented target figure, either a simple geometric shape (Dalton et al. 1974) or pictures of familiar objects (Dalton & Crapper-McLachlan, 1984), to one of a pair of test stimuli. Test stimuli were visible when the target was presented (simultaneous match) or were presented following a delay of from 0 to 60 seconds. Results indicated that performance was stable with advancing age among adults without Down syndrome. In contrast, some adults with Down syndrome showed age-associated deterioration in delayed matching-to-sample tasks. Mean age of onset of this deterioration was 49 (ranging from 41.5 to 59), and preceded roughly by two years the appearance of other clinical symptoms of dementia. Based upon their studies of 149 adults with Down syndrome, Dalton and Crapper-McLachlan estimated that the incidence (i.e., rate of new cases over a specified time period) of onset of memory deterioration among adults with Down syndrome over 40 years of age was 9% per year.

Haxby (1989) employed an extensive neuropsychological test battery to assess performance among 24 adults with Down syndrome ranging from 19 to 54 years of age. He divided his sample of non-demented adults into two groups based upon age: under 35 (n = 19) and 37 and over (n = 5). Results indicated that the older group did not differ from the younger group on overall intelligence (Stanford-Binet mental age), immediate verbal and visuospatial memory spans, or language. Age-associated differences in performance were evident for tests of visual perception (e.g., WISC-R Block and Extended Block Design, Hiskey Nebraska Block Patterns), as well as tests focusing on the incorporation of new information into memory (e.g., Hidden Object Memory, Recognition Memory for Designs), with older adults with Down syndrome exhibiting poorer performance when compared to younger age adults. Because all tasks that revealed systematic variations in performance associated with age appeared to demand either storage or manipulation of information that is not easily encoded verbally, these aspects of cognitive processing seem most sensitive to aging effects in this population. However, generalization of these results should await reports of longitudinal studies of a larger sample of older adults with Down syndrome. In fact, Haxby and Shapiro (1992) recently presented longitudinal data on 21 adults with

Down syndrome (8 over 40 years of age), and no clear relationship was found between age and change within individuals.

Muir et al. (1988) employed evoked response measures (to auditory stimuli) to assess aging and cognition among adults with Down syndrome or Fragile X syndrome. They examined late components of evoked responses, primarily focusing on P300, assumed to be a sensitive measure of post-perceptual processing that reflects the ability to differentiate infrequent from frequent stimulus events, and related their findings to those from a study conducted two years earlier in their laboratory (Blackwood, St. Clair, Muir, Oliver, & Dickens, 1988). Among adults with Fragile X syndrome, no subjects exhibited a change in P300. For 7 of the 40 nondemented adults with Down syndrome (17.5%), significant change was observed in P300 during the two years that intervened between initial and subsequent testing. Thus, P300 changes were seen in individuals with no clinical indication of dementia, and therefore this measure may be a useful indicator of cognitive changes related to aging. Unfortunately, results explicitly relating age to the prevalence of P300 change among nondemented participants were not presented. However, the combined data for demented and nondemented participants indicated that the likelihood of P300 change was unrelated to age once people with Down syndrome reach age 30.

In summary, studies examining the effects of aging on specific cognitive processes suggest that performance typically is stable among adults without Down syndrome until they reach their 60s. In contrast, some adults with Down syndrome begin to show signs of performance decline in their mid to late 40s. These findings are consistent with results of studies relating aging to changes in IQ test performance and also provide some limited suggestions that aging may differentially affect some specific aspects of cognitive processing (e.g., Haxby, 1989). However, results are far from definitive. It is evident that many more studies employing cross-sequential and longitudinal designs are needed in order to provide a clearer understanding of how aging affects specific aspects of the cognitive capabilities of adults with mental retardation.

Mental Health Problems Associated With Aging

Little is known about the relationship between aging and the manifestation of psychiatric disorders or maladaptive behaviors in older persons with mental retardation. Whereas the last two sections of this chapter reviewed numerous studies that examined age-associated changes in adaptive behavior and cognitive processes, this section reviews the limited number of studies conducted on age-associated changes in mental health status among older adults with mental retardation.

General Issues Relevant to Mental Health of Persons With Mental Retardation

Before reviewing relevant studies focusing explicitly on aging, several issues of major significance for the broader field of mental retardation merit discussion. First, the paucity of literature on this topic may be related to the fact that professionals in the field of mental retardation have focused their attention primarily on IQ and adaptive behavior. Both of these hypothetical constructs have been used for decades as the criteria for diagnosing and treating persons with mental retardation (American Association on Mental Retardation, 1992). In contrast, mental health problems of people with mental retardation appear to be diagnostically "overshadowed" by the presence of their mental retardation (Reiss, Levitan, & Szysko, 1982). The presence of behaviors and symptoms that would likely be classified as reflecting an underlying mental disorder in other populations typically have been erroneously attributed to mental retardation *per se*, rather than to the presence of two co-occurring conditions.

In addition, the criteria generally employed to diagnose particular mental disorders in the nonretarded population are likely to require modification or significant redevelopment for persons with mental retardation, particularly for persons with severe disabilities (Borthwick-Duffy & Eyman, 1990; Davidson et al., in press; Sovner, 1986). Because clinical presentation is often atypical, observable problem behaviors (signs) and verbally reported distress or dysfunctions (symptoms) can be difficult to classify with regard to their mental health implications in this population. Indeed, it is often not possible to obtain reliable verbal reports of the symptoms that are associated with a mental health problem because of limitations in expressive language skills. Determination of these signs and symptoms is the critical antecedent to developing a diagnostic nosology of psychiatric disorders for people with mental retardation (Bruininks, Hill, & Morreau, 1988; Menolascino, 1988), but, in contrast to the situation common for people without mental retardation, the determination of a psychiatric disorder may rest solely on the observation of maladaptive behavior. Davidson et al. (in press) reinforced the fact that this constitutes an important limitation by noting that receiving psychiatric care is only partially related to having a psychiatric diagnosis.

The presence of maladaptive behaviors is not related to a psychiatric diagnosis in any simple way (Borthwick-Duffy & Eyman, 1990; Bouras & Drummond, 1992; Sovner & Hurley, 1983). It is often difficult to determine the extent to which maladaptive behaviors are related to the neuropathic processes of mental retardation or to psychopathological processes of mental illness. Some multivariate studies have indicated that maladaptive and adaptive behaviors are separate and distinct constructs (Bruininks & McGrew, 1987; McGrew, Ittenbach, Bruininks, & Hill, 1991). This finding, that maladaptive behaviors are not the inverse of adaptive behaviors, supports the hypothesis that there is a unique process, perhaps related to psychopathology, occurring when maladaptive behaviors significantly interfere with daily functioning.

Yet despite all of the nosological and diagnostic difficulties, studies of mental illness among persons with mental retardation find higher than expected prevalence rates, which have been estimated to be anywhere from four to six times that of the general population (Gualtieri, Matson, & Keppel, 1989; Jacobson, 1982; Matson & Barret, 1982; Rutter, Tizard, Yule, Graham, & Whitemore, 1976). For example, depression occurs frequently in persons with mental retardation (Harper & Wadsworth, 1990; Senatore, Matson, & Kazdin, 1985; Sireling, 1986; Sovner & Hurley, 1983). However, estimates of prevalence compared to schizophrenia suggest that differential diagnosis is particularly difficult. Some studies suggest that depression occurs less frequently (Benson, 1985; Fraser, Leuder, Gray, & Campbell, 1986; Jacobson, 1990), but others suggest the reverse (e.g., Borthwick-Duffy & Eyman, 1990; Eaton & Menolascino, 1982; Reiss, 1982). Of course, this type of diagnostic imprecision makes it difficult to determine whether the prevalence of depression, schizophrenia, or other mental disorders increases with age.

We do know, though, that among people with mental retardation there are clear associations between the presence of maladaptive behaviors and psychiatric diagnoses on the one hand (Jacobson, 1990) and between the diagnosis of a psychiatric problem and receipt of psychiatric services on the other. However, not all persons with behavior problems are given a psychiatric diagnosis, nor are psychiatric diagnoses necessary for receipt of psychiatric services. Unfortunately, in this population psychiatric services are often limited to receipt of psychoactive medications rather than the range of therapeutic interventions to be expected for people without retardation (Seltzer & Essex, 1993).

The questionable use of psychoactive medications, particularly antipsychotic medications, is an issue of particular concern. These medications, which have the potential to produce significant adverse reactions, especially among older persons, are often prescribed for control of maladaptive behaviors, with or without determination of an appropriate psychiatric diagnosis (Anderson & Polister, 1993; Davidson et al., in press; Seltzer, Finaly, & Howell, 1988). Overreliance on behavioral observations, particularly maladaptive behaviors, may complicate and confuse the diagnostic process considerably. As Sovner and Hurley (1983) noted, overt and attention drawing behaviors might hide an underlying psychiatric disorder such as depression. This process of "behavioral highlighting" of maladaptive behaviors may be related to the inappropriate use of psychoactive medications. Finally, there is some evidence that the presence of discrete maladaptive behaviors may be related to age, but in a complex and nonlinear fashion (McGrew et al., 1991). These data indicate that total reliance on linear regression based analyses for inferring relationships between age and selected indicators of mental health must be avoided.

Age-Associated Mental Health Problems

There are very few empirical studies that have investigated the relationship between older age and specific types of mental health problems. Among the few studies that have addressed relevant age-associated issues there is some disagreement about whether the occurrence of behavior problems changes as persons with severe levels of mental retardation age. Several researchers have reported finding an inverse relationship between age and the presence of adaptive behaviors (Bouras & Drummond, 1992; Davidson et al., in press; Jacobson, 1982), although Day (1985) found no relationship between age and problem behaviors.

Jacobson (1982), for example, conducted a cross-sectional analysis of over 30,000 persons residing in community and institutional settings in New York State. His sample included persons with a variety of developmental disabilities, some of whom were also labeled as having a psychiatric diagnosis. He found that persons aged 60 or older displayed fewer behavior problems than persons age 13 through 59. Bouras & Drummond (1992), Davidson, et al. (in press), and Jacobson (1982) all employed cross-sectional designs to make inferences about changes over time. Therefore, their results need to be interpreted cautiously because of potential problems of cohort and healthy survivor effects noted earlier in this chapter.

Davidson et al. (1992) examined age-associated changes in maladaptive behaviors in a cohort of persons referred to a crisis intervention team specializing in dual diagnosis. They found that 25% of their sample exhibited some psychiatric symptoms regardless of age. However, with increasing age there was an increasing likelihood of having two referral problems rather than the one typically found in younger subjects. The vast majority of referral problems were for aggression, psychiatric symptoms, and noncompliance, the latter being a problem that increased particularly in older persons with mild mental retardation. Unfortunately, these investigators did not report which maladaptive behaviors were more frequently associated with which type of psychiatric disorder.

Day (1985) found that neurotic disorders occurred frequently among older persons with mild mental retardation who had resided in the community. In contrast, Borthwick-Duffy and Eyman (1990) conducted a discriminant analysis to determine the best predictors of dual diagnosis and found that once aggression, cognitive abilities, and social skills were entered into the model, age was not related to dual diagnosis. Neither study was designed specifically to study mental health changes in older age longitudinally.

We may assume that many older persons with mental retardation, like their age contemporaries, face new emotional challenges related to physical and functional losses associated with age and a shrinking social support system (Seltzer, 1985). Although there is some debate about whether older persons are more likely to become depressed than younger persons (Newmann, 1989), depression does occur frequently in this age cohort and is one of the most treatable functional disorders of older age. In contrast, methods for assessment, diagnosis, and treatment of depression in persons with mental retardation are poorly developed (Gualtieri, 1989).

As with other age-related changes in persons with mental retardation, the incidence of affective disorders may be related to the etiology of the mental retardation. Clinical evidence suggests that older persons with Down syndrome display a complex of symptoms when depressed that includes impairments in adaptive, memory, and intellectual functioning (Burt et al., 1992; Collacott et al., 1992; Sovner & Hurley, 1983; Szymanski & Biederman, 1984; Warren, Holroyd, & Folstein, 1989). These impairments are also characteristic of dementia in this population. Thus, both researchers and clinicians face an important diagnostic challenge in differentiating dementia and depression in persons with Down syndrome, as illustrated in case studies of five adults with Down syndrome whose symptoms of severe depression resulted in erroneous diagnoses of Alzheimer disease (Warren et al., 1989).

Both Burt et al. (1992) and Collacott et al. (1992) examined the presentation of dementia and depression in persons with Down syndrome in comparison to a matched control sample. Burt et al. found depression to be a problem In persons with Down syndrome, but the prevalence of depression was slightly higher in their non-Down syndrome group. The Burt et al. study examined the relationship between decline in function, depression, and dementia, and found that all individuals with Down syndrome who were behaviorally declining were also depressed. These researchers suggest that depression is either a risk factor for dementia in Down syndrome or is a symptom that accompanies dementia.

Collacott and his colleagues found a significantly increased risk of depression, dementia, and personality disorders in persons with Down syndrome and a different set of psychiatric disorders among persons without Down syndrome. They also examined the issue of co-occurrence of dementia and depression but arrived at a different conclusion than Burt et al. They compared the mean age of onset of depression and dementia in their sample of persons with Down syndrome and found that it was 29 years of age for the onset of depression and about 54 years of age for dementia. They concluded that dementia is therefore unlikely to account for the higher rate of depression in this population. Clearly, more research needs to be conducted in this area so that researchers and clinicians can determine when persons with Down syndrome are experiencing an affective disorder without a dementia, an affective disorder with a dementia, or a dementia without an affective disorder.

Since dementia is an age-associated disorder, we should expect to find an increase in dementia in all diagnostic groups as the proportion of older persons with mental retardation increases. The question arises as to whether to classify dementia as a psychiatric disorder (as it is in DSM-III-R) or as a progressive neurological disorder, a label that emphasizes the biological basis for the cognitive decline. Given this classificatory uncertainty, the treatment of persons with mental retardation and dementia might fall within the purview of the aging network, the mental health system, or the developmental disabilities network. The determination of which of the three service systems has the responsibility to support the long-term care needs of persons with mental retardation and dementia therefore entails resolution of difficult political and economic issues. The funding dilemmas associated with the ever increasing number of older persons with mental retardation and dementia have already begun to surface and are likely to be one of the most hotly debated issues related to mental health associated with aging.

Earlier, the pattern of inappropriate use of psychiatric medications in persons with mental retardation was noted. The severity of this problem increases as persons with mental retardation age. With aging, all persons have a decreasing "therapeutic window" within which the dosage of medication produces an effective response. As a consequence, the likelihood of adverse drug reactions is increased in older persons (see Seltzer & Luchterhand, chapter 7 this volume). Because of the potential iatrogenic problem of adverse drug reactions, a lower use of psychoactive drugs should be observed with advancing age. Instead, the few studies available suggest just the opposite. Seltzer et al. (1988) found that older persons with mental retardation who lived in nursing homes received substantially more psychotropic medications than persons who were living in the community even though persons who lived in the community had more severe and frequent behavior problems. In the nursing homes, these medications were used primarily to control behavior problems that nursing home staff felt incompetent to handle. In the community settings, staff usually felt competent to handle these behavior problems without psychotropic medication.

In a study of Medicaid recipients who lived in large residential facilities, Buck and Sprague (1989) also found that middle aged and older persons with mental retardation were significantly more likely to receive psychotropic (particularly antipsychotic) medications compared to younger persons who lived in the same facilities. Finally, in a national survey of psychotropic medication use among older persons with mental retardation who lived in state and federally supported residential settings, Anderson and Polister (1993) found that approximately 20% of the persons surveyed were using antipsychotic medication, but 78% of this medicated group were not diagnosed as having a psychosis. In addition, nearly as many people who were diagnosed with a psychosis were not given antipsychotic medication. These findings suggest rather clearly that in older persons with mental retardation, there seems to be a disturbingly low association between patterns of psychoactive medication use and the presence of the psychiatric disorders for which these medications are intended.

In summary, little is known about age-related mental health changes among older adults with mental retardation. One reason for this dearth of knowledge is the absence of good epidemiological research. Borthwick-Duffy and Eyman (1990) applied the three conditions described by Keily and Lubin (1983) for evaluating epidemiological data on the occurrence of mental illness and mental retardation: the sample must be representative; the data must reflect accurate diagnoses; and the individuals without the diagnoses should be known not to have the mental illness being measured. The representativeness of the data reviewed herein are limited because of the sampling strategies used in most studies of dual diagnosis. Study samples were typically drawn from the treatment roster of agencies providing psychiatric care to the sample members (e.g., Davidson et al., in press; Day, 1985) or from statewide data sets (e.g., Borthwick-Duffy & Eyman, 1990; Jacobson, 1990; McGrew et al., 1991). Selection bias is a major problem with these sampling strategies. That is, persons who are included in the rosters of psychiatric facilities or who receive state supported services differ from persons who are not enrolled in these service systems. One study that controlled for selection bias is the study conducted by Collacott et al. (1992). These researchers used a population-based sampling approach with all persons with Down syndrome who lived in Leicestershire, England, as potential participants.

Keily and Lubin's second and third criteria, referring to the accuracy of both positive and negative diagnostic decisions, highlight problems that have been discussed throughout this section. The limitations of diagnostic instruments and conventions, as well as the questionable appropriateness of standard diagnostic criteria for persons with mental retardation, suggest that analyses based upon differentiation between persons who have or do not have a mental disorder were only partially valid, at best. Thus, due to these methodological limitations, studies reviewed in this section need to be put into proper perspective. Hopefully, future research on the mental health problems associated with aging will be able to address these limitations more successfully.

Future research should also study whether there are subgroups of older persons with mental retardation, other than persons with Down syndrome, who by virtue of the etiology of their mental retardation or because of their life experiences are at greater risk for mental health problems in old age. Another critical area for future research is the development of a diagnostic nosology of mental disorders based on maladaptive behaviors (signs) exhibited by persons with mental retardation and their relationship to standard classification systems. Lastly, there are very few reports in the literature describing outcomes of interventions designed to improve the mental health of older persons with mental retardation. Future research should investigate all the alternative intervention strategies, especially the effective use and misuse of pharmacotherapies, that maintain the overall mental health status of this population.

Summary of Methodological Issues in the Study of Age-Associated Changes

Much of the literature presented above utilized cross-sectional research designs and some was descriptive in nature (i.e., statistical analyses were not conducted). Interpretation of results from cross-sectional research designs, which are always subject to confounds associated with "cohort" and "healthy survivor" effects, is especially difficult in investigations of aging processes. Because true longitudinal research is not a practical option for assessing development across the life span, cross-sequential designs seem best suited for studies focusing on age-associated changes in the characteristics of adults with mental retardation. However, although these designs do provide information regarding individuals' changes over time, there remains a potential confound between life experience, survival, and change in status. Individuals who died because they were prone to deterioration at comparatively early ages, had they survived, may have lowered the estimated performance levels of comparatively younger groups. Analyses of obtained data can address this potential confound by examining performance levels of cohorts overlapping in age. If performance of each age cohort at its last assessment approximates that of the next oldest cohort at its initial assessment, it is much more likely that age trends across the entire range sampled would mirror those to be found in a true longitudinal study.

The current predominance of a behavioral over a medical model in our field has had the effect of reducing interest in etiology of mental retardation. Consequently, there has been a reduction in the inclusion of etiology as a factor in many research designs. Yet, for the many diverse causes of "organic" mental retardation that have been identified (Burack, Hodapp, & Zigler, 1988), there is reason to expect systematic variations in aging patterns. Therefore, future studies should make every effort to classify subjects based upon etiology.

The vast number of scales, instruments, and measurement methodologies employed in the extant literature on aging and mental retardation makes direct comparison of research results difficult. Reliability and validity estimates of measures rarely are reported, if indeed they are available. If we are to develop a core of research that will be of practical significance in the development of new programs, technologies, and treatments, we must advocate for research that utilizes a common core of well-validated, reliable measures.

Implications for Research, Policy Development, and Service Provision

The future holds many promises for the aging adult with mental retardation. However, a great deal needs to be learned about all aspects of the aging process to ensure a high quality of life throughout the "senior" years. To aid in achieving this goal, future research on the issue of adaptive, cognitive, and mental health changes with age needs to address a number of key issues. First, the quality of assessment instruments that are being utilized to document characteristics of aging in people with mental retardation needs to be improved. There are well researched and validated tools that have been used within the field of gerontology that may be applicable or modifiable for use with people with mental retardation. These established methods represent a valuable resource. Second, additional prospective cohort studies need to be funded. Only through the use of such longitudinal research designs will the effects of aging be clearly differentiated. Given the current paucity of knowledge about aging among adults with mental retardation, it may be cost effective at this time to fund large scale studies that examine multiple measures from a multidisciplinary perspective. While these study designs typically do not permit testing of specific hypotheses, they provide a breadth of information that can be used as a foundation for more focused efforts.

For example, it is critical to explore whether there are interactions between the individual and his or her environment and age-related changes. Currently, we do not know whether the profusion of new residential and programmatic alternatives for adults with mental retardation differentially affects adaptive, cognitive, and mental health outcomes. It must be noted that considerable prior research was conducted on institutional samples or samples of people who had spent a significant proportion of their lives resident in an institution. Although some data suggest that there are similar patterns of skill loss regardless of institutional history (e.g., Collacott, 1992), further research must thoroughly investigate the full relationship between residential and day programming placements and age-associated changes.

Third, there are many areas in which little or no research has been conducted. Broadly focused exploratory studies are needed to increase our knowledge about aging in adults with mental retardation and the influence of such factors as (a) health and diet, (b) risk factors for mortality, (c) behavioral/psychiatric disorders, (d) history of service receipt, (e) use of psychotropic medications, (f) demographics, etc.

Fourth, autopsies should be arranged for any study participants who die during the course of longitudinal research in order to allow the collection of neuropathological data. These findings can be related to clinical measures to improve development of valid methods for differential diagnosis of age-associated problems.

Fifth, researchers in the field of aging and mental retardation must develop strong linkages with service providers to transfer new technologies. Service providers may not be aware of developing intervention technologies because of the extended period that elapses between scientific reports and broad dissemination. Researchers must look to aiding development of or participating in staff training programs in order to ensure that providers are kept abreast of the latest relevant information. In addition, channels of communication must be developed to permit providers to inform researchers about the effectiveness of interventions and the nature of issues that demand development of improved applications. Technology transfer can then be optimized, which will both help shape the direction of future research and insure that innovative findings have a direct impact on the quality of life of adults with developmental disabilities during their senior years.

References

Abuelo, D. N. (1983). Genetic disorders. In J. L. Matson & J. A. Mulick (Eds.), *Handbook of mental retardation* (pp. 105–120). New York: Pergamon.

American Association on Mental Retardation. (1992). *Mental retardation: Definition, classification, and systems of support.* Washington, DC: Author.

American Psychiatric Association. (1987). *Diagnostic and statistical manual of mental disorders* (3rd ed. rev.). Washington, DC: Author.

Anderson, D. J., & Polister, B. (1993). Psychotropic medication use among older adults with mental retardation. In E. Sutton, A. R. Factor, B. A. Hawkins, T. Heller, & G. B. Seltzer (Eds.), *Older adults with developmental disabilities: Optimizing choice and change* (pp. 61–76). Baltimore, MD: Brookes.

Ball, M. J., & Nuttall, K. (1980). Neurofibrillary tangles, granuovacuolar degeneration, and neuron loss in Down syndrome: Quantitative comparison with Alzheimer dementia. *Annals of Neurology, 7,* 462–465.

Barcikowska, M., Silverman, W. P., Zigman, W. B., Kozlowski, P. B., Kujawa, M., Rudelli, R., & Wisniewski, H. M. (1989). Alzheimer-type neuropathology and clinical symptoms of dementia in mentally retarded people without Down syndrome. *American Journal on Mental Retardation, 93,* 551–557.

Bell, A., & Zubek, J. (1960). The effect of age on the intellectual performance of mental defectives. *Journal of Gerontology, 15,* 285–295.

Benson, B. A. (1985). Behavior and mental retardation: Associations with age, sex, and level of functioning in an outpatient clinic sample. *Applied Research in Mental Retardation, 6,* 79–85.

Blackwood, D. H. R., St. Clair, D. M., Muir, W. J., Oliver, C. J., & Dickens, P. (1988). The development of Alzheimer's disease in Down's syndrome assessed by auditory event-related potentials. *Journal of Mental Deficiency Research, 32,* 439–453.

Borthwick-Duffy, S. A., & Eyman, R. K. (1990). Who are the dually diagnosed? *American Journal on Mental Retardation, 94,* 586–595.

Bouras, N., & Drummond, C. (1992). Behaviour and psychiatric disorders of people with mental handicaps living in the community. *Journal of Intellectual Disability Research, 36,* 349–357.

Bruininks, R. H., Hill, B. K., & Morreau, L. E. (1988). Prevalence and implications of maladaptive behavior and dual diagnosis in residential and other service programs. In J. A. Stark, F. J. Menolascino, M. H. Abarelli, & V. C. Gray (Eds.), *Mental retardation and mental health: Classification, diagnosis, treatment, service* (pp. 3–30). New York: Springer.

Bruininks, R. H., & McGrew, K. S. (1987). *Exploring the structure of adaptive behavior* (Report No. 87–1). Minneapolis: University of Minnesota, Department of Educational Psychology.

Buck, W. J., & Sprague, R. L. (1989). Psychotropic medication of mentally retarded residents in community long-term facilities. *American Journal on Mental Retardation, 93,* 618–623.

Burack, J. A., Hodapp, R. M., & Zigler, E. (1988). Issues in the classification of mental retardation: Differentiating among organic etiologies. *Journal of Child Psychology and Psychiatry, 29,* 765–779.

Burt, D. B., Loveland, K. A., & Lewis, K. R. (1992). Depression and the onset of dementia in adults with mental retardation. *American Journal on Mental Retardation, 96,* 502–511.

Butler, R. N. (1980). Introduction. In S. G. Haynes & M. Feinleib (Eds.), *Second conference on the epidemiology of aging* (pp. 14). Bethesda, MD: National Institutes of Health.

Carter, G., & Jancar, J. (1983). Mortality in the mentally handicapped: A 50 year survey at the Stokes Park group of hospitals. *Journal of Mental Deficiency Research, 27,* 143–156.

Collacott, R. A. (1992). The effect of age and residential placement on adaptive behaviour of adults with Down's syndrome. *British Journal of Psychiatry, 161,* 675–679.

Collacott, R. A. (1993). Epilepsy, dementia and adaptive behaviour in Down's syndrome. *Journal of Intellectual Disability Research, 37,* 153–160.

Collacott, R. A., Cooper, S. A., & McGrother, C. (1992). Differential rates of psychiatric disorders in adults with Down's syndrome compared with other mentally handicapped adults. *British Journal of Psychiatry, 161,* 671–674.

Cooke, L. (1988). Hearing loss in the mentally handicapped: A study of its prevalence and association with ageing. *British Journal of Mental Subnormality, 34,* 112–116.

Dalton, A. J., & Crapper-McLachlan, D. R. (1984). Incidence of memory deterioration in aging persons with Down's syndrome. In J. M. Berg (Ed.), *Perspectives and progress in mental retardation: Vol. II. Biomedical aspects* (pp. 55–62). Baltimore, MD: University Park Press.

Dalton, A. J., & Crapper-McLachlan, D. R. (1986). Clinical expression of Alzheimer's disease in Down's syndrome. *Psychiatric Perspectives on Mental Retardation: Psychiatric Clinics of North America, 9,* 659–670.

Dalton, A. J., Crapper, D. R., & Schlotterer, G. R. (1974). Alzheimer's disease in Down's syndrome: Visual retention deficits. *Cortex, 10,* 366–377.

Dalton, A. J., & Wisniewski, H. M. (1990). Down's syndrome and the dementia of Alzheimer disease. *International Review of Psychiatry, 2,* 43–52.

Davidson, P. W., Cain, N. N., Sloane-Reeves, J. E., Speybroech, A. V., Segal, J., Gutkin, J., Quijano, L. E., & Kramer, B. M. (in press). Characteristics of community-based clients with mental retardation and aggressive behavior disorders. *American Journal on Mental Retardation.*

Davidson, P. W., Cain, N. N., Sloane-Reeves, J. E., Kramer, B., Quijano, L., VanHeyningen, J., & Giesow, V. (1992, November). *Aging effects on severe behavior disorders in community-based clients with mental retardation.* Paper presented at the Annual Meeting of the Gerontological Society of America, Washington, DC.

Day, K. A. (1985). Psychiatric disorder in the middle-aged and elderly mentally handicapped. *British Journal of Psychiatry, 147,* 660–667.

Day, K. A. (1987). The elderly mentally handicapped in hospital: A clinical study. *Journal of Mental Deficiency Research, 31,* 131–146.

Demaine, G. C., & Silverstein, A. B. (1978). Mental age changes in institutionalized Down's syndrome persons: A semi-longitudinal approach. *American Journal of Mental Deficiency, 82,* 429–432.

Devenny, D. A., Hill, A. L., Patxot, O., Silverman, W. P., & Wisniewski, K. (1992). Ageing in higher functioning adults with Down syndrome: An interim report in a longitudinal study. *Journal of Mental Deficiency Research, 36,* 241–250.

Eaton, I. F., & Menolascino, F. J. (1982). Psychiatric disorders in the mentally retarded: Types, problems and challenges. *American Journal of Psychiatry, 139,* 1297–1303.

Evenhuis, H. M. (1990). The natural history of dementia in Down's syndrome. *Archives of Neurology, 47,* 263–267.

Eyman, R. K., & Widaman, K. F. (1987). Life-span development of institutionalized and community-based mentally retarded persons, revisited. *American Journal of Mental Deficiency, 91,* 559–569.

Fenner, M. E., Hewitt, K. E., & Torpy, D. M. (1987). Down's syndrome: Intellectual and behavioral functioning during adulthood. *Journal of Mental Deficiency Research, 31,* 241–249.

Fisher, M. A., & Zeaman, D. (1970). Growth and decline of retardate intelligence. In N. R. Ellis (Ed.), *International review of research in mental retardation* (Vol. 4, pp. 151–191). New York: Academic Press.

Fraser, J., & Mitchell, A. (1876). Kalmuc idiocy: Report of a case with autopsy, with notes on sixty-two cases. *Journal of Mental Sciences, 22,* 169-179.

Fraser, W. I., Leuder, I., Gray, J., & Campbell, L. (1986). Psychiatric and behavior disturbance in mental handicap. *Journal of Mental Deficiency Research, 30,* 49–57.

Goate, A. M., Haynes, A. R., Owen, M. J., Farrall, M., James, L. A., Lai, L. Y. C., Mullan, M.J., Roques, P., Rossor, M. N., Williamson, R., & Hardy, J. A. (1989). Predisposing locus for Alzheimer's disease on chromosome 21. *Lancet, i,* 352–355.

Grossman, H. J. (1983). *Classification in mental retardation.* Washington, DC: American Association on Mental Deficiency.

Gualtieri, C. T. (1989). Affective disorders. In *Treatment of psychiatric disorders: A task force report of The American Psychiatric Association* (pp. 10–13). Washington, DC: American Psychiatric Association.

Gualtieri, C. T., Matson, J. L., & Keppel, J. M. (1989). Psychopathology in the mentally retarded. In *Treatment of psychiatric disorders: A task force report of the American Psychiatric Association* (pp. 4–8). Washington, DC: American Psychiatric Association.

Harper, D. C., & Wadsworth, J. S. (1990). Dementia and depression in elders with mental retardation: A pilot study. *Research in Developmental Disabilities, 11,* 177–198.

Hauber, F. A., Rotegard, L. L., Bruininks, R. H. (1985). Characteristics of residential services for older/elderly mentally retarded persons. In M. P. Janicki & H. M. Wisniewski (Eds.), *Aging and developmental disabilities: Issues and approaches* (pp. 327–350). Baltimore, MD: Brookes.

Haveman, M. J., & Maaskant, M. A. (1989). Defining fragility of the elderly severely mentally handicapped according to mortality risk, morbidity, motor handicaps and social functioning. *Journal of Mental Deficiency Research, 33,* 389–397.

Haveman, M., Maaskant, M. A., & Sturmans, F. (1989). Older Dutch residents of institutions, with and without Down syndrome: Comparisons of mortality and morbidity trends and motor/social functioning. *Australia and New Zealand Journal of Developmental Disabilities, 15,* 241–255.

Haxby, J. V. (1989). Neuropsychological evaluation of adults with Down's syndrome: Patterns of selective impairment in non–demented old adults. *Journal of Mental Deficiency Research, 33,* 193–210.

Haxby, J. V., & Schapiro, M. B. (1992). Longitudinal study of neuropsychological function in older adults with Down syndrome. In L. Nadel & C. Epstein (Eds.), *Down syndrome and Alzheimer disease* (pp. 35–50). New York: Wiley–Liss.

Hewitt, K. E., Carter, G., & Jancar, J. (1985). Ageing in Down's syndrome. *British Journal of Psychiatry, 147,* 58–62.

Hewitt, K. E., Fenner, M. E., & Torpy, D. (1986). Cognitive and behavioral profiles of the elderly mentally handicapped. *Journal of Mental Deficiency Research, 30,* 217–225.

Jacobson, J. (1982). Problem behavior and psychiatric impairment within a developmentally disabled population: 1. Behavior frequency. *Applied Research in Mental Retardation, 3,* 121–139.

Jacobson, J. W. (1990). Do some mental disorders occur less frequently among persons with mental retardation? *American Journal on Mental Retardation, 94,* 596–602.

Janicki, M. P. (1989). Aging, cerebral palsy, and older persons with mental retardation. *Australia and New Zealand Journal of Developmental Disabilities, 15,* 311–320.

Janicki, M. P., & Hogg, J. H. (1989). International research perspectives on aging and mental retardation: An introduction. *Australia and New Zealand Journal of Developmental Disabilities, 15,* 161–164.

Janicki, M. P., & Jacobson, J. W. (1986). Generational trends in sensory, physical, and behavioral abilities among older mentally retarded persons. *American Journal of Mental Deficiency, 90,* 490–500.

Janicki, M. P., & MacEachron, A. E. (1984). Residential, health, and social service needs of elderly developmentally disabled persons. *The Gerontologist, 24,* 128–137.

Jervis, G. A. (1948). Early senile dementia in mongoloid idiocy. *American Journal of Psychiatry, 105,* 102–106.

Kaplan, O. (1943). Mental decline in older morons. *American Journal of Mental Deficiency, 47,* 277–285.

Keily, M., & Lubin, R. A. (1983). Epidemiological methods. In J. L. Matson & J. A. Mulick (Eds.), *Handbook of mental retardation* (pp. 541–556). New York: Pergamon Press.

Krauss, M. W., & Seltzer, M. M. (1986). Comparison of elderly and adult mentally retarded persons in community and institutional settings. *American Journal of Mental Deficiency, 91,* 237–243.

Lai, F., & Williams, R. S. (1989). A prospective study of Alzheimer disease in Down syndrome. *Archives of Neurology, 46,* 849–853.

Lott, I. T. (1983). Perinatal factors in mental retardation. In J. L. Matson & J. A. Mulick (Eds.), *Handbook of mental retardation* (pp. 97–103). New York: Pergamon.

Lund, J. (1988). Psychiatric aspects of Down's syndrome. *Acta Psychiatrica Scandinavia, 78,* 369–374.

Maaskant, M., & Haveman, M. (1989). Aging residents in sheltered homes for persons with mental handicap in the Netherlands. *Australia and New Zealand Journal of Developmental Disabilities, 15,* 219–230.

Malamud, N. (1972). Neuropathology of organic brain syndrome associated with aging. In C. M. Gaitz (Ed.), *Aging and the brain* (pp. 67–87). New York: Plenum.

Matson, J. L., & Barret, R. P. (1982). *Psychopathology in the mentally retarded.* New York: Grune & Stratton.

McGrew, K. S., Ittenbach, R. F., Bruininks, R. H., & Hill, B. K. (1991). Factor structure of maladaptive behavior across the lifespan of persons with mental retardation. *Research in Developmental Disabilities, 12,* 181–199.

Menolascino, F. J. (1988). Mental illness in the mentally retarded: Diagnostic and treatment issues. In J. A. Stark, F. J. Menolascino, M. H. Abarelli, & V. C. Gray, (Eds.), *Mental retardation and mental health: Classification diagnosis, treatment, services* (pp. 109–123). New York: Springer.

Meyers, C. E., Nihira, K., & Zetlin, A. (1979). The measurement of adaptive behavior. In N. R. Ellis (Ed.), *Handbook of mental deficiency, psychological theory and research* (pp. 431–481). Hillsdale, NJ: Erlbaum.

Muir, W. J., Squire, I., Blackwood, D. H. R, Speight, M. D., St. Clair, D. M., Oliver, C., & Dickens, P. (1988). Auditory P300 response in the assessment of Alzheimer's disease in Down's syndrome: A 2–year follow–up study. *Journal of Mental Deficiency Research, 32,* 455–463.

Newmann, J. P. (1989). Aging and depression. *Psychology and Aging, 4,* 150–165.

Nihira, K. (1969). Factional dimensions of adaptive behavior in adult retardates. *American Journal of Mental Deficiency, 73,* 868–878.

Nihira, K., Foster, R., Shellhaas, M., & Leland, H. (1974). *AAMD adaptive behavior scale.* Washington, DC: American Association on Mental Deficiency.

Popovitch, E. R., Wisniewski, H. M., Barcikowska, M., Silverman, W., Bancher, C., Sersen, E., & Wen, G. Y. (1990). Alzheimer neuropathology in non–Down's syndrome mentally retarded adults. *Acta Neuropathologica (Berlin), 80,* 362–367.

Reiss, S. (1982). Psychopathology and mental retardation: Survey of a developmental disabilities mental health program. *Mental Retardation, 20,* 128–132.

Reiss, S., Levitan, G. W., & Szysko, J. (1982). Emotional disturbance and mental retardation: Diagnostic overshadowing. *American Journal of Mental Deficiency, 86,* 567–574.

Robakis, N. K., Wisniewski, H. M., Jenkins E. C., Devine–Gage, E. A., Houck, G. E., Yao, X. L., Ramakrishna, N., Wolfe, G., Silverman, W., & Brown, W. T. (1987). Chromosome 21q21 sublocalization of gene encoding beta amyloid peptide in cerebral vessels and neuritic (senile) plaques of people with Alzheimer's disease and Down syndrome. *Lancet, i,* 384–385.

Rutter, M., Tizard, J., Yule, W., Graham, O., & Whitemore, K. (1976). Research report: Isle of Wight studies, 1964–74. *Psychological Medicine, 6,* 313–332.

Schupf, N., Silverman, W. P., Sterling, R. C., & Zigman, W. B. (1989). Down syndrome, terminal illness and risk for dementia of the Alzheimer type. *Brain Dysfunction, 2,* 181–188.

Seltzer, G. B. (1985). Selected psychological processes and aging among older developmentally disabled persons. In M. P. Janicki & H. M. Wisniewski (Eds.), *Aging and developmental disabilities: Issues and approaches* (pp. 211–228). Baltimore, MD: Brookes.

Seltzer, G. B., & Essex, E. (1993). *Service needs of persons with mental retardation and other developmental disabilities* (Robert Wood Johnson Foundation Report). Providence, RI: Brown University, Center for Gerontology and Health Care Research.

Seltzer, G. B., Finaly, E., & Howell, M. (1988). Functional characteristics of elderly mentally retarded persons in community settings and nursing homes. *Mental Retardation, 26,* 213–217.

Seltzer, G. B., & Luchterhand, C. (1994). Health and well-being of older persons with developmental disabilities: A clinical review. In M. M. Seltzer, M. W. Krauss, & M. P. Janicki (Eds.), *Life course perspectives on adulthood and old age* (pp. 109–142). Washington, DC: American Association on Mental Retardation.

Seltzer, M. M., Seltzer, G. B., & Sherwood, C. C. (1982). Comparison of community adjustment of older vs. younger mentally retarded adults. *American Journal of Mental Deficiency, 87,* 9–13.

Senatore, V., Matson, J. L., & Kazdin, A. E. (1985). An inventory to assess psychopathology of mentally retarded adults. *American Journal of Mental Deficiency, 89,* 459–466.

Silverstein, A. B., Herbs, D., Miller, T. J., Nasuta, R., Williams, D. L., & White, J. F. (1988). Effects of age on the adaptive behavior of institutionalized and non-institutionalized individuals with Down syndrome. *American Journal of Mental Retardation, 92,* 455–460.

Silverstein, A. B., Herbs, D., Nasuta, R., & White, J. F. (1986). Effects of age on the adaptive behavior of institutionalized individuals with Down syndrome. *American Journal of Mental Deficiency, 90,* 659–662.

Sireling, L. (1986). Depression in mentally handicapped patients: Diagnosis and neuroendocrine evaluation. *British Journal of Psychiatry, 149,* 274–278.

Solitaire, G. C., & LaMarche, J. B. (1966). Alzheimer's disease and senile dementia as seen in mongoloids: Neuropathological observations. *American Journal of Mental Deficiency, 70,* 840–848.

Sovner, A. (1986). Limiting factors in the use of DSM-III criteria with mentally retarded persons. *Psychopharmacology Bulletin, 22,* 1055–1059.

Sovner, A., & Hurley, A. D. (1983). Do the mentally retarded suffer from affective illness? *Archives of General Psychiatry, 40,* 61–67.

St. George-Hyslop, P. H., Tanzi, R. E., Polinsky, R. J., Haines, J. L., Nee, L., Watkins, P. C., Myers, R. H., Feldman, R. G., Pollen, D., Drachman, D., Growdon, J., Bruni, A., Foncin, J. F., Salmon, D., Frommelt, P., Amaducci, L., Sorbi, S., Placentini, S., Stewart, G. D., Hobbs, W., Conneally, P. M., & Gusella, J. F. (1987). The genetic defect causing familial Alzheimer's disease maps on chromosome 21. *Science, 235,* 885–890.

Szymanski, L. S., & Biederman, J. (1984). Depression and anorexia nervosa of persons with Down syndrome. *American Journal of Mental Deficiency, 89,* 246–251.

Terry, R. D., & Katzman, R. (1983). Senile dementia of the Alzheimer type. *Annals of Neurology, 14,* 497–506.

Thase, M. E., Liss, L., Smeltzer, D., & Maloon,

J. (1982). Clinical evaluation of dementia in Down's syndrome: A preliminary report. *Journal of Mental Deficiency Research, 26,* 239–244.

Thase, M. E., Tigner, R., Smeltzer, D. J., & Liss, L. (1984). Age-related neuropsychological deficits in Down syndrome. *Biological Psychiatry, 19,* 571–585.

Ulrich, J. (1985). Alzheimer changes in nondemented patients younger than sixty-five: Possible early stages of Alzheimer's disease and senile dementia of Alzheimer type. *Annals of Neurology, 7,* 273–277.

Walz, T., Harper, D., & Wilson, J. (1986). The aging developmentally disabled person: A review. *The Gerontologist, 26,* 622–629.

Warren, A. C., Holroyd, S., & Folstein, M. F. (1989). Major depression in Down's syndrome. *British Journal of Psychiatry, 155,* 202–205.

Widaman, K. F., Gibbs, K. W., & Geary, D. C. (1987). The structure of adaptive behavior: I. Replication across fourteen samples of nonprofoundly retarded persons. *American Journal of Mental Deficiency, 91,* 348–360.

Wisniewski, H. M., & Rabe, A. (1986). Discrepancy between Alzheimer-type neuropathology and dementia in people with Down syndrome. *Annals of the New York Academy of Science, 477,* 247–259.

Wisniewski, H. M., Rabe, A., & Wisniewski, K. E. (1987). Neuropathology and dementia in people with Down's syndrome. In *Molecular neuropathology of aging* (Banbury report 27, pp. 399–408). Cold Spring Harbor, NY: Cold Spring Harbor Laboratory.

Wisniewski, K. E., Wisniewski, H. M., & Wen, G. Y. (1985). Occurrence of neuropathological changes and dementia of Alzheimer's disease in Down syndrome. *Annals of Neurology, 17,* 278–282.

Young, E. C., & Kramer, B. M. (1991). Characteristics of age-related language decline in adults with Down syndrome. *Mental Retardation, 29,* 75–79.

Zigman, W., Rabe, A., Schupf, N., Sersen, E., Silverman, W., Zigman, A., & Wisniewski, H. M. (1990). Clinical diagnosis of Alzheimer dementia in mentally retarded people (abstract). *Neurobiology of Aging, 11,* 276.

Zigman, W. B., Schupf, N., Lubin, R. A., & Silverman, W. P. (1987). Premature regression in adults with Down syndrome. *American Journal of Mental Deficiency, 92,* 161–168.

Zigman, W. B., Schupf, N., Silverman, W. P., & Sterling, R. C. (1989). Changes in adaptive functioning of adults with developmental disabilities. *Australia and New Zealand Journal of Developmental Disabilities, 15,* 277–287.

Zigman, W. B., Schupf, N., Zigman, A., & Silverman, W. (1993). Aging and Alzheimer disease in people with mental retardation. In N. W. Bray (Ed.), *International review of research in mental retardation* (Vol. 19) (pp. 41–70). New York: Academic Press.

Preparation of this chapter was supported by funds provided by New York State through its Office of Mental Retardation and Developmental Disabilities, as well as by Grants R29 HD24170, PO1 HD22634, P01 AG11531, and R01 AG09439 from the National Institutes of Health, and by Grants 07DD0273-18 and 90DD0185-02 from the Administration on Developmental Disabilities, Department of Health and Human Services. Work completed at the NYS Institute for Basic Research in Developmental Disabilities was part of a large Institute-wide program for the study of aging processes in people with mental retardation and developmental disabilities under the overall direction of Dr. Henry M. Wisniewski. The insightful comments by Drs. Nicole Schupf, April Zigman, and Henry Wisniewski on a previous version of this chapter are gratefully acknowledged.

Chapter 6

Trends in Mortality Rates and Predictors of Mortality

Richard K. Eyman, University of California at Riverside
Sharon A. Borthwick-Duffy, University of California at Riverside

As the research evidence presented in this chapter will demonstrate, persons with moderate to profound mental retardation are likely to have shorter life expectancies than their nonhandicapped peers. Studies of mortality have consistently shown an inverse relationship between severity of retardation and longevity. In fact, people with mild forms of retardation have been found to have life expectancies that are close to those of people with average intelligence (Dupont, Vaeth, & Videbech, 1987). Although low intelligence per se does not increase the risk of an early death, secondary handicaps and concomitant health problems present additional risk factors, such as nonmobility and the lack of basic self-help skills, that are more common among people with severe intellectual handicaps than in those with milder forms of retardation or in the general population. This chapter focuses on people who, as a group, are at the greatest risk of having shorter than normal life expectancies, i.e., those with severe intellectual deficits or secondary handicapping conditions. Persons with mild retardation may seem to be excluded from consideration; however, this is because their life expectancies have been found to be similar to people of average intelligence and the risk factors are assumed to be similar in both groups. This assumption, of course, is subject to empirical confirmation and is discussed in the chapter.

Although some factors associated with mortality are common among persons of all ages, other predictors of life expectancy have been found to differ across the life span for people with mental retardation. Eyman, Call, and White (1989), for example, found different subsets of risk factors among individuals who were either older or younger than age 50. Other age-related issues relate to the predisposition to premature aging that has been found among persons with Down syndrome.

The study of life expectancy is important for both scientific and practical reasons. The identification of risk factors has contributed and will continue to contribute to efforts to reduce mortality rates among persons with mental retardation. For a number of practical reasons, estimates of life expectancy for subgroups with different characteristics have proven to be extremely useful to service systems, families, and professional groups. The purpose of this chapter is to review the historical and current findings related to the life expectancy of persons with mental retardation. Risk factors that are unrelated to the age of the individual are discussed separately from those that have been found to be important only within certain age groups. The acquisition and regression of basic skills that are associated with mortality have been found to impact survival, over and above the presence or absence of these abilities. A review of recent research in this area follows the discussion of specific predictors. Finally, we discuss implications for research, policy development, and service provision.

Historical Background

Historically, the survival of people with mental retardation drew attention because it was found that many of these individuals died before reaching adulthood (Carter & Jancar, 1983; Richards & Sylvester, 1969; Tarjan, Wright, Eyman, & Keeran, 1973). For example, Richards and Sylvester (1969) reported overall death rates in institutions for people with mental retardation in Great Britain and New York to be double those of the general population in England and Wales. These results were confirmed in another institutional sample in Canada by Balakrishnan and Wolf (1976). More recently, it has been found that medical advances, such as the introduction of antibiotics, and improved diets, medical care, and environments have increased the longevity of people with mental retardation in general (Carter & Jancar, 1983) and in particular of those with Down syndrome, whose survival has increased by more than 30 years (Thase, 1982).

O'Brien, Tate, and Zaharia (1991) compared mortality rates for two time intervals, 1974 through 1979 and 1980 through 1985, and found significant improvement in survival between the two time periods. Respiratory disease was reported to be the most common cause of death for persons with profound mental retardation, supporting the earlier findings of Chaney, Eyman, and Miller (1979). In contrast, O'Brien et al. (1991) found that heart disease and cancer were the most common causes of death among persons with mild, moderate, or severe mental retardation among the institutionalized people they studied.

It is apparent that medical advances have reduced mortality connected with heart disease and cancer, which in turn has improved survival over the past 50 years for people with moderate and mild mental retardation, as stated by Carter and Jancar (1983) and Thase (1982). However, research studies have consistently found that people with profound retardation who are not ambulatory remain at high risk for an early death from respiratory infection (Carter & Jancar, 1983; Eyman, Borthwick-Duffy, Call, & White, 1988; Eyman, Grossman, Tarjan, & Miller, 1987). Carter and Jancar (1983) found that respiratory infections had increased over the past 50 years as a major cause of death. However, since many more people are designated as having mild or moderate mental retardation in comparison to those who have profound retardation and are nonambulatory, it is not surprising that overall mortality rates have decreased over the past 50 years.

These findings imply that large numbers of people with mild and moderate mental retardation, and, to a lesser extent, ambulatory individuals with severe and profound mental retardation, will survive to older ages. This fact led Carter and Jancar (1983) to contend that the majority of community placements that were suitable for relatively young individuals would be less appropriate for an aging population in terms of both services offered and space available: "As with the general population, geriatric mentally handicapped persons will thus constitute a serious problem in terms of resource availability" (Carter & Jancar, 1983, p. 155).

Despite the improved longevity for many people with mental retardation, there are still large numbers of nonambulatory individuals with severe or profound mental retardation whose life expectancies are very limited (Eyman et al., 1987). As noted above, most of these people (about 70%) will die of a respiratory illness which in turn is related to swallowing difficulties, disturbances in coughing and gagging, and shallow respiration. Moreover, even though the longevity of people with mental retardation has increased, most of them still do not have a normal life expectancy of 75 or more years. As Simila, von Wendt, and Rantakallio (1986) reported, mental retardation *per se* is not necessarily associated with an increased death rate, but additional complicating medical conditions and disorders predispose the individual to infections and the like.

Methods of Determining Life Expectancy

Life expectancy is usually defined as the remaining life-time (in years) for a person who survives to the beginning of the indicated age interval (period life table). If one is dealing with a survival analysis, the life expectancy estimate is commonly set where 50% of a specified age cohort has died.

Terminology used to describe survival is related in part to the methodology used to compute life expectancy. There are several methodological issues surrounding the computation of mortality and survival, which can be found in selected texts on this topic. For example, mortality rates and life tables are usually the province of demography and are discussed in books such as Shryock, Siegel, and Associates (1976) and Schoen (1988). These texts discuss the use of different measures of mortality for estimating life expectancy. Although it is beyond the scope of this chapter to provide a detailed description of the statistical procedures involved in the construction of life tables, brief descriptions of the more common methods used are provided so the reader can best interpret the research presented. Demographers commonly distinguish between two types of life tables according to the reference year of the table—the current or period life table and the generation or cohort life table. The *period or current life table* is based on the experience of a sample or population over a short period of time, e.g., one or three years. To quote Shryock et al. (1976):

> This type of table, therefore, represents the combined mortality experience by age of a population in a particular short period of time (treated synthetically or viewed cross-sectionally); it does not represent the mortality experience of an actual cohort. Instead it assumes a hypothetical cohort that is subject to the age specific death rates observed in a particular period. (p. 249)

Therefore, a current life table may be viewed as a "snapshot" of current mortality.

The *generation life table* is based on the mortality rates experienced by a cohort of people. A common cohort for demographers would include all persons born in a given city or state in a year, such as 1920. According to this type of table, individuals in a given cohort would be followed and the number dying each year observed from birth to the point where all persons were dead. Since data are needed over a long period of years to complete a single table, it is rarely used as described above. Instead, a *survival analysis* is employed in which the investigator can estimate 5-, 10-, or 20-year cumulative sur-

vival rates for a cohort of people followed for 5, 10, or 20 years.

Both of these types of tables can be found in the mental retardation literature. Balakrishnan and Wolf (1976), Eyman, Call, and White (1991), and Eyman, Grossman, Chaney, and Call (1990) provide examples of period or current life tables. Examples of survival analyses include studies by Eyman et al. (1987) and Eyman, Grossman, Chaney, and Call (in press). Based on our experience (Eyman et al., 1990) the period table provides similar estimates to survival analysis. Differences in results only appear when sample sizes become small or wide age ranges are combined to form a single cohort (survival analysis) and compared with smaller age ranges in a period table. Even then, discrepancies are moderate to small, i.e., 4 to 5 years' difference in a life expectancy estimate using the two methods.

Identifying Predictors of Mortality

Predictors That Are Stable Across the Life Span

It is clear from the literature cited on mortality and survival that life expectancy is closely linked to age, level of retardation, cerebral palsy, degree of immobility, feeding, incontinence, and associated medical problems, i.e., seizures, chronic infections, etc. Even in a study of people with Down syndrome, Eyman et al. (1991) found that some of these people were immobile, tube fed, and incontinent, and demonstrated a short life expectancy. However, most individuals with Down syndrome *did not* have these profound disabilities and were noted to be likely to survive into their 40s and 50s. Consequently, life expectancy in the different etiologies is also determined to a large extent by mobility, feeding, and toileting status. The exceptions to this generalization are certain chromosomal or neurodegenerative diseases which, however, comprise a very small percentage of the population of people with a label of mental retardation.

Among the attributes of people with mental retardation that influence their mortality regardless of age are certain etiologies, level of mental retardation, epilepsy, cerebral palsy, major medical problems (such as the tendency to choke, gastrointestinal infections, heart conditions, chronic respiratory infection, hepatitis, etc.), the lack of mobility or feeding skills, and incontinence. With the exception of mobility, feeding skills, and incontinence, these conditions are generally permanent and influence longevity across the life span.

Probably the most frequently studied predictors of death have been etiology and level of retardation (Eyman, Borthwick, & Tarjan, 1984; Forssman & Åkesson, 1965; McCurley, MacKay, & Scally, 1972; Primrose, 1966; Richards & Sylvester, 1969; Sabagh, Dingman, Miller, & Tarjan, 1959; Tarjan, Eyman, & Miller, 1969). For example, Down syndrome represents a chromosomal abnormality that has received considerable attention with regard to longevity. Thase (1982) documented that early studies on the life expectancy of individuals with Down syndrome suggested a poor outcome, usually 10 years or less. More recent studies (Baird & Sadovnick, 1987; Eyman et al., 1991; Richards & Siddiqui, 1980) provide data indicating a life expectancy into the late 40s and early 50s for most individuals with Down syndrome. However, mortality rates increase dramatically after the age of 50 such that few persons with Down syndrome will be found alive by age 70 (Eyman et al., 1989; Richards & Siddiqui, 1980; Thase, 1982). Furthermore, a substantial number of people with Down syndrome suffer from congenital heart disease that, if left untreated, shortens longevity to about 30 years (Baird & Sadovnick, 1987; Eyman et al., 1991). Still another subset of individuals with Down syndrome has profound handicaps: They are immobile, fed by others, incontinent, and have a life expectancy of under 8 years (Eyman et al., 1991).

Individuals with developmental cranial anomalies, particularly hydrocephalus, historically have had a very poor prognosis for survival if shunting cannot be performed (Eyman et al., 1987). Moreover, persons with severe brain damage are also likely to die early

(Eyman et al., 1990). Other etiologies have less clear effects on mortality. For example, etiology of mental retardation is often indeterminate (Chaney & Eyman, 1982). Some causes can be established, such as certain chromosomal or neurodegenerative diseases, which, however, comprise a small percentage of the population of people with mental retardation. But many etiologies remain unknown because of a lack of accurate gestational or birth history, or absence of appropriate diagnostic tests.

Level of retardation also relates to mortality and has been studied extensively (Eyman et al., 1987). However, level of retardation has also been shown to be related to the acquisition of basic skills such as ambulation, toilet training, etc. (Eyman, Silverstein, & McLain, 1975; Eyman, Tarjan, & Cassady, 1970; O'Connor, Justice, & Payne, 1970). Hence, the causative factors for early mortality are more likely a consequence of associated handicaps and medical problems than level of retardation *per se* (Eyman et al., 1987). Nevertheless, level of retardation has still emerged as a strong predictor of mortality in recent studies (O'Brien et al., 1991).

Another group of risk factors for mortality across the age range of people with mental retardation includes cerebral palsy, seizures, and major medical problems. Evans, Evans, and Alberman (1990), Kudrjavcev, Schoenberg, Kurland, and Groover (1985), and Roboz (1972) have examined the impact of cerebral palsy on survival of people with severe mental retardation and impaired mobility. All of these studies confirmed poor survival for people with severe cerebral palsy associated with nonmobility in contrast to less impaired individuals with more moderate levels of mental retardation. Of additional interest here is the Carter and Jancar (1983) finding that deaths due to status epilepticus have decreased with a concomitant increase in those due to carcinoma, myocardial infarction, and cerebrovascular accident. Eyman et al. (1988, 1990) found these medical problems to be subordinate to other more powerful predictors of early mortality, including mobility, feeding, and toileting deficits.

However, only mobility has been found to predict mortality well across all ages, in contrast to toileting and eating skills. Thus, it is important at this juncture to examine differential prediction of mortality depending on the age of the individual.

Predictors That Are Different Across the Life Span

The attributes that define mortality risk are somewhat different across the age range. Eyman et al. (1988) found that immobility and tube feeding were very strong predictors of early mortality through age 50; after age 50, toileting and eating skills predicted mortality best. Furthermore, mortality rates were highest between the ages of 0 and 10 years and after 50 years. In another study specifically devoted to mortality of elderly persons with mental retardation, Eyman et al. (1989) found an overall prevalence rate of 4.4% for people with developmental disabilities over age 55 who were served in California between 1984 and 1987. The mortality rates for individuals 55 years or older were over 19% for nonmobile people, 23% for persons who could not feed themselves, and 18% for individuals who were not toilet trained.

Haveman and Maaskant (1989) examined 5-year mortality rates over the life span for institutionalized people with severe mental retardation in Holland compared to the overall Dutch population. The individuals with severe mental retardation exhibited very high mortality rates during their early years, i.e., ages 0–4 years, declining to a low point between the ages of 30 and 39 and then rising sharply again after 40 years of age. In contrast, the general population mortality was very low until 70 years of age. Haveman and Maaskant (1989) concluded that the mortality risk for persons with severe mental handicaps between ages 50 and 59 was comparable with that for 60- to 69-year-old people in the Dutch population as a whole. Haveman and Maaskant further concluded that if there is a need for defining a turning-point according to age and mortality risk, the age of 50 seems a reasonable one. These results agree with studies by Eyman et al. (1987), Richards and Siddiqui (1980), and Thase (1982).

More recent studies have further refined estimates of life expectancy by including new predictors such as the ability to voluntarily move one's body or extremities and the need for tube feeding. Eyman et al. (1990), for example, found immobile subjects had a much shorter life expectancy than those who could move about. Those who also required tube feeding had a very short life expectancy, i.e., 4 to 5 additional years from the time of evaluation, regardless of age. Those who were able to eat with assistance from others and were immobile had an average life expectancy of about 9 additional years. Finally, those who were mobile and fed by others, though not ambulatory, had a life expectancy of about 23 more years. The sample sizes of these subgroups ranged between 1,000 and 4,500.

An even more recent study by the above authors (Eyman, Grossman, Chaney, & Call, 1993) focused on additional precision by examining the importance of mobility and arm-hand use. For persons who could roll over but were otherwise nonmobile (i.e., could not crawl), survival was relatively good; about 70% to 80% of the sample of more than 2,000 individuals (mostly children) were still alive after 11 years. Those individuals who could not roll over but had some functional use of their arms or hands still had a relatively short life expectancy, i.e., will live about 10 more years, although it was much improved compared to people who could not roll over and had no arm-hand use, i.e., will live 6 more years. Moreover, children who could not roll over or crawl and required tube feeding had the worst survival rates, i.e., will live 1 to 5 more years. Voluntary rolling, which usually requires some arm-hand use, is apparently very critical to survival.

For persons with restricted mobility the resultant early death is mainly due to respiratory complications (Chaney et al., 1979). Pulmonary ventilation is lessened, causing the high incidence of respiratory infection (Roboz, 1972). Blisard, Martin, Brown, Smialek, Davis, and McFeeley (1988) reported that 72% of deaths of persons with profound disabilities who resided in an institution were due to respiratory complications, especially pneumonia, and also aspiration with or without pneumonia. It is becoming evident, as Carter and Jancar (1983), Chaney et al. (1979) and O'Brien et al. (1991) reported, that respiratory complications leading to death are most prevalent among individuals with severe mental retardation in contrast to heart disease and cancer, which are more common among people with less severe forms of retardation.

Dupont et al. (1987) specifically studied the life expectancy of people with mild retardation in Denmark. In general, the longevity of this population averaged 65 to 73 years, depending on the age interval examined. These survival times are still less than the 75 to 84 years used as estimates of longevity for the general population.

Acquisition and Regression of Basic Skills Related to Mortality

Eyman, Olmstead, Grossman, and Call (1993) studied the probabilities of attaining mobility and feeding skills over a 5-year period for subgroups of about 8,000 individuals (mostly children). The sample was chosen based on a lack of skills at an initial time point (1980–1985). The results focused on change in skill level or death 5 years later. The sample was further stratified by the need for tube feeding versus being able to eat if fed by others. Although most children with mental retardation would be expected to achieve the basic skills examined, there are a substantial number of these individuals who will not acquire self-help ability. It is evident from previous studies that the probability of attaining self-help skills is related to IQ (Eyman et al., 1970; Lohmann, Eyman, & Lask, 1967; O'Connor et al., 1970; Tarjan, Dingman, & Miller, 1960). In other words, people with profound or severe mental retardation are much less likely to have attained self-help skills than individuals who have mild or moderate mental retardation.

The results suggested critical ages (usually about 6 years of age) at which self-help skills should be attained if they are likely to be acquired later in time. It was also apparent that failure to attain mobility, self-feeding, or toileting ability dramatically reduces the chances for survival. Of particular importance was the role of tube feeding in predicting early mortality. Among people being fed by gastrostomy tube, mortality was high (over 50%) in the very young ages, declining to about 40% in the older age groups. Conversely, for people not on a gastrostomy tube, but being fed by others, mortality rates over a 5-year period were between 20% to 30%. These mortality trends over age were inversely related to the likelihood of improvement in basic skills. Individuals being fed by gastrostomy tube demonstrated very low probabilities of acquiring any of the skills studied regardless of their age. Individuals being fed by others showed a much higher chance of attaining the self-help skills, particularly if they were less than 3 years of age.

Of particular interest were the findings reported by Eyman et al. (1989) regarding regression of basic skills among individuals with mental retardation 55 years of age or older. About 5% of this older age group were found to have lost their mobility, eating, and toileting skills over a 5-year period. When regression in these skills occurred, the mortality rates rose from 7.5% (no change) to 20% to 30% (regression). Loss of eating ability was especially devastating, as the mortality rate increased to 30%. Although declines in competence have been previously shown to decrease survival (Eyman et al., 1987), it was not apparent that a loss of ability in these areas would be even more predictive of death for older individuals with mental retardation. On medical grounds, these results are not surprising even though definitive statistical evidence concerning the morbid consequences of self-help regression among older persons with mental retardation has not been well publicized.

Implications for Research, Policy, and Practice

Implications for Research

Need for accurate estimates of survival and identification of risk factors. Although workers in the field of mental retardation have generally been aware of the high risk of early mortality of many persons with mental retardation, there is considerable controversy among physicians and other professionals as to how long medically fragile children and adults with mental retardation can survive if provided good medical care. This disagreement has become very apparent to the present investigators through consultation in medical malpractice lawsuits in which the life expectancy of a child with a disability is frequently a central issue. Interviews with a sample of parents of children with profound handicaps also have revealed varying estimates of survival for the same child given by different physicians. Life expectancy is a major issue to these parents for many reasons, but particularly because children are usually in need of total care and frequent hospitalizations. Although some answers are available at this time regarding survival of severely handicapped children and adults, it is critical that accurate estimates of life expectancy based on relatively current data become available to professionals in the field of mental retardation. This will require longitudinal data on large enough groups of people to allow for analysis within subgroups of people with different characteristics. Further, predictors of mortality must continue to be examined and efforts should be made to distinguish causal factors from correlates of survival.

Residential placement issues. Decisions regarding the selection of the most appropriate residential placement continue to confront workers in the field of mental retardation. With regard to survival, questions have arisen regarding the advantages and disadvantages of individuals with severe handicaps living at home with their families as opposed to being placed in institutions or skilled nursing facilities. Some parents will go to extraordinary lengths to keep their children at home regardless of the degree of handicap and presence of serious medical problems. We have been asked on several occasions by professionals in the field whether or not we have found differences in mortality rates between individuals living in their own homes versus other residential alternatives. This question is difficult to answer because individuals who are more medically fragile are most often found in institutions and skilled nursing facilities; i.e., it is difficult to find comparable groups to study in other settings. Hence, a definitive answer requires additional in-depth studies that control for factors associated with placement decisions as well as the presence of the known factors that place an individual at risk of an early death. Moreover, these in-depth studies should continue to search for new risk factors that may be placement-specific and may not have been identified in previous comparative studies.

Medical care and interventions. Chapman, La Plante, and Wilensky (1986) concluded that little is known about the relative impact of medical care on mortality and morbidity versus other determinants of health, e.g., genetics, lifestyle, environment, etc. St. George (1986) argued that it is widely accepted that medical interventions have only a marginal effect on population mortality, mainly at a very late stage, after death rates have already fallen strikingly. However, as was noted previously, medical advances such as the introduction of antibiotics, better diets, improved living conditions, and better medical care have increased the longevity of people with mental retardation in general, and in particular, those with Down syndrome (Carter & Jancar, 1983; Eyman et al., 1987; Thase, 1982). As is true in the general population, it is not difficult to conclude that a combination of many factors has improved survival. However, it is next to impossible to separate out the effect of a single intervention, such as medical care, as a major reason for improved life expectancy. Given the limitations on sound experimental designs dictated by humane considerations, this situation is not likely to change. Furthermore, there is a paucity of literature concerned with interventions for children with disabilities that have demonstrated positive effects. The major goal of future research on mortality should be to identify subsets of factors that predict positive outcomes rather than to attempt to claim that a particular intervention or broad placement category, etc., will improve prognosis.

Focus on aging persons with mental retardation. Even though most of the interest in survival has concerned younger children, interest has been increasing in the continued survival of older people with mental retardation. Older adults were noted by Haveman and Maaskant (1989) to have mortality rates comparable to those of nonretarded people aged 60 years or more in the Dutch population. The special needs of the current population of elderly adults with mental retardation have been emphasized throughout this volume. For example, people with Down syndrome have been singled out as a unique population with a known predisposition to premature aging. As others have noted, longitudinal same-subject studies are needed to help provide additional information on the effects of aging on the health status of this population (Zigman, Seltzer, & Silverman, chapter 5 this volume).

Increasing generalizability. In terms of the representativeness of study populations, the majority of early studies focused on institutionalized groups. More recently, investigators have studied persons receiving services from state agencies for people with mental retardation. These studies have included people living at home and those living in the full range of community residential placements. From these data, the life expectancy of persons receiving state services has varied from about 4 years from the present for people with the most profound handicaps to about 55 years from the present for individuals with mild handicaps who are receiving state services.

In general, persons with moderate mental retardation through profound mental retardation are well represented in state service systems. However, individuals designated as having mild retardation in schools are often not known to state mental retardation or developmental disabilities service systems. Others lose their formal labels following their school years and do not seek additional services. It is reasonable to assume that people with mild retardation who *are* part of state service systems are those with the greatest needs (and would therefore be more likely to be more at risk). Thus, the life expectancies reported in this chapter for served people would be lower than for the total group of people with mild retardation. However, it is also possible that additional risk factors could be present among the group of people with below average intelligence who are living without a formal support system, e.g., their health may be jeopardized due to poor nutrition or lack of health care (see Edgerton, chapter 4 this volume). Depression and other mental health problems among persons with mild retardation (who may not be part of service systems) have also been suggested as being linked to suicide or accidental death. Hence, we would have to say that the life expectancy and mortality rates reported in this chapter are generalizable primarily for individuals with more severe forms of retardation who are represented in state service systems. Certainly, factors associated with the life expectancy of the "elusive" group of persons with mild retardation who do not receive formal services should become a focus of future empirical study.

Use well-defined subgroups for study. It is not very informative for present day investigators to discuss life expectancy or mortality within the broad category of mental retardation. When research is based on subgroups comprised of heterogeneous groups of people, some people may have severe disabilities while others may have only mild handicaps. The mortality and survival rates computed on these groups represent a weighted average (based on the number of people with and without severe disabilities) of two very different mortality experiences. Given our current state of knowledge, such estimates are not useful. Furthermore, since people with fewer disabilities outnumber individuals with profound disabilities, the resulting mortality estimates of heterogeneous groups will reflect the survival experience of people with fewer disabilities. Future samples need to be separated according to known risk factors for specific subgroups, such as age, level of retardation, and ambulation status at a minimum, and some known etiologies, such as Down syndrome. More precise subgroups using several risk variables concerning mortality will furnish more informative survival estimates than poorly defined subgroups.

Statistical methods. In addition to life tables and mortality *per se*, there have been several new developments in the methodology that evaluates predictors of mortality. Wells, Feinstein, and Walter (1990), Feinstein, Wells, and Walter (1990), and Walter, Feinstein, and Wells (1990) compared several multivariate mathematical methods for predicting survival relative to the statistical selection of prognostic variables. Specifically, logistic regression (used by Eyman et al., 1989) was compared with regression methods, i.e., discriminant function analysis and the Cox proportional hazard regression techniques. Overall, these methods gave identical results except in instances where too many variables were entered into the prediction equation. Thus, if a prudent selection of prediction variables are considered to begin with (a strong suggestion in most statistics textbooks), these methods will generally give the same results. However, some additional problems can arise when using proportional hazard procedures (Singer & Willett, 1991). Therefore, it seems safe to conclude that methods of computing survival using selected predictor variables are very robust. As new statistical methods are developed for estimating survival and identifying predictors of mortality, future research in this area should continue to cross-validate and confirm that different methods provide similar results.

Implications for Policy Development

Correctly interpreting life expectancy data. Demographers and statisticians have specified fairly robust procedures for estimating longevity. Although it is a common practice, it is not correct to use the age distribution of a residual population of institutionalized people or community residents as an estimate of how long such individuals are likely to survive, because some members of the cohort have already died. Residual populations suffer these cohort effects that can differentially impact who is available for tabulation. For example, most high-risk children die young and do not reach an older age category. Hence, an investigator might find at some arbitrary time point that 30% of the people who are immobile in institutions are over 25 years of age and naively assume that 30% of such people can be expected to survive past 25 years. These cross-sectional tabulations ignore a large at-risk population who have previously died and were not counted in the at-risk group versus those who actually died. Moreover, residual populations capitalize on others who represent "outliers" to the general mortality experience. Interpreting such tabulations relative to probability of survival is misleading and incorrect. It is for this reason that the current or period life table is preferred to estimate age-specific mortality rates as a way of obtaining the average number of years remaining. Similarly, average age at death cannot estimate life expectancy.

Because service system administrators often attempt to forecast the survival time of specific groups of individuals with disabilities for the purpose of projecting needs for future services and medical care, it is important that accurate estimates of life expectancy are considered in this process. Therefore, developers of policy (as well as those who utilize survival data for other reasons) must recognize the flawed logic that leads to life expectancies based on cross-sectional data and residual populations.

Training self-help skills. Some children in a profoundly impaired state do become stronger, gain basic skills, and survive, while others do not (Eyman, Olmstead et al., 1993). For example, there is some evidence that with special training selected people with mental retardation will show improvement in self-help, social, and communication skills (Eyman et al., 1970, 1975; Roos, 1965, 1970; Watson, 1967). However, there is no evidence that all of these individuals will develop self-help skills as a result of such programs. Rather, the more profound the level of retardation, the less likely changes in skills will be achieved, especially after a certain age (Eyman et al., 1970; Eyman & Widaman, 1987).

Public Law 94-142 assures that educational opportunities will not be denied because of the severity of an individual's disability. Since this federal law has been enforced in California by both the school systems and the Department of Developmental Services for the past 16 years, the vast majority of people in the samples used in the Eyman, Olmstead et al. (1993) study would have been in some kind of educational programs during the school years. However, the results of this investigation demonstrated that, even with training, many people with mental retardation had not achieved minimal skill levels over time and subsequently had much higher than normal mortality rates. Certainly all individuals should be given the advantage of appropriate training and habilitation programs. Unfortunately, though, skill acquisition is not a guaranteed outcome, especially among persons with the most severe intellectual deficits (Eyman, Olmstead et al., 1993). Moreover, improved medical care has not altered significantly the poor prognosis for those individuals with profound disabilities and without self-help ability (Eyman et al., 1990). This is likely explained by the presence of other risk factors than basic skills.

A more realistic approach to improving longevity for this group might be to focus on the prevention of the underlying brain damage that leads to skills deficits and the improvement of physical therapies designed to prevent restricted mobility. Just as P.L. 94–142 has guaranteed the right to education for all individuals, regardless of handicap, it might be that policies for persons with mental retardation who are at risk of an early death should emphasize the need for therapy that will increase body movement.

Residential placement issues. The need for in-depth studies on the impact of various characteristics of health care provided by different residential settings types has already been discussed. The policy implications should be obvious. The current emphasis on placing people in the least restrictive environment and ideally leaving them in their natural homes has resulted in formal and informal policies that make health facilities and institutions a placement of last resort. It is important, however, that these humanistic policies that are based on the principle of normalization be continuously evaluated as data become available on the potential impact of setting characteristics on the life expectancy of persons already at risk.

To date, there is no conclusive evidence to suggest that the care in one residential setting type is associated with higher (or lower) mortality rates for individuals with similar characteristics. Licensing and other standards of care for facilities that serve individuals with mental retardation provide some assurance that the health needs of these people will be met. However, continued research in this area may provide information that will lead to additional or revised standards, and may also lead to a reconceptualization of what provides the least restrictive environment for individuals who are at great risk of an early death.

Implications for Practice

Focus on basic skills. Although the relationship of some basic skills to survival may be indirect, the importance of mobility and ambulation and of toileting and eating skills extends beyond the development of independence and appears to influence the risk of mortality for individuals with mental retardation. Knowledge of these relationships should encourage professional therapists and other direct care workers to focus on the acquisition of these skills, especially for persons with other identified risk factors. Previous research has shown that in some cases intensive programs designed to improve mobility have been successful where traditional therapies have not. Thus, continued efforts to design and use programs that will increase mobility and even lead to the development of other basic skills may extend the life expectancy of some individuals with mental retardation.

Recognizing risk factors. The identification of individuals who display characteristics that place them at a higher risk of an early death, such as lack of basic skills and the need for tube feeding, should alert practitioners to the need for careful monitoring of these vulnerable individuals. Continued research will hopefully identify additional factors that will make it possible to more accurately "flag" these individuals and then intervene to the extent possible to improve skills and reduce health-related problems.

Providing more accurate estimates. We have already discussed the importance of providing families with realistic expectations for the survival of their children with severe disabilities. Recognizing that this information may not always be viewed as helpful, we believe that for parents and others who wish to know how long their children might live, estimates must be as accurate as possible. Physicians and other professionals who are involved in informing or counseling families must have some understanding of life tables and must recognize dangers of reporting figures that are based on heterogeneous groups or cross-sectional data using residual samples.

References

Baird, P. A., & Sadovnick, A. D. (1987). Life expectancy in Down syndrome. *Journal of Pediatrics, 110,* 849–854.

Balakrishnan, T. R., & Wolf, L. C. (1976). Life expectancy of mentally retarded persons in Canadian institutions. *American Journal of Mental Deficiency, 80,* 650–662.

Blisard, K. S., Martin, C., Brown, G. W., Smialek, J. E., Davis, L. E., & McFeeley, P. J. (1988). Causes of death of patients in an institution for the developmentally disabled. *Journal of Forensic Sciences, 33,* 1457–1462.

Carter, G., & Jancar, J. (1983). Mortality in the mentally handicapped: A 50 year survey at the Stoke Park group of hospitals (1930–1980). *Journal of Mental Deficiency Research, 27,* 143–156.

Chaney, R. H., & Eyman, R. K. (1982). Etiology of mental retardation: Clinical vs. neuroanatomic diagnosis. *Mental Retardation, 20,* 123–127.

Chaney, R. H., Eyman, R. K., & Miller, C. R. (1979). Comparison of respiratory mortality in the profoundly mentally retarded and in the less retarded. *Journal of Mental Deficiency Research, 23,* 1–7.

Chapman, S. H., La Plante, M. P., & Wilensky, G. (1986). Life expectancy and health status of the aged. *Social Security Bulletin, 49,* 24–48.

Dupont, A., Vaeth, M., & Videbech, P. (1987). Mortality, life expectancy, and causes of death of mildly mentally retarded in Denmark. *Upsala Journal of Medical Sciences, 44* (Suppl.), 76–82.

Edgerton, R. B. (1994). Quality of life issues: Some people know how to be old. In M. M. Seltzer, M. W. Krauss, & M. P. Janicki (eds.), *Life course perspectives on adulthood and old age* (pp. 53–66). Washington, DC: American Association on Mental Retardation.

Evans, P. M., Evans, S. J. W., & Alberman, E. (1990). Cerebral palsy: Why we must plan for survival. In B. Valman & M. Chiswick (Eds.), *Archives of diseases in childhood* (Vol. 65, pp. 1329–1333). London: British Medical Association.

Eyman, R. K., Borthwick, S. A., & Tarjan, G. (1984). Current trends and changes in institutions for the mentally retarded. *International Review of Research in Mental Retardation, 12,* 177–203.

Eyman, R. K., Borthwick-Duffy, S. A., Call, T. L., & White, J. F. (1988). Prediction of mortality in community and institutional settings. *Journal of Mental Deficiency Research, 32,* 203–213.

Eyman, R. K., Call, T. L., & White, J. F. (1989). Mortality of elderly mentally retarded persons in California. *The Journal of Applied Gerontology, 8,* 203–215.

Eyman, R. K., Call, T. L., & White, J. F. (1991). Life expectancy of persons with Down syndrome. *American Journal on Mental Retardation, 95,* 603–612.

Eyman, R. K., Grossman, H. J., Chaney, R. H., & Call, T. L. (1990). The life expectancy of profoundly handicapped people with mental retardation. *New England Journal of*

Medicine, 323, 584–589.

Eyman, R. K., Grossman, H. J., Chaney, R. H., & Call, T. L. (1993). Survival of profoundly disabled people with severe mental retardation. *American Journal of Diseases of Children, 147,* 329–336.

Eyman, R. K., Grossman, H. J., Tarjan, G., & Miller, C. R. (1987). *Life expectancy and mental retardation* (Monograph No. 7). Washington, DC: American Association on Mental Deficiency.

Eyman, R. K., Olmstead, C. E., Grossman, H. J., & Call, T. L. (1993). Mortality and the acquisition of basic skills by children and adults with severe disabilities. *American Journal of Diseases of Children, 147,* 216–222.

Eyman, R. K., Silverstein, A. B., & McLain, R. (1975). Effects of treatment programs on the acquisition of basic skills. *American Journal of Mental Deficiency, 79,* 573–582.

Eyman, R. K., Tarjan, G., & Cassady, M. (1970). Natural history of acquisition of basic skills by hospitalized retarded patients. *American Journal of Mental Deficiency, 72,* 120–129.

Eyman, R. K., & Widaman, K. F. (1987). Lifespan development of institutionalized and community-based mentally retarded persons, revisited. *American Journal of Mental Deficiency, 91,* 559–569.

Feinstein, A. R., Wells, C. K., & Walter, S. D. (1990). A comparison of multivariable mathematical methods for predicting survival — I. Introduction, rationale, and general strategy. *Journal of Clinical Epidemiology, 43,* 339–347.

Forssman, H., & Åkesson, H. O. (1965). Mortality in patients with Down's syndrome. *Journal of Mental Deficiency Research, 9,* 146–149.

Haveman, M. J., & Maaskant, M. A. (1989). Defining fragility of the elderly severely mentally handicapped according to mortality risk, morbidity, motor handicaps and social functioning. *Journal of Mental Deficiency Research, 33,* 389–397.

Kudrjavcev, T., Schoenberg, B. S., Kurland, L. T., & Groover, R. V. (1985). Cerebral palsy: Survival rates, associated handicaps, and distribution by clinical subtype (Rochester, MN, 1950–1976). *Neurology, 35,* 900–903.

Lohmann, W., Eyman, R. K., & Lask, E. (1967). Toilet training. *American Journal of Mental Deficiency, 71,* 551–557.

McCurley, R., MacKay, D. N., & Scally, B. G. (1972). The life expectation of the mentally subnormal under community and hospital care. *Journal of Mental Deficiency Research, 16,* 57–67.

O'Brien, K. F., Tate, K., & Zaharia, E. S. (1991). Mortality in a large southeastern facility for persons with mental retardation. *American Journal on Mental Retardation, 95,* 497–503.

O'Connor, G., Justice, R. S., & Payne, D. (1970). Statistical expectations of physical handicaps of institutionalized retardates. *American Journal of Mental Deficiency, 74,* 541–547.

Primrose, D. A. A. (1966). Natural history of mental deficiency in a hospital group and in the community it serves. *Journal of Mental Deficiency Research, 10,* 159–189.

Richards, B. W., & Siddiqui, A. Q. (1980). Age and mortality trends in residents of an institution for the mentally handicapped. *Journal of Mental Deficiency Research, 24,* 99–105.

Richards, B. W., & Sylvester, P. E. (1969). Mortality trends in mental deficiency institutions. *Journal of Mental Deficiency Research, 13,* 276–292.

Roboz, P. (1972). Mortality rate in institutionalized mentally retarded children. *The Medical Journal of Australia, 1,* 218–221.

Roos, P. (1965). Development of an intensive habit training unit at Austin State School. *Mental Retardation, 3,* 12–15.

Roos, P. (1970). Evolutionary changes of the residential facility. In A. A. Baumeister & E. C. Butterfield (Eds.), *Residential facilities for the mentally retarded* (pp. 29–58). Chicago: Aldine.

Sabagh, G., Dingman, H. F., Miller, C. R., & Tarjan, G. (1959). Differential mortality in a hospital for the mentally retarded: A study of mortality among patients admitted to Pacific State Hospital, 1948–1956. In L. Henry & W. Winkler (Eds.), *Proceedings of the International Population Conference* (pp. 460–468). Vienna, Austria: Union internationale pour l'étude scientifique de la population.

Schoen, R. (1988). *Modeling multigroup populations*. New York: Plenum Press.

Shryock, H. S., Siegel, J. S., and Associates. (1976). *The methods and materials of demography*. New York: Academic Press.

Simila, S., von Wendt, L., & Rantakallio, P. (1986). Mortality of mentally retarded children to 17 years of age assessed in a prospective one-year birth cohort. *Journal of Mental Deficiency Research, 30,* 401–405.

Singer, J. D., & Willett, J. B. (1991). Modeling the days of our lives: Using survival analysis when designing and analyzing longitudinal studies of duration and the timing of events. *Psychological Bulletin, 110,* 268–290.

St. George, D. (1986). Life expectancy, truth, and the ABPI. *The Lancet, 2,* 346.

Tarjan, G., Dingman, H. F., & Miller, C. R. (1960). Statistical expectations of selected handicaps in the mentally retarded. *American Journal of Mental Deficiency, 65,* 335–341.

Tarjan, G., Eyman, R. K., & Miller, C. R. (1969). Natural history of mental retardation in a state hospital revisited: Releases and deaths in two admission groups, ten years apart. *American Journal of Diseases of Children, 117,* 609–620.

Tarjan, G., Wright, S. W., Eyman, R. K., & Keeran, C. V. (1973). Natural history of mental retardation: Some aspects of epidemiology. *American Journal of Mental Deficiency, 77,* 369–379.

Thase, M. E. (1982). Longevity and mortality in Down's syndrome. *Journal of Mental Deficiency Research, 26,* 177–192.

Walter, S. D., Feinstein, A. R., & Wells, C. K. (1990). A comparison of multivariable mathematical methods for predicting survival — II. Statistical selection of prognostic variables. *Journal of Clinical Epidemiology, 43,* 349–359.

Watson, L. S., Jr. (1967). Application of operant conditioning techniques to institutionalized severely and profoundly retarded children. *Mental Retardation Abstracts, 4,* 1–18.

Wells, C. K., Feinstein, A. R., & Walter, S. D. (1990). A comparison of multivariable mathematical methods for predicting survival — III. Accuracy of predictions in generating and challenge sets. *Journal of Clinical Epidemiology, 43,* 361–372.

Zigman, W. A., Seltzer, G. B., & Silverman, W. (1994). Behavioral and mental health changes associated with aging. In M. M. Seltzer, M. W. Krauss, & M. P. Janicki (Eds.), *Life course perspectives on adulthood and old age* (pp. 67–91). Washington, DC: American Association on Mental Retardation.

Community Services
for An Aging Population

Chapter 7

Health and Well-Being of Older Persons With Developmental Disabilities: A Clinical Review

Gary B. Seltzer, University of Wisconsin–Madison
Charlene Luchterhand, University of Wisconsin–Madison

During the last decade, professionals in the field of mental retardation have recognized that older persons are an underserved group, particularly in regards to health care (Howell, Gavin, Cabrera, & Beyer, 1989). Clinical services have been dominated by pediatric practitioners, and very few programs have been established to educate and train professionals in the provision of health care services to older persons with developmental disabilities (Seltzer & Essex, 1993).

One purpose of this chapter is to describe the health care services that this group needs as gleaned from the authors' experience in operating a specialized, tertiary care clinic for older persons with developmental disabilities and their families. The chapter opens with a description of this clinic and then, to place the clinic and the health care problems it sees in the broader context of the health care needs of this population, the chapter moves to an overview of the institutional barriers faced by older persons with developmental disabilities when they have to access the health care system. In addition, the authors examine the personal characteristics of older persons with developmental disabilities and their families that may influence their experiences with the health care system. Taken together, institutional barriers and characteristics of the population, accurately perceived or not, represent the larger context in which the specialized clinical services described in this chapter exist.

Because the content of this chapter is heavily influenced by the use of information gathered at a specialized, tertiary care clinic for older persons with developmental disabilities, the clinical problems described may represent a skewed sample of all the clinical problems experienced by this population. The skew probably favors problems that are severe or of a special nature, problems that could not be treated in a person's home community. In addition, the topics described in this chapter reflect the expertise of the authors and the disciplines represented on the clinic's team. Again, these may not be representative of the topics that a differently configured interdisciplinary team might select.

Case studies from the clinic are used to amplify points and to illustrate the relationship of treatment recommendations to the resultant course of treatment over time. When possible, the authors use information from the generic, geriatric health care literature and the specialized, but very limited, health care literature that describes the needs of older persons with developmental disabilities.

Another purpose of the chapter is to describe an assessment methodology for clinicians and others to use when they evaluate clinical problems and formulate treatment recommendations. Specifically, the authors describe the functional assessment methodology used to analyze both the personal characteristics of individuals and the environmental supports that affect the functional potential of older individuals with developmental disabilities. One particular functional assessment tool, OT FACT, is described in depth. It is used by the clinic staff as a blueprint to collect and analyze clinical data and formulate treatment recommendations. The chapter concludes with a brief discussion of the dilemmas that emerge in providing tertiary level care in a health care system that has only begun to recognize the needs of older persons with developmental disabilities.

The Aging & Developmental Disabilities Clinic

The Aging & Developmental Disabilities Clinic was organized at the Waisman Center University Affiliated Program at the University of Wisconsin–Madison to respond to problems of health care access and delivery, to provide interdisciplinary training for students and professionals, and to research and document special health care needs of this population. Partial funding for the clinic comes from an Administration on Developmental Disabilities Training Initiative Project. Because the goals of the project go far beyond the delivery of services, clinic staff are engaged in a variety of other community-based activities. Thus the clinic operates on a part-time basis about eight months of the year. The clinic opened in the fall of 1989, has seen approximately 72 individuals with developmental disabilities and their families, and is a joint venture with the University of Wisconsin Geriatrics Clinics. It is located in a satellite outpatient facility of the University of Wisconsin Hospital and Clinics. This location maximizes the opportunity for consumers[1] to receive health assessment and treatment in the same manner as do other older persons.

Referrals to the clinic have come through a variety of sources: family members, case managers, residential or vocational providers, health care providers, and the legal system. Individuals are accepted for clinic evaluation if they are experiencing a functional decline thought to be related to the effects of aging, if health care personnel in their local community have had difficulty in understanding or treating the decline, or if

family members are aging and need assistance with long term planning. When the presenting problem does not meet these criteria, callers are referred to other services. Since the clinic staff deliver tertiary care, they seek to preserve, or in some cases establish, primary care within the individual's local community.

All of the individuals seen in the clinic have been found to have multiple clinical problems, ranging in nature through physical, cognitive, psychological, social, and emotional. The range and complexity of these problems have reinforced the usefulness of an interdisciplinary team in the assessment process. The core team of the Aging & Developmental Disabilities Clinic includes an audiologist, geriatrician, nurse, occupational therapist, psychologist, and social worker. Consultations from other specialists, such as low vision specialists, psychiatrists, physical therapists, speech and language pathologists, and lawyers, are sought when needed. Diagnosis and recommendation of treatment strategies are a collective effort with team members building on each other's suggestions. As in all interdisciplinary work, the most critical component, other than competence in one's own discipline, is the ability to interact cooperatively with other team members (Adlin & Seltzer, in press).

After several years of writing lengthy reports, the team developed an easy-to-complete form on which the clinical findings are summarized (see Figure 1). This form is completed at the conclusion of each consumer's evaluation. After the consumer's or guardian's written consent is obtained, a summary report, consisting of this form, a printout on functional status (OT FACT), and interdisciplinary recommendations, is provided to the consumer, the family, and service providers, as appropriate. Oftentimes, consumers and their families are also given written, "user-friendly" information on health and well-being. In addition, health practitioners who are involved with the consumer system

---

[1] Various terms are used to refer to the person who requires assessment, e.g., patient or client. In keeping with current ideology, we use the term "consumer" throughout this chapter to serve as a reminder that individuals are consumers of health care.

Figure 1. Interdisciplinary Evaluation Summary

Waisman Center on Mental Retardation and Human Development
Aging & Developmental Disabilities Clinic

Interdisciplinary Evaluation Summary

Client: _____

DOB: ___ /___ /____   DOE:___ /___ /____   UWH#: __ __ __ – __ __ – __ __ –☐

	YES	NO	?[a]
1. Systems assessed:	**Normal Range?**		
_____ Cardiovascular	☐	☐	☐
_____ Gastrointestinal	☐	☐	☐
_____ Genitourinary	☐	☐	☐
_____ Head and Neck	☐	☐	☐
_____ Musculoskeletal	☐	☐	☐
_____ Neurological	☐	☐	☐
_____ Skin	☐	☐	☐
_____ Other _____	☐	☐	☐

2. Blood tests obtained:	**Normal Range?**		
_____ CBC	☐	☐	☐
_____ Chemistry & Electrolytes	☐	☐	☐
_____ Thyroid	☐	☐	☐
_____ B12, Folate	☐	☐	☐
_____ VDRL	☐	☐	☐
_____ Hepatitis B	☐	☐	☐
_____ Drug Levels	☐	☐	☐
_____ Other _____	☐	☐	☐

3. X-rays obtained:	**Normal Range?**		
_____ Abdomen	☐	☐	☐
_____ Chest	☐	☐	☐
_____ CT Scan	☐	☐	☐
_____ MRI	☐	☐	☐
_____ Other_____	☐	☐	☐

4. Medical tests obtained:	**Normal Range?**		
_____ Echocardiogram	☐	☐	☐
_____ EEG	☐	☐	☐
_____ EKG	☐	☐	☐
_____ Sleep Study	☐	☐	☐
_____ Other_____	☐	☐	☐

5. Hearing sensitivity/ function meets average daily needs? ☐ ☐ ☐

	YES	NO	?[a]
6. Vision appears to meet average daily needs?	☐	☐	☐
7. Communication skills (verbal or alternative method) are adequate?	☐	☐	☐
8. Nutrition is adequate?	☐	☐	☐
9. Dental health is adequate?	☐	☐	☐
10. Findings suggest that medication changes be initiated?	☐	☐	☐

11. Portions of the following cognitive tests were administered: Scores:

WAIS-R	_____
Peabody (PPVT)	
Stanford Binet	_____
Other _____	_____

12. Testing was consistent with mental retardation in the following range (protocol filed in chart):
☐ Mild   ☐ Moderate ☐ Severe
☐ Profound ☐ Not applicable

	YES	NO	?[a]
13. Is there evidence of dementia?	☐	☐	☐

14. Psychological tests administered:
_____ Beck Depression Inventory
_____ Geriatric Depression Screen
_____ Other _____

[a]? indicates findings are inconclusive

Figure 1. (continued)

	YES	NO	?[a]
15. Mental status exam revealed: Depression?	☐	☐	☐
Other mental diagnoses? Specify: _____	☐	☐	☐
Other mental status problems? Specify: _____	☐	☐	☐
16. S/he understands and expresses emotions adequately?	☐	☐	☐
17. S/he is capable of learning how to express emotions?	☐	☐	☐
18. Her/his social support system is adequate (i.e. s/he has sufficient family members and/or friends who provide emotional support)?	☐	☐	☐
19. S/he has adequate opportunities (& assistance if needed) to: interact with family and friends?	☐	☐	☐
participate in group activities?	☐	☐	☐
pursue individual leisure activities?	☐	☐	☐
participate in religious activities?	☐	☐	☐
20. Current vocational or day programming is consistent with her/his needs and desires at this time?	☐	☐	☐
21. S/he has the capability to increase her/his independence with daily living skills (e.g. dressing, meal preparation, grooming)?	☐	☐	☐

22. S/he would benefit from the following supports to maintain or promote his/her optimal functioning?

	Continue	Obtain	Not Needed
Behavioral specialist	☐	☐	☐
Counseling/ psychotherapy	☐	☐	☐
Home health nurse	☐	☐	☐
Personal care assistance	☐	☐	☐
Occupational therapy	☐	☐	☐
Physical therapy	☐	☐	☐
Speech therapy	☐	☐	☐
Other _____	☐	☐	☐

23. Assessment indicates the need for further care or evaluation from the following specialists:

☐ Not applicable ☐ Neurologist
☐ Audiologist ☐ Ophthalmologist
☐ Cardiologist ☐ Primary care physician
☐ Dentist ☐ Psychiatrist
☐ ENT specialist ☐ Other

24. S/he would benefit from additional planning at this time in the following areas:

☐ Not applicable ☐ Residential
☐ Financial ☐ Safety
☐ Health Promotion ☐ Social
☐ Legal ☐ Vocational

_____   _____
Marilyn Adlin, M.D.   Gary B. Seltzer, Ph.D.
Geriatrician   Psychologist

[a]? indicates findings are inconclusive

are provided consultation about aging and developmental disabilities as are service providers (e.g., case managers, residential and employment providers). Written resources and consultation help individuals and their support system members to design preventative health interventions, to promote the early detection of health problems, and to assist individuals when they need to advocate for access to health services.

Access and Delivery Problems in Obtaining Health Care Services

The need for health care generally increases in importance as persons age. Individuals who survive to old age are more likely to have persistent, age-associated, chronic illnesses that require health care interventions (Lehmann, 1968). Access to age-appropriate health care has become a critical issue for older persons who have developmental disabilities because inclusion in an effective health care system may differentiate those who remain in the community from those who are institutionalized in nursing homes or ICFs-MR even when there are no differences in functional abilities and severity of the medical conditions between the two groups (Hayden & DePaepe, 1991; Lakin, Anderson, Hill, Bruininks, & Wright, 1991; Seltzer, Finaly, & Howell, 1988).

In the following section, we will discuss access and problems in delivering health care services to older persons with developmental disabilities. Barriers to service include lack of training for health care providers; financial constraints; personal characteristics of some people with developmental disabilities; past experiences of individuals with developmental disabilities, their family caregivers or service providers; and multiple care providers with differing viewpoints.

Institutional Barriers: Lack of Training for Health Care Providers

Health care is generally accessed in two ways: through an ongoing relationship with a primary care physician and through an awareness of a specific health care problem

that may require assessment and treatment from a tertiary care provider. Primary health care is thought to be practiced best when it is delivered in a comprehensive, coordinated, and continuous fashion (Granger, Seltzer, & Fishbein, 1987). Comprehensive care combines the delivery of preventive, curative, and palliative care and includes a coordinated response to the psychological, social, residential, recreational, and economic well-being of the whole individual (Haggerty, 1971). Primary care practitioners provide comprehensive care when they develop a mechanism for coordinating and integrating a treatment plan that includes multidisciplinary services (Seltzer, Granger, Wineberg, & LaCheen, 1984). Continuous care is provided when an individual's health care is monitored and modified according to changing needs. Continuous care is particularly important when the health care problems require long-term management rather than only short-term and cure-oriented treatment (Granger et al., 1987).

Unfortunately, several researchers have reported that primary care remains generally unavailable to older persons with developmental disabilities in their home communities (Buehler, Menolascino, & Stark, 1986; Crocker, 1992). Furthermore, as persons with developmental disabilities reach old age, they are more likely to need not only primary care, but also tertiary care that is delivered by an interdisciplinary group of practitioners. These practitioners should be familiar with age-associated disorders that then interact with the lifelong presence of impairments. Examples include musculoskeletal impairments (such as those seen in persons with cerebral palsy) or other pathological processes that occur with higher frequency in older age (such as Alzheimer disease). The delivery of this type of age-related care is rarely available, primarily because most health care professionals receive little, if any, education and training about the health care needs of adults with developmental disabilities (Crocker, 1989, 1992; Jaskulski, Metzler, & Zierman, 1990; Kuehn, Powers, Dolan, & Cohen, 1988). The delivery of age-appropriate health care services thus presents a major challenge for individuals with developmental disabilities, their families, professionals, and advocates.

Geriatrics and gerontology are the specialty disciplines that treat the health problems of older adults. The geriatric specialty developed out of the recognition that illness in older individuals often presents with vague, nonspecific, or seemingly trivial symptoms. Sometimes older individuals experience conditions in an altered manner (e.g., depression without sadness, or myocardial infarction without chest pain) or symptoms are tolerated and not reported to health practitioners (Kane, Ouslander, & Abrass, 1984). The specialty of geriatrics recognizes the need for careful interdisciplinary investigation of symptoms and functional status. Training in geriatrics has been available to physicians in Great Britain for over 40 years, but the medical establishment in the United States did not initiate training programs in geriatrics until the late 1970s (Adlin & Seltzer, in press), and very few older individuals with developmental disabilities are treated by trained geriatricians (Adlin, 1993).

Institutional Barriers:
Financial Constraints

Another barrier to obtaining assessment and other health care services for an older individual with developmental disabilities is health care costs. Almost all of the individuals seeking services at the Aging & Developmental Disabilities Clinic have Medicaid or Medicare. Few have been able to pay privately for health care costs or to obtain other health insurance. Reliance on these public benefits can preclude early detection of medical conditions. Carnes, Gunter-Hunt, Hess, and Drinka (1987), in a review of recommendations for preventive health interventions in the general elderly population, discovered marked discrepancies between recommendations and reimbursement policies. Medicare covered only 1 of 18 recommended preventive procedures. Other insurance, including Medicaid, covered these procedures either partially or fully, and their performance was at the discretion of the physician.

Personal Characteristics
as Barriers to Health Care

Health care for older persons with developmental disabilities is further complicated by the limited and sometimes unreliable verbal reports of some individuals. Frequently, people with developmental disabilities do not know how to monitor their own health needs or to interpret and report symptoms. In addition, Biersdorff (1991) suggests that a high percentage of people with developmental disabilities (25%) may exhibit elevated pain thresholds. Failure to react to pain decreases the chances of identifying a medical problem and obtaining appropriate medical intervention. Thus, access to appropriate health care may be dependent upon someone else recognizing that the person with developmental disabilities has a health problem.

Personal Characteristics:
Past Experiences

Problems might be identified by family members, friends, case managers, medical, residential or vocational providers. Knowledge of health care, belief systems, and past experiences with health care providers may influence how informants decide to assist a person with developmental disabilities to seek medical attention. For example, if a careprovider assumes a symptom to be a normal aspect of aging rather than an indication of a medical condition, the symptom may never come to the attention of a health practitioner. In another scenario, fear or concern that a health care assessment might result in recommendations that are difficult to implement or accept might make a family member or other care provider reluctant to seek assessment. Older parents of adults with developmental disabilities never forget that physicians often recommended institutionalization in years past. Faced again with the involvement of professionals, older parents are justifiably leery of assessments that may again suggest a temporary separation or permanent placement of their adult child out of their home. Feeling this way, they may not seek health care until they face a health care crisis, their own or that of their children.

Clinicians should be aware that an evaluation may be anxiety-provoking for older persons with developmental disabilities, in part because they may recall similar situations from the past that resulted in uncomfortable medical procedures or personal changes, such as residential transitions. Thus, cooperation with different parts of the assessment process may be variable, as illustrated in the following example. A consultant physician to a nursing home referred a 79-year-old woman with mild retardation to the Aging & Developmental Disabilities Clinic for a complete physical and medication review. He reported that over the past year she had become increasingly irritable, aggressive, and "noncompliant." However, during the evaluation, the woman reported that she was generally happy. Staff learned that, despite the fact that she had lived in the nursing home for the past 30 years and a residential transition was not being considered, the evaluation reminded her of activities that had occurred in the past, i.e., testing sessions that had resulted in transitions to new residences. She feared that the evaluation might mean that another transition was imminent, and reported that she at least "knew what to expect" at her current residence. It seemed that her fears biased her responses.

Personal Characteristics: Multiple Care Providers

When both families and service providers are involved in making decisions about the health care of a person with developmental disabilities, there can be conflicting opinions. Staff of the Aging & Developmental Disabilities Clinic have witnessed encounters in which families and service providers were polarized, both groups believing that they wanted what was "in the best interests" of the person with developmental disabilities. Yet, with limited verbal input from the person with developmental disabilities, the groups have held differing opinions as to what constituted "best interests." In one instance, it became clear that both the family members of a 79-year-old man with mental retardation and his service providers (residential, day program, and case management) cared a great deal

about this man and wanted to promote his well-being. He was essentially nonverbal and acquiescent, characteristics which allowed opposing viewpoints to develop between his family and service providers regarding appropriate day programming and nutrition. People close to him had become so embroiled in these issues that they had difficulty putting aside their viewpoints during subsequent consultation by clinic staff, rendering clinical opinions and recommendations ineffective.

Functional Assessment

The primary assessment approach used in the Aging & Developmental Disabilities Clinic is functional assessment. Function is defined most broadly as a person's ability to perform age and culturally appropriate tasks and to fulfill social roles. Factors that typically contribute to an analysis of function include relevant diagnoses; anatomical, physiological, psychological, and cognitive deficits and strengths; a delineation of available social roles; family and social support systems; and other environmental supports. The functional approach used in the clinic has been influenced by the disability models of Nagi (1975) and Wood (1975). Both models require that a functional analysis include the influence of personal, environmental, and social factors on task and role performance. The Nagi model generally includes the following constructs: pathology, impairment, functional limitations, and disability. A typical functional analysis determines the extent to which one's impairments are sufficient to explain one's behavioral limitations or functional limitations as assessed by a functional assessment instrument. If they are not, the clinician tries to determine the reasons for the discrepancy, be they personal characteristics such as motivation or environmental obstacles such as demands that exceed the person's capabilities. Some theorists define disability as the gap between a person's capabilities and the environmental demands (Nagi, 1979; Verbrugge, 1990). In this formulation, disability is inherently a relational construct, the meaning of which varies according to whether or not a functional balance is struck between individuals and their environments. For example, when functional limitations are unlikely to be affected by changing personal characteristics, such as when someone has Alzheimer disease, environmental supports such as assistive devices, environmental modifications, or personal care attendants may be needed to meet the person's daily needs. Individuals who use this analytic schema can recognize the potential for some persons to gain skills and maintain social roles while appreciating that for others, an appropriate treatment goal is to support the maintenance of personal abilities or to slow down their deterioration by implementing environmental changes.

This model has recently been adopted in the Institute on Medicine Report, *Disability in America* (Pope & Tarlov, 1991). The Report also stressed two additional classes of variables that may result in disablement. The first includes *risk factors associated with poor health* (e.g., biological, environmental, lifestyle, and behavioral). These variables can be used to anticipate and in some cases prevent excess or secondary disabilities. For example, if we knew more about the trajectory of effects on ambulation due to the aging process in persons with cerebral palsy, we might be able to prevent secondary disabilities such as falls or fractures by encouraging persons to use alternative means of ambulation, if ambulation problems were in fact found as one reached middle age.

The second class of variables described in the Institute of Medicine Report (Pope & Tarlov, 1991) broadens the scope of analysis of function. The Report suggested that recommendations go beyond considerations of how to help a person with activities of daily living skills and move to include *quality of life factors* (e.g., life satisfaction, standard of living, housing, and employment). The addition of these two classes of variables gives more weight to the investigation of an individual's residential and social circumstances, a topic that has had broad ideological appeal in the field of developmental disabilities since the deinstitutionalization movement in the early 1970s.

In order to implement the above described functional assessment schema, the staff of the Aging & Developmental Disabilities Clinic collaborated on a new version of a computerized functional assessment instrument called OT FACT. OT FACT has been under development for the past eight years (Smith, 1990a, 1990b) and is distributed by the American Occupational Therapy Association. OT FACT was designed as a generic functional assessment instrument that could be used to assess almost any type of person with an impairment that resulted in functional limitations. After reviewing the items in Version 1.0 of OT FACT, staff of the clinic contributed to the development of additional items for Version 2.0 of the software. Increased question detail was added to items that are particularly relevant to both a thorough geriatric assessment and the assessment of persons with developmental disabilities. A generic geriatric assessment team could use the new version of OT FACT to evaluate older persons with developmental disabilities.

OT FACT is a computer-tailored assessment instrument that provides specific definitions of each of the items being assessed. OT FACT allows the clinician to gather the diagnostic information with whatever procedures he or she typically uses. That is, there are no checklists or specific protocols that tell the user how to gather the information on functioning. In effect, OT FACT provides a blueprint for organizing the information gained and for scoring and summarizing statistically the individual's functional abilities within each of the domains assessed. OT FACT provides assessment data in an Environmental domain and in the four domains that are delineated in Figure 2.

Computerization allows for the synthesis of vast amounts of consumer data (there are 800 items in the program). The OT FACT functional assessment is structured in an outline format. The computer branches into greater detail when a deficit is identified and omits detailed questions when such questions are not needed (i.e., when there is either a total deficit or no deficit on an item). Where a deficit is noted, the computerized branching

Figure 2. Performance domains of OT FACT

Performance Domains of OT FACT

INTEGRATED ROLES OF PERFORMANCE
Performance, Integration, Balance, Integration Over Time

ACTIVITIES OF PERFORMANCE
Personal Care Activities
Occupational Role Related Actilties

INTEGRATED SKILLS OF PERFORMANCE

Motor Integration Skills:
Gross Motor, Fine Motor, Postural Control, Activity Tolerance

Sensory Motor Integration Skills:
Perceptual, Perceptual-Motor

Cognitive Integration Skills:
Problem Solving, Generalization of Learning, Sequencing, Concept Formation, Categorization
Intellectual Operations in Space, Learning Style Breadth

Social Integration Skills:
Peer Interactions, Authority/Subordinate Interactions, Family Interactions,
Pet and Animal Interactions

Psychological Integration Skills:
Coping, Stress Management, Time Use/Planning, Initiation and Termination,
Maintains Physical Integrity

UNDERLYING COMPONENTS OF PERFORMANCE

Neuromuscular Components:
Muscle Tone, Reflexes, Range of Motion, Strength, Endurance, Soft Tissue Integrity

Sensory Awareness Components:
Tactile, Proprioceptive, Kinesthetic, Ocular Control, Vestibular, Auditory, Olfactory, Gustatory

Cognitive Components:
Level of Arousal, Memory, Orientation, Attention Span, Recognition, Thought Processes, Flexibility

Social Components:
Group Interaction, Dyadic Interaction

Psychological Components:
Personal Responsibility/Motivation, Initiative, Termination of Action, Body Image, Value Identification,
Interest Identification, Goal Setting, Attending Behavior, Emotional Self-Regulation

expands the category and subsequently expands the sensitivity of the partial deficit scoring.

An additional benefit of computerization is the ability to efficiently score performance ability relative to different environmental demands. Thus, OT FACT can be completed and scored so that it measures a person's level of performance under different environmental conditions, for example, a person's functional performance without the assistance of environmental supports versus with needed environmental supports. The data summarized by OT FACT can help determine the type and intensity of services needed by an individual to optimize his or her functional abilities. These stored data can be retrieved in individual form for clinical purposes or in aggregate form to describe the population or to evaluate the effectiveness of the suggested treatment interventions.[2]

On average, our interdisciplinary team can complete an OT FACT assessment in about 30–40 minutes. Of course, collecting the consumer data that are entered takes a great deal longer. In our clinic, some of these data are gathered by a mailed questionnaire and a structured telephone interview before the clinic appointment. Most of the remaining information is gathered from assessments completed during the clinic visit. After the visit, the team completes OT FACT together by viewing and responding to items on a computer screen. Some items are more likely to be assessed by a single discipline while others may be transdisciplinary. Completing OT FACT as an interdisciplinary team gives members the opportunity to integrate information from other disciplines and tends to add to each discipline's formulation of the findings. An ancillary benefit of completing OT FACT in this manner relates to the training of disciplinary interns. Trainees who participate learn to appreciate the contribution of their disciplines' information relative to the integrated findings of the interdisciplinary team. In this way, trainees are given the opportunity to synthesize their findings with those of other disciplines and then to make recommendations that contribute to a comprehensive understanding of the consumer's needs.

Physical Health Assessment

Medical Assessment

The majority of older persons with developmental disabilities have health care needs that are similar to those of other older persons. As the severity of the impairments underlying the developmental disability increases, however, the need for specialized health care grows (Crocker, 1989). Guidelines that specify the frequency of various health screening procedures and examinations for the general elderly population are appropriate for most older people who have developmental disabilities as well. Some of the age-associated physical health problems of the elderly include sensory losses (e.g., vision and hearing), musculoskeletal changes (e.g., arthritis, osteoporosis, loss of muscle), cardiovascular problems (e.g., high cholesterol, hypertension, heart disease), and gastrointestinal problems (e.g., constipation).[3]

---

[2] Data from OT FACT can be used to formulate as recommendations the type and intensity of the needed services as required by the new classification system of the American Association on Mental Retardation (1992). Studying the extent to which these recommendations are implemented over time may provide feedback to the assessment team about the quality of the recommendations or the need for resources. Failure to implement the recommendations may occur because they were of poor quality or because resources within the individual's program were unavailable. In the latter case, the service provider receives information that documents the need for additional resources to implement a service plan. Implementation of the recommendations and failure to achieve projected outcomes may reflect the poor quality of the recommendations, a finding that might reflect on the competence of the interdisciplinary team. The above are but a few examples of the use of OT FACT as a program evaluation tool.

[3] Recently, a number of training guides and other types of literature have been written to describe what is known about normative and nonnormative age-related health changes experienced by older persons with developmental disabilities. Some examples are Gambert, Liebeskind, & Cameron, 1987; Hawkins et al., 1989; Kultgen, Rinck, & Pfannenstiel, 1987; Machemer & Overeynder, 1993; Zigman, Seltzer, & Silverman (chapter 5 this volume).

A thorough physical examination for persons with developmental disabilities is important because of the difficulties some individuals have in understanding and reporting symptoms. Prior to a consumer's visit to the Aging & Developmental Disabilities Clinic, records are reviewed to determine how complete a physical examination is warranted during the consultation assessment. For persons who have primary physicians, portions of the physical examination, blood studies, and other medical tests may be deferred. Epidemiological data on the trajectory of increases in physical impairments and functional losses among older persons with developmental disabilities are unavailable. We do know that certain disorders, usually those with an organic etiology, result in an accelerated aging process (Adlin & Seltzer, in press; Zigman, Seltzer, & Silverman, chapter 5 this volume). For example, persons with Down syndrome have been observed to experience physical changes and functional losses that are often associated with "premature aging" (Dalton, Seltzer, Adlin, & Wisniewski, in press; Zigman et al., chapter 5 this volume). For persons with Down syndrome or cerebral palsy, modification of general medical screening guidelines may be needed. Both of these conditions are associated with unique physiology and premature aging.

Down Syndrome and Aging

Individuals with Down syndrome are apt to need more frequent cognitive, adaptive behavior, and physiological testing compared to the general aging population, and they are likely to benefit from these at an earlier age. Zigman et al.'s (chapter 5 this volume) review of the literature on cognitive, adaptive behavior, and mental health changes in adults with Down syndrome provides ample data to support the need for vigilance in assessing these domains. Adults with Down syndrome experience age-associated disorders at an earlier age than would normatively be expected. One of the most frequently occurring of these is thyroid disease. In a community sample of 138 persons with Down syndrome being seen for routine health care, Friedman, Kastner, Pond, and O'Brien (1989)

found that 20% of the sample had previously unrecognized hypothyroidism. Estimates of hypothyroidism in the adult population of persons with Down syndrome vary, with some estimates as high as 40% (Dinani & Carpenter, 1990). For this reason, Lott and McCoy (1992) recommend that thyroid function tests be performed annually.

Persons with Down syndrome experience early degenerative changes in the spine so that by their mid 20s, they have disc space narrowing. They also have signs of osteoarthritic changes throughout the spine (Diamond, 1992). Clinicians and caregivers should be alert to symptoms indicating possible musculoskeletal or neurological changes. In particular, researchers have found problems with the cervical spine such that even slight trauma might result in weakness, paralysis, and sometimes death (Burke et al., 1985; Pueschel & Scola, 1987). It is not known whether cervical spine instability increases with age or is static. Prevention of trauma is important, and thus contact sports and sudden acceleration or deceleration place adults with Down syndrome at risk for serious injury. Diamond (1992) suggests that X rays should be taken about every five years to evaluate progressive changes.

Obstructive sleep apnea has been reported in both children and adults with Down syndrome (Pueschel, 1992). Sleep apnea is related to physiological characteristics such as generalized hypotonia (deficient tension or tone), which can result in airway collapse, tongue hypotonia, and enlargement of the adenoids and tonsils caused by frequent infections. In the general population, the likelihood of sleep apnea increases with age (Ancoli-Israel, Kripke, & Mason, 1987). Thus older persons with Down syndrome are at greater risk of developing this condition by virtue of both their special physiological characteristics and their premature aging (Adlin, 1993). Consequences of sleep apnea include excessive daytime sedation, behavioral disturbances, failure to thrive, declining functional skills, and disrupted sleep patterns. Clinic staff often recommend that sleep studies be performed when investigating a diagnosis of Alzheimer disease in an older adult with Down syndrome.

The greatest dental problem faced by the adult with Down syndrome is periodontal disease (Sterling, 1992). Sterling reports that the incidence of severe, destructive periodontal disease in persons with Down syndrome has been reported to be as high as 96%. Periodontal disease is clearly in evidence by the age of 30. Unfortunately, standard treatments of this problem have generally not been successful in reversing the pathological process, a finding that suggests that periodontal disease goes beyond the issue of dental hygiene. Immunologic deficiencies in persons with Down syndrome are thought to be related to the increased prevalence and severity of this problem (Hann, Deacon, & London, 1979; Wittingham, Pitt, Sharma, & MacKay, 1977). Because the severity of periodontal problems varies markedly among adults with Down syndrome, it is recommended that an aggressive, preventive, dental health program be instituted for this population (Sterling, 1992). Prevention is particularly important because the oral structures in persons with Down syndrome generally predict a poor response to dental prostheses.

Cerebral Palsy and Aging

Very little is known about the effect of aging on the health care needs of persons with cerebral palsy (Brown, Bontempo, & Turk, 1991). Only anecdotal information is available about the medical, psychological, social, and functional issues related to adulthood and aging in persons with cerebral palsy (Overeynder, Turk, Dalton, & Janicki, 1992). In one of the few studies to investigate the health status of adults with cerebral palsy, Bax, Smyth, and Thomas (1988) reported that the health of their subjects was poor, with problems such as contractures of the lower and upper joints evident among the majority of subjects. They found that although over half of their sample had health problems that warranted intervention, less than a third were receiving any type of health care services.

The variability among persons with cerebral palsy is such that it is difficult to determine the trajectory of age-related changes in this group. Persons with cerebral palsy who do not have cognitive and motor problems have a very different aging process than that of persons with cerebral palsy and comorbid conditions such as severe mental retardation, severe spastic quadriplegia, and epilepsy.

The anecdotal reports of persons with cerebral palsy belie the description of cerebral palsy as a neurological condition that is *nonprogressive*. Many middle aged and older persons with cerebral palsy are experiencing an atypical aging process that may occur as a result of the interactions between their normative age-associated changes and their preexisting impairments. The outcome of these interactions increases the likelihood that they will experience a decline in functional performance, physiological changes, pain, and restrictions in their daily social and emotional activities at an earlier age than their age peers without cerebral palsy. On the other hand, cerebral palsy is not a progressive disorder in the same way as are other neurological disorders such as multiple sclerosis or Parkinson disease. The lesion of the brain responsible for the cerebral palsy remains unchanged. Although professionals in the field have yet to coin a word that describes this interactive process between the preexisting condition of cerebral palsy and age-associated changes, the common assertion that cerebral palsy is a non-progressive disorder may be misleading to professionals and consumers alike.

June Kailes (1992) commented that *"When I, a person with CP, would speak my concerns to friends who were medical professionals, I felt that my descriptions sounded vague and slightly bizarre. When I explained I'm not walking as fast, my balance is not as good, I have more spasticity and many more aches and pains all I received were blank looks. I decided to initiate my own informal survey of friends and colleagues with disabilities. My results confirmed that I was not alone."* (p. 75)

Ambulation and balance seem to decline at an earlier age in persons with cerebral palsy than in the general population (Pimm, 1992).

Changes in the vestibular system make it difficult to retain balance as people age, and persons with cerebral palsy, whose vestibular system may become impaired sooner than age peers, are at risk for falls. A further complication of aging in persons with cerebral palsy is deconditioning after a hip fracture or some other event that reduces the amount of daily activities. This occurs because oftentimes persons with cerebral palsy have difficulty resuming their ordinary activities and level of functioning after these events (Sherk, Pasquariello, & Doherty, 1983). Compression fractures of the spine may also cause immobility and can be very painful. During this time there is muscle strength loss. The following statement made by a 44-year-old woman with cerebral palsy at a recent conference illustrates the above noted complications:

"I have discovered that I am a new kind of statistic. I know several other women with cerebral palsy who are about my age who have also broken their hips and who now need to use a wheelchair. All my life, I have been told to equate independence with ambulation and although I realize the bias in this message, I still feel robbed, overly dependent, and in physical and emotional pain."

There are also age-related changes in joint function and bone density. A contributing factor for hip and other fractures is osteoporosis. One risk factor is immobility. Older persons with cerebral palsy who have been inactive may not have developed adequate bone density and mass at a younger age and are therefore likely to experience an accelerated loss of bone density and mass as they age. Additionally, there is evidence that medications used to treat seizure disorders may increase the likelihood that adults with cerebral palsy will experience decrements in their bone mineral density (Root et al., 1992). The coexistence of seizure disorders and cerebral palsy is fairly high (Hauser & Hesdorffer, 1990), and persons with both these disorders are at substantially greater risk for osteoporosis. This condition is further complicated by the problem of hip dislocation or subluxation (Pritchett, 1983; Trainer, Bowser, & Dahm, 1986). Degenerative joint disease, osteoporosis, and hip fractures are the most prevalent conditions that result in immobility among the elderly (Kane, Ouslander, & Abrass, 1984). Again, persons with cerebral palsy are at increased risk for falls and fractures at an earlier age than their contemporaries, events that often lead to a decrements in mobility (Turk & Machemer, 1993).

Persons with cerebral palsy also appear to have increased difficulty in swallowing as they age and greater chances of aspiration. Ferrang, Johnson, and Ferrara (1992) found that over half of the adults with cerebral palsy they interviewed reported feeding problems. Persons seen in the clinic report that they have less control of their tongue than in the past, and thus food may slide uncontrollably down the throat. The person with swallowing problems takes more time to eat and may even need assistance. These needs, particularly when resisted, may impact negatively on the psychological, nutritional, and functional status of older persons with cerebral palsy.

Finally, it is not uncommon for adults with cerebral palsy to have an increased number of urinary tract infections, incontinence, and urinary retention. The bladder can become more spastic with age, often resulting in a hyperreflexic bladder that is likely to contract more frequently, a common cause of incontinence in older persons (Mayo, 1992). These urological problems are more common in persons with cerebral palsy and happen at a younger age than in the general population. The presence of these problems may limit a person's willingness to engage in social activities or even remain employed.

Sensory Losses: Audiologic and Vision Assessment

Hearing and visual impairments are two of the most prevalent, age-associated changes for aging adults. Yet, they may be significantly underdiagnosed among older people with developmental disabilities. If they are diagnosed, their consequences may not be recognized by family and care providers, and this population may not receive the state-of-the-art assistance necessary to remediate the problems. If not addressed, symptoms can lead to misdiagnosis (e.g., behavioral problems or dementia). These impairments can also result in social withdrawal, decreases in functional abilities, and depression. Adults with developmental disabilities, especially mental retardation, may rely on auditory or visual cues to help them function in their day-to-day lives. When senses become impaired and familiar cues are no longer available, a person's functional abilities in other areas can be affected.

Hearing. Prevalence studies indicate that 25–40% of individuals over 65 years of age exhibit some degree of hearing loss (Bess, Lichtenstein, & Logar, 1991). Individuals with developmental disabilities may be more likely to develop hearing loss than the general population. Hearing loss can be associated with various genetic and metabolic conditions that result in developmental disabilities (e.g., Down syndrome) (Northern & Downs, 1991). Personal characteristics, such as limited communication abilities, and a sheltered life-style for some people with developmental disabilities can contribute to "hiding" the hearing loss. In addition, the knowledge and technical skills that are now available in this area were not available when the current generation of older adults was younger. Accordingly, many aging adults with developmental disabilities may not yet be identified as having hearing loss. More than half of the consumers who have been evaluated at the Aging & Developmental Disabilities Clinic have been assessed as having significant hearing losses. For many of these individuals, family and local service providers had not suspected hearing loss.

All consumers who are evaluated at the Aging & Developmental Disabilities Clinic receive audiologic testing. Indications of hearing function are obtained by direct and indirect measurements. Direct measurements include hearing screenings and tympanometric procedures. Tympanometric procedures provide an indication of middle-ear dysfunction. Indirect measurements include interviews with consumers and caregivers. If concerns are noted, a referral is made for further audiological assessment or medical attention. Some types of hearing loss can be corrected or improved by medical or surgical intervention. Other types of loss can be helped by hearing instruments, although, as with the population in general, it may not be easy for the person who needs a hearing aid to adapt to it. A third category of loss cannot be helped by either medical intervention or hearing instruments; however, there are strategies for minimizing hearing difficulties that can be used to help the person retain social contact.

Vision. With aging, a person's abilities are sometimes compromised due to a decrease in vision. Close to 95% of people over the age of 65 who participated in the 1984 National Health Interview Survey wore glasses or reported that they needed corrective lenses to improve their visual acuity (Kovar, 1986). But, only 45% of people over the age of 85 reported that their glasses corrected all of their visual problems. Decreased vision may be related to the normal aging process or to pathology. Frequently, physiological changes that develop as people age, in tandem with environmental and disease factors, cause impairment in vision (Heath, 1992).

It is possible that a greater number of people with developmental disabilities have uncorrected visual impairments than the general population. Much has been written about the assessment of multihandicapped children who have visual impairments, but a search of a comprehensive, low-vision bibliographic database of about 5,000 references (*Low Vision—The Reference,* Goodrich & Jose, 1993) was 100% negative for articles on serving older people with developmental disabilities who have low vision.

The geriatrician conducts a limited vision screening during evaluations at the Aging & Developmental Disabilities Clinic. When appropriate, referrals are made to conventional eye-care providers (i.e., ophthalmologists and optometrists) who are able to detect and treat refractive errors and disease without subjective input from the patient. However, it is not always possible to determine how well individuals can see, especially when they are unable to respond to a standard eye chart consisting of letters, numbers, or words. Determining how well or poorly non-responding persons use their functional vision and what aids will help remediate their problems requires a specialized assessment. Frequently clinic staff make referrals to a low-vision rehabilitation specialist, who assesses and instructs people with low vision in how to maintain or regain independence in a variety of environments.

Medication Review

As we age, the therapeutic window in which drug therapy is effective is likely to decrease because of the physiological changes that accompany normal aging, changes that affect the absorption, distribution, and metabolism of medication. One outcome of these changes is the increased likelihood that medications will be toxic, causing adverse reactions. These iatrogenic reactions to medication are estimated to result in as many as 20% of hospital admissions for older persons (McGinnis, 1988). Contributing to this phenomenon is the fact that the elderly tend to have several specialty physicians, a consequence of which is taking multiple medications. Symptoms related to adverse drug interactions are often non-specific. In some cases, another medication is prescribed to treat these symptoms. This cascade of medication usage leads to polypharmacy, a problem that, according to our observations, may be even more prevalent among older persons with developmental disabilities than in the general older population.

There are a number of reasons why this group is at risk for polypharmacy. First, persons with a known organic etiology for their developmental disabilities may be more sensitive to medication usage at an earlier age. This may be a problem for persons with Down syndrome particularly. Because of their premature aging process, they may have a greater likelihood of experiencing adverse reactions to medications at an earlier age than expected in the general population. Second, persons with developmental disabilities may not be able to accurately describe their symptoms; thus physicians might have to experiment with different medications and medication dosages until something seems to work. This process is further complicated by the need for informants, who can only be reporting vicariously on medication effects.

Adlin (1993) notes that older persons with developmental disabilities are at very high risk because of the types of drugs that are prescribed. One type of medication with side effects that is often prescribed for persons with developmental disabilities for an indefinite amount of time is psychotropic medication. Prevalence estimates of use among samples in community residential facilities run as high as 36% (Hill, Balow, & Bruininks, 1985). The estimated prevalence of use of all types of psychoactive medications by those who live in the community runs from 36% to 48% (Anderson & Polister, 1993; Intagliata & Rinck, 1985). In one of the only studies to examine medication use in older persons with developmental disabilities, Anderson and Polister (1993) found a national prevalence rate of 27% for the use of psychotropic medications, excluding seizure medications, and a rate of 19% for the use of antipsychotic medications. Furthermore, they found that there was a poor correspondence between the type of psychoactive medications being prescribed and the diagnosis of the recipient. In short, older persons with developmental disabilities are at great risk for experiencing the adverse effects of overmedication, inappropriately prescribed medications, and medication interactions. Therefore, the clinic staff routinely review medications and assess their efficacy with individuals, families, and primary care physicians.

Dental Care

Barriers to dental care for older individuals parallel those for general health care. DeBiase (1991) identifies the following barriers for elderly persons: financial cost, physical inaccessibility of services, lack of dental awareness, misconceptions, fear of treatment, illness, and neglect of this area by caregivers. She distinguishes lack of dental awareness and misconceptions as the most disconcerting of the barriers because they may result in ageist behavior. For example, older people may not seek the dental services they need because they incorrectly believe that tooth loss or poor oral health are natural consequences of growing older.

Figure 3. Patient Discharge Dental Summary

Waisman Center on Mental Retardation and Human Development
Aging & Developmental Disabilities Clinic

Patient Discharge Dental Summary

Patient Name _____ Age _____

Dentist Name _____ Date _____

I. General Condition of Teeth

Missing _____

Migration _____

Caries: Crown _____

Root _____

Recurrent (Forming around old fillings) _____

Decay: Broken _____

Crown erosion _____

Root erosion _____

Stains _____

Loose or displaced _____

Other _____

	YES	NO
II. Condition of Soft Tissue Showing Presence of the Following:		
Dental plaque	☐	☐
Calculus (tartar)	☐	☐
Gingivitis or lower gingiva	☐	☐
Periodontal pockets	☐	☐
Gums bleed when brushed	☐	☐
Red, swollen, or tender gums	☐	☐
Pus between teeth and gums	☐	☐
Persistent bad taste	☐	☐
Pyorrhea (periodontal disease)	☐	☐
Gums have pulled away from teeth	☐	☐

Gingival tissue (gums)
☐ Normal ☐ Inflamed ☐ Hypertrophied

III. Prosthetic Condition

	YES	NO
Needs dental prosthesis	☐	☐
Uses dental prosthesis	☐	☐
Takes out dentures daily	☐	☐

Condition of dentures
☐ Good ☐ Fair ☐ Poor

	YES	NO
IV. Other		
Occlusive problems	☐	☐
Temporomandibular joint problems	☐	☐
Clenching or grinding the teeth (bruxism)	☐	☐

Saliva (dry mouth) ☐ Normal ☐ Abnormal

Lips ☐ Normal ☐ Abnormal

Tongue ☐ Normal ☐ Abnormal

Oral hygiene ☐ Good ☐ Fair ☐ Poor

Cooperation ☐ Good ☐ Fair ☐ Poor

Diet ☐ Good ☐ Fair ☐ Poor

V. Oral Physiological Condition

Tasting ☐ Good ☐ Fair ☐ Poor

Chewing ☐ Good ☐ Fair ☐ Poor

Swallowing ☐ Good ☐ Fair ☐ Poor

Speaking ☐ Good ☐ Fair ☐ Poor

Perceiving pain ☐ Good ☐ Fair ☐ Poor

Appearance ☐ Good ☐ Fair ☐ Poor

Family members and service providers may be more motivated to promote dental care once they learn that tooth loss is *not* a part of the natural aging process and that a person who is edentulous will continue to require dental care in order to maintain the health of the soft tissues. Tooth loss is caused by extensive caries or periodontal disease. The elderly are a high risk group for root caries. A common characteristic of those developing root caries (Banting, 1991) and periodontal disease (Suzuki, Niessen, & Fedele, 1991) is reduced ability or interest in maintaining oral hygiene. People with developmental disabilities frequently have had lifelong problems in maintaining oral hygiene. Regular dental care is a vital component in maintaining health in later life when people experience the additional impacts of medication, illness, and further disability resulting from such conditions as arthritis or strokes.

Over 400 medications have been identified as having oral side effects (Niessen & Jones, 1991). In addition, medical conditions that generally affect older people frequently alter the health of the oral cavity (DeBiase, 1991). Disorders of the oral cavity are often found to be a major contributor to poor eating habits in the elderly. Older persons who have experienced impairments in the functioning of their dominant hands related to a stroke, those with visual problems, and those with dementia may have difficulty maintaining good oral hygiene with consequent deleterious effects on their dental health (Niessen & Jones, 1986).

Because so few resources exist to evaluate oral health, we have included a Dental Summary, developed for use in the Aging & Developmental Disabilities Clinic by Fernando Saenz-Forero, faculty of the Dental School, University of Costa Rica (see Figure 3). This tool helps dental specialists summarize the condition of the patient's teeth, soft tissue, prosthetic devices, oral physiology, and related characteristics and conditions (e.g., occlusive problems, oral hygiene, diet, and cooperation). It may also serve as a checklist of concerns for caregivers to use when seeking dental care.

Assessment of Cognitive Functioning

Almost half of the referrals made to the clinic ask for an evaluation of a person's cognitive status. Most often, the specific concern is dementia. The diagnosis of dementia is a clinical diagnosis in that there are no specific laboratory or neuropsychological tests that can confirm or deny with certainty the diagnosis of dementia (National Institutes of Health, 1987). Only on autopsy can that occur, and even then there is such diversity among the diseases that cause dementia that about 20% of the cases of dementia in persons under the age of 60 are categorized as unclassified dementia (Heston & White, 1983).

Almost every person referred to the clinic with Down syndrome is suspected by someone as having dementia. Service providers and families have become aware that persons with Down syndrome have an accelerated aging process, one consequence of which may be an early onset of Alzheimer disease. The differential diagnosis of dementia in persons with Down syndrome is complicated by the high prevalence of depression, sensory loss, hypothyroidism, and sleep apnea.

The use of neuropsychological tests are among the most critical clinical tools for diagnosing dementia. The presence of preexisting baseline cognitive data or the use of prospective reexaminations of cognitive function greatly increases the clinician's confidence when making a diagnosis of dementia. Unfortunately, many persons with Down syndrome who are age 45 or older (the age at which symptoms of Alzheimer disease typically begin to appear [Dalton & Wisniewski, 1990]) have not had previous cognitive testing, and if they have, the specific test scores needed for comparison of past and present performance are unavailable. Because many persons with Down syndrome show "floor effects" when tested with a standardized instrument, the test scores often do not show decrements in cognitive functioning over time. That is, persons in the moderate or lower ranges of mental retardation score with a zero on many items or subtests, thereby making their scores indistinguishable from one testing period to another (Dalton et al., in press). Sometimes the presence of the previous test protocol or the use of raw rather than scaled scores adds comparative information. It is for the purpose of these prospective analyses that we administer the WAIS-R or encourage others to administer this standardized intelligence test or some other intelligence test when an individual has the potential to show variability on the test.

Mental status exams and other global cognitive measures are not sensitive measures of the early stages of dementia in this population. Another approach for assessing early stage dementia is therefore needed. In almost all cases of dementia, there are significant declines of memory and of one or more other intellectual functions such as judgment, abstract thought, or orientation. A structured interview with or a questionnaire completed by a parent or other caregiver who has observed specific changes in behavior and intellectual functioning is the best way to identify changes in judgment, abstract thought, and orientation outside of the clinic visit. The most useful clinical tool we have found to measure memory, particularly secondary memory, is the Fuld Object Memory Test (Fuld, 1977). This test uses common objects such as a ball, a nail, and a finger ring. The test was designed to assess storage, retrieval, and retention in an older population. It has been normed for impaired and unimpaired individuals. It is designed to minimize the effects of hearing and vision impairments common in adults with Down syndrome. The test can be modified to accommodate different cognitive abilities by changing the number of items, determining how many trials it takes to recall the items, and by varying the length of the period of distraction in which the person can remember and identify common objects.

Some additional cognitive areas are assessed and then scored on OT FACT. One cluster of cognitive skills, cognitive integration skills, includes the person's ability to comprehend, synthesize, and evaluate environmental information and then incorporate it into goal-directed behavior. Some other functions assessed are problem solving abilities, generalization of learning, sequencing, concept formation, categorization, and intellectual operations in space. Clinic staff also evaluate the person's learning style to determine whether he or she can use a variety of methods and media to learn new information. The latter area is particularly important in the assessment of dementia and for giving feedback to all concerned about what seem to be the best modalities to use when maintaining or slowing down deterioration of skills.

Lastly, some of the more fundamental mental status functions are assessed, including arousal, memory function, orientation, attention span, recognition of familiar objects, thought processes (form and content), and cognitive flexibility. These cognitive components are usually the prerequisite abilities for the acquisition of more complex cognitive tasks.

Psychological Health

A thorough review of the literature related to the mental health of older persons with developmental disabilities can be found in Zigman et al., chapter 5 in this volume. Therefore, we will focus mainly on the primary assessment domains included in OT FACT and then highlight two of the psychological disorders commonly present among individuals referred to the clinic.

An individual's coping and stress management are investigated. Clinic staff assess the extent to which an individual responds to environmental demands in a personally and socially satisfying manner. Challenging behaviors are examined and coded on OT FACT as skill competencies. For example, rather than asking if someone is self abusive on OT FACT, the examiner asks whether the individual can maintain physical integrity by acting in ways that will not cause physical harm to his or her own body. Other psychological components that are assessed include the person's initiative, body image, value identification, goal setting, and emotional self-regulation.

Depression is the most frequently occurring psychiatric disorder seen in the clinic. The lifetime expectancy of unipolar depression in the general population is approximately 20% for women and 10% for men (Kaplan & Sadock, 1988). As many as 10% of all elderly people are significantly depressed (Gurland, 1976). However, it is particularly difficult to diagnose depression in older people with developmental disabilities. Family members and care providers frequently attribute symptoms of depression to other causes (e.g., character traits, dementia, the "aging process") and often do not recognize that depression can be readily treated and reversed.

Assessment of depression is an integral part of almost every consultation evaluation in the Aging & Developmental Disabilities Clinic. This is important because so many consumers have an undetected depression and because it helps in making a differential diagnosis with dementia. Interviews with consumers, collateral information, and scores from tools such as the Geriatric Depression Screen (Yeasavage, Brink, & Rose, 1983) all assist in the mental health assessment.

One of the most dramatic changes in functional ability experienced by a consumer of the clinic followed the diagnosis and treatment of depression. A 62-year-old woman with mental retardation and a seizure disorder was referred to the clinic because of a drastic decline in her functional abilities subsequent to an illness. At the time of her clinic evaluation, she was residing in a nursing home, was wheelchair dependent, unable to transfer independently to and from the wheelchair, and unable to feed herself. Just several months earlier she had lived in a small group home with other older adults, independently performed all activities of daily living, and enjoyed participating in community activities. At the clinic she was given a thorough physical, neurologic, and psychological assessment. After finding no evidence for an organic etiology to account for the severity of her functional losses and deconditioned state, the geriatrician prescribed an antidepressant medication and physical therapy (which previously had been discontinued). She responded well to both and later was discharged from the nursing home to the same small group home where she regained her former lifestyle.

This woman's sister and the personnel in the service system had assumed that her decline was physiological and were determined to have her remain in the nursing home. They wondered why it was necessary to push someone at her age. They did not appreciate the impact that their hopelessness had on her psychological state. In part her depression was reflective of their perception of her as hopelessly ill and helpless.

One disorder that clinic staff have observed is in need of more attention is obsessive-compulsive disorder, particularly as it presents among middle-aged and older persons with Down syndrome. Clinic staff have been surprised by the number of persons referred for behavioral decline and sometimes aggressive behavior who have many of the symptoms of this disorder. At a younger age, individuals may manifest less severe behavioral symptoms of this disorder and are often described as stubborn or as having a rigid type of response pattern. By the time some of these individuals are seen in the clinic, however, they have become considerably more dysfunctional than "stubborn" or "rigid" implies.

Obsessive thoughts are harder to elicit than compulsive behaviors because of language impairments in this group; however clinic staff have had individuals tell them that they have recurrent thoughts or ideas that bother them and frequently lead to repetitive acts. Generally, compulsions are more obvious, diagnostically. Individuals seem to engage in repetitive and intentional behaviors in order to cope with their anxiety. When these acts are interrupted, the person may become quite upset, anxious, and sometimes physically aggressive. In addition, the person's daily routine is punctuated by certain rituals that tend to be excessively performed and are time-consuming. Sometimes these rituals interfere with the person's occupation or social functioning and reduce the person's opportunities to learn new skills and even perform those which he or she is capable of performing.

Clinic staff have recommended that this disorder, once recognized, be treated behaviorally by gradually redirecting the person and supporting his or her ability to successfully engage in other activities. They have also recommended the short-term use of medication when the behavior has placed a person at risk for a more restrictive residential placement. Lastly, clinic staff have recommended the use of augmentative communication to help the individuals express the thoughts that are making them anxious and leading to repetitive behaviors.

Assessment of Social/ Emotional Functioning

Examination of a consumer's affect, behavior, social interactions, work performance, involvement in day programming, leisure, and religious activities will indicate if a consumer needs assistance regarding expression and coping with his or her feelings and social involvement. This area of functioning is assessed in the clinic through direct observation and interaction with the individual and through the verbal and written reports of people who interact with the consumer on a regular basis (e.g., family members and residential, vocational, and case management providers). Visits to the consumer's home and vocational setting are sometimes conducted to supplement data gathered in the clinic and by written report. The following topics represent salient social/emotional issues for the consumers who have been evaluated in the clinic: communication skills, expression of emotion, and sexuality.

Communication Skills

As clinic staff interact with the consumer throughout the day of evaluation, they assess his or her communication skills with the following questions in mind. Does the person have the ability to adequately communicate her or his wants and needs? If not, would he or she be able to learn and utilize an alternative method? If the consumer has an alternative method, is she or he skilled in using that method and are there other people who will

communicate with her or him in this manner? The following vignette will illustrate the importance of assessment in this area.

A 31-year-old man with Down syndrome was referred to the clinic because residential staff feared that he was developing dementia. They reported that he was forgetful, at times disoriented, and that his behaviors were obsessive. They were particularly concerned about increasingly aggressive behavior. During the course of the evaluation, it became clear that the man did not have a dementia, but in fact he seemed to want more control over his life. The man had great difficulty with expressive language. Although he tried to answer questions, he withdrew when others found it difficult to understand him. Clinic staff learned that a communication book had been given to him, but that it did not seem to be helpful. A communication consultation was arranged. One of the findings from the consultation was that his communication booklet was actually a copy of a book that had been designed for someone else. In order for him to use such a tool effectively, it needed to be tailored with pictures and words appropriate to his life. Staff who worked with him daily came to realize how frustrated he was with his lack episodes decreased following modification of his communication booklet and with increased encouragement and support regarding expressive communication from the staff who worked with him daily. This case represents one of many that have been seen at the clinic where a person with Down syndrome is referred because of a suspected dementia and in fact has a reversible type of problem.

Expression of Emotion

It is not unusual for individuals with developmental disabilities to verbalize that everything is fine and that they are happy when their affect and behavior indicate just the opposite. And it is not unusual for their family members or care providers to accept their verbalizations at face value and then to be perplexed by inconsistent behavior. Therefore, when clinic staff work with this population, they attend to their affect and behavior and attempt to learn sufficient details about their lives to identify possible sources of emotional distress.

Observations of older persons with developmental disabilities who come to the clinic indicate that the ability to learn how to express emotions knows no age limit. Many older people with developmental disabilities may have always had the ability, but the knowledge and assistance to help them develop this ability in earlier years was lacking. This inability will impact their lives lifelong, unless they are helped to learn these skills. A 79-year-old woman, who resided in a nursing home, was becoming increasingly irritable, aggressive, and "noncompliant." Clinical assessment indicated that the woman's skills in understanding and managing her emotions were much less developed than might be expected given her strong cognitive abilities. Thus, she had the intellectual capability to learn to recognize and deal with her emotions, but she needed assistance in this area. Nursing home staff were provided with information on areas of concern to her as well as recommendations for how to help her communicate her feelings. These recommendations included tactics such as helping her to identify emotions by describing and labeling feelings, encouraging her to share her feelings with staff verbally, reinforcing her discussing her concerns rather than her incidents of inappropriate behavior, and initiating discussions with her about aging issues that would be expected to trouble her (e.g., her health and capabilities, the declining health of family members, her feelings about death, etc.).

One area of emotion that deserves particular attention is that of grief and bereavement. Little is known about how people with developmental disabilities conceptualize or interpret their emotions about death. However, their reactions are very similar to those of the general population (Wadsworth & Harper, 1991). There is a tendency in our culture to shy away from the subject of death and dying. Therefore, many families and service providers are unfamiliar with characteristics of grieving that are normative. The consequences of ignoring feelings of grief and bereavement in older persons with developmental disabilities are frequently a diminished quality of life and the functional decline associated with depression (Averill & Wisocki, 1981).

Close family members of a 45-year-old woman with Down syndrome denied that she was grieving the death of her mother; they reported that she had not been emotionally close to her mother. Yet, she refused to visit her sister's house where her mother had been living, and she displayed increased anxiety and agitation. During the clinic evaluation, the woman responded strongly to questions related to her mother and cried readily when she talked about her. Clinic staff, therefore, discussed the need for grief counseling with the family.

Family members and service providers may also want to "protect" the person with developmental disabilities from the subject of death. One adult family home provider for a 61-year-old woman with mental retardation did not plan to tell her about the death of her mother. "I want her to have only happy days," he indicated. He assumed that she would not note the cessation of visits to her mother or conversations about her mother with care providers.

During the consultation evaluation, clinic staff investigate whether a consumer has experienced the death of a loved one or some other loss, the meaning of this loss, what coping skills she or he uses, and what assistance she or he could use. Some guidance for staff and family who are assisting the person with developmental disabilities can be inferred from the individual's developmental stage (Seltzer, 1989). Persons at a high stage of cognitive development, who can reason abstractly, understand that death is irreversible, universal, and inevitable (Seltzer, 1989). Not understanding these maxims about death may lead to erroneous thoughts about what has happened to a loved one who has died. Another predictor of understanding the meaning of death is age. Lipe-Goodson and Goebel (1983) studied whether older persons with developmental disabilities understand the concept of death better than younger persons with developmental disabilities. Controlling for IQ, they found that a larger percentage of older adults understood the concept of death than did younger adults.

Older persons with developmental disabilities might benefit from grief therapy that is adapted to meet their cognitive and emotional needs. Although it is not always clear how best to assist individuals who are coping with loss, they will need permission and support to express their emotions. Art therapy is likely to be very helpful for people who lack verbal abilities or whose verbal skills are limited. Hospice care organizations are also excellent resources. Hospice care agencies vary greatly in their organizational structure and mission. Some may be able to counsel directly with individuals who are grieving and may utilize a variety of therapeutic techniques. Others may provide consultation to care providers or make available a list of private practitioners or agencies who assist in the area of grief and bereavement.

Sexuality

Sexually motivated behavior continues throughout the life span as do problems related to sexuality. Most of the current cohort of older adults with developmental disabilities have not had the opportunity to engage in open discussions regarding sexuality or to attend health or sex education classes and therefore may be unclear about issues of appropriate sexual expression. This has implications for both their behavior and their safety.

People with developmental disabilities seem to progress through the same sexual developmental stages as do people without disabilities (Eaton & Burdz, 1984); however, progress through these stages is at a slower pace. This may mean that their experiences are substantially different from their age peers without disabilities. Patterson (1991) reports that there is very little research about the sexual expression of people with disabilities, only a small amount of research that describes sexual behaviors of people with disabilities, and almost no literature on differences of sexual behavior based on levels of handi-

cap. This means that care providers are relying on their personal experiences and beliefs to help them provide service in this area.

Clinic staff have evaluated a range of sexual problems including the expression of appropriate behaviors in inappropriate settings, inappropriate behaviors, lack of intimacy in couples, and sexual abuse. Cases of sexual abuse included incidents in which people with developmental disabilities were perpetrators and others in which they had been victims. Assessment of sexuality problems identifies the problem, its severity, and environmental factors that support its continuation. Recommendations are made to families and local service providers that will foster change and provide support for the individual regarding sexuality. Some situations require consultation from a sex therapist or psychotherapist. In most situations, it is recommended that consumers receive education regarding sexuality.

For example, Heighway, Kidd-Webster, and Shaw (1990) report, "People with developmental disabilities have unique learning needs in many aspects of their lives—sexuality is no exception" (p. 5). Therefore, "Individualized guidance and education for promoting positive sexuality and the prevention of sexual abuse is essential" (p. 5). These authors developed a sexuality training program that clinic staff frequently recommend to clients, their families, and service providers. The program was developed after the authors learned that issues of sexual abuse were interconnected with other issues such as self-esteem, assertiveness, understanding of sexuality, opportunities to develop relationships, and the attitudes and actions of family, friends, and service providers. They developed a model, Skills Training for Assertiveness, Relationship-Building and Sexual Awareness (STARS), that focuses on four areas in which competencies are developed: understanding relationships, social interaction, sexual awareness, and assertiveness.

Assessment of Environmental Supports

Employment, Retirement, Leisure

Because many individuals spend significant portions of their days in work-related or day program activities, performance in these settings is assessed. Increases or decreases in work productivity, changes in interaction with peers, attendance, stamina, and comparing behavior at work or day programs with behavior in other settings provides information about a possible functional problem. An important question is whether there is a "goodness of fit" between the individual's physical and emotional needs and the day program. Is the individual happy with her or his daytime programming? Is she or he capable of the physical demands in the setting?

Janicki (1989) states that of all the transition issues related to aging, retirement is the most vexing. Janicki (1989) and Kultgen et al. (1987) discuss the benefits that work provides and the importance of developing plans so that older workers with disabilities have something to "retire to." Work can provide a source of income, self-esteem, means for social interaction, and a way of structuring time. Alternatives to these benefits must be identified if an individual is to have an optimal retirement experience.

One alternative activity for older persons with developmental disabilities is exercise (Hall, 1992). Many losses in function are attributed mistakenly to the aging process when in fact they occur because of the lack of exercise and the resultant deconditioning of muscle strength and other physical abilities. Proper exercise promotes health and well-being and prevents deconditioning. Therefore, retirement plans are best designed with activities that include a formal exercise program or require movement.

The timing of retirement needs to be reviewed on an individual basis for older persons with developmental disabilities, rather than assessed categorically (i.e., on the basis of age). Individuals who did not have work opportunities until later in life and who are enjoying these activities may not want to retire. Others may prefer retirement or partial retirement because of health problems or other reasons. Rinck, Torner, Griggs, and Cohen (1992) have developed a *Work and Retirement Planning Curriculum,* which provides guidance for service providers and family members as they assist a person with developmental disabilities to decide whether to continue working or transition to retirement.

A 69-year-old woman with mental retardation in the mild range was referred to the clinic by a nurse in her residential setting, an ICF-MR. Staff had noted increased memory loss and nervousness as well as decreased social interaction. The suggestion was made that she retire from her daily participation in a sheltered workshop. According to her vocational provider, her work was of excellent quality, and she had one of the highest productivity rates in the agency. She was enthusiastic about her work. She liked what she did, and the monetary rewards were important to her. She usually spent her leisure time in individual pursuits and participated in few social activities. After evaluation, clinic staff strongly recommended that she not be forced to retire, but that she should be offered preretirement counseling. Important aspects of this counseling would be discussions about retirement (e.g., the meaning of retirement, that it is a reward and not a punishment), exploration and development of leisure pursuits (e.g., visiting a Senior Center, participating in a community recreation program, seeking a volunteer companion who could assist her in attending community activities, and learning financial planning). The goal was to allow her to make informed choices about work versus retirement.

Choice was a major theme for another woman, 71 years old, who had cerebral palsy with spastic quadriplegia. She was an excellent candidate for retirement. Although she enjoyed attending a sheltered workshop, the most important aspect for her was socializing with others. Her functional abilities had declined recently and she no longer had the stamina to attend the workshop on a daily basis. She did not have enough money to pay for transportation to both her job and leisure activities. She also did not have the stamina to engage in leisure activities everyday. She needed a part-time leisure program. Her group home, however, required residents to have a full-time daytime program out of the home, and the vocational provider required full-day attendance. Because of these rules and her health status, she feared that she would be expected to go to a nursing home. Earlier in her life, she had advocated for a long time to leave a nursing home, and returning was the last thing she wanted to happen. A person-centered planning process might have enabled her to retire and not fear placement in a more restrictive setting because of her age. Her problem, which is still unresolved after more than a year, illustrates the need for interagency planning and problem-solving that increases the flexibility of human service agencies to meet the needs of individuals with developmental disabilities who, as they age, may not fit into programmatic structures that were developed for younger individuals.

As noted earlier, leisure activities play a strong role in helping people transition from work to retirement. Hawkins, Eklund, & Gaetani (1989) describe the importance of leisure activities for older persons with developmental disabilities: "When human beings are denied opportunities to engage in meaningful leisure, individual psychological, physical, and social well-being diminishes and the likelihood of aberrant conditions increases" (p. 5). Leisure activities can vary from individual pursuits to group interactions and from relaxation to complex endeavors. Hallmarks of leisure are freedom of choice and the opportunities to pursue activities that are pleasurable and personally fulfilling. During the clinic assessment, information is collected about the activities in which a person engages, if he or she finds them enjoyable, and what other activities he or she might like to try. Sometimes people with developmental disabilities have difficulty identifying or initiating pleasurable pursuits and will need staff assistance in this area. Utilizing tools such as Kivnick's (1991) Inventory of Life Strengths or Rinck's (1991) pictorial booklet of activities, or obtaining a consultation from a recreation therapist or an occupational therapist may be helpful.

Social Supports

Older persons with developmental disabilities are likely to experience a different pattern of social supports than older people in general; usually, they do not marry or have children or grandchildren. They tend to have fewer friends than other older people. According to Krauss, Seltzer, and Goodman (1992), only about 25% of adults with developmental disabilities who lived with their parents had friends who were not also friends of their mothers. Some older adults with developmental disabilities have lacked opportunities to participate in activities where they might meet others and develop friendships. Even when they participate in day programming, though, the large majority of them do not seem to develop friendships that extend beyond the programs' hours (Krauss et al., 1992). Some persons have difficulty initiating friendships because they have poor social skills. However, the latter and other explanations available in the literature do not explain the pervasiveness of this problem in the lives of persons with developmental disabilities. The dwindling of social supports as one ages coupled with the absence of friendships is likely to result in significant loneliness among older persons with developmental disabilities.

A 61-year-old woman with Down syndrome and mild mental retardation was referred to the clinic by her group home staff, who were observing memory loss, symptoms of depression, episodes of crying, mood swings, and aggressive behavior toward a peer. During the evaluation, she displayed very good social skills. She reported feeling sad and lonely, and especially seemed to miss her parents. She related anecdotes about her parents in great detail. These anecdotes seemed to have a common theme of being supported physically and emotionally by her parents. Her parents had died 10 years earlier; she had no siblings. Her cousin and his family had been her primary source of social support for the past 10 years. However, their interactions were decreasing markedly because of health problems, travel, and involvement with their own grandchildren. At the conclusion of the interview, the woman offered to bring the interviewers flowers and gifts. She said, "It gets lonely without you." Although this woman lived in a group home with very caring and committed staff, she gave strong indications that she was missing the support and special attention that she had previously received from family members, the type of support that may have been approximated by close friendships with peers.

The following example supports an observation that clinic staff have made regarding some middle-aged persons who are at home with their elderly parents. A 49-year-old woman with cerebral palsy and mental retardation in the mild range was referred to the clinic by her parents because of a decline in her self-care activities and aggressive behavior. She had become depressed. During the evaluation, we learned that this woman, who had many capabilities, had functioned for many years as her father's helper after he retired, while her mother continued to work. She had no friends and had become reclusive except for contact with other immediate family members. After her mother's retirement, she seemed to have lost her one role in life as her father's helper. She acted with considerable anger towards her parents, particularly her mother, seeming to blame them for her isolation. Her parents recognized the problem and sought assistance to help her become involved in other meaningful activities and relationships. Gradually, she began to participate in a few activities, but the protective tug of war that her parents had waged for so long continued to limit her ability to gain independent friendships. The family did begin to appreciate the scope of their problems and decided to seek family counseling, an option that reduced their daughter's identification as the only family problem.

Sufficient evidence exists to suggest that the availability of social support can have beneficial effects on the immune system, the cardiovascular system, and longevity (Goleman, 1992). Because of the importance of social supports to health and well-being, a complete interdisciplinary evaluation includes an assessment of a consumer's social support system and offers suggestions for enhancement, if needed. The following questions are among those investigated. Who are members of the individual's social support system—family members, friends, service providers? How has the composition of the support system changed over the years? Are paid service providers the only supportive people in the consumer's life? Does she or he have adequate opportunities and assistance (if needed) to interact with people who are close to her or him? Is there conflict between supportive people that affects the individual with disabilities? Is the individual grieving? These and other questions lead to specific recommendations for health promotion via interventions targeted at the individual's social support system.

Religious Activities

Religious activities are very important to some people with developmental disabilities, just as they are important to some people in the general population. Participation in church service and social activities can help reduce stress, add meaning to life, and be a source for socialization (Bearess, 1989). In our secular professional roles, we may forget that persons with developmental disabilities search, like others, for the meaning of their existence; they struggle with existential questions of who they are, where they came from, why their lives have unfolded as they have, and what will happen to them when they die.

According to Bearess, a spiritual assessment for persons with developmental disabilities should include the following four domains: learning about the individual's life history; exploring important relationships; listening to hopes and dreams; and discussing worship history. To many clinicians, assessing these domains may seem routine. However, the "analytic framework" with which one understands these self-reports differs from the psychosocial framework that underlies standard professional theory and practice. An individual who explores these domains for the purpose of understanding the individual's spiritual self expects to appreciate another's values, images of power and order, and the meaning ascribed to faith, ritual, worship, and one's very existence.

Understanding a person's faith and desire to worship usually leads to determining if she or he desires to participate in religious activities more often and, if so, whether activities are accessible. Obstacles to access often include transportation, physical and attitudinal barriers. Oftentimes, these can be overcome by finding someone within the congregation who can become an advocate. For example, an adult family home provider for a 31-year-old man with Down syndrome reported that he was not fully accepted by the pastor of the church or members of the congregation until she helped him demonstrate that he could adequately perform the duties of an usher. After he demonstrated his competency the pastor publicly praised his efforts. He was greeted warmly by other congregation members and encouraged to continue to actively participate.

Attending the place of worship one chooses, a seemingly basic constitutional right, is often denied to older persons with developmental disabilities who live in long-term care facilities. Worship is often institutionalized by making the option to worship available only in the facility. A 62-year-old man with mental retardation and brain injury subsequent to a traffic accident seemed to be depressed and was quite unhappy living in a large intermediate care facility. Although he had an extremely slow, perseverative speech pattern, he seemed to enjoy verbal communication. During the evaluation when given his choice of topics to discuss, he spent most of the allotted time describing the beautiful church he used to attend. The church was located across the street from a previous residence. He no longer attended a church. Direct care staff reported that worship services were available to him at the facility, but his very slow behavior and his daily schedule precluded even his attendance at this "generic" place of worship. The irony of this example is that the staff were trying to find a way to motivate this gentleman to engage in activities that would elevate his depressed mood.

Accessing Formal Services

It is nearly always the case that consumers assessed in the Aging & Developmental Disabilities Clinic need assistance from other service agencies. Sometimes individuals have not been connected previously to any formal services. Others may be receiving services from agencies within the developmental disabilities service sector. Yet others may be participating in programs sponsored by the aging network (e.g., health services, senior centers, day care programs).

Each system has some unique benefits for older persons with developmental disabilities. A role of the clinic is to encourage the aging network and the developmental disabilities service system to form alliances in the provision of services to older people with developmental disabilities.

For example, a 75-year-old woman who lived with her younger sister was referred to the clinic. She had moderate mental retardation, seizure disorder, partial hearing loss, osteoarthritis, and degenerative joint disease. She received excellent nursing, case management, outreach, and adult day services from two agencies that serve the elderly, although the sister refused in-home assistance. Adult day center staff reported that they did not know how best to support this woman. At times she displayed such strong episodes of agitation that staff found it difficult to assist her as well as continue programming for their other consumers. She also seemed to be declining in her cognitive abilities. She frequently arrived at the center with unexplained bruises and other injuries. An evaluation was completed that included a home visit, interactions with adult protective services, and the interdisciplinary evaluation in our clinic. An array of recommendations resulted from this evaluation. Among these, clinic staff suggested that the woman be referred to the county developmental disabilities intake unit. Once she was determined to be eligible for developmental disabilities services, additional resources were made available to staff in the aging network, including specific consultation regarding how to work with her challenging behaviors and possible residential alternatives to living with the sister.

One of the services that sometimes falls under the rubric of formal service is transportation. Oftentimes, the availability of transportation will make the difference as to whether someone can retire and attend a generic senior program or remain in the present vocational setting. Transportation also plays a very important role in relation to who gets what kind of health care service.

Short-Term and Long-Term Planning

Clinic staff provide comprehensive consultations, rather than primary care, and take great care in identifying both short-term and long-term goals that will promote the health and well-being of older individuals with developmental disabilities over a period of time. Generally, recommendations are made in the following areas: financial, health promotion, legal, residential, safety, social and vocational. As the topic of long-term planning is covered elsewhere in this volume (Freedman & Freedman, chapter 9; Heller & Factor, chapter 3), we will only highlight a few issues.

Consistent with the finding of Heller and Factor (1991), clinic staff have seen that parents frequently have great difficulty in addressing long-term planning issues in categories other than financial. Residential planning in particular seems to be stressful. Parents frequently have a hard time believing that their children with disabilities may outlive them. Addressing future residential planning also means focussing on their own decreasing abilities or mortality. Some parents report that they have been forced to live one day at a time and they are accustomed to doing so. Others report faith in God that supports their belief that everything will work out. Some families have had previous experiences with professionals that resulted in recommendations or actions that they believe were not in the best interest of the individual or the family, a circumstance that now inhibits them from trying again. Other families note that the instability of plans precludes planning; community programs change, staff turn over, state surveyors make decisions affecting eligibility for various programs. Parents question the value of developing plans that they expect might not materialize. Lastly,

some families need to remain intact for pragmatic reasons. In these instances clinic staff have had difficulty determining who is caring for whom. Adults with disabilities and their aging parents have developed a symbiosis based on complementary needs; to think about planning for a son or daughter would also greatly affect a parent's living arrangements.

Seltzer and Seltzer (1992) note the importance of letting families know that plans, once made, can later be changed as circumstances change. Although this may seem evident to the present generation of families, the older generation of families missed the opportunity to utilize federal legislation such as P.L. 94–142 and P.L. 99–457, legislation that supported the role of families in the planning process. This older generation of families have not been "empowered" to make important decisions with the formal service system, and, given the lack of legislated entitlements for adults, they have reason to be cautious. Nevertheless, engaging in planning may provide more options than relying on others during a crisis; therefore, clinic staff emphasize the need for short and long-term planning with parents, siblings, or guardians. Resources that are used or given to families include a handbook published by The Arc (Berkobien, 1991) and materials on personal futures planning (Mount, 1985; Mount & Zwernik, 1988).

Discussion

In this time of concern about health care cost and availability, the dilemma of how best to provide health care to older persons with developmental disabilities is complicated by the dearth of health care professionals who are trained to treat this population. Throughout the operation of the clinic, the team has struggled with its mission to serve persons as much as possible within their preestablished health care and social service systems. Frequently, conducting a thorough assessment is far less of a challenge than helping families identify health care practitioners, behavioral specialists, and psychiatrists in consumers' home communities who can help implement the findings of the Aging & Developmental Disabilities Clinic.

Lack of available resources and funding for community-based services raises questions about the broader issue of generic versus specialized services. Geriatric health care practitioners generally think in terms that overlap with that of professionals in the field of developmental disabilities. Geriatricians and other geriatric health personnel usually examine function and also think of the long-term needs of their patients. Families often play a critical role in the care of an older individual as happens in families with a member with developmental disabilities. Additionally, geriatricians and other geriatric practitioners try to develop solutions that promote an individual's quality of life, a goal also emphasized in the field of developmental disabilities. Since there are these overlapping practice approaches, geriatric professionals may be receptive to providing services to older persons with developmental disabilities and may do so competently when specialized training is available.

Presently, though, a generic geriatric assessment team is unlikely to agree to evaluate older persons with developmental disabilities and often for very good reasons. These health professionals do not feel competent to do so. Although this perception of incompetence may be reinforced by stereotypes about the differences between older persons with developmental disabilities and the patients they usually treat, the fact remains that these practitioners have had very little, if any, training to treat this population. The need to train generic health care personnel to treat older persons with developmental disabilities supports the need for specialized settings where low incidence consumers and health care problems are routinely treated and where generic health providers can go for training. However, sufficient funding for inter-disciplinary clinics (particularly those providing services under Medicaid) is generally unavailable unless obtained in conjunction with some other research or training grant. These fiscal constraints limit the feasibility of designing specialized services.

Because the future of health care design and finance has so many unknowns, this dilemma is unlikely to be resolved soon. In the meantime, one method for bridging the gap between the lack of training related to the delivery of heath care to older persons with developmental disabilities and their need for generic services is to find some common clinical tool that helps generic geriatric practitioners feel more competent to treat older persons with developmental disabilities. As both fields utilize a functional approach to assessment, OT FACT may help professionals bridge the two fields of practice. With the proper training and supportive consultation on the use of OT FACT, professionals in generic geriatric assessment units might be able to treat many of the commonly occurring health and related problems of older persons with developmental disabilities.

Conclusions

Although this chapter focuses on a particular age stage—old age—the topic covered may be better understood by adopting a life-span perspective. Health and well-being in old age are a function of health promotion and lifestyle modifications adopted at early ages. Although we lack the longitudinal data to support a life-span perspective on health and well-being, we can assume that persons with developmental disabilities and their families who have had access to quality health care are much more likely to have made life style modifications that enhance their later life physical functioning and successful aging. There is probably no better example of the effect of prevention than that of dental care. We have the technology to prevent or slow the deterioration of teeth, but often persons with developmental disabilities do not have access to dental care. The majority of the individuals seen at our clinic are edentulous or very close to it. For this older generation, prevention is too late, but not for younger adults and children.

Other areas described in this chapter that need to be viewed from a life-span perspective are retirement, leisure, and social supports. Individuals are more likely to retire to something if they have developed the financial, social, and leisure resources at a younger age. Research and, to some extent, clinical practice in the field of developmental disabilities have focused on children, on young adult transitions from educational systems to employment, and most recently on old age. The middle adult years are the time when leisure activities, social supports, and fiscal means are expected to be developed and yet professionals have paid very little attention to these critical years (Seltzer, 1993).

The descriptive nature of this chapter is also testimony to the fact that we need to engage in more research on age-related changes in old age. As this is the first generation whose aging process is being described in the literature, we can only begin to draw inferences about how earlier developmental and health related occurrences have influenced this generation's aging process. Although these inferences are limited by cohort and healthy survivor effects, they are the only source of data we will have for some time. The present generation of older persons with developmental disabilities are survivors. They are also often referred to as pioneers. In effect though, they are persons who have no role models as they and others close to them anticipate the challenges of their later years of life. The same might also be said about professionals in the field of developmental disabilities who, for the first time, are supporting the needs of this group of older persons with developmental disabilities.

References

Adlin, M. (1993). Health care issues. In E. Sutton, T. Heller, A. Factor, B. A. Hawkins, & G. B. Seltzer (Eds.), *Older adults with developmental disabilities: Toward community integration* (pp. 49–60). Baltimore, MD: Brookes.

Adlin, M., & Seltzer, G. B. (in press). Gerontology. In H. G. Garner & F. Orelove (Eds.), *Teamwork in human services.* Stoneham, MA: Andover Medical Publishers.

American Association on Mental Retardation. (1992). *Mental retardation: Definition, classification and systems of support.* Washington, DC: Author.

Ancoli-Israel, S., Kripke, D. F., & Mason, W. (1987). Characteristics of obstructive and central apnea in the elderly: An interim report. *Biological Psychiatry, 22,* 741–750.

Anderson, D. J., & Polister, B. (1993). Psychotropic medication use among older adults with mental retardation. In E. Sutton, T. Heller, A. Factor, B. A. Hawkins, & G. B. Seltzer (Eds.), *Older adults with developmental disabilities: Toward community integration* (pp. 61–75). Baltimore, MD: Brookes.

Averill, J. R., & Wisocki, P. A. (1981). Some observations on behavioral approaches to the treatment of grief among the elderly. In H. Sobel (Ed.), *Behavior therapy in terminal care: A humanistic approach* (pp. 125-150). Cambridge, MA: Ballinger.

Banting, D. W. (1991). Management of dental caries in the older patient. In A. S. Papas, L. C. Niessen, & H. H. Chauncey (Eds.), *Geriatric dentistry: Aging and oral health* (pp. 141–167). St. Louis, MO: Mosby Year Book.

Bax, M. C., Smyth, D. P., & Thomas, A. P. (1988). Health care of physically handicapped young adults. *British Medical Journal of Clinical Research and Education, 296,* 1153–1155.

Bearess, B. (1989). Pastoral care and the assessment of spiritual needs. In M. C. Howell, D. G. Gavin, G. A. Cabrera, & H. A. Beyer (Eds.), *Serving the underserved: Caring for people who are both old and mentally retarded. A handbook for caregivers* (pp. 73–78). Boston, MA: Exceptional Parent Press.

Berkobien, R. (1991). *A family handbook on future planning.* Arlington, TX: Association for Retarded Citizens of the United States.

Bess, F. H., Lichtenstein, M. J., & Logar, S. A. (1991). Audiologic assessment of the elderly. In W. F. Rintelmann (Ed.), *Hearing assessment* (2nd ed., pp. 511-548). Austin, TX: PRO-ED.

Biersdorff, K. K. (1991, May). *Significantly altered pain experience: More common than you may think*. Paper presented at the 115th Annual Meeting of the American Association on Mental Retardation, Washington, DC.

Brown, M. C., Bontempo, A., & Turk, M. A. (1991). *Secondary consequences of cerebral palsy: Adults with cerebral palsy in New York State*. Albany: New York State Office of Mental Retardation and Developmental Disabilities.

Buehler, B. A., Menolascino, F. J, & Stark, J. A. (1986). Medical care of adults with developmental disabilities. In W. E. Kiernan & J. A. Stark (Eds.), *Pathways to employment for adults with developmental disabilities* (pp. 241–249). Baltimore, MD: Brookes.

Burke, S. W., French, H. G., Roberts, J. M., Johnston, C. E., Whitecloud, T., & Edmunds, J. O. (1985). Chronic altanto-axial instability in Down syndrome. *Journal of Bone and Joint Surgery, 67-A*, 1356–1360.

Carnes, M., Gunter-Hunt, G., Hess, J., & Drinka, T. (1987). Preventive health maneuvers for the elderly: Recommendations vs. reimbursement policies. *Wisconsin Medical Journal, 86*, 27–29.

Crocker, A. C. (1989). The spectrum of medical care for developmental disabilities. In I. L. Rubin & A. C. Crocker (Eds.), *Developmental disabilities: Delivery of medical care for children and adults* (pp. 10–22). Philadelphia: Lea & Febiger.

Crocker, A. C. (1992). Expansion of the health-care delivery system. In L. Rowitz (Ed.), *Mental retardation in the year 2000* (pp. 163–183). New York: Springer.

Dalton, A. J., Seltzer, G. B., Adlin, M. S., & Wisniewski, H. M. (in press). Association between Alzheimer disease and Down syndrome: Clinical observations. In J. M. Berg, A. J. Holland, & H. Karlinsky (Eds.), *Alzheimer disease and Down syndrome*. New York: Oxford University Press.

Dalton, A. J., & Wisniewski, H. M. (1990). Down's syndrome and the dementia of Alzheimer's disease. *International Review of Psychiatry, 2*, 43–52.

DeBiase, C. B. (1991). Dental health education for the elderly. *Dental health education theory and practice* (pp. 243–264). Philadelphia, PA: Lea & Febiger.

Diamond, L. S. (1992). Orthopedic disorders in Down syndrome. In I. T. Lott & E. E. McCoy (Eds.), *Down syndrome: Advances in medical care* (pp. 111–126). New York: Wiley Liss.

Dinani, S., & Carpenter, S. (1990). Down's syndrome and thyroid disorder. *Journal of Mental Deficiency Research, 34*, 187–193.

Eaton, W. O., & Burdz, M. (1984). Gender understanding and the similar sequence hypothesis. *American Journal of Mental Deficiency, 89*, 23–38.

Ferrang, T. M., Johnson, R. K., & Ferrara, M. S. (1992). Dietary and anthropometric assessment of adults with cerebral palsy. *Journal of the American Dietary Association, 92*, 1083–1086.

Freedman, R. I., & Freedman, D. N. (1994). Planning for now and the future: Social, legal, and financial concerns. In M. M. Seltzer, M. W. Krauss, & M. P. Janicki (Eds.), *Life course perspectives on adulthood and old age* (pp. 167–184). Washington, DC: American Association on Mental Retardation.

Friedman, D. L., Kastner, T., Pond, W. S., & O'Brien, D. R. (1989). Thyroid function in individuals with Down syndrome. *Archives of Internal Medicine, 149*, 1990–1993.

Fuld, P. A. (1977). *Fuld object-memory evaluation (cat. no. 33925M): Instruction manual*. Wood Dale, IL: Stoelting.

Gambert, S. R., Liebeskind, S., & Cameron, D. (1987). Lifelong preventive health care for elderly persons with developmental disabilities. *The Journal of the Association for Persons with Severe Handicaps, 12*, 296–296.

Goleman, D. (1992, December 15). New light on how stress erodes health. *New York Times*.

Goodrich, G., & Jose, R. T. (Eds.). (1993). *Low vision—The reference* (2nd ed.). New York: The Lighthouse.

Granger, C. V., Seltzer, G. B., & Fishbein, C. (1987). *Primary care of the functionally disabled: Assessment and management*. Philadelphia: Lippincott.

Gurland, B. F. (1976). The comprehensive frequency of depression in various adult age groups. *Journal of Gerontology, 31,* 283–292.

Haggerty, R. (1971). Does comprehensive care make a difference? Introduction: Historical perspectives. *American Journal of Diseases of Children, 122,* 467–486.

Hall, N. K. (1992). Health maintenance and promotion. In R. J. Ham & P. D. Sloane (Eds.), *Primary care geriatrics* (pp. 95–118). St. Louis, MO: Mosby Year Book.

Ham, R. J. (1992). Characteristics of the ill elderly patient. In R. J. Ham & P. D. Sloane (Eds), *Primary care geriatrics: A casebased approach* (pp. 40–63). St. Louis, MO: Mosby Year Book.

Hann, H. W., Deacon, J. C., & London, W. T. (1979). Lymphocyte surface makers and serum immunoglobulin in persons with Down syndrome. *American Journal of Mental Deficiency, 84,* 245–251.

Hauser, W. A., & Hesdorffer, D. C. (1990). *Epilepsy: Frequency, causes and consequences.* New York: Demos.

Hawkins, B. A., Eklund, S. J., & Gaetani, R. P. (1989). *Aging and developmental disabilities: A training inservice package.* Bloomington: Indiana University Institute of the Study of Developmental Disabilities.

Hayden, M. F., & DePaepe, P. A. (1991). Medical conditions, level of care needs and health-related outcome of persons with mental retardation: A review. *The Journal of the Association for Persons with Severe Handicaps, 16,* 188–206.

Heath, J. M. (1992). Vision. In R. J. Ham & P. D. Sloane (Eds.), *Primary care geriatrics* (pp. 482–489). St. Louis, MO: Mosby Year Book.

Heighway, S., Kidd-Webster, S., & Shaw, M. (1990). *STARS: Skills training for assertiveness, relationship-building and sexual awareness* (2nd ed.). Madison: Wisconsin Council on Developmental Disabilities.

Heller, T., & Factor, A. (1991). Permanency planning for adults with mental retardation living with family caregivers. *American Journal on Mental Retardation, 96,* 163–176.

Heller, T., & Factor, A. (1994). Facilitating future planning and transitions out of the home. In M. M. Seltzer, M. W. Krauss, & M. P. Janicki (Eds.), *Life course perspectives on adulthood and old age* (pp. 39–50). Washington, DC: American Association on Mental Retardation.

Heston, L. L., & White, J. A. (1983). *Dementia: A practical guide to Alzheimer's disease and related illnesses.* New York: W. H. Freeman.

Hill, B. K., Balow, E. A., & Bruininks, R. H. (1985). A national study of prescribed drugs in institutions and community residential facilities for mentally retarded people. *Psychopharmacological Bulletin, 21,* 279–284.

Howell, M. C., Gavin, D. G., Cabrera, G. A.,& Beyer, H. A. (Eds.). (1989). *Serving the under-served: Caring for people who are both old and mentally retarded. A handbook for care-givers.* Boston, MA: Exceptional Parent Press.

Intagliata, J., & Rinck, C. (1985). Psychoactive drug use in public and community residential facilities for mentally retarded persons. *Psychopharmacological Bulletin, 21,* 279–284.

Janicki, M. P. (1989). Transition from worklife to retirement. For a Presidential forum, *Citizens with mental retardation and community integration* (pp. 150–155). Washington, DC: President's Committee on Mental Retardation.

Jaskulski, T., Metzler, C., & Zierman, S. A. (1990). *Forging a new era: The 1990 reports on people with developmental disabilities.* Washington, DC: National Association of Developmental Disabilities Councils.

Kailes, J. I. (1992). Aging with a disability: Educating myself. *Generations,* Winter 1992, 75–77.

Kane, R. L., Ouslander, J. G., & Abrass, I. B. (1984). *Essentials of clinical geriatrics.* New York: McGraw-Hill.

Kaplan, H. I., & Sadock, B. J. (1988). *Synopsis of psychiatry.* Baltimore, MD: Williams & Wilkins.

Kivnick, H. Q. (1991). *Living with care, caring for life: The inventory of life strengths* (assessment update). Minneapolis: University of Minnesota, Long-Term Care DECISIONS Resource Center.

Kovar, M. G. (1986). Aging in the eighties. Preliminary data from the supplement on aging to the National Health Interview Survey, U.S., January–June 1984. *Advance data from vital and health statistics* (No. 115). Hyattsville, MD: U.S. Public Health Service.

Krauss, M. W., Seltzer, M. M., & Goodman, S. J. (1992). Social support networks of adults with mental retardation who live at home. *American Journal on Mental Retardation, 96,* 432–441.

Kuehn, M. L., Powers, J., Dolan, T. D., & Cohen, H. (1988). *Report on the health care needs of adults with developmental disabilities.* Madison: University of Wisconsin.

Kultgen, P., Rinck, C., & Pfannenstiel, D. (1987). *Training guide for aging specialists.* Kansas City, MO: UMKC Institute for Human Development, University Affiliated Facility for Developmental Disabilities.

Lakin, K. C., Anderson, D. J., Hill, B. K., Bruininks, R. H., & Wright, E. A. (1991). Programs and services received by older persons with mental retardation. *Mental Retardation, 29,* 69–74.

Lehmann, J. (1968). Patient care needs as a basis for development of objectives of physical medicine and rehabilitation medicine teaching in undergraduate medical schools. *Journal of Chronic Diseases, 21,* 340–352.

Lipe-Goodson, P. S., & Goebel, B. L. (1983). Perception of age and death in mentally retarded adults. *Mental Retardation, 21,* 68–75.

Lott, I. T., & McCoy, E. E. (Eds.) (1992). *Down syndrome: Advances in medical care.* New York: Wiley Liss.

Machemer, R. H., & Overeynder, J. C. (Eds.). (1993). *Understanding aging and developmental disabilities: An in-service curriculum.* Rochester, NY: University of Rochester.

Mayo, M. E. (1992). Lower urinary tract dysfunction in cerebral palsy. *Journal of Urology, 147,* 419–420.

McGinnis, M. J. (1988). The Tithonus syndrome: Health and aging in America. In R. Chernoff & D. A. Lipschitz (Eds.), *Health promotion and disease prevention in the elderly* (pp. 1–16). New York: Raven Press.

Mount, B. (1985). *Person-centered planning: Finding directions for change by listening to the lives of people using the process of personal futures planning.* West Hartford, CT: Graphic Futures, Inc.

Mount, B., & Zwernik, K. (1988). *It's never too early, it's never too late: A booklet about personal futures planning* (Publication No. 421–88–109). St. Paul, MN: Metropolitan Council.

Nagi, S. Z. (1975, May). *Disability concepts and prevalence.* Paper presented at the First Mary Switzer Memorial Seminar, Cleveland, OH.

Nagi, S. Z. (1979). The concept and measurement of disability. In E. D. Berkowitz (Ed.), *Disability policies and government programs* (pp. 1–15). New York: Praeger.

National Institutes of Health. (1987). *Differential diagnosis of dementing diseases.* National Institutes of Health Consensus Developmental Conference Statement, 6(11).

Niessen, L. C., & Jones, J. A. (1991). Facing the challenge: The graying of America. In A. S. Papas, L. C. Niessen, & H. H. Chaney (Eds.), *Geriatric dentistry: Aging and oral health* (pp. 3–13). St. Louis, MO: Mosby Year Book.

Northern, J. L., & Downs, M. P. (1991). *Hearing loss in children* (4th ed.). Baltimore, MD: Williams & Wilkins.

Overeynder, J., Turk, A. J., Dalton, A. J., & Janicki, M. P. (1992). *I'm worried about the future: The aging of adults with cerebral palsy.* Albany: New York State Developmental Disabilities Council.

Patterson, P. M. (1991). *Doubly silenced: Sexuality, sexual abuse and people with developmental disabilities.* Madison: Wisconsin Council on Developmental Disabilities.

Pimm, P. (1992). Cerebral palsy: "A non-progressive disorder"? *Education and Child Psychology, 9,* 27–33.

Pope, A. M., & Tarlov, A. R. (Eds.). (1991). *Disability in America: Toward a national agenda for prevention*. Washington, DC: National Academy Press.

Pritchett, J. W. (1983). The untreated unstable hip in severe cerebral palsy. *Clinical Orthopedics, 173,* 169–72.

Pueschel, S. M. (1992). The person with Down syndrome: Medical concerns and educational strategies. In I. T. Lott & E. E. McCoy (Eds.), *Down syndrome: Advances in medical care* (pp. 53–60). New York: Wiley Liss.

Pueschel, S. M., & Scola, F. H. (1987). Altantoaxial instability in individuals with Down syndrome. Epidemiologic, radiographic, and clinical studies. *Pediatrics, 80,* 555–560.

Rinck, C. (1991). *What do you like to do? A selection book of activities*. Kansas City, MO: UMKC Institute for Human Development, University Affiliated Program for Developmental Disabilities.

Rinck, C., Torner, R. S., Griggs, P. A., & Cohen, G. J. (1992). *WARP curriculum*. Kansas City, MO: UMKC-Institute for Human Development.

Seltzer, G. (1989). A developmental approach to cognitive understanding of death and dying. In M. C. Howell, D. G. Gavin, G. A. Cabrera, & H. A. Beyer (Eds.), *Serving the underserved: Caring for people who are both old and mentally retarded. A handbook for caregivers* (pp. 331–338). Boston, MA: Exceptional Parent Press.

Seltzer, G. B. (1993). Psychological adjustment in midlife: Developmental and quality of life issues for persons with mental retardation. In E. Sutton, T. Heller, A. Factor, B. A. Hawkins, & G. B. Seltzer (Eds.), *Older adults with developmental disabilities: Toward community integration* (pp. 157–184). Baltimore, MD: Brookes.

Seltzer, G. B., & Essex, E. L. (1993). *Service needs of persons with mental retardation and developmental disabilities* (Robert Wood Johnson Foundation Report). Providence, RI: Brown University, Center for Gerontology and Health Care Research.

Seltzer, G. B., Finaly, E., & Howell, M. (1988). Functional characteristics of elderly mentally retarded persons in community settings and nursing homes. *Mental Retardation, 26,* 213–217.

Seltzer, G. B., Granger, C. V., & Wineberg, D. E., & LaCheen, C. (1984). Functional assessment in primary care. In C. V. Granger & E. Gresham (Eds.), *Functional assessment in rehabilitation medicine* (pp. 289–304). Baltimore, MD: Williams & Wilkins.

Seltzer, M. M., & Seltzer, G. B. (1992). Aging in persons with developmental disabilities. In F. J. Turner (Ed.), *Mental health and the elderly: A social work perspective* (pp. 136–160). New York: The Free Press.

Sherk, H. H., Pasquariello, P. D., & Doherty, J. (1983). Hip location in cerebral palsy: Selection for treatment. *Developmental Medicine and Child Neurology, 25,* 738–746.

Smith, R. O. (1990a). *OT FACT software and operating manual*. Rockville, MD: American Occupational Therapy Association.

Smith, R. O. (1990b). *OT FACT administration and tutorial manual*. Rockville, MD: American Occupational Therapy Association.

Sterling, E. S. (1992). Oral and dental considerations in Down syndrome. In I. T. Lott & E. E. McCoy (Eds.), *Down syndrome: Advances in medical care* (pp. 135–146). New York: Wiley Liss.

Suzuki, J. B., Niessen, L. C., & Fedele, D. J. (1991). Periodontal diseases in the older adult. In A. S. Papas, L. C. Niessen, & H. H. Chauncey (Eds.), *Geriatric dentistry: Aging and oral health* (pp. 189–201). St. Louis, MO: Mosby Year Book.

Trainer, N., Bowser, B. L., & Dahm, L. (1986). Obturator nerve block for painful hip in adult cerebral palsy. *Archives of Physical Medicine and Rehabilitation, 67,* 829–830.

Turk, M. A., & Machemer, R. H. (1993). Cerebral palsy in adults who are older. In R. H. Machemer & J. C. Overeynder (Eds.), *Understanding aging and developmental disabilities: An in-service curriculum* (pp. 111–129). Rochester, NY: University of Rochester.

Verbrugge, L. M. (1990). The iceberg of disability. In S. M. Stahl (Ed.), *The legacy of longevity: Health and health care in later life* (pp. 55–76). Newbury Park, CA: Sage Publications.

Wadsworth, J. S., & Harper, D. C. (1991). Grief and bereavement in mental retardation: A need for a new understanding. *Death Studies, 15,* 281–292.

Wood, P. (1975). *Classification of impairments and handicaps.* Geneva: World Health Organization.

Wittingham, G. H., Pitt, D. B., Sharma, D. L. B., & MacKay, I. R. (1977). Stress deficiency of the T-lymphocyte system exemplified by Down's Syndrome. *Lancet 1,* 163–166.

Yeasavage, J. A., Brink, T. L., & Rose, T. L. (1983). Development and validation of a geriatric depression screening scale: A preliminary report. *Journal of Psychiatric Research, 17,* 37–49.

Zigman, W. B., Seltzer, G. B., & Silverman, W. P. (1994). Behavioral and mental health changes associated with aging in adults with mental retardation. In M. M. Seltzer, M. W. Krauss, & M. P. Janicki (Eds.), *Life course perspectives on adulthood and old age* (pp. 67–91). Washington, DC: American Association on Mental Retardation.

The work described in this chapter has been supported in part by Grants #07DDO273-18 and #90DDO185-02 from the U.S. Department of Health and Human Services, Administration on Developmental Disabilities. We would like to acknowledge our other team members whose collegiality and collaboration over the past four years made possible the interdisciplinary assessment process that is described in this chapter. They include Marilyn Adlin, M.D.; Jean Baker, Ph.D.; Ronaldo Hirsch, M.Sc., D.D.S.; Mary Musholt, M.S.N., R.N.; Robert Nellis, M.A., CCC-A; Kathleen Rust, M.S., O.T.R.; and Fernando Saenz-Forero, D.D.S. Also thanks to Marshall Flax, M.S., Wisconsin Council of the Blind, for his consultation regarding low vision assessment, and to our trainees who, in addition to learning, have provided valuable insights as the Clinic evolved.

Chapter 8

Policies and Supports for Older Persons With Mental Retardation

Matthew P. Janicki, New York State Office of Mental Retardation
and Developmental Disabilities

Older persons with mental retardation represent a diverse population. The types of cognitive and physical impairments and capabilities they have vary greatly, as do their needs for community supports and services (Hogg, Moss, & Cooke, 1988a; Stroud & Sutton, 1988). In some instances, the degree of intellectual handicap determines the types of supports or programs needed; in other instances, the degree of dysfunction in physical and social abilities is more determinant. As with developing programs for America's overall older population, the challenge to administrators, planners, service providers, and others is to define constructive public policies and to offer an array of options and supports that can accommodate the variety of needs of older persons with mental retardation and promote the fullest community involvement. Thus, the concern of this chapter: What is the policy context for aging services, what are the age-related issues that affect supports and service needs of older persons with mental retardation, and what are the community support options that appear most viable to meet their needs?[1]

National and State Policies

Who is considered to be "elderly" among persons with mental retardation is still open to discussion (Factor, 1993; Seltzer & Krauss, 1987; Sison & Cotten, 1989), with no clear cut definitional agreement. However, the inclusion of specific provisions for older persons with disabilities in the 1987 reauthorization of the Older Americans Act of 1965 (P.L. 89–73, as amended; National Association of State Units on Aging [NASUA], 1985) may eventually lead to definitional consistency by the public sector. Because the Older Americans Act specifies age 60 as the age of eligibility for services and requires equal access to services by older individuals with disabilities, including adults with mental retardation, many states have adopted age 60 as a basis for planning. However, many analysts also recognize that premature or precocious aging is a major concern among certain persons with a disability, as it is among nondisabled persons who age prematurely (Overeynder, Turk, Dalton, & Janicki, 1992). Because problems and needs posed by individuals with disabilities who age prematurely also need to be considered, some have proposed using a younger age (possibly 55, as recommended by Seltzer & Krauss, 1987) for definitional purposes and provision of compensatory services.

The 1987 amendments to the Older Americans Act included several changes that enabled older persons with disabilities to be served within regular services normally provided under the Act. Other changes included a specific mandate to the state units on aging and the area agencies on aging to cooperatively plan and develop services for older persons with disabilities in conjunction with state and local mental retardation/develop-

---

[1] Although aging issues relate to all people with mental retardation, irrespective of degree of impairment or capabilities, most of this chapter addresses issues, supports, and options that apply to older adults with minimal or moderate needs for assistance or supports. This is particularly true with reference to structures and activities within the aging network and generic community amenities.

mental disabilities agencies. The amendments also enabled disabled, dependent adults under the age of 60 to be served at congregate meal sites when accompanying their eligible parent or caregiver. The 1992 amendments to the Act went even further and, stressing older caregiver needs, authorized the Administration on Aging to set up demonstration programs that promote the community involvement of older adults with developmental disabilities and provide supports to home-based caregivers (Janicki, 1993).

Over the past few years many changes in national policy can be attributed to the initiatives of federal agencies responsible for administering the Developmental Disabilities Assistance and Bill of Rights Act and the Older Americans Act, that is, the federal agencies for developmental disabilities and aging within the U.S. Department of Health and Human Services. Two of the initiatives included the signing of a joint agreement on how to approach this population, and the support of university-based training centers in aging and developmental disabilities.

At the state level, a number of state mental retardation/developmental disabilities agencies have also begun to show a concern about aging. Some have held networking conferences (Janicki, 1991), conducted interagency planning (Hawkins & Eklund, 1989), established policies on aging (University of Akron, n.d.), designated key program development staff, and developed program models that specifically serve older persons with mental retardation (Factor, 1993; Janicki & Bradbury, 1993). Additionally, the promotion (Cotten, 1985; Spirrison & Cotten, 1989) and subsequent adoption by state agencies of statements of principles affirming the basic rights of older persons with developmental disabilities (e.g., Connecticut Department of Mental Retardation—see University of Akron, n.d.) have had an influence on program practices. Such policy documents, designed to define public policy and influence public perceptions, often include an affirmation that elderly people with mental retardation have an equal opportunity to participate in the activities in which they choose to be involved, that they have the right to be integrated with peers, and that supports and services obtained should be provided in a manner that is flexible, accessible, and appropriate and that reflects the free choice and promotes the dignity of each individual (Lakin et al., 1989).

In addition, community program development has been spurred by a variety of national groups, including the National Association of State Units on Aging (which passed a resolution requesting directors of state units to seek to work cooperatively with their counterparts administering mental retardation/developmental disabilities agencies), the National Association of Area Agencies on Aging (which distributed background materials on aging and developmental disabilities to its membership), and the National Association of State Directors of Developmental Disabilities Services (which has disseminated information about policies and innovative services and supports).

However, notwithstanding these national developments that have helped shape public policy in aging and mental retardation, individual states are confronted by several dilemmas. Because people with disabilities are surviving longer (Maaskant, 1993), as are people in the general population (due to improved health care, social conditions, and housing), concerns have been raised that increased longevity has created a demand for services and special attention that many states are ill-prepared to address (Factor, 1993). Because many states had given much of their attention to developing child-oriented developmental and remedial educational services and adult-oriented vocational and social developmental services, the new demand for senior-oriented mental retardation services presents an expansion of current service initiatives. And, when attention has been focussed on this population, controversy has ensued among mental retardation policymakers and administrators regarding whether to create a parallel senior services track within mental retardation services or to collaborate with the aging network in the use of existing or augmented senior services within that network (Ansello & Rose, 1989). The use of the Older Americans Act amendments in opening up aging network services has only intensified this debate (Clark, 1988; Quirk & Aravanis, 1988). Representatives of the aging network raise concerns that mental retardation providers will overwhelm local aging network programs with referrals and that involvement with the mental retardation system will deplete scarce dollar resources allocated to the aging network's most needy. Counter arguments are that able seniors with mental retardation are easily integrated into generic aging programs and are lawfully eligible to use senior programs. It is argued further that because senior centers, nutrition sites, and senior housing generally accommodate the well elderly, their use by older adults with severe cognitive and physical limitations will be minimal (Roberto & Nelson, 1989).

Thus, policy-related problems posed to public administrators stem from needing to identify new sets of age-related services for older adults with mental retardation, indemnifying mental retardation providers who may "lose" clientele to aging network programs, and developing workable arrangements with counterparts in aging agencies to share resources and enhance program acceptability. Reasons for these problems are many. For example, some mental retardation providers are reluctant to part with their clientele for a variety of reasons, including opposition from parent-based boards, concern over loss of income (due either to lost "worker" productivity or diminished per capita payments from government funding sources), or a sense of superiority (feeling that aging network programs are insufficiently dynamic and challenging). Another reason is that although public policy stresses integration and the use of aging network programs, in reality this policy may only apply to those older adults capable of independent activities. Thus, older adults with severe limitations in independent functioning still need structured programs and services that may be provided only by the mental retardation system.

Other areas of policy concern relate to the beliefs underpinning senior programs and supports that influence how the specific needs of older adults with mental retardation are addressed (Blaney, 1992; Hawkins, 1993; Janicki, 1991; 1992; Janicki, Moss, & Lucchino,

1992; van Walleghem, 1993). These concerns stem from two important questions: How can we best design interventions and support? Are the needs and abilities of older adults with mental retardation uniform? For example, with regard to the first question, current practice in the United States has been to use the developmental model with younger age persons with mental retardation as the basis for services and programming and to practice pedagogical techniques to impart that learning (Henning, 1993). Under this model, new learning is viewed as probable and continuous, with an invariable striving to promote ever greater independence and self-direction capacities. The process, using a pedagogical approach, defines outcome goals and objectives built on teaching techniques that use predetermined, sequential, and prerequisite skills. Learning is defined as mastering these predetermined skills. Further, most jurisdictions, due to state or federal regulations, also use "team-driven" planning to define habilitation plans. As applied to older adults, some of these underlying beliefs have been questioned, and different foundations have been offered (Hawkins, 1993). Indeed, adopting an andragogical approach has been suggested, where function takes on more importance than form (Henning, 1993) and person-centered, rather than "team-driven," approaches are the norm (Wilson, 1992). In this approach, learning is linked to use and need, and a mentoring model is employed that teaches skills that are congruent with the person's own life objectives. In large part this is due to a recognition that with advancing age competition is not as important as it was with younger persons, nor are vocational competence and personal independence the sole goals for most programmatic activities. With advanced age, different values come into play—partly because of physiological changes and partly due to social role expectations. Thus, the focus of activities and the means of engagement take on different meanings and manifestations, including more of an emphasis on social interactions. Indeed, the argument is made that involvement with the aging network offers a richer, if not potentially more varied, social environment for older persons with mental retardation. However, this argument is not universal; Blaney (1992), for example, has argued against age-integrated experiences and services with age peers because of the perceived devalued status of older people.

With regard to the second area of questioning, experience has shown that many workers perceive old age as a uniform entity and believe that all older people have the same needs and abilities irrespective of life course or chronological age. Thus, they do not differentiate between third age and fourth age life-span aspects. According to Laslett (1991), the "third age" characterizes that period of the life span when work takes on less importance and avocational endeavors, friendships, and retirement occupy more time. Generally, adults in the third age are healthy, have reasonable financial resources, and experience a change in the focus of life activities. Some term people in this stage of life the "well-elderly." This same characterization, except for the financial aspects, applies to older persons with mental retardation. The notion of the "fourth age" characterizes that period of life when greater prominence is given to increasing infirmity and frailty and decreasing ability for self-care. Because, generally, physical and psychological functioning, rather than chronological age, differentiate these two life stages, it is useful to understand that older people differ markedly. Thus, when these notions are applied to older adults with mental retardation, it becomes evident that they are not a homogeneous or uniform population and that their needs and abilities will differ widely, based not only upon age, but upon experience and how the physical aging process is affecting them.

From a policy perspective, what ties together programmatic planning and these life-span concepts? There are several issues with regard to adults in the third age. One is the concept of *successful aging*, which is defined in terms of an individual retaining his or her capabilities to function as independently as possible into old age and promoting the belief that persons who age successfully are able to remain out of institutions, maintain their autonomy and competence in all their activities of daily living, and continue to engage in productive endeavors of their own choosing. Another relevant concept is *rehabilitative intent*. With younger persons with mental retardation, the rehabilitative intent is to promote skill development to assist that individual to be as independent as possible so that he or she can be a competitive member of society, effectively using social amenities, working, and enjoying the freedom of having his or her own household. With persons in middle age or later, independence still remains an important goal; however, it is now moderated by another complementary goal, interdependence, which is realized by fostering social skills that maintain personal independence and promote involvement with others, be they age peers or younger or older persons. Thus, among individuals who are elderly, independence is now no longer stated in terms of vocational competitiveness, but in terms of continued social and personal competence (that is, maintaining self-care skills and avoidance of institutionalization) and survivability. Thus, if community involvement is to be successful, it needs to meld together the tenets behind successful aging and social interdependence, while continuing to foster personal independence and sound physical and mental health. Nested within this belief is the recognition that planning for one's own immediate use of time and defining one's future in terms of lifestyle, housing, and community involvement, as well as having access to a full range of options to exercise that planning, is crucial to productive aging.

Although more thought has been given to third age aspects, there are also policy questions related to fourth age issues. In large part, fourth age concerns are linked to problems related to a combination of aging in place and increased frailty (which we discuss below); however, fourth age issues also correspond to concerns about long-term care and the role of nursing facilities for people with mental retardation (Anderson, 1993b). Concerns about the abuse of admissions to nursing facilities in some states led Congress to amend the provision of federal law which has become known as the "Nursing Home Reform Act" (Gettings, 1990). Of particular import are the PASARR aspects—the preadmission screening and annual resident review requirements. These aspects prohibit admission without prior review and assessment for appropriateness by state mental retardation authorities (Gettings, 1990). Although designed to apply in most part to younger age persons with mental retardation, applications to older adults who are experiencing advancing age, physical debilitation, and increased frailty have raised many unresolved questions about the role of nursing facilities with regard to old people with mental retardation and how to best handle increased infirmity. Such questions range from the general appropriateness of admission to nursing facilities of persons with mental retardation, whether agencies should be encouraged to develop dedicated nursing facilities for elderly adults with mental retardation, and at what point should elderly adults be "ACD'd"[2] out of ICFs-MR and transferred to nursing facilities.

Policies are also affected by the emerging reality that as our nation moves toward the beginning of a new millennium, a dramatic increase in the number of older adults is expected (Bureau of Census, 1988). The 1990 population census revealed that there were approximately 248 million Americans, some 17% of whom were age 60 or older. It also showed that the character of the nation's demographics was marked by a bulge among persons currently in their 30s and 40s (the "baby boomers," that is, those persons born shortly after World War II and into the mid-1960s). This particular generation has contributed to a growing number of persons in the early middle age group. Demographers predict a major shift in the character of the population over the next 20 years as this group ages and expect an even greater number of elderly persons age 85 and older, as well. The aging of this generation will create a population

surge resulting in a "senior boom," which will peak in numbers by 2035. These same changes will affect today's population of persons with mental retardation.

Future demands upon the nation's community services for elderly persons will be in large part determined by today's baby boom generation. Much of the increased demand will be evident in the decade following the year 2000, when the first wave of the baby boomers will begin to enter the younger-senior, or 60+, age group. Demographers have estimated that although the number of older Americans is currently at about one of out nine, this proportion will shift to about one out of five within the next 30 to 40 years. There is a similar expectation for older adults with mental retardation. Consequently, consideration of these changing needs over the next 10 to 15 years is critical if appropriate supports and services are to be available.

Another impetus for policy consideration is the change in how society has viewed people with mental retardation and specifically older adults with mental retardation. Historically, the aging of persons with mental retardation was rarely considered even to the degree that pioneers like Dybwad (1962), who was among the first to consider aging issues, did so— that is, only with regard to problems facing young adults. Until relatively recently, persons with severe disabilities have had relatively short life expectancies, most older adults with mental retardation spent much of their lives out of sight in public institutions, and community sheltered workshops had not yet experienced a "greying" of their workers. These factors contributed to the lack of awareness of and concern for older and elderly adults with mental retardation (Malone, 1990). With improved health and social conditions, as well as new programs and technologies, persons with mental retardation are now living longer and are more numerous and conspicuous in natural community settings; thus their aging has become a more prominent system issue.

---

[2] ACD'd means alternate care determined—a concept in ICFs-MR whereby it is determined that someone residing in an ICF-MR can no longer benefit from it, due either to improvement or to deterioration.

A number of health policy concerns have been raised as well. One such concern stems from whether the individual characteristics of aging adults with mental retardation are similar or dissimilar from those of other aging persons (Eklund & Martz, 1993). The policy implication of this question is whether generic health services can serve all older people or whether specialized health services for older people with lifelong disabilities are needed (Jacobson, Janicki, & Ackerman, 1989). With regard to mental retardation, there are more similarities than dissimilarities, with some differences found in the areas of physiological and psychological aging (Hogg, Moss, & Cooke, 1988b; Seltzer & Krauss, chapter 1 this volume; Zigman, Seltzer & Silverman, chapter 5 this volume.) It has also been noted that having a mental or physical handicap over a lifetime has consequences for personal functioning in adulthood and into old age (Kailes, 1992; Maaskant, 1993; Overeynder et al., 1992; Zola, 1988). Probably the most defined differences are found in certain age-associated features among older persons with Down syndrome, including problems arising from premature aging and the higher rate of age-related Alzheimer disease (Lott, 1988; Wisniewski & Merz, 1985). On the positive side, with increased life expectancy, persons with Down syndrome are surviving past their 40s. This increased longevity, however, has led to an increased occurrence of precocious or premature aging and has raised questions about definitions of aging based upon chronological age and legislated age floors for the receipt of senior services. Health policy considerations are thus affected by knowing that as people age, irrespective of background, many of their social and physical needs are the same, and yet in some instances compensations have to be considered for some segment of adults who age earlier or need special services before their age peers need them.

Another health policy consideration is the co-incidence of Alzheimer disease among persons with mental retardation, which among age peers is markedly higher in persons who have Down syndrome (Lott, 1988; Noelker & Somple, 1993). Reports indicate that between 1.5% and 2.5% of adults with mental retardation, age 40 and older, have suspected or diagnosed Alzheimer disease, with increased frequency tied to advancing age; of these, about 60% are persons with Down syndrome (Janicki & Dalton, 1993a, 1993b). It has been reported that one in three persons with Down syndrome age 50 and older will manifest the behavioral symptomology of Alzheimer disease (Wisniewski & Merz, 1985). Thus more attention will need to be given to screening and clinical diagnostic strategies among older persons with Down syndrome to detect early signs of Alzheimer disease; more training of direct care staff will be needed so that they can observe and intervene effectively; and more planning will be required for fourth age services for a group of individuals whose chronological age normally would not call for such services (Janicki & Dalton, 1993b).

Thus, given that the demographic characteristics of this population will change dramatically over the next 10 to 20 years, the demands upon public and voluntary agencies will also change (Factor, 1993; Zola, 1988). We expect that the seniors of tomorrow will have different characteristics and needs than today's seniors and that these changes will place new demands upon health and social services. Public policy considerations thus need to take into account these changes in demographics and the changing character of successive generations of aging adults. Certainly, the growing similarities of the needs of older people, whether in the third or fourth age, and the desire to accommodate older people with mental retardation in a range of common community programs and services warrant further exploration of these policy considerations.

Program Issues

Concerns of Families
In the general population, families provide most of the informal supports (or "services") to elderly persons (Roberto, 1993). Because of these efforts, most impaired elderly adults live outside of institutions and most of their service needs are met by an informal sup-

port network, generally composed of a spouse or an adult daughter or son (Commonwealth Fund Commission, 1988). Unlike other elderly persons, older persons with mental retardation generally do not have children or a spouse on whom they can depend for support. In some cases, they live with very old parents who still provide their day-to-day supports (Jennings, 1987). In other instances, it is siblings or the children of siblings who provide care. Although the numbers of elderly persons with mental retardation who live with their families is estimated to be modest, if localities expand supports to families, continue to sustain adults with mental retardation in family settings, and provide more options for community involvement, then the numbers of persons with mental retardation growing older within their family homes is expected to increase in the future (Seltzer, 1992).

The two-generation elderly family, where the parents are in their 70s or 80s and a son or daughter with mental retardation is in his or her 50s or 60s, is a programmatic challenge because each family member may need specific aging services. Many older sons or daughters with mental retardation may not be known to service providers because they have remained at home and may not be currently involved with human services agencies (Smith, Fullmer, & Tobin, chapter 2 this volume). Service providers all too commonly are alerted to the existence of these individuals only after the death or hospitalization of a parent. Thus, the problems faced by parents who continue to care for an older adult son or daughter with mental retardation pose a difficult dilemma (Kaufman, 1989). Many states have yet to link available aging services with developmental disabilities services in such situations. During the past decade, the need of families for support in general, and for respite care in particular, has emerged as one of the most pronounced issues in the field of mental retardation (Turnbull et al., 1993). Although older families of persons with mental retardation have always had support needs, more attention is being paid to these needs as a result of several factors: increasing numbers of older families caring for a son or

daughter with a disability at home, the return to family life of older adults discharged from institutions, and the aging and increasing impairment of caregivers.

Although more attention has been devoted to the structure of American families and their capacity to provide care for dependent family members of all ages in recent years (Turnbull et al., 1993), provider agencies are still experiencing difficulties in identifying such older families and linking them to services. Several investigators (e.g., Smith et al., chapter 2 this volume; Tobin, 1992) have noted the problems inherent in finding families and older adults unknown to formal services. Indeed, older families have concerns that are different than those of younger parents. They are more worried about guardianship and conservator issues, permanency planning, and deciding whether or not to engage or avoid contact with mental retardation agencies. Many have led successful lives after making the decision not to institutionalize their infant or youngster with mental retardation. Thus, these "adaptive copers" in their later years present a different set of needs than do new parents facing the potentially richer array of supports offered to parents today (Krauss & Seltzer, 1993; see also Heller & Factor, chapter 3, and Seltzer & Krauss, chapter 1, this volume). Programmatic considerations thus could include extensive outreach to locate heretofore unknown families, collaboration among mental retardation, aging, and social services agencies to jointly serve older caregivers, and assistance to aid families in futures planning (see Smith et al., chapter 2 this volume).

Aging in Place

Generally, "aging in place" (or growing old where you live) refers to the problem of frailty of older individuals living in a community setting and the demands that increased frailty makes upon the support systems and the environment. As older persons with mental retardation who reside in group homes, apartments, or with their families have aged, their abilities and needs for supports have changed.

Some older persons experience medical complications or frailty that accompany the normal aging process as they enter the fourth age. Frailty has been defined in the Older Americans Act as having a physical or mental disability that restricts the ability of an individual to perform normal daily tasks and threatens the capacity of an individual to continue to live in a community setting (Janicki, 1993). In the general population, increased frailty may lead to admission to a long-term care setting; however, in many instances such an action can be precluded by targeted interventions that provide informal or formal supports or by environmental adaptations to enhance the individual's ability to continue to care for him or herself. Support intervention may mean providing in-home supports or finding an alternative living situation. Environmental intervention may mean adapting or changing buildings to compensate for the older individual's difficulties in ambulation, sensitivity to temperature changes, diminished vision and hearing, or impairments in fine motor dexterity. Such adaptations or modifications can include providing ramps and carpets, changing the height of cabinets, installing grab bars in bathrooms, replacing door knobs with door handles, installing air conditioning or zoned heating, etc. (New York State Office for the Aging [NYSOFA], 1990). These types of environmental modifications may be appropriate for any residential situation that includes people with mental retardation. Modifications can also include augmenting staff capacities by offering cross-training related to physical aging and special medical and nursing care practices (Gibson, Rabkin, & Munson, 1992; Janicki, 1991; Maaskant, 1993). Modifications may also be assistive devices and may include glasses or hearing aids for sensory deficits and wheelchairs and other mobility aids for ambulation deficits for persons who may experience losses due to chronic diseases or skill losses (Maaskant, 1993).

With aging in place, differing demands are placed upon family caregivers and residential setting staff. In natural settings, increasing frailty may jeopardize continued independent living because of concerns about the inability for self-care, potential harm due to falls or misuse of household appliances, or poor nutrition due to lack of access to meals or foodstuffs. In contrast, supervised community residential settings may in fact offer an alternative to institutionalization for older adults with mental retardation in their fourth age. With increased frailty, older adults with mental retardation living alone may lose important self-care capacities; however, in a staffed group setting these losses may not jeopardize continued stay. Thus, whereas small group or supportive living settings may have had a different purpose for younger age persons, with increasing age and frailty, they may be the lifeline to continued community living. The programmatic challenge to staff and other caregivers is to accommodate changes among individuals as they grow older and to view alternative residential options as a means of providing supports to those individuals for as long as possible. When leaving the residence is warranted, the primary reason is typically an illness or medical condition that requires acute hospitalization. Programmatic considerations thus could include promoting activities that are directed toward adapting the residence, retraining the staff rather than forcing a change in residence, and providing the financial underpinnings for continued stay.

Retiring

Retirement for older persons with mental retardation is a relatively novel concept. To retire, one needs to have been actively involved in work or work programs, and many older adults with mental retardation have not been. In such situations does retirement have conceptual validity? Moss (see Janicki, Moss, & Lucchino, 1992), citing the British experience, has argued that retirement may *not* be a normal life stage transition in situations where adults with mental retardation do not normally participate in work programs and questions whether there will be any changes in daily activities or routines if they are deemed to be "retired." However, when work has been a primary activity (as it has been for some older adults with mental retardation), choosing to retire often marks a major life transition that is fraught with conflicting demands. For older persons in general a number of issues are involved in the choices made. Understanding the options under any retirement scheme is important to deciding what one will give up or gain. Many people, because of the importance of *primary and secondary gains* associated with their work, are vexed by questions about what will happen when wages or salary are no longer received (primary gain), what will happen to friendships, having a place to go each workday, and the personal identity that is defined by one's job (secondary gains). With most people, wages or salary are usually substituted by Social Security benefits or a pension, and friendship circles are expanded and status redefined by new affiliations and life activities.

The social and personal changes associated with retirement can be traumatic, especially when some bridging or transitioning has not occurred. This may be particularly true for persons with a lifelong disability, some of whom have become dependent upon their workplace both for discretional monies and social supports (Janicki, 1989; Sutton, Sterns, & Park, 1993). Thus, precipitous loss of income or change in friendships after leaving a workplace and becoming involved in new settings can be a problem. Compounding this problem in the United States is the lack of any change in funding or claimant status under the Social Security Act when a person who has been on Supplemental Security Income (SSI) "retires." (An adult on SSI due to lifelong disability does not become a Social Security pension recipient.) Indeed, most individuals on SSI who live in group quarters do not see the monies received (except for a small personal allowance), as these are generally kept by caregivers or host agencies to cover room and board costs. Thus, monies earned in sheltered work or other employment settings may be the only tangible discretionary income for such older adults. This loss of money upon retirement can pose a problem. In either instance, whether the earned money has real or symbolic value, its loss is felt and may pose a major impediment to wanting to retire. The lack of a "pension policy" (or any substitution scheme for earned income) can pose problems for agencies working with individuals who are of retirement age, as most individuals with a lifelong disability do not receive earned Social Security benefits or pensions to use as income in retirement (New York State Developmental Disabilities Planning Council [NYSDDPC], 1988).

Being a retiree without discretionary monies poses other problems as well. Inclusion in senior group activities, such as an outing or a trip, may involve a nominal fee. Even participating in a congregate meal program involves some cost, since nutrition sites ask for a modest donation per meal. One can argue that older people should have the dignity associated with "paying my own way." This is particularly touchy among those persons trying to "fit in" who are of limited means, because many senior activities are peer-oriented and what one contributes is closely watched by the other seniors. Thus, having money to spend in such situations can be crucial to an older individual's dignity and self-respect.

Many states have not yet developed policies or supports that permit individuals with a lifelong disability to retire from programs or activities in which they may have been involved for all or part of their adult life and move to an alternate set of programs or activities (Rinck, Tomer, Griggs, & Cohen, 1992; Sutton, Sterns, & Park, 1993). Thus, one concern related to retirement is ensuring that appropriate policies and structures are in place to ease retirement, encourage personal planning for the later years, and invite greater involvement in the community. Another concern is underwriting the costs of programs that aid in the transition to retirement and of programs that can maintain retirement (Factor, 1993). In some instances, this involves finding a way to pay for housing and day services; in others it may mean finding ways to fund pensions (NYSDDPC, 1988). In still others, it may mean planning for alternatives to traditional long-term care services to accommodate older persons as they become frail and more infirm with increasing age (Ansello & Rose, 1989).

Integrating Services

There have been major changes in public attitudes toward adults with mental retardation over the past ten years (Anderson, 1993a). Many local providers are thus trying to accommodate new thinking related to community living philosophies and practices. The reality, however, is that state and local agencies are faced with the problem of fierce competition for resources for people of different ages and the question of whether to operate integrated or segregated services (Hogg, 1990). It has been argued that the aging and mental retardation networks can work together with respect to aging people with mental retardation (Ansello & Rose, 1989; Lepore & Janicki, 1990; McDowell, 1988; Ossofsky, 1988).

In comparisons of services for people with mental retardation and those for elderly people, it has been noted that these two populations are similar with respect to the need for health services, income maintenance, and social supports, and dissimilar with respect to the total life-span needs (Gettings, 1988, 1989; Hogg & Moss, 1991; Janicki et al., 1985). In addition, people with mental retardation may require at an earlier stage of their lives services that are usually provided to elderly people. Thus, given the convergence of needs with older age, use of generic programs may ensure age-appropriateness of activities and environment, flexibility, normalized social engagement with nonhandicapped people, and wider integration in the community (Hawkins, 1993; Seltzer, 1988).

A number of workers have demonstrated the feasibility of integrating people with mental retardation into a range of generic aging network and other day services (Ansello, Coogle, Wood, & Cotter, 1992; de Thibault, 1993; Ern, 1993; Janicki, 1991; LePore & Janicki, 1990; Stroud & Sutton, 1988). However, these efforts, as Seltzer (1988) and LePore and Janicki (1990) have argued, may be subject to certain weaknesses because of obstacles to integration efforts that derive from the lack of appropriate staff training, lack of receptiveness in staff or other users at the programs,

and inappropriateness of activities or programming found at the sites for people with mental retardation. Other factors may be operating as well, such as the exclusivity of developmental disability services, a sense of superiority on their part, or simply an unwillingness to face the problems aging poses to an agency (Janicki, 1988). Others have noted another problem: the lack of adequately trained professionals who know about both aging and mental retardation and who understand the means to provide comprehensive services for older people with mental retardation (Cotten & Spirrison, 1988; Davidson, Janicki, Seltzer, & Rose, 1988; Gibson, Rabkin, & Munson, 1992; Janicki, 1988, 1991; Kultgen & Rominger, 1993; Seltzer, 1988).

With respect to community involvement, Hogg et al. (1991) have noted several classes of variables that have shown to have an influence, including the following: (a) age *per se* has been shown to be associated with residential settings that tend to restrict community integration, whereas a variety of aspects of adaptive behavior will also affect both social contacts and extent to which community facilities are accessed; (b) people with moderate to minimal mental retardation can maintain themselves independently or semi-independently; however, it is equally clear from studies that the quality of life in many "normalized" community settings is generally of a low order; (c) type of residential setting has been shown to impact a variety of aspects of social and community integration, though it is clear that it is the operating policy or social mode of the residence, rather than the residential type *per se*, that encourages integration; (d) a growing body of data indicate that integration can be facilitated through direct personal intervention, notably through paid or volunteer companion schemes; (e) leisure activities have increasingly become the foci for social and community integration; several surveys have demonstrated the importance of leisure pursuits as contributors to this process and to the development and expansion of the emotional lives of people with mental retardation; and (f) in areas where they exist, generic community seniors programs have been shown to be an effective program model for older persons with mental retardation when the program milieu accommodates new entrants.

In examining the variability of community services for seniors with mental retardation, Janicki (1992) noted that some services have evolved or been developed through strategies that start at the governmental level and others have evolved through the interest of local groups or service providers. At the governmental level he noted efforts at planning and bridging—that is, efforts at identifying common concerns, numbers of potential clientele, and cooperative endeavors between government departments that provide for the elderly and those that provide for persons with mental retardation. In many such cases, these government activities can be considered somewhat fundamental; in others, these activities have taken on noteworthy features.

In many instances, efforts are directed at aiding third age activities—whether they are defined programs or simply individual assistance efforts. Others are directed at fourth age problems, like extended care needs and supportive medical services. In those instances where third age needs are recognized and the social system can accommodate targeted activities, many of these efforts are directed toward integration activities, like the ones noted below. In other instances, national or local efforts are a response to an elderly segment of a population without much focus on strategies (for example, situations that are reactive, possibly resulting from aging in place).

In those instances where specific organized strategies were available to aid older adults with retirement or a shifting of programmatic focus, Janicki (1992) noted that they took on the following facets: *retirement assistance ventures* that aid with the task of retiring and using leisure time; *pull-out programs* that draw two or more groups of people together for a common purpose during a set time; *senior companion ventures* that involve a senior friend or companion helping someone with a disability to use the common senior services; *senior center ventures* that aid an older person with mental retardation with using a neighborhood or community senior services center; *social model site programs* that provide a day service composed of activities and supervision for seniors with special needs (often persons with dementia or other mentally debilitating conditions); and *health model site programs* that provide a day service composed of activities and supervision for seniors with physical or mental needs under the direction of a physician.

In any given locality, the extent of community involvement among persons with disabilities and the nature of senior services program development are functions of public policy. Localities define how they view involvement and development; thus, to expand either, they determine which program development approach (integration, specialty programs, or a blending of these two) they want to pursue. Experience has shown that no one method can sufficiently address the support needs of all older persons with developmental disabilities in a given community. Further, the question of how individual choice is factored into this policy mechanism has yet to be fully explored on a research level.

Involvement in Ordinary Life

The promotion of community involvement is not new, having been part of social policy, agency practices, research, and personal needs for many years. Involvement in older age has witnessed providers and seniors seeking out retirement activities and options within the broader community and, more narrowly, within the aging network. There is nothing magical about looking to the aging network for such options—most recognize the variability of the options within this network. Indeed, with time and perseverance, anyone can find things to do in his or her community (whether the activity is specifically accommodating seniors or more generally persons of all ages) and these may not need to be specifically linked to aging network programs.

In the United States, community aging network programs offer a variety of options supported by public funds. In many communities, congregate meal sites, senior clubs, and retiree activity centers have been around for some time (National Council on the Aging [NCOA], 1990). In 1965, Congress made a commitment to the elderly population of the United States by providing for social settings that could serve as gathering places for persons with limited options or of limited means (NASUA, 1985; Quirk & Aravanis, 1988). These modest social settings, over the years, have expanded to the varied types of multipurpose senior centers found in many of our communities today (Krout, 1993). Some evolved from preexisting senior clubs while others were specifically developed to serve a particular neighborhood or community. These types of settings exist in other countries as well, where such senior or pensioner clubs, neighborhood social centers, autumn clubs, and luncheon clubs are often underwritten by public funds or supported by membership fees.

Why focus on these? Community involvement means being part of one's community, having the same opportunities to use public amenities as one's peers, and using these opportunities to live an ordinary life. Further, it means being involved with and an intimate part of the scene of any community and party to the same experiences as other persons of one's age. Being accepted, befriended, and free to pick and choose from what is available are all part of being included—as are the risks of failure, rejection, and frustration. Senior services within the United States can provide a rich and varied choice of environments for meeting others of like age, developing new friendships, and being able to recreate, socialize, and learn new things. Thus, these types of settings can offer ripe opportunities for community involvement.

Programs specifically designed to accommodate the needs of older persons with mental retardation involve a careful blending of the needs of the individual and available resources. Oftentimes, program needs can be met via existing program models that can range from drop-in recreation/ social centers for persons who are retired or who only work part-time, to home supports, preretirement training projects, or social/

health model adult day care programs. These programs can be age-specific or multigenerational.

There is growing recognition that among the elderly there is a diversity of need, especially among those individuals with late-life disabilities or age-associated impairments (Ansello & Rose, 1989). Although mental retardation provider agencies are beginning to respond with community support services, such as home health and respite, most aging network services have not sufficiently evolved to accommodate persons with long-term dependency or physical care needs. The mental retardation system, however, does have the capability to continue to provide long-term care services to individuals with severe disabilities. It also has the potential to provide social recreational services to persons minimally impaired when no aging network alternatives exist. For example, in some communities, social model day-care programs run by mental retardation agencies are open to all functionally impaired seniors, irrespective of impairment etiology (see Janicki, 1992). In this vein, providers of services to persons with mental retardation can also become community resources to other seniors who need adult day services. Many states are considering such program options where there are limited senior services, where there is a reluctance to overwhelm existing services with many older persons with lifelong disabilities, thus changing the character of those services, or where existing aging network services are of poor quality.

Day Activities and Program Options

Adjusting one's lifestyle to age-specific wants or demands may mean engaging in a variety of activities, including becoming involved in work or volunteering. With regard to work, many older persons continue to work beyond traditional retirement age in the jobs they hold; others may retire from full-time employment and seek part-time jobs to occupy time and provide supplemental income (Stout Vocational Rehabilitation Institute [SVRI], 1990). Informal and formal work options can range from continuing or starting work, involvement in an older worker program, volunteering, involvement in other community aging network programs, or participation in specialty retirement or activity programs operated by a community social or disability agency.

Employment programs, such as the Senior Community Employment Services Program, can help place income-eligible seniors within community and government agencies in part-time positions (SVRI, 1990). This program, under Title V of the Older Americans Act, is directed toward seniors age 55 and older whose incomes are within 125% of poverty level. Other agencies, such as state employment service and vocational rehabilitation agencies also can aid in locating full-time or part-time employment (SVRI, 1990). The advantages of continued employment are that it can ease the transition to retirement as it provides money for bills, other expenses, and discretionary spending. It can also provide gainful activity, intergenerational socialization opportunities, and continued involvement with other persons. Unfortunately, employment or work supports may not always be available, or seniors may come up against the federal annual allowable earned income limits or find that work availability is highly dependent upon the local economy. Further, a substantial barrier to continued employment is the ageism practiced by the many employment and vocational rehabilitation agencies that do not offer older applicants tangible assistance in locating work or job training (SVRI, 1990).

Volunteering activities can range from informally giving time and helping in community activities or participating in formal programs like Green Thumb, Foster Grandparents, or Senior Companions (Rinck et al., 1992). The advantages of volunteering include involvement in programs that (a) provide outlets for wanting to help, (b) offer opportunities for socializing and making new friends, and (c) tender something back to the community. Additionally, volunteering usually occurs within a supervised program and thus may offer gentle guidance for volunteers. Volunteering may also provide a small income (if a stipend is available) and a chance for formal involvement with community activities. How-

ever, there are also disadvantages to volunteering; for example, volunteering requires an ability to function independently and exercise judgement; volunteering opportunities may not always be available; transportation to volunteer sites may be a problem; and not all volunteer supervisors are capable of overseeing seniors with disabilities.

Qualitatively, senior service settings will vary as much as the people who administer and populate them. Some are housed in spacious buildings, rich in variety and opportunities and open to a spectrum of the community. Others, more humble, may offer the barest essentials and opportunities—often only a place to meet and share a cup of morning coffee or afternoon tea (Standards and Guidelines Committee, 1993). Begun in 1943 in New York City, senior centers are places that typically offer a slate of weekly activities for seniors, often accompanied by a daily, hot lunch (Oriol, 1993). Some sites have TV, game, craft, and other activity rooms where multiple activities occur simultaneously. Depending on the center site, some activities may be directed by paid or volunteer leaders. It is estimated that senior centers are used by between 10 and 20% of America's elderly population (Krout, 1993). Participation in activities is voluntary and on a first-come, first-served basis. Senior center site users generally tend to be healthy, active, and self-selecting as to what they do or do not want to do while at the center. For older adults with mental retardation, getting involved with senior centers may have advantages, including a "right at home, right in the community" experience, a diversity of activities and an environment that can be stimulating, a chance to make new friends, and opportunities to socialize and be part of a daily community group. There are disadvantages, however, including a limited staff who may not have had experience with older persons with mental retardation, supervision that may be minimal, some activities too complex or not of interest, an environment that is relatively unstructured, and the potential for bias and discrimination against participants with mental retardation or physical disabilities (Ossofsky, 1988).

Nutrition programs (or congregate meal sites) are places where a hot midday meal is provided in a congregate setting to persons aged 60 and over. Persons under age 60 may be served if they are a spouse or are disabled and live with or are under the care of a person age 60 or older. The setting may be at a day care program, senior center, or a community location such as a church, school, town hall, or community center. The primary purpose of a nutrition site is to serve a noontime meal to those who wish to participate. Nutrition sites serve as a focal point and meeting place for seniors and often may be the only available social setting in a community where seniors can meet. Many sites have activities and programs timed to occur around the meal. For seniors with mental retardation, senior centers offer many advantages; for example, such programs are found in most communities, they provide hot meals in the company of age peers, and offer a social atmosphere that provides opportunities to make new friends. They also offer a chance for volunteering (for example, serving as the greeter at the door, collecting meal donations, setting up the tables for the meal, cleaning up afterwards, or helping with the home delivered meals program, if food preparation is done on site). In general, the advantages outweigh the disadvantages. However, there are also some disadvantages; for example, most nutrition sites are open only a few hours a day (thus, offering limited engagement for persons needing a full day activity), activity programming at sites may be limited or nonexistent, openness to new participants may be a problem, and the expected donation per meal may be an impediment to regular attendance for persons on limited incomes.

In contrast to these informal social settings, formal day services like social adult day care or day services programs are sites that typically provide daytime care and activities for seniors who require supervision or who may be frail (NCOA, 1990). Such programs provide assessments and formal admissions, and activities tend to be individualized. They can serve as respite for families who must provide for their elderly relatives or as a program site for others in need of a social program. The advantages of using such sites are that programming is oriented on the basis of individual need; staff generally have experience with persons who have various disabilities and impairments; and program participants who are not mentally retarded share similarities in functional abilities with older persons with mental retardation. The disadvantages of using such sites are that staff ratios at day care sites are lower than those found in the specialist disability network day programs, social adult day care programs may not operate under a fixed set of standards (so program quality may vary from site to site), and, because categorical funding for social adult day care programs does not exist (most programs are only supported by their funding source and participant fees), cost may be a problem.

Supports to Families

Most older persons with mental retardation, if still living at home, reside with an elderly parent or parents and experience "aging in place." Such a two-generation elderly family often requires special services from both the aging and developmental disabilities networks (Janicki, Krauss, Cotten, & Seltzer, 1986). In some communities, disability agencies have developed special outreach efforts to aid such families. In some instances, the disability agencies have developed joint efforts with aging network agencies because, under the Older Americans Act, the state's area agencies on aging are responsible for providing a number of family supports (Ansello & Rose, 1989). Thus, when looking for support possibilities to aid older families with a member with mental retardation, the local area agency on aging might be a good resource. The local aging services agencies can offer a range of support services to elderly caregivers, including access assistance (transportation, outreach, and information and referral), in-home services (homemaker and home health aide, visiting and telephone reassurance, chore maintenance, and supportive services for families of elderly victims of Alzheimer disease and neurological and organic brain disorders of the Alzheimer type), and legal assistance (NASUA, 1985; Quirk & Aravanis, 1988).

Housing Options

A number of community housing options may become opportunities for older individuals with mental retardation, who functionally may have the same abilities or limitations as other elderly individuals needing special housing (Ansello & Rose, 1989). In some instances, age along with income and functional level (but not categorical disability) are the criteria used to determine eligibility; in others, age alone may determine eligibility.

Housing options range from generic housing that may be used by any older person who may be no longer living in his or her own home to specialist housing, such as supportive apartments and family care/personal care homes provided by disability agencies (Stone, 1989). Typical senior housing options may include shared housing, assisted-living, senior citizen housing, ECHO units, home equity conversions, and on a much broader scale, any of these occurring within naturally occurring retirement communities (American Association of Retired Persons [AARP], 1984). Housing programs may also include in-home supports that help older persons to continue to live in their own homes.

Shared housing or group living residences for older adults who share household responsibilities and living expenses, usually with no live-in supervision provided (AARP, 1984), have a number of advantages including normalized living with other seniors. They are similar to group homes (but without staff), usually free of local site selection requirements, operated by not-for-profit groups, and relatively inexpensive to operate. The disadvantages are that this model has been tried with seniors with mental retardation in only limited areas, and when it has been tried it has been limited to seniors with high independence capacity and skills. In addition, there may be some difficulty in finding housemate matches, reticence on the part of disability agencies to make referrals (for fear of losing 'clientele'), or the need for an agency to provide oversight and supports. In some communities, restrictive zoning ordinances may also pose a barrier.

A variation on the above is an "assisted-living development" where a for-profit developer, often a hotel corporation, transforms a former hotel (or may build a new one) to a residence for adults, generally 70 years of age or older (New York Times, 1993a). Assisted-living units, seen as an alternative for nursing homes, are more functional because they are open to older adults who are not seriously ill or infirm and who do not want to live on their own, but want to enjoy some privacy and control and be in the company of others their age. Residents of such programs receive meals, transportation, housekeeping, personal care, and medication management while living in their own apartments. Advantages and disadvantages for participation in this type of arrangement are similar to those for shared housing, with the exception that, because these types of programs are usually operated by for-profit entities, having sufficient funds to "buy in" may be an obstacle.

Privately or publicly operated congregate housing for a locality's senior citizens offers independent living with the provision of some on-site supports (Prosper, 1987). Some 5% of the nation's seniors live in congregate housing programs (AARP, 1984). For older adults with mental retardation, the advantages of seeking to live in public congregate housing include nondiscriminatory eligibility (generally age and residency and not disability), living with age peers, availability of support services on premises, physically accessible apartments, and the availability of meals in a common dining area. There are disadvantages, however, including competition with other elderly persons for scarce units, needing to be on a waiting list and possibly needing own transportation, variable housing quality (depending upon town), and needing to secure supports from an outside agency.

Accessory apartments built into family homes or freestanding units placed on property adjacent to a family home (AARP, 1984) are another housing option that promotes greater autonomy. Also called ECHO units (ECHO stands for Elder Cottage Housing Opportunities—originated in Australia, they are also known as "granny flats"), these apartments offer the advantage of living independently near a relative, alone, or with housemates. Generally these are set up in a garage or other freestanding building or in an addition to the regular family home—but offer private access, independent utilities, and a sense of being on one's own. They are relatively economical to live in, usually unencumbered by regulatory constraints, and provide easy eligibility for in-home aging network support services. Among the disadvantages, however, is that this type of apartment is not permitted in some communities, due to zoning restrictions. Further, there may be no "program" support monies available, there may be a need to tie in to day services, and most importantly, there is the potential for loss of the residence when the family moves or the parents die or themselves become frail and leave the family's primary residence.

Home equity conversion is a means of converting assets of a high equity home by a homeowner to provide monthly support funds for living in the home (AARP, 1987; NYSOFA, 1987). The advantages are that parents who do not need the equity in their home for their own retirement can set up their son or daughter in their own home for a determinant period of time. Indeed, the son or daughter can be designated a co-owner, can continue to live in his or her own family's home, and can have a regular monthly allowance on which to live. The home can also be used to support a shared housing unit. On the other hand, although this arrangement provides guaranteed security for a set time, a significant problem may be the loss of the home when equity runs out. Other disadvantages may include a need for agency tie-in for supports and outside help for home maintenance and inaccessibility of amenities if located in a suburban or rural area. Also, obtaining an fair equity mortgage (and finding low closing costs) is highly dependent upon location and housing market.

Naturally occurring retirement communities (or NORCs as they have come to be known) are places not originally planned or intended as communities for older people, but due to various reasons half or more of the residents are now age 60 or older (AARP, 1984). Such communities can consist of a single building, a development, an entire neighborhood, or even a small town or resort community (New York Times, 1993b). They are formed either by older people who have remained after younger people have moved away or by older people moving in after retirement. It is estimated that about one in four older Americans live in this type of community and the expectation is that the number will grow over the next twenty years. For seniors with mental retardation, the advantages of living in NORCs can include availability of some social and health services, informal supports, continued living in a community and neighborhood setting, and greater chances of friendships, socialization, and potential for participation in age-peer clubs and activity groups. There are some potential disadvantages as well; these include living with mostly other seniors, sometimes only informal community services, a lack of special services, and lack of special funding to secure housing within the NORC.

Implications for Policy, Research, and Service Provision

Public policy will need to accommodate anticipated changes in both the demographics and the character of successive generations of adults maturing into old age. The growing similarities of the needs of older people whether in the third or fourth age, irrespective of whether they have had a lifelong disability or not, and the desire to accommodate older people with mental retardation in a range of common community programs and services are areas that require further research and exploration.

Government, at all levels, needs to make a commitment to services for people with mental retardation who are aging. One measure of the impact of public policy commitments is the extent of community involvement among persons with disabilities and the nature of senior services program development. Discussed, but unresolved, is the question of how future public policy will define involvement and development: Will we see in the future an expansion of integration approaches or an intensified development of specialty programs? Or perhaps we'll see a blending of the two? Experience showing that no one method can sufficiently address the support needs of all older persons with mental retardation in a given community argues for a variety of approaches. Further, individual choice needs to be factored into this policy mechanism; yet, this has not been fully explored on a research level.

The future of greater community involvement of older people is based upon building a system of supports that listens and responds to the stated needs of the individuals it is designed to aid. This will mean going beyond traditional models of care and services to ensure that older persons with mental retardation can define what they need, get supports and services in a manner that makes them part of the greater community, and promotes the highest quality of their lives as far into old age as possible.

Thus, the continued reassessment of public policies that impede involvement and enhanced participation have to be undertaken. To this end, several iterations of federal law (in particular the Older Americans Act) have stimulated federal initiatives for older persons with mental retardation. More focused attention at the federal, state, and local levels will have to occur; specifically more initiatives that promote interagency training, staff exchanges, and greater awareness and sensitivity to aging among persons with mental retardation among administrators, agency staff, and mainstream seniors using aging network services (Ansello & Rose, 1989; Gibson, Rabkin, & Munson, 1992; Ossofsky, 1988). At the federal level, the federal administrations concerned with developmental disabilities and aging need to request that state advisory councils (to the state units on aging) specifically include older persons with a disability and persons who have caregiving responsibility for older persons with mental retardation or a person with mental retardation; encourage cross-training between the aging network and the mental retardation system, particularly involving local agencies and university programs; and stress that the plans of the state units on aging and area agencies on aging include consideration of older adults with mental retardation and other disabilities.

At the state level, state units on aging and mental retardation authorities need to encourage senior centers to consider the needs of older adults with cognitive disabilities and offer programs, classes, and activities that will appeal to them and further encourage them to attend the centers; encourage area agencies on aging to provide technical assistance to local mental retardation agencies if they want to set up retirement activity programs; and support projects that provide models for renovation or re-construction of senior centers to make them fully accessible to people with cognitive and physical disabilities, including adaptive signage and changes in physical amenities, entrances, communication systems, and dining facilities.

With regard to research, unfortunately, aging remains a stepchild within the mainstream disability research community. Research efforts with regard to programmatic issues have been particularly scant. More research is needed to identify factors that ease involvement and greater participation in aging network programs and increase the variability of programs so that people with all types of personal competencies and capabilities will be able to use such community resources freely. In addition, studies need to be undertaken that examine adaptability within the aging network as applied to seniors with mental retardation. Studies also need to include participant satisfaction measures, examining the outcome of current integration strategies. Research is also needed on more general individual decision making and futures planning to examine the processes and outcomes from initiatives currently being undertaken to enable older adults to take active control over their lives.

Research is also needed that examines specialist versus generalist approaches to providing services and individual assistance.

Indeed, from a broader public policy perspective, research is needed to examine directions and commitments of personnel and fiscal resources by state mental retardation authorities to aging related services and individual supports. With successive reauthorizations of the Older Americans Act showing more responsibility to people with disabilities, research is also needed to examine the impact of existing initiatives and approaches of compliance with this legislation. Further, continued examination of the lives of older parents who have perpetual parenting responsibilities is needed to identify the factors of aging network supports that are most helpful in maintaining family integrity and survival.

As states wrestle with the fundamentals of whether, or how, to provide integrated or specialist services, avenues for stable funding will have to be worked out to enable a full range of age-specific options to become available and the mechanisms offered to provide supports for their use. Importantly, once states (via their mental retardation authorities) have devoted full attention to aging related services, we will truly see cradle-to-grave (that is, life-span) services and supports for people with mental retardation. Thus, older adult services or supports will no longer stop with work options or workshops, but continue on to facilitate broader third age options, such as retirement and the living out of productive ordinary lives as older citizens, and creative and innovative fourth age options that offer dignity to old age.

References

American Association of Retired Persons. (1984). *Housing options for older Americans.* Washington, DC: Author.

American Association of Retired Persons. (1987). *Home made money: Consumer's guide to home equity conversion.* Washington, DC: Author.

Anderson, D. (1993a). Health issues. In E. Sutton, A. R. Factor, B. Hawkins, T. Heller, & G. Seltzer (Eds.), *Older adults with developmental disabilities: Optimizing choices and change* (pp. 29–48). Baltimore, MD: Brookes.

Anderson, D. (1993b). Social inclusion of older adults with mental retardation. In E. Sutton, A. R. Factor, B. Hawkins, T. Heller, & G. Seltzer (Eds.), *Older adults with developmental disabilities: Optimizing choices and change* (pp. 79–94). Baltimore, MD: Brookes.

Ansello, E. F., Coogle, C. L., Wood, J. B., & Cotter, J. J. (1992, September). *Partners II: Aging and developmental disabilities in Virginia.* Paper presented at the Second Lexington Conference on Aging and Developmental Disabilities, Lexington, KY.

Ansello, E. F., & Rose, T. (1989). *Aging and lifelong disabilities: Partnership for the twenty-first century.* College Park: University of Maryland, Center on Aging.

Blaney, B. C. (1992). The search for a conceptual framework. In S. Moss (Ed.), *Aging and Developmental Disabilities: Perspectives from Nine Countries* (Monograph #52). Durham, NH: World Rehabilitation Fund/University of New Hampshire.

Bureau of Census. (1988). *Aging in the Third World.* Washington, DC: U.S. Department of Commerce.

Clark, S. (1988). Room in the aging network? A view from the aging system. *Perspective on Aging, 17*(5), 13,22.

Commonwealth Fund Commission. (1988). *Aging alone: Profiles and projections.* Baltimore, MD: Commonwealth Fund.

Cotten, P.D. (1985). The elderly mentally retarded (developmentally disabled) population: A challenge for the service delivery system. In S. J. Brody & G. E. Ruff (Eds.), *Aging and rehabilitation: Advances in the state of the art* (pp.159–187). New York: Springer.

Cotten, P. D., & Spirrison, C. L. (1988). Development of services for elderly persons with mental retardation in a rural state. *Mental Retardation, 26,* 187–190.

Davidson, P. W., Janicki, M. P., Seltzer, M. M., & Rose, T. (1988, March). *Proceedings of "Aging and Developmental Disabilities: Windows to the Aging Network."* (Symposium presented at the ADD Commissioner's Annual Forum, New Orleans, LA). Rochester, NY: University of Rochester, University Affiliated Program in Developmental Disabilities.

de Thibault, T. (1993, May). *Outline of a program preparing mentally handicapped persons for retirement*. Paper presented at the 4th International Roundtable on Aging and Mental Handicap (Training Staff for Work with Ageing Mentally Handicapped Persons), Lyon, France.

Dybwad, G. (1962). Administrative and legislative problems in the care of the adult and aged mental retardate. *American Journal of Mental Deficiency, 66*, 716–722.

Eklund, S. J., & Martz, W. L. (1993). Maintaining optimal functioning. In E. Sutton, A. R. Factor, B. Hawkins, T. Heller, & G. Seltzer (Eds.), *Older adults with developmental disabilities: Optimizing choices and change* (pp. 3–28). Baltimore, MD: Brookes.

Ern, M. (1993, May). *Service networks for the aged, for the disabled: The problem of coming together of older persons with mental handicaps sharing services with the elderly*. Paper presented at Fondation de France (Paris) Conference on Disability and Old Age — How Do They Add Up? International Contrasts and Parallels, Lyon, France.

Factor, A. (1993). Translating policy into practice. In E. Sutton, A. R. Factor, B. Hawkins, T. Heller, & G. Seltzer (Eds.), *Older adults with developmental disabilities: Optimizing choices and change* (pp. 257–276). Baltimore, MD: Brookes.

Gettings, R. (1988). Barriers to and opportunities for cooperation between the aging and developmental disability services. *Educational Gerontology, 14*, 419–429.

Gettings, R. M. (1989). Barriers to and opportunities for cooperation between the aging and developmental disabilities service delivery systems. In E. F. Ansello & T. Rose (Eds.), *Aging and lifelong disabilities: Partnership for the twenty-first century* (pp. 27–30). College Park: University of Maryland, Center on Aging.

Gettings, R. M. (1990). *Eliminating inappropriate nursing home placements: An analysis of federal/state implementation of OBRA/87's PASARR requirements*. Alexandria, VA: National Association of State Mental Retardation Program Directors.

Gibson, J. W., Rabkin, J., & Munson, R. (1992). Critical issues in serving the developmentally disabled elderly. *Journal of Gerontological Social Work, 19*, 35–49.

Hawkins, B. (1993). Leisure participation and life satisfaction of older adults with mental retardation and Down syndrome. In E. Sutton, A. R. Factor, B. Hawkins, T. Heller, & G. Seltzer (Eds.), *Older adults with developmental disabilities: Optimizing choices and change* (pp. 141–156). Baltimore, MD: Brookes.

Hawkins, B. A., & Eklund, S. J. (1989). Aging and developmental disabilities: Interagency planning for an emerging population. *Journal of Applied Gerontology, 8*, 168–174.

Heller, T., & Factor, A. (1994). Facilitating future planning and transitions out of the home. In M. M. Seltzer, M. W. Krauss, & M. P. Janicki (Eds.), *Life course perspectives on adulthood and old age* (pp. 39–50). Washington, DC: American Association on Mental Retardation.

Henning, D. (1993, May). *Designing a staff training program to meet your goals*. Paper presented at the 4th International Roundtable on Aging and Mental Handicap (Training Staff for Work with Ageing Mentally Handicapped Persons), Lyon, France.

Hogg, J. (1990). *International sources and directions in the study of ageing and severe intellectual impairment (mental handicap)*. Paper presented at the symposium "Growing Up and Growing Older," Institute for Research on Mental Retardation and Brain Aging, Troina, Italy.

Hogg, J., & Moss, S. (1991). Social and community integration. In M.P. Janicki & M. M. Seltzer (eds.), *Aging and developmental disabilities: Challenges for the 1990s* (Proceedings of the Boston Roundtable on Research Issues and Applications in Aging and Developmental Disabilities) (pp. 25–51).

Washington, D.C: American Association on Mental Retardation, Aging Special Interest Group.

Hogg, J., Moss, S., & Cooke, D. (1988a). *Ageing and mental handicap.* London: Croom-Helm.

Hogg, J., Moss, S., & Cooke, D. (1988b). From mid-life to old age: Ageing and the nature of specific life-transitions of people with mental handicap. In G. Horobin & D. May (Eds.), *Living with mental handicap: Transitions in the lives of people with mental handicap* (pp. 148–165). London: Jessica Kingsley.

Jacobson, J. W., Janicki, M. P., & Ackerman, L. (1989). Health care services usage by older persons with developmental disabilities living in community settings. *Adult Residential Care Journal, 3,* 181–191.

Janicki, M. P. (1988). Aging and persons with mental handicap and developmental disabilities. *Journal of Practical Approaches to Developmental Handicap, 12* (2), 9–13.

Janicki, M. P. (1989). Transition from worklife to retirement for older persons with mental retardation. *Proceedings of the Presidential Forum: Citizens with mental retardation and community integration* (pp. 150–155). Washington, DC: President's Committee on Mental Retardation.

Janicki, M. P. (1991). *Building the future: Planning and community development in aging and developmental disabilities.* Albany: New York State Office of Mental Retardation and Developmental Disabilities (Community Integration Project in Aging and Developmental Disabilities).

Janicki, M. P. (1992). *Integration experiences casebook: Program ideas in aging and developmental disabilities.* Albany: New York State Office of Mental Retardation and Developmental Disabilities (Community Integration Project in Aging and Developmental Disabilities).

Janicki, M. P. (1993). *Building the future: Planning and community development in aging and developmental disabilities* (rev. ed.). Albany: New York State Office of Mental Retardation and Developmental

Disabilities (Community Integration Project in Aging and Developmental Disabilities).

Janicki, M. P., & Bradbury, S. (1993). *Creating choices: New York's third age programs.* Albany: New York State Office of Mental Retardation and Developmental Disabilities.

Janicki, M. P., & Dalton, A. J. (1993a). Alzheimer disease in a select population of older adults with mental retardation. *Irish Journal of Psychology, 14,* 37–46.

Janicki, M. P., & Dalton, A. J. (1993b, August). *Clinical/training implications of Alzheimer disease among older adults with mental retardation.* Paper presented at the 101st Annual Meeting of the American Psychological Association, Toronto, Ontario, Canada.

Janicki, M. P., Knox, L. A., & Jacobson, J. W. (1985). Planning for an older developmentally disabled population. In M. P. Janicki & H. M. Wisniewski (Eds.), *Aging and developmental disabilities: Issues and approaches* (pp. 143–160). Baltimore, MD: Brookes.

Janicki, M. P., Krauss, M. W., Cotten, P., & Seltzer, M. M. (1986). Respite services and the older developmentally disabled adult. In C. L. Salisbury & J. Intagliata (Eds.), *Respite care: Support for persons with developmental disabilities and their families* (pp. 51–68). Baltimore, MD: Brookes.

Janicki, M. P., & MacEachron, A. E. (1984). Residential, health and social service needs of elderly developmentally disabled persons. *The Gerontologist, 24,* 128–137.

Janicki, M. P., Moss, S., & Lucchino, R. (1992). *Adult day programs for seniors with developmental disabilities in the United States and England.* Paper presented as part of the symposium, "Adult Day and Respite Care Programs," at the 120th Annual Meeting of the American Public Health Association, Washington, DC.

Janicki, M. P., Otis, J. P., Puccio, P. S., Rettig, J., & Jacobson, J. W. (1985). Service needs among older developmentally disabled persons. In M. P. Janicki and H. M. Wisniewski (Eds.), *Aging and developmental disabilities: Issues and approaches* (pp. 289–304). Baltimore, MD: Brookes.

Janicki, M. P., & Seltzer, M. M. (1991). *Aging and developmental disabilities: Challenges for the 1990s* (Proceedings of the Boston Roundtable on Research Issues and Applications in Aging and Developmental Disabilities). Washington, DC: American Association on Mental Retardation, Aging Special Interest Group.

Jennings, J. (1987). Elderly parents as caregivers for their adult dependent children. *Social Work, 32,* 430–433.

Kailes, J. I. (1992). Aging with a disability: Educating myself. *Generations, 16,* 75–77.

Kaufman, A. V. (1989). Social work services for elderly persons with mental retardation: A case example. *Social Work in Health Care, 14,* 67–80.

Krauss, M. W., & Seltzer, M. M. (1993). Coping strategies among older mothers of adults with retardation: A life-span developmental perspective. In A. P. Turnbull, J. M. Patterson, S. K. Behr, D. L. Murphy, J. G. Marquis, & M. J. Blue-Banning (Eds.), *Cognitive coping, families & disability* (pp. 173–182). Baltimore, MD: Brookes.

Krout, J. A. (1993). Do senior centers serve 7 million elders? *Perspective on Aging, 22*(2), 8–9.

Kultgen, P., & Rominger, R. (1993). Cross training within the aging and developmental disabilities services systems. In E. Sutton, A. R. Factor, B. Hawkins, T. Heller, & G. Seltzer (Eds.), *Older adults with developmental disabilities: Optimizing choices and change* (pp. 239–256). Baltimore, MD: Brookes.

Lakin, K. C., Jaskulski, T. M., Hill, B. K., Bruininks, R. R., Menke, J. M., White, C. C., & Wright, E. A. (1989). *Medicaid services for persons with mental retardation and related conditions.* Minneapolis: University of Minnesota, Center for Residential and Community Services.

Laslett, P. (1991). *A fresh map of life: The emergence of the third age.* Cambridge, MA: Harvard University Press.

Lepore, P., & Janicki, M. P. (1990). *The wit to win: How to integrate older persons with developmental disabilities into community aging programs.* Albany: New York State Office for the Aging.

Lott, I. T. (1988). Down's syndrome, aging, and Alzheimer's disease: A clinical review. *Annals of the New York Academy of Science, 396,* 15–26.

Maaskant, M. A. (1993). *Mental handicap and ageing.* Dwingeloo, The Netherlands: KAVANAH.

Malone, D. M. (1990). Aging persons with mental retardation: Identification of the needs of a special population. *Gerontological Review, 3,* 1–14.

McDowell, D. (1988). Aging and developmental disabilities: Personal reflections on policy for persons. *Educational Gerontology, 14,* 465–470.

National Association of State Units on Aging. (1985). *An orientation to the Older Americans Act* (rev. ed.). Washington, DC: Author.

National Council on the Aging. (1990). *Standards and guidelines for adult day care.* Washington, DC: Author.

New York State Developmental Disabilities Planning Council. (1988). *On the feasibility of different pension support systems for New York State residents with a developmental disability.* Albany, NY: Author.

New York State Office for the Aging. (1990). *Design features: Housing older New Yorkers.* Albany: Author.

New York State Office for the Aging. (1987). *Home equity conversion.* Albany, NY: Author.

New York Times. (1993a). Former hotel is recast as housing for elderly. August 6, 1993, p. A21.

New York Times. (1993b). English retirement resort is a model for Europe. July 13, 1993, p. A3.

Noelker, E. A., & Somple, L. C. (1993). Adults with Down syndrome and Alzheimer's: Clinical observations of family caregivers. In K. A. Roberto (Ed.), *The elderly caregiver: Caring for adults with developmental disabilities* (pp. 81–94). Newbury Park, CA: Sage.

Oriol, W. (1993). The first half-century of senior centers charts the way for decades to come. *Perspective on Aging, 22*(2), 2–7.

Ossofsky, J. (1988). Connecting the networks: Aging and lifelong disabilities. *Educational Gerontology, 14,* 389–397.

Overeynder, J., Turk, M., Dalton, A. J., & Janicki, M. P. (1992). *I'm worried about the future... A report on the aging of adults with cerebral palsy.* Albany: New York State Developmental Disabilities Planning Council.

Prosper, V. (1987). *A review of congregate housing in the United States.* Albany, NY: New York State Office for the Aging.

Quirk, D., & Aravanis, S. (1988). State partnerships to enhance the quality of life of older Americans with lifelong disabilities. *Educational Gerontology, 14,* 431–438.

Rinck, C., Tomer, R. S., Griggs, P. A., & Cohen, G. J. (1992). *WARP curriculum.* Kansas City: University of Missouri at Kansas City, Institute for Human Development.

Roberto, K. A. (1993). Review of the caregiving literature. In K. A. Roberto (Ed.), *The elderly caregiver: Caring for adults with developmental disabilities* (pp. 3–20). Newbury Park, CA: Sage.

Roberto, K. A., & Nelson, R. E. (1989). The developmentally disabled elderly: Concerns of service providers. *Journal of Applied Gerontology, 8,* 175–182.

Rose, T., & Janicki, M. P. (1986). Older mentally retarded adults: A forgotten population. *Aging Network News, 3*(5), 17–19.

Seltzer, G. B. (1985). Selected psychological processes and aging among older developmentally disabled persons. In M. P. Janicki & H. M. Wisniewski (Eds.), *Aging and developmental disabilities: Issues and approaches* (pp. 211–227). Baltimore, MD: Brookes.

Seltzer, M. M. (1988). Structure and pattern of services utilization by elderly persons with mental retardation. *Mental Retardation, 26,* 181–185.

Seltzer, M. M. (1992). Family caregiving across the full lifespan. In L. Rowitz (Ed.), *Mental retardation in the year 2000* (pp. 85–100). New York: Springer.

Seltzer, M. M., & Krauss, M. W. (1987). *Aging and mental retardation: Extending the continuumrom* (Monograph No. 9). Washington, DC: American Association on Mental Retardation.

Seltzer, M. M., & Krauss, M. W. (1994). Aging parents with coresident adult children: The impact of lifelong caregiving. In M. M. Seltzer, M. W. Krauss, & M. P. Janicki (Eds.), *Life course perspectives on adulthood and old age* (pp. 3–18). Washington, DC: American Association on Mental Retardation.

Sison, G. F. P., & Cotten, P. D. (1989). The elderly mentally retarded person: Current perspectives and future directions. *Journal of Applied Gerontology, 8,* 151–167.

Smith, G. S., Fullmer, E. M., & Tobin, S. S. (1994). Living outside the system: An exploration of older families who do not use day programs. In M. M. Seltzer, M. W. Krauss, & M. P. Janicki (Eds.), *Life course perspectives on adulthood and old age* (pp. 19–38). Washington, DC: American Association on Mental Retardation.

Spirrison, C. L., & Cotten, P. D. (1989). The bill of rights for the elderly person with mental retardation. *Journal of Applied Gerontology, 8,* 148.

Standards and Guidelines Committee. (1993). Standards and guidelines help centers do their work better for more people: Accreditation now a likely next step. *Perspective on Aging, 22*(3), 16–19.

Stone, J. A. (1989). Housing options for older people with developmental disabilities: Implications for adult residential care. *Adult Residential Care Journal, 3,* 193–207.

Stout Vocational Rehabilitation Institute. (1990). *Aging in America: Implications for vocational rehabilitation and independent living* (Report of the 17th Institute on Rehabilitation Issues). Menomonie: University of Wisconsin–Stout, Research and Training Center, Stout Vocational Rehabilitation Institute.

Stroud, M., & Sutton, E. (1988). *Expanding options for older adults with developmental disabilities.* Baltimore, MD: Brookes.

Sutton, E., Sterns, H., & Park, L. S. S. (1993). Realities of retirement and pre-retirement planning. In E. Sutton, A. R. Factor, B. Hawkins, T. Heller, & G. Seltzer (Eds.), *Older adults with developmental disabilities: Optimizing choices and change* (pp. 95–106). Baltimore, MD: Brookes.

Tobin, S. S. (1992). *Non-normative aging.* Paper presented at the 45th Annual Meeting of the Gerontological Society of America, Washington, DC.

Turnbull, A. P., Patterson, J. M., Behr, S. K., Murphy, D. L., Marquis, J. G., & Blue-Banning, M. J. (Eds.). (1993). *Cognitive coping, families & disability.* Baltimore, MD: Brookes.

University of Akron. (n.d.). *Memoranda of agreements: Federal, state and local agreements for older persons with developmental disabilities.* Akron, OH: University of Akron, Institute for Life-Span Development and Gerontology.

van Walleghem, M. (1993). Ageing people with intellectual disabilities: A new challenge for our society. *Irish Journal of Psychology, 14,* 2–4.

Wilson, M. (1992). *Respecting the past, enjoying now, and embracing the future.* Madison: University of Wisconsin, Wisconsin Lifelong Planning Initiative.

Wisniewski, H. M., & Merz, G. S. (1985). Aging, Alzheimer's disease, and developmental disabilities. In M. P. Janicki & H. M. Wisniewski (Eds.), *Aging and developmental disabilities: Issues and approaches* (pp. 177–184). Baltimore, MD: Brookes.

Zigman, W., Seltzer, G., & Silverman, W. (1994). Behavioral and mental health changes associated with aging in adults with mental retardation. In M. M. Seltzer, M.W. Krauss, & M.P. Janicki (Eds.), *Life course perspectives on adulthood and old age* (pp. 67–91). Washington, DC: American Association on Mental Retardation.

Zola, I. K. (1988). Aging and disability: Toward a unifying agenda. *Educational Gerontology, 14,* 365–387.

Partial support for this chapter was provided by the Administration on Aging and the Administration for Developmental Disabilities, U.S. Department of Health and Human Services, through Project of National Significance Grant No. 90-AJ-2012.

Chapter 9

Planning for Now and the Future: Social, Legal, and Financial Concerns

Ruth I. Freedman, Boston University
Donald N. Freedman, Concannon, Rosenberg, Freedman, Goldstein & Magence

The purposes of this chapter are to discuss the long-term planning issues, conflicts, and dilemmas faced by families caring for adult children with mental retardation and to identify key social, legal, and financial principles of long-term planning. Long-term planning refers to the process of making arrangements for the long-term or future well-being of the person with mental retardation. This is often referred to as life planning, permanency planning, or future planning. Such planning by family caregivers, service providers, and persons with mental retardation may involve decision-making in the areas of living arrangements, services and supports, and legal and financial matters.

Families face pressing questions and dilemmas regarding long-term care, such as these:

- Where will the relative live when the parents are no longer able to provide care?

- What services and informal supports does the relative need?

- Who will oversee, secure, and provide appropriate services?

- Who will pay for living arrangements and services?

These questions often require family decision-making and action related to government benefits, health and life insurance coverage, trusts and wills, legal competency, guardianship and alternatives to guardianship. Families and persons with mental retardation require practical information, assistance, and support in negotiating the maze of legal, financial, and social policies.

Background

Families caring for adults with mental retardation serve in a variety of roles, such as advocate, case manager, counselor, companion, guardian, financial manager, community liaison, medication monitor, transportation provider. For many persons with mental retardation and other disabilities, family members, usually parents, are the lifeblood, the backbone of their community support system. Without the supports provided by their families, many persons with mental retardation would be unable to function independently in the community. In many cases, families serve as an alternative to institutionalization or help to delay out-of-home placement.

Family caregivers express serious concern about what will happen when they are no longer able to provide care due to illness, death, financial hardship, or other circumstances. As family caregivers age, uncertainty about the future becomes an increasing source of concern. Parents face the "dual strain of planning for and adjusting to their own aging and the aging of the relative who may outlive them" (Seltzer, Krauss, & Heller, 1991, p. 23). It is not uncommon for parents to express the hope that the family member with mental retardation will predecease them. Numerous studies and needs assessments have cited this unease about the future as a frequent source of worry, stress, anxiety and "subjective burden" for parents (Gollay, Freedman, Wyngaarden, & Kurtz, 1978; Goodman, 1978; Grant, 1986; Seltzer et al., 1991; Turnbull, Turnbull, Bronicki, Summers, & Roeder-Gordon, 1989).

Yet in spite of enormous concern about the future, research indicates that few families of adults with mental retardation make concrete long-term plans (Heller & Factor, 1991; Kaufman, Adams, & Campbell, 1991). Seltzer et al. (1991) note that this finding is consistent with research regarding elderly persons in general. There are several possible reasons for lack of long-term planning. First, long-term planning is emotionally and socially difficult for many families to undertake. Such planning raises critical personal and ethical issues that families may not feel emotionally "ready" to tackle, such as deciding who will care for the child when the parents are no longer able and determining whether siblings or other relatives are available and willing to assume caregiving roles.

Frequently, parents expect or assume that a sibling will take over responsibility when they are no longer able, but many parents do not discuss these future arrangements with siblings or other relatives (Goodman, 1978; Heller & Factor, 1991; Kaufman et al., 1991; Krauss, 1990). Seltzer and Krauss (1989) found that mothers who made explicit plans for a sibling to assume caregiving responsibility reported substantially less stress than mothers who had not made long-term care arrangements. However, Turnbull et al. (1989) discuss the possibility that long-term planning may actually increase anxiety and stress in the short term, although decrease over the long term.

Few families have discussed long-term planning issues with the mentally retarded adult or obtained his or her preferences for future living and other arrangements (Heller & Factor, 1991; Seltzer et al., 1991; Smith & Tobin, 1989). When planning is done, it is often done *for* the mentally retarded individual, rather than with him or her. This lack of involvement of the mentally retarded family member runs counter to current programmatic and legal principles that stress the importance of autonomy, independent decision-making, self-advocacy, and least restrictive environment.

Families have often coped by taking a one-day-at-a-time approach to caregiving (Goodman, 1978; Grant, 1986; Turnbull et

al., 1989). An inadequate, disjointed service system has forced families to take a crisis orientation approach, not a long-term planning perspective. Many families feel that they cannot afford the luxury of planning beyond tomorrow.

When families do undertake long-term planning, they may experience frustration and despair. They find it difficult to plan rationally in a system that at times seems irrational or to make plans for programs and services that may not exist now or in the future. There is a general level of distrust and lack of confidence among many families regarding the availability, adequacy, and long-term security of the existing service system. Families lack information on legal and financial issues as well as information on ways to maximize access to entitlements and supports (Gollay et al., 1978; Goodman, 1978; Heller & Factor, 1991; Smith & Tobin, 1989). Lack of information and misinformation on the part of families and care providers may lead to inappropriate efforts to obtain guardianship in derogation of the individual's rights and to inefficient and duplicative utilization of personal and family financial resources and government entitlements.

The inability of a family to continue providing care, given the individual's functional competency, has major implications in three spheres: for the relative with mental retardation, for other persons in the family, and for the service delivery system. Persons with mental retardation must face the trauma and crisis of a parent's death or illness, as well as the removal of much of their support system. Often, family members are placed in emergency living arrangements or respite facilities, if available, but typically they face long waiting lists. Often, they are inappropriately placed because of the lack of other alternatives. For example, they may be placed in an institutional facility or nursing home for lack of an appropriate community setting. Heller (1988) describes the "transfer trauma" and lack of psychological preparation associated with such emergency residential relocations. Also, guardianship or other protective mechanisms may be established for the individual as a crisis response, severely limiting the individual's legal rights. This in some cases may not be appropriate or justified. Siblings or other family members are the "next-of-kin" who often willingly or unwillingly inherit caregiving responsibilities. The siblings may be asked to assume significant emotional, social, legal, and financial responsibility for the relative. For the service delivery system, emergency or crisis placements and supports may not be available. The needs of these families may not have been identified to the service system prior to the crisis (Janicki, Otis, Puccio, Rettig, & Jacobson, 1985) or families may have already been on long waiting lists, but to no avail. Long-term planning on the part of families and service providers is needed to minimize trauma and crisis for the mentally retarded adult, other family members, and the service delivery system.

Planning From A Life-Span Perspective

Planning is an ongoing, lifelong process that must address both the short-term and long-term needs of the individual and family. Families should attempt to be proactive, instead of reactive—planning for now and the future. Too often, planning does not occur until a major crisis has already happened (for example, the illness or death of a family caregiver). Appropriate options may be very limited or nonexistent in a crisis situation. Families and persons with mental retardation may have more opportunities for choice, autonomy, and control if planning is initiated at an early stage.

Planning should be an ongoing process, with periodic monitoring to assess changes over time—for example, changes in the individual's or family's situation, in resources, laws, programs, or policies. There is an emerging interest in the mental retardation field in the changing needs of persons with mental retardation and their families across the life span (Seltzer & Krauss, chapter 1 this volume). Similarly, legal procedures that require periodic review of court treatment orders and limited terms of guardianship reflect a perspective of persons with mental retardation as being subject to change and development. Life-span developmental theory looks at changes in the family life cycle, experienced either by the family as a whole or by individuals within the family unit. Long-term planning ideally responds to the dynamic and changing needs of the family and its members.

Long-term planning must address the needs of individual family members and the family as a unit at various stages of the individual's and family's life cycles. Specific legal or financial issues and concerns may arise that require planning at each stage. Turnbull, Summers, and Brotherson (1986) have identified the following developmental stages and transitions faced by families in general, based on the family systems research of Olson et al. (1984): couple, childbearing, school age, adolescence, launching, postparental, and aging. Unfortunately, no systematic research has been conducted on the specific life cycle stages and transitions faced by families with children with mental retardation. In any event, each of these stages, which may involve major shifts in family functions, responsibilities, and interactions, is often characterized by heightened family stress. In families of persons with mental retardation, family members may face specific stressors at each stage relating to their additional roles and responsibilities and the long-term nature of their responsibilities. For example, Suelzle and Keenan (1981) noted heightened levels of family stress during transition points in the mentally retarded child's life, particularly at the beginning and completing of school.

Parents with children who do not have disabilities ordinarily expect that parental responsibility will diminish over time as their children mature and become more independent. Parents of children with significant mental retardation, however, anticipate the need to continue to assume a substantial degree of responsibility for their children, even in adulthood. Transitional periods become more complex for these families. Milestones often differ in content and in timing from families with nondisabled children. Equally important from a planning perspective, whereas in other cases life stages for individuals and for families diverge as one generation succeeds to the next, the stages of families and members with mental retardation remain enmeshed, encompassing two and sometimes three generations.

Family members face many legal and financial issues at the various stages of the family's and individual's life cycles, starting immediately upon birth and identification of the child's special needs. During the earliest years of child-rearing, parents need to plan for alternative care for their children in the event of parental death or incapacity. Such planning involves legal components, particularly in identifying the person or persons to assume legal responsibility for decision-making on the child's behalf. Planning also must involve financial and entitlements components to try to ensure that sufficient personal and governmental resources are available in a complementary way to meet the child's lifetime needs. Specifically, parents will need to consider a will, both to direct the overall management and distribution of family assets and to nominate a guardian with ongoing legal responsibility for decision-making on the child's behalf. They may also consider a trust, to manage assets for the benefit of the child over his or her lifetime, and life insurance, to enhance the share of the parents' estate which can be committed to the child's support. Most importantly, they will need to take into account government programs for early intervention and special education services, as well as particular programs—like Supplemental Security Income, Medicaid, and Social Security Survivor's Benefits—that might provide income or services to the child in the absence of one or both parents. As children reach puberty and adolescence, families may face decisions regarding sex education and birth control. Potential legal and ethical conflicts may arise regarding the roles of the parent and the child in making decisions about birth control, abortion, or sterilization.

A critical milestone with significant legal implications is the child's reaching legal majority, now age 18 in most states. Generally speaking, and subject to some important exceptions, a person under age 18 does not have the legal capacity to enter into binding contracts, give informed consent, or otherwise assume responsibility for his or her own decisions. Parents of persons under age 18 ordinarily, and without court process, have the right and responsibility to make decisions on the child's behalf. Age, not physical or mental capacity, is the determining factor.

When any individual reaches the age of majority, however, he or she is presumed by law to have the physical and mental capacity to manage his or her own personal and financial affairs. Normal parental guardianship of the child ends; at this point, guardianship continues only on the basis of specific court action in appointing a guardian with ongoing responsibilities. Therefore, if there is concern that a family member with mental retardation who is approaching the age of majority does in fact lack the capacity to make informed decisions about the management of his or her personal and financial affairs, the need for guardianship or less restrictive alternatives to guardianship should be evaluated. Evaluating an individual's capacity and need for guardianship, determining who should serve as guardian and successors, and planning the case to be made to the court for guardianship or other substitute decision-making mechanisms involve coordinated clinical, social, and legal planning on the part of the family and helping professionals. Reaching the age of majority also has implications for entitlements planning. Persons with mental retardation may become eligible for certain financial benefits on their own for the first time, independent of their family's financial status. Potential examples include Supplemental Security Income, Medicaid, and Social Security Childhood Disability Benefits. Some entitlement programs targeted only to children will end; others, most notably vocational rehabilitation programs, may be newly available.

Another critical stage is the end of the child's formal public schooling, ordinarily at age 22 unless a high school diploma has been awarded earlier. The transition from public schooling to adulthood, the world of work and independent living, may be particularly stressful for families with mentally retarded children, because "launching" of their children at this stage may be delayed or different than for families with nonhandicapped children. This is often the time when vocational and residential decision-making occurs. Although some children with mental retardation may move out of their family homes to independent living or supervised residential programs as they enter adulthood, many remain at home well into their adult years, due to the family's or child's preference or to lack of appropriate residential alternatives in the community. Legal and financial planning at this stage typically involves determination of the individual's eligibility for rehabilitation and job training programs, residential programs, health care, and income and housing assistance. Whereas special education services are mandated by federal and state law and by many state constitutions for all handicapped children, regardless of type or level of disability, the service system for adults with mental retardation and other disabilities is more fragmented, complex, and often exclusionary. Families may find that their child is ineligible for certain programs and benefits or the benefits may be time-limited, or they may face extensive waiting lists for appropriate programs in their communities.

As the adult family member with mental retardation ages, additional issues may emerge, such as possible changes in living arrangements or preferences, job situations, or family supports. The health status of the individual may deteriorate, increasing the need for medical care and personal assistance with activities of daily living. In later years, if the individual is working or in a day program, retirement possibilities and preferences should be explored. Retirement planning is particularly problematic for individuals with mental retardation because their work histories are unlikely to support substantial levels of Social Security Retirement Benefits, private pensions, or savings for retirement. Furthermore, diminished capacity for independent living may make the individual ineligible, fairly or not, for special supported living arrangements available to other elders, such as congregate care facilities, retirement homes and life care communities.

In addition to the developmental milestones outlined above in the life of the family member with mental retardation (and the response by the parents and family as a unit), there is a simultaneous progression of milestones in the lives of the parents and other family members. As the person with mental retardation changes and develops across the life span, so too do the parents and siblings. Other family members have their own developmental needs to consider and plan for. For example, at the same time that the person with mental retardation may be in transition from school to adulthood, parents may face critical decisions regarding their own jobs and careers, personal and social relationships, and health and well-being. Also, parents may have primary caregiving responsibilities for other family members, such as younger children, or, with increasing likelihood, their own parents. Long-term planning must therefore address multiple overlapping life-span trajectories—of the individual with mental retardation, of the parents and other family members, of the family unit as a whole. As the parents enter their middle years, they need to plan for their own potential future needs, as well as their children's, in the areas of life and health insurance, trusts and estates, advanced health directives, and retirement. Because the various family members are likely at different stages or developmental milestones, addressing their various sets of needs is a complex and at times conflicting task. For example, parents approaching retirement may have reached the stage where ordinary expectations would have them wanting to "wrap up loose ends" at home and at work at the very time that their adult child with mental retardation is just in transition to adulthood and is experiencing increasing independence in adult services. The adult child's primary goal at this stage may be increased independence or socialization opportunities, while the parents' primary concern may be for increased economic security and peace of mind.

We have outlined the various developmental stages of the family and its members across the life span and identified potential legal and financial planning issues that occur at each stage. However, little systematic research is available on the nature, extent, and timing of legal and financial planning by families with children with mental retardation. As discussed earlier in this chapter and in chapter 3 by Heller and Factor, it seems that legal and financial planning by families with children with mental retardation is not widespread and that this lack of future planning is consistent with the fact that most elderly persons do not plan for themselves in the areas of health, living arrangements, or finances. Families often postpone legal and financial planning until the later stages of their life span, when the death or poor health of a parent necessitates a change in living and other arrangements for the child with mental retardation.

Some data on state guardianship policies and procedures are available from a recent national survey (Cohen, 1992). States identified some of the potential initiation points or "triggers" for guardianship, including the client reaching the legal age of majority; initiation of guardianship by parents or other family members; the perceived need for significant medical or behavioral treatment; entry into a state residential facility; entry into community-based facilities; initiation of guardianship by the individual habilitation team; and inability of the client to manage finances. Many of these seven "triggers" correspond to various points in the life-span cycle.

Limited data also are available from this survey on the approximate percentage of clients served by state agencies who are under guardianship. Six states reported that over 80% of their clients residing in public institutions were under guardianship; only a few states reported fewer than 20% of their clients being under guardianship. Guardianship is more widely used for clients in institutions than in community facilities, perhaps because state policies and regulations may require assessment of the legal competency of institutional residents but not of residents of community facilities or of individuals living with their families or independently. Fifteen states reported that they lack data on guardianship, and six states noted that their data did not include individuals in community placement or under family or private guardianship.

In another national study of 370 elderly residents (aged 63 and older) with mental retardation living in state residential facilities, it was estimated that between 13% and 36% of residents were considered legally competent (Anderson, Lakin, Bruininks, & Hill, 1987). For those residents not considered legally competent (that is, 64% to 87% of the residents surveyed), the state was the most frequent guardian or conservator, followed by relatives.

Neither of these surveys collected data on the extent of guardianship among persons with mental retardation living with their families or independently. It is likely that legal guardianship is not as widely utilized by these families, particularly while the parents are alive, for several reasons. First, many programs, agencies, and professionals perceive parents as having the authority to make decisions on behalf of their adult child with mental retardation, even in the absence of legal guardianship. In contrast, parents of persons in institutions or community residential programs may pursue guardianship to secure a degree of control or leverage in affecting agency decision-making. Second, the availability and willingness of many family members to assist the relative with mental retardation with decision-making may mitigate the practical need for guardianship, independent of the individual's capacity. And finally, as discussed earlier, few families engage in long-term planning in which the need for guardianship is evaluated.

Principles of Long-Term Planning

Based on research about families' concerns and needs, we have developed a series of principles regarding long-term planning to serve as guidelines. The social, legal, and financial ramifications of these principles are discussed in the following sections. By integrating these principles into the long-term planning process, persons with mental retardation, their families, and service providers will, we hope, develop more responsive and appropriate plans for now and the future.

1. Planning must be undertaken with a recognition that individuals with mental retardation have distinct legal rights to services and benefits and to personal autonomy.

It is plainly beyond the purpose or scope of this chapter even to synopsize the law as it affects persons with mental retardation and their families, but certain broad principles bear directly on long-term planning. For example, the equal protection clause of the Fourteenth Amendment to the United States Constitution focuses on the similarities among all individuals as citizens with equal rights and on the use of the law as an instrument to minimize differences. The thrust is that segregation is inherently discriminatory. Separate supposedly special services and protections like guardianship—however well-intentioned — are inherently suspect. To the extent that the individual is to be the recipient of the mixed blessings of governmental largesse, it must be on the basis either of his or her voluntary action or of clear and present need.

Another legal mandate based on a constitutional requirement is that the individual not be deprived of liberty without "due process of law." The basic idea is straightforward. The power of the state is so great in relation to that of the individual that without structural constraints on state power in its dealings with the individual, the individual would always lose. We usually think of the due process clause in the context of the application of criminal law, involving incarceration and fines. But the law has grown to recognize more subtle exercises of government power that have the effect, although usually not the intent, of depriving the individual of his or her freedom. Appointment of a guardian, administration of psychotropic drugs, forced institutionalization, and transfer of control of government entitlements to another are examples of exercises of government control subject to constitutional limitation on behalf of the individual. Otherwise expressed, the individual has a legally recognized right to the least restrictive form of services or protection necessary for the shortest time possible.

Lawyers advocating on behalf of the rights of persons with mental retardation to appropriate habilitative services have applied due process principles. Without education, treatment, training, protection from harm, special services, and substitute decision-making mechanisms for people unable to act on their own, persons with mental retardation are deprived of freedom of action, no less effectively than through imprisonment. This principle thus focuses on the responsibility of government to identify the special needs of persons with mental retardation, and to intervene effectively to ameliorate them. In programmatic terms, this legal mandate translates into the right to treatment, based on a view of the state as a protective parent.

2. Planning should involve the family member with mental retardation to the maximum extent of his or her capacity.

For most persons, including persons with severe disabilities, the ability and opportunity to make choices and decisions is an important and cherished component of their lives, reflecting favorably on their perceived independence, dignity, and self-worth (Guess, Benson, & Siegel-Causey, 1985). However, it is often a challenge to take into account the individual's desires, values, and aspirations. Turnbull et al. (1989) have developed a Preference Checklist designed to help persons with mental retardation identify their preferences or choices in four major areas of daily life: social-interpersonal concerns; community and leisure participation; residential placement; and vocational area. The goal of the Checklist is to involve persons with mental retardation to the maximum extent possible in expressing preferences and making choices regarding long-term planning issues. Similarly, current "person-centered" and "futures planning" strategies focus on the needs and preferences of the individual and on ways to assist the individual to gain control over daily life activities (Factor & Anderson, 1992; O'Brien, 1987; O'Brien, Forest, Snow, & Hasbury, 1989).

Too often, service or treatment plans are based primarily or solely on a "deficit" model in which the individual's problems or limitations are the focal point of the plan. Long-term planning should identify and build upon the strengths and competencies of the individual as well as his or her limitations and needs. For example, if members of the planning team believe that an individual is unable to make decisions independently about financial matters, they should ask whether supports, training activities, or assistance can be made available to assist the individual with managing his or her financial affairs.

To the extent that the individual is competent to make and communicate decisions, they should be honored. To the extent that an individual lacks the competency to make or communicate decisions, they should be based on a determination of what he or she would have decided, based on all pertinent available evidence of preference. This is often referred to as the "substituted judgment" approach. In the absence of evidence of preference, decisions must be based on an objective determination of what would be in the individual's "best interests."

So much for broad principle. The real problem lies in applying these concepts to the range of persons with mental retardation, from the person with the mildest to those with much more severe degrees of impairment. What we mean by competency, and how it is determined, lies at the heart of the determining the nature and extent of appropriate involvement of the individual in decision-making. The term "competency" is used differently in many contexts, however, and is a source of much confusion. As noted by Beyer and Howell (1989), the word should be pluralized to allow distinction between *legal competency,* that is, the legal right to make decisions and speak for oneself, and *functional competency,* the ability to make decisions. Legal competency, with regard to adults, involves a determination by a court as to whether the individual meets the legal criteria for guardianship under state law, ordinarily expressed in general terms like "capacity to manage one's personal and/or financial affairs." Assessment of functional competency, on the other hand, encompasses a number of dimensions, including the capacity to accept and learn essential information, apply newly acquired information to make

decisions, contemplate the risks and outcomes of alternative courses of action, and accept responsibility for a "wrong choice" (Beyer & Howell, 1989, p. 124). Also relevant to assessment of functional competency is the capacity to generalize to new environments and situations, recall and apply past experiences, and communicate decisions.

Unfortunately, the law does not reflect the fact that people in the real world occupy a range of functional competency in a variety of domains. For example, the same person who may be severely lacking in his or her capacity to manage personal finances or medical treatment may nonetheless have the capacity to participate meaningfully in decisions relating to residency and occupational and social activities. Case law and some state statutes now do allow for limited guardianship tailored to meet specific areas of incompetency, at least within broad domains.

Another source of confusion in planning arises from the tendency of many to assume that because an individual is classified as having mental retardation, he or she is not competent and therefore needs a guardian. The problem is one of taking a definition and classification system like that of the AAMR (American Association on Mental Retardation, 1992) and applying it uncritically in a variety of personal, social, and legal domains, for which it was not intended. The AAMR definition of mental retardation looks to the interaction of significantly subaverage general intellectual functioning and deficits in adaptive skill areas manifested during the developmental period. Mental retardation is determined on the basis of admittedly imprecise test measures of intellectual functioning and adaptive behavior, among other factors. Thus, it certainly cannot be said that persons with mental retardation, as defined by the AAMR, are necessarily incapable of appropriate participation in decision-making.

Given the reality that many persons with mental retardation are limited to some extent in being able to participate in decision-making, and given the desirability to the individual of receiving needed services, perhaps the most sensitive task in long-term planning is to seek an appropriate balance of the scales of paternalism versus protection, of undue risk versus loss of autonomy, in individual real-world cases. With many, we may move too quickly to abandon hopes of the individual participating in decision-making, at least in some domains and to some degree. As with anyone, participation by the individual with mental retardation depends in part on his or her own functional competencies, interest, and verbal communication skills. The presence of even a severe degree of disability does not in itself put the issue of participation to rest. To the contrary, the more severe the disability, the more responsibility devolves to parents and others to take affirmative steps to facilitate participation—to make, in the terms of the Americans with Disabilities Act, "reasonable accommodations" to the individual's areas of incapacity. This may require, for example, greater understanding of and reliance on the particular communication modes displayed or preferred by the individual, whether or not verbal, to ascertain the individual's preferences. It would also require more attention to the education and training of persons with mental retardation in decision-making (Guess et al., 1985).

In situations where the individual's incapacity to comprehend or communicate is so great that responsibility for decision-making must be delegated to a surrogate, without realistic possibility of meaningful participation by the individual, decision-making must be based on a determination of what would be in the "best interests" of the individual. Decisions can then only be based on a determination of what, from the perspective of family and professionals, would be best for the individual, balancing the potential risks, benefits, and side effects of alternative courses of action. The "best interest" approach is typically viewed as objective, based on medical, psychological, and social facts. However, the risk remains of imposing one's own and societal values on the decision-making process, particularly with regard to the importance often given high cognitive functioning as an aspect of quality of life.

Rather, even in being objective, we must strive to base decisions on the best interests of the individual from his or her own perspective. An individual's particular cognitive capacity to appreciate the world, however limited or different, does not make his or her life less to be valued.

Leading court cases, furthermore, illustrate how difficult it is to apply these conceptual models in actual life circumstances, however easily the underlying principles may be elucidated. For example, in *Superintendent of Belchertown State School* v. *Saikewicz,* the court struggled with the application of the "substituted judgment" approach to the circumstances of an individual with severe mental retardation seemingly lacking the capacity to make or communicate the decision as to whether he should undergo chemotherapy for cancer to prolong his life somewhat, where treatment would necessarily involve stressful side effects and physical restraints the purpose of which he could not comprehend. The court, without possibility of communication from Saikewicz or evidence based on past behavior, nonetheless decided against treatment on the basis that Saikewicz would have reached this conclusion had he been able. The dilemmas posed by "substitute judgment" are discussed in Apolloni and Cooke (1984).

3. Planning should involve all family members and other persons who may play a future role in providing or managing care on a long term basis.

Siblings and other relatives, as well as parents and close friends, need to be involved in planning from the earliest possible time in order to make realistic the expectation that they will have the knowledge, sensitivity, and confidence to assume direct responsibilities for providing or managing long term care when the parents are no longer available. Their concerns, issues, and questions need to be raised and addressed in the planning process. Planning should also involve members of the formal support system who currently play a role or may potentially play a role in the long-term care of the relative. For example, social workers, case managers, advocates, and community residence staff may be helpful in assessing needs and identifying possible resources for the relative and his or her family. Involvement of the formal service system in the planning stages may help prevent, delay, or minimize crises later.

To the extent that the individual lacks the capacity to make major decisions about his or her personal and financial affairs, it will be necessary to identify decision-makers to act on his or her behalf in roles such as trustee, representative payee, and guardian. All such roles require a long-term commitment, a sensitivity to the particular needs of the individual, involvement in providing and monitoring services, advocacy regarding personal and financial entitlements, and care in spending so as to avoid or minimize entitlement conflicts. Family members are ordinarily in the best position to take on these roles. Families should consider professional fiduciaries (banks, attorneys, or accountants) only as a last resort, in the absence of other available resources. Professionals are expensive and typically will not have the time, background, or inclination to function effectively in this context. On the other hand, siblings face a conflict of interest to the extent that distributions on behalf of the family member with mental retardation will ordinarily lessen the amount available for ultimate distribution to themselves or their children. In some situations, exercise of the responsibilities of guardian or trustee may foster dependency or resentment inconsistent with an optimal sibling relationship. Family members may live far away or may be preoccupied with their own family circumstances. They may fear they are not able to take on the responsibilities of trustee or guardian. If the problem is fear of assuming responsibility and potential financial liability, this concern may be addressed in the trust itself by explicitly insulating a family member trustee (although not a bank or professional trustee) from any possible claim of negligence as long as he or she acts in good faith.

Guardians and trustees can share their responsibilities. This will lessen the risk of burnout from one person's attempting too much. It will also provide a degree of mutual oversight and assistance. Sharing can be accomplished informally by designation of coguardians or cotrustees. A more formal approach would be to name one fiduciary as "guardian of the person only" of the ward, thereby limiting responsibilities to health, education, welfare, residential, and other personal aspects of the individual's needs. Another individual might have responsibility for financial matters, either through a trust or as representative payee. Further elaboration of the roles of the trustee is possible, given enough volunteers. For example, one cotrustee (the "financial trustee") might have responsibility for investment, accounting, and tax management of the trust. The other cotrustee (the "personal trustee") would have responsibility for deciding how the trust is to be used to benefit the beneficiary. This approach is particularly useful with larger trusts, where a financially unsophisticated family member who knows the child best may be unwilling to assume full responsibility as trustee, including tax, accounting, and investment issues. A second family member could perhaps handle the financial issues, despite living at a distance or being unfamiliar with the child. It thus may be possible to tailor long-term responsibilities to the special talents and interests of different family members.

Where family members are not able or willing to assume direct responsibility as trustees, there may nevertheless be other roles that they can play. Family members (usually brothers or sisters) can be assigned the role of advisor to the trustee, particularly in matters involving how the trust is to be used. Similarly, they can be named to receive notification by the trustee of planned trust actions and copies of trust accounts and tax returns. These kinds of involvement give the family members both the right and the encouragement to stay involved over time without creating responsibilities or expectations they cannot realistically meet.

In situations where family members are not appropriate or available to serve in these roles, there is in many states an alternative often developed by parents' groups themselves.

Nonprofit corporations or collective trusts may be formed by parents for the sole purpose of serving as trustee for families in need of such services. Various corporate guardianship and community trust programs are discussed in a survey of financial planning programs by Agosta, Feinberg, and Bradley (1985) and in Apolloni and Cooke (1984).

4. One must reconcile or in any event recognize the potentially conflicting goals of the individual and his or her family.

Long-term planning may involve balancing the goal of independence expressed by the person with mental retardation versus the goal of protection from harm expressed by the parents. Similarly, family financial dependence on the individual's entitlements may conflict with the desirability of the relative attempting more competitive employment activities. Parents may face the dilemma of balancing the long-term needs of the person with mental retardation with the shorter-term needs of other children for education, for example, or with the parents' own needs for a secure retirement and old age, particularly in light of the risk they may face of catastrophic health care needs. Determining what is in the person's "best interest" is a complicated issue, often involving an intergenerational balancing of legitimate and appropriate interests among the various parties affected.

For example, in an area of frequent conflict, pressures for and against guardianship often reflect more than purely clinical concerns. The interests of parents, siblings, service providers, and government agencies are often involved, often in subtle ways. Parents may pursue guardianship in the belief that, as guardians, they will have greater power in dealing with agencies or simply more control over the future. Siblings may seek guardianship to protect a future financial interest. An agency providing direct care to an individual who is particularly independent and therefore perceived as "difficult" may pursue guardianship to give it access to a more cooperative decision-maker within the family. In such cases, reliance of the agency upon the family for decision-making derogates from the individual's autonomy and basic rights.

Or, the agency may oppose guardianship, where a client is particularly compliant, in the interest of administrative ease; inappropriate reliance on the individual, beyond his or her capacity, can be used as an excuse for arbitrary action. Given the multifaceted nature of the issues involved in guardianship, it is imperative that all interests be disclosed and dealt with openly.

Similarly, conflicts may well arise from the allocation of family resources in relation to the special needs of the family member with mental retardation. The allocation has two dimensions. The first is intergenerational. The parents must decide how much they should try to retain for their own needs in their later years. And second, the parents must decide whether they should allocate the remainder of their assets among their children equally or on the basis of relative need. Transfer of assets to the trust during the parents' lifetime may help protect family resources from the financial needs and risks to which the parents themselves, and the rest of the family, might be exposed—business necessity, rainy-day savings, educational support of other children, future retirement, possible need for long-term nursing home care or other health catastrophe, and so forth. On the other hand, such transfers may adversely affect the parents' capacity to meet their own needs.

A similar conflict arises regarding the allocation of family resources among the children. On the one hand, parents most frequently wish to make equal gifts to their children, to avoid apparent favoritism and jealousies that might make it less likely that the siblings will help the disabled child in the future. On the other hand, making equal gifts just to be "fair" may leave the child with special needs at risk and may result in windfall inheritances to other children who do not need them.

Relative future need for assistance cannot be gauged with precision. It varies over time, with changes in the circumstances of the individual and other family members, and in the array of available governmental benefits and services develop. Nonetheless, projections of need can be made on the basis of the individual's needs today, current and projected financial and other entitlements, current rates of return on investments, and conservative projections of future trends, as well as the possibility of currently unforeseen future developments.

5. The individual has a right to services and protection in the least restrictive and intrusive form possible, appropriate to his or her needs.

Various legal mechanisms are available to assist the individual who, to some degree, is not fully capable of making long-term decisions on his or her own behalf. These mechanisms reflect different balances of autonomy and protection and can be utilized in individual cases with proper effect. In order of generally increasing degree of restrictiveness, they include the following:

1. Use of an advocate or advisor in personal and financial matters.

2. Use of limited withdrawal accounts.

3. Use of cosignatory bank accounts (requiring two signatures on bank accounts for withdrawal).

4. Use of a trust (allowing control only over funds actually transferred into a trust, tailored to meet individual needs).

5. Use of a representative payee (allowing control only over funds from the Social Security Administration).

6. Limited guardianship of property only (for example, with the authority of the guardian limited to accumulations of assets, but not to normal income).

7. Full guardianship of property (allowing control of all funds in which the individual has an interest).

8. Limited guardianship of the person only (that is, with the guardian's authority limited to identified areas of individual need, such as consent to medical services).

9. Full (or "plenary") guardianship of the person only.

10. Full guardianship of the person and property.

Even if "limited guardianship" is not available in a particular jurisdiction, it is still often possible for the guardian to tailor the implementation of guardianship powers in a manner that maximizes the role and participation of the ward. The attitude of the decision-maker toward the ward and the manner in which the decision-maker projects that attitude may well be as important from the perspective of the ward as the extent of the decision-maker's legal power. Similarly, most states do not require periodic review of the need for guardianship. Nonetheless, the guardian can, on his or her own initiative, reassess whether his or her implementation of guardianship responsibilities is as consistent as possible with the goal of maximizing the ward's developmental potential. Counseling of the decision-maker is thus often a key to the decision-maker's maintaining an appropriate and constructive role.

6. Planning involves a realistic assessment of the individual's and family's personal, social, and financial resources and of the availability of public resources to assist and support the individual and his or her family.

Long-term planning cannot effectively be accomplished in a vacuum. A thorough assessment of personal needs and resources is necessary in order to plan for and maximize eligibility for public resources and entitlements. Given the reality that few persons with mental retardation, or their families, have the financial resources to provide all necessary services themselves, it is essential to assess strategies to stretch personal and family resources by means of maximizing governmental entitlements. Governmental entitlements, like Social Security Disability Benefits, Supplemental Security Income (SSI), and Medicaid, are ordinarily essential for persons with mental retardation. Entitlements are not sufficient, however. Entitlement programs contain many gaps which, if left unfilled, may leave basic needs unmet. Therefore, without integration of governmental entitlements with personal and family resources, planning will be incomplete.

Complicating the matter, however, entitlements may conflict with other aspects of long-term planning geared to maximizing individual development. Eligibility for SSI, for example, requires an emphasis on the individual's incapacity, rather than strengths, which risks undercutting efforts of care providers toward enhancing self-esteem and independence. Financial conflicts also can occur. With elder parents on fixed incomes or siblings concerned about draining a potential future inheritance, intense pressure to keep a disabled adult child on benefits may outweigh the desirability of the individual risking competitive employment and possible loss of benefits.

Hoping to avoid dealing with such conflicts altogether, some parents consider leaving funds to a sibling or other relative with the "understanding" that he or she will use the property for the benefit of the person with mental retardation. This approach is seldom satisfactory and is fraught with risk. Even assuming utmost good faith on the part of the relatives (not an assumption that should be comfortably made, unfortunately), the property, held by the relatives without legal restriction, is subject to risks of loss beyond the relative's control. Divorce, death, disability, business failure, injury liability, foreclosure, or other circumstances beyond the relative's control may deprive the relative of the power to use the property for the benefit of the family member with mental retardation, regardless of best intentions. The temptation to "borrow" the funds for personal use during periods when it may not be needed by the family member may be too great to bear, especially if the relative encounters a financial emergency or "opportunity" or feels pressure from his or her own immediate family to use the funds.

The situation encountered by the substitute caretakers of the family member with mental retardation—the guardians and trustees—is vastly different from that encountered by guardians and trustees in more ordinary circumstances. The plain and common sense that one might think to apply, based on more typical parenting experiences, may be just wrong. Given the choice between a community and institutional training program, the first being more normal but the second be-

ing more intensive, for which should the guardian advocate? Should the guardian approve a work attempt, knowing that the person may lose SSI as a result of a successful, though part-time, work experience? Parents of children with mental retardation make these hard decisions every day and may well have developed very clear and effective, if not articulated, approaches to dealing with such issues. Instruments such as wills and trusts stand as certainly the last, if not necessarily the best, opportunity for parents to give guidance on such matters.

Trusts have proven to be effective in addressing the concerns of families in this area. Trusts can be used to establish a mechanism for the ongoing management of family financial resources on behalf of the individual with mental retardation; to provide personal direction to decision-makers so as to improve the quality of judgments made on the individual's behalf; and to assign responsibilities for overall care and management in a secure and balanced manner complementing the strengths of involved family members.

A trust is an arrangement in which a person (or persons) called the "settlor" or "grantor" enters an agreement with a second person or financial institution, called the "trustee," to hold, manage, and use identified assets, called "trust principal and income," for the benefit of a third person, the "beneficiary." The trust instrument itself spells out the principles and rules that are to guide the trustee in making decisions about the investment and use of trust property. A "living trust" is established during the lifetime of the settlor but may or may not be then funded. Living trusts are often funded as a result of a "pour-over" provision in the settlor's will or by naming the trust as the beneficiary of a life insurance policy. A "testamentary trust" is a trust that is established and funded in the individual's will. It thus does not go into effect until the individual's death.

Living trusts may be revocable or irrevocable. A revocable trust can be canceled or amended by the settlor at any time during his or her lifetime. This makes for great flexibility. However, special circumstances may support the use of a trust that is irrevocable, that cannot be canceled or amended by the settlor. Such special circumstances may include income tax or estate tax considerations, as only property in irrevocable trusts can be treated as separate from the taxpayer. Also, for gifts to qualify for the annual gift tax exclusion of up to $10,000, the gifts must be to individuals or to irrevocable trusts containing special provisions. Similarly, if a parent is particularly concerned about his or her health or potential need for long-term nursing home care or other liability concerns, then consideration of an irrevocable trust, at least partially funded during the parent's lifetime, may be warranted. Otherwise, substantially all of the assets of the parent may have to be spent on his or her nursing or medical care before Medicaid eligibility may be established. Also, irrevocability is usually more appropriate in the event that other persons, such as grandparents, may make transfers to the trust, either through lifetime gifts or their wills.

Trusts have several advantages over guardianship as a means of managing assets and income on behalf of the individual with mental retardation. A trust is basically a private agreement, which can be tailored flexibly to meet the individual's particular needs. In contrast, the discretion of a guardian is determined by statutes and case law of general application. The need for court involvement may add uncertainty, expense and delay, and thus has a chilling effect on innovation and risk-taking. Secondly, use of a trust does not require or imply legal incompetency of the beneficiary. One may thus use a trust in a situation where the individual has a diminished capacity to function independently but is not so incapable that guardianship is appropriate. Lastly, being the beneficiary of a trust does not necessarily render the individual ineligible for means-sensitive programs. In contrast, property held by a guardian is generally counted when an eligibility determination is made.

Rules determining the effect of trusts on eligibility for benefits and services vary among programs and states and can certainly be expected to change over time. Nonetheless, it is possible to discern certain principles of general application for trusts in this context.

A. Distribution of trust income and principal must be solely in the hands of the trustee. The beneficiary must not have any explicit or implied right, power, or authority to control trust expenditures or distributions, directly or indirectly.

B. The language of the trust must explicitly reflect the "supplemental" intent of the trust. The trustee must have the power to spend from the trust only to obtain goods or services that the individual is unable to obtain from any other source, including public benefit programs. This statement of supplemental intent is necessary to avoid the possible claim that the trustee's failure to spend from the trust constitutes an abuse of discretion by the trustee.

C. In light of the possibility of changes in the law involving eligibility for many programs, which might render the individual ineligible for important benefits or services as a result of particular provisions in the trust, some form of "safety valve" provision should be included, allowing or requiring the trustee to terminate or amend the trust in specified ways so as to avoid unanticipated and needless depletion.

D. In response to the possibility of changes in the needs of the individual, perhaps as a result of his or her clinical status, or in the array of available supportive services, the trust should provide for periodic review to consider modifications of the implementation of the trust.

E. Even if trust principal is not counted in determining the beneficiary's eligibility, distributions from the trust may be counted as income to the beneficiary even where the distribution is not cash to the individual, but a payment on his or her behalf (so-called "in-kind" payments). This treatment may reduce benefit levels. Language should be included in the trust to target this concern or make certain that the trustee is aware of the potential problem.

Service and Policy Implications

There is a critical need for long-term planning on the part of families and service providers in order to minimize trauma and crisis for the adult with mental retardation, other family members, and the service delivery system. In many cases, lack of planning results in unanticipated and possibly overwhelming service demands on an already strained service system (Kaufman et al., 1991). Families and service providers lack updated information on long-term planning options—particularly regarding residential, legal, and financial arrangements. Services and supports that are needed to assist persons with mental retardation, their families, and service providers with long-term planning include the following:

- improved case management with a focus on long-term planning and life-span developmental concerns;
- information, referral, and training for families and service providers regarding legal and financial issues involved in long-term care planning such as guardianship, less restrictive alternatives to guardianship, governmental entitlements, and trust and estate planning;
- support to individuals and families in planning and preparing for critical transition stages such as reaching the age of majority or adulthood, transition from special education services to vocational and other adult services, moving out of the family's home to an outside residential placement or independent living, retirement, or old age;
- assisting families in assessing the availability and capacity of their informal support networks (family members, friends, neighbors) as well as formal services and resources in terms of providing long-term care;
- training and supports for individuals with mental retardation to enhance their decision-making capacity and autonomy regarding long-term plans and preferences;
- supportive counseling for families and individuals with mental retardation who must deal with the emotional, social, and interpersonal dimensions of long-term planning as well as the legal and financial aspects;
- development of strategies to facilitate communication and coordination among service providers, family members, and persons with mental retardation in development of long-term plans;
- information, counseling, and support to siblings who currently or may potentially assume a caregiving role;
- development of flexible residential alternatives and functional supports to assist individuals in living where they choose to and participating in community life;
- expansion of continuing legal education programs for attorneys involved in family estate planning, who may have as clients families with members with mental retardation, and for judges, guardians, trustees, representative payees, and advocates, to facilitate consideration of the special social, personal, emotional, legal, and entitlements issues discussed in this chapter;
- review and reform of guardianship statutes and procedures to ensure that the authority of court-appointed guardians is tailored to meet the needs of the individual;
- expansion of collaborative, corporate, and governmental alternatives to provide necessary guardianship and trust services for persons with mental retardation who lack effective family advocacy support.

The availability of such services and supports would enable and empower individuals, families, and service providers to engage in proactive planning rather than delaying decision-making until a crisis in the family support system has occurred.

Research Implications

Few studies have addressed the subject of long-term planning by persons with mental retardation and their families. Current data are primarily descriptive, cross-sectional, and based on small nonprobability samples. Only a few studies have been explanatory in purpose, analyzing factors associated with or determinants of long-term planning. There is a need to move beyond existing descriptive research to explanatory research in order to examine the following kinds of issues: factors associated with long-term planning by family members; circumstances or factors that facilitate or impede the planning process; the short-term and long-term impacts of the planning process on caregiver and family well-being; and the roles and effectiveness of various professionals in the planning process.

Longitudinal research is needed to study the changing needs of families and children with mental retardation over the life span. Using a developmental life-span perspective, studies could examine the changes experienced by the family as a whole (such as changes in family functions, roles, resources, capacities, supports) as well as changes experienced by individuals within the family unit. Long-term planning is a dynamic process that should respond to the changing needs of the family and its members. Certain changes in the course of the family life cycle or in the development of individuals within the family may precipitate the need for long-term planning. And conversely, long-term planning may bring about certain changes or adaptations in the family unit and its members.

It is important for research to incorporate the various perspectives of the persons involved in the planning—the parents, the family member with mental retardation, other family members who are or may eventually be involved, and the service providers and professionals. There may be significant discrepancies in the perceptions, preferences, and concerns of the various parties involved. Research in this area has typically involved interviewing only the primary caregiver, typically the mother.

There is a need for multidimensional measures of long-term planning. Typically, studies have used a dichotomous measure of planning—plan/don't plan. The various aspects and dimensions of planning need to be assessed including the areas of planning, types of planning activities, level of involvement in planning, extent of planning efforts, and planning preferences.

Comparative research on family caregivers and service providers across different population groups would provide a broader framework for understanding long-term planning issues. For example, families caring for frail elderly relatives or relatives who are mentally ill or physically disabled face similar legal and financial concerns. One key area of cross-disability research would be an analysis of governmental policies as they affect family caregiving across the life span—for example, an analysis of the incentives and disincentives for family care and long-term planning created by current federal and state legislation and funding mechanisms.

Research incorporating the methodological issues described above would greatly enhance the knowledge base in this field and would assist service providers and policy makers in the development of responsive programs.

References

Agosta, J., Feinberg, B., & Bradley, V. (1985). Families and future financial planning: National survey results. In J. Agosta & V. Bradley (Eds.), *Family care for persons with developmental disabilities: A growing commitment* (pp. 149–164). Cambridge, MA: Human Services Research Institute.

American Association on Mental Retardation. (1992). *Mental retardation: Definition, classification, and systems of support* (9th ed.). Washington, DC: Author.

Anderson, D. J., Lakin, K. C., Bruininks, R. H., & Hill, B. K. (1987). *A national study of residential and support services for elderly persons with mental retardation* (Report No. 22). Minneapolis: University of Minnesota, Department of Educational Psychology.

Apolloni, T., & Cooke, T. P. (Eds.) (1984). *A new look at guardianship: Protective services that support personalized living.* Baltimore, MD: Brookes.

Beyer, H. A., & Howell, M. C. (1989). Decision making by and for individuals of questionable competence. In M. C. Howell, D. G. Gavin, G. A. Cabrera, & H. A. Beyer (Eds.), *Serving the underserved: Caring for people who are both old and mentally retarded* (pp. 118–130). Boston: Exceptional Parent Press.

Cohen, G. J. (1992, October). *Guardianship and an aging population of persons with developmental disabilities*. Kansas City: University of Missouri, Kansas City Institute for Human Development.

Factor, A., & Anderson, D. (1992, May). *Person-centered planning: Innovative approaches in case management and habilitation planning*. Paper presented at the 116th Annual Meeting of the American Association on Mental Retardation, New Orleans, LA.

Gollay, E., Freedman, R., Wyngaarden, M., & Kurtz, N. (1978). *Coming back: The community experiences of deinstitutionalized mentally retarded people*. Cambridge, MA: Abt Books.

Goodman, D. M. (1978). Parenting an adult mentally retarded offspring. *Smith College Studies in Social Work, 48*, 209–234.

Grant, G. (1986). Older carers, interdependence and care of mentally handicapped adults. *Aging and Society, 6*, 333–351.

Guess, D., Benson, H. A., & Siegel-Causey, E. (1985). Concepts and issues related to choice-making and autonomy among persons with severe disabilities. *Journal of the Association for Persons with Severe Handicaps, 10*, 79–86.

Heller, T. (1988). Transitions: Coming in and going out of community residences. In M. P. Janicki, M. W. Krauss, & M. M. Seltzer (Eds.), *Community residences for persons with developmental disabilities: Here to stay* (pp. 149–158). Baltimore, MD: Brookes.

Heller, T., & Factor, A. (1991). Permanency planning for adults with mental retardation living with family caregivers. *American Journal on Mental Retardation, 96*, 163–176.

Heller T., & Factor, A. (1994). Facilitating future planning and transitions out of the home.

In M. M. Seltzer, M. W. Krauss, & M. P. Janicki (Eds.), *Life course perspectives on adulthood and old age* (pp. 39–50). Washington, DC: American Association on Mental Retardation.

Janicki, M. P., Otis, J. P., Puccio, P. S., Rettig, J. S., & Jacobson, J. W. (1985). Service needs among older developmentally disabled persons. In M. P. Janicki & H. M. Wisniewski (Eds.), *Aging and developmental disabilities: Issues and approaches* (pp. 289–304). Baltimore, MD: Brookes.

Kaufman, A. V., Adams, J. P., & Campbell, V. A. (1991). Permanency planning by older parents who care for adult children with mental retardation. *Mental Retardation, 29*, 293–300.

Krauss, M. W. (1990, May). *Later life placements: Precipitating factors and family profiles*. Paper presented at the 114th Annual Meeting of the American Association on Mental Retardation, Atlanta, GA.

O'Brien, J. (1987). A guide to life-style planning. In G. T. Bellamy & B. Wilcox (Eds.), *A comprehensive guide to the activities catalog: An alternative curriculum for youth and adults with severe disabilities* (pp. 175–189). Baltimore, MD: Brookes.

O'Brien, J., Forest, M., Snow, J., & Hasbury, D. (1989). *Action for inclusion*. Toronto, Canada: Frontier College Press.

Olson, D. H., McCubbin, H. I., Barnes, H., Larsen, A., Muxen, M., & Wilson, M. (1984). *One thousand families: A national survey*. Beverly Hills: Sage Publications.

Seltzer, M. M., & Krauss, M. W. (1989). Aging parents with mentally retarded children: Family risk factors and sources of support. *American Journal on Mental Retardation, 94*, 303–312.

Seltzer, M.M., & Krauss, M.W. (1994). Aging parents with coresident adult children: The impact of lifelong caregiving. In M.M. Seltzer, M.W. Krauss, & M.P. Janicki (Eds.), *Life course perspectives in adulthood and old age* (pp. 3–18). Washington, DC: American Association on Mental Retardation.

Seltzer, M. M., Krauss, M. W., & Heller, T. (1991). Family caregiving over the life course. In M.P.

Janicki & M.W. Krauss (Eds.), *Aging and developmental disabilities: Challenges for the 1990s* (Proceedings of the Boston Roundtable on Research Issues and Applications in Aging and Developmental Disabilities) (pp. 3–24). Washington, DC: American Association on Mental Retardation, Aging Special Interest Group.

Smith, G. C., & Tobin, S. S. (1989). Permanency planning among older parents of adults with lifelong disabilities. *Journal of Gerontological Social Work, 14,* 35–59.

Suelzle, M., & Keenan, V. (1981). Changes in family support networks over the life cycle of mentally retarded persons. *American Journal of Mental Deficiency, 86,* 267–274.

Superintendent of Belchertown State School v. Saikewicz, 373 Mass. 728, 370 N.E.2d. 417 (1978).

Turnbull, A. P., Summers, J. A., & Brotherson, M. J. (1986). Family life cycle: Theoretical and empirical implications and future directions for families with mentally retarded members. In J. J. Gallagher & P. M. Vietze (Eds.), *Families of handicapped persons: Research, programs, and policy issues* (pp. 45–65). Baltimore, MD: Brookes.

Turnbull, H. R., Turnbull, A. P., Bronicki, G. J., Summers, J. A., & Roeder-Gordon, C. (1989). *Disability and the family: A guide to decisions for adulthood.* Baltimore, MD: Brookes.

Future Directions

Chapter 10

Methodological Challenges in the Study of Life-Span Development of Persons With Mental Retardation

Keith F. Widaman, University of California at Riverside
Sharon A. Borthwick-Duffy, University of California at Riverside
Justina C. Powers, University of California at Riverside

Over the past quarter century, the scope of research and theory regarding developmental phenomena has broadened considerably, encompassing the description and explanation of the development of persons across the life span. Prior to that time, separate age-graded subdisciplines seemed to dominate the way the field of developmental psychology was conceived. Some researchers were identified as child psychologists, others as adolescent psychologists, still others as gerontologists. Thus, instead of the domain of variables or constructs, the age of the participants provided the stronger demarcation of one's research area, and rather different theoretical models and processes were proposed to explain phenomena at the disparate stages of the life span.

This trend has been evident in the field of mental retardation as well. For example, sizable bodies of research have accumulated in relation to the early attachment of infants (Blacher & Meyers, 1983) and the development of specific abilities in infancy (Cicchetti & Ganiban, 1990), the development of abilities during school-age years including adolescence (Hodapp et al., 1992; Smith & Phillips, 1992), age-related declines among older individuals (Silverstein, Herbs, Miller, Nasuta, & Williams, 1988; Silverstein, Herbs, Nasuta, & White, 1986), potential relationships of Down syndrome to Alzheimer disease (Dalton & Wisniewski, 1990; Zigman, Seltzer, & Silverman, chapter 5 this volume), and life expectancy of persons with mental retardation (Eyman & Borthwick-Duffy, chapter 6 this volume). In contrast, few studies have examined the development of persons with mental retardation over the life span (but see Eyman & Arndt, 1982; Eyman & Widaman, 1987).

With the advent of a life-span perspective on the development of persons (cf. Goulet & Baltes, 1970), the need arose to bring the array of theories and results from the subdisciplines under a common developmental framework that could integrate findings across the human life span. Not surprisingly, this attempt is fraught with difficulties of various kinds. Diverse findings deriving from the study of persons at different points in the life span may require theories and models that include a wide array of processes or mechanisms that influence or underlie development. In addition, the particular subset of mechanisms that influence growth or decline in any given domain of behavior may vary with life stage. For example, early in life, certain types of basic biological mechanisms, aided by crucial environmental inputs, appear to lead to an unfolding of preprogrammed sequences of development. During childhood and adolescence, social and educational experiences seem to drive many of the changes observed in behavior (McCall, 1981). Finally, during aging, the gradual breakdown of the physical or biological systems supporting life and basic psychological functioning, a deterioration that may have both genetic and experiential contributions, seems to affect the relative speed of decline in various capabilities (Horn, 1989). Providing comprehensive theories and models of human development that encompass the necessary array of biological and psychological processes and the ways these processes interact across the life span is a daunting challenge, yet one that must be confronted if we are to characterize well the ontogenetic progress of behavioral development and change.

The developmental trajectory for the acquisition of cognitive skills by persons with mental retardation has been the subject of ongoing discussion for many years. According to the developmental position proposed by Zigler (1969; Zigler & Hodapp, 1986), both IQ and chronological age are responsible for determining the rate of development and the eventual asymptotic level of performance that is reached. Thus, the study of development in persons with mental retardation is complicated by the need to include the influences of both aging and level of intelligence on the acquisition of skills during the developmental period and the decline in skills during old age. Moreover, other factors, such as etiology of mental retardation and secondary handicapping conditions, are also likely to interact with the mechanisms that influence development and decline (e.g., Zigman et al., chapter 5 this volume). These additional factors must become part of a life-span theory that encompasses the processes influencing development and that applies uniquely to persons with mental retardation.

In this chapter, we will discuss a number of challenges that confront researchers employing life-span approaches to the study of the development of persons with mental retardation. We contend that these challenges are endemic to research on any population of persons, although the study of persons with mental retardation may lead to unique considerations with regard to certain problems. In our chapter, we will provide concrete contexts for the explication of challenges in research by using examples from the behavioral domains of intelligence and adaptive behavior, domains of great importance in our field due to their centrality in the definition of mental retardation and practical significance in the lives of persons with mental retardation (Widaman, Borthwick-Duffy, &

Little, 1991). However, our use of examples in the domains of intelligence and adaptive behavior should not be construed as limiting in any way the importance of these challenges for research in other domains or on other units of observation. That is, life-span developmental investigations may study various types of observations—individuals, families, careproviders, or service systems, among others—and the key variables may be wide ranging as well—encompassing intellectual or social skills, health status, family functioning, or patterns of service utilization. Thus, the challenges we identify accompany any search for adequate theories of the life-span development or change of persons with mental retardation and the social and institutional systems with which they interact.

When investigating the development of behaviors, such as adaptive behaviors, across the life span, a number of important issues arise. These issues include principally at least the following: (a) the nature of the theoretical propositions investigated; (b) the design of the empirical investigations of life-span development; (c) the types of analyses of data from the study; and (d) the interpretation and evaluation of results. Each of these issues will be discussed in turn in the remainder of this chapter.

Life-Span Theory and Mental Retardation

General Developmental Issues

Basic research questions. The study of behavioral development begins with the stating of the fundamental issues confronted by a proposed study, issues that provide the motivation for the investigation. Several kinds of general issues provide a standard frame of reference for developmental researchers, issues involving the nature of the developmental changes to be studied. One way of construing the question of the nature of developmental change is in terms of the mean level of behavior observed, changes that are largely or solely quantitative in nature (Widaman, 1991). Across a very wide array of behavioral domains, marked changes in mean level are observed during infancy, childhood, and adolescence. Once an asymptotic level of behavior is reached during early adulthood, there is often relative stability, with small increases or decreases during the middle years of adulthood. Then, with the advent of aging, declines begin to be observed, declines that accelerate with advancing age (e.g., Horn, 1989; Schaie, 1983). Similarly, age-related changes in adaptive behavior during the developmental and middle adult periods have been found in studies of persons with mental retardation (Eyman & Widaman, 1987; Little & Widaman, 1991; Widaman et al., 1991; Zigman et al., chapter 5 this volume). In studies of aging persons with Down syndrome, there has been some evidence to support the hypothesis of age-related declines. However, most studies have been cross-sectional and have found losses in specific adaptive skills rather than a generalized decline in competence (Zigman et al., chapter 5 this volume).

A second way of interpreting the question of the nature of developmental change is to investigate the evolution of the formal or structural properties of the processes underlying behavior. Here, the change studied is a change in form or structure, change that is qualitative, rather than quantitative (Widaman, 1991). Perhaps the clearest example of a theory of structural change is that of Piaget (1970), who hypothesized that cognitive structures evolve during infancy, childhood, and adolescence through a series of four major stages. These stages, or periods, include the sensorimotor period of infancy, the preoperational and concrete operational periods of childhood, and the formal operational period that typically emerges during early adolescence. Not surprisingly, the ontogenetic evolution of the forms or structures underlying behavior is often at least as important for theory as are the observed changes in mean levels of behavior.

Yet another important distinction in developmental research is whether theories attempt to explain the mean developmental function, individual differences in development, or both (Baltes & Nesselroade, 1979). From

infancy through adolescence, remarkable changes in mean levels of behavior occur; developmental theories that provide explanations of these changes are therefore quite attractive. However, explanations of the mean developmental trend may yield little information about development of individuals (Wohlwill, 1973). That is, strikingly high and distressingly low levels of performance by many individuals may be consistent with a moderate developmental trend. Moreover, considerable individual differences in growth rate can occur in the presence of moderate levels of longitudinal stability of individual differences about the mean. Life-span curves for adaptive behavior domains, for example, are based on mean levels of performance at each age across the life span and provide profiles of trajectories of development for subgroups of people with specific characteristics (e.g. Eyman & Arndt, 1982; Eyman & Widaman, 1987). These curves are useful for characterizing typical, or average, developmental trends and form the basis for a theory of life-span development. However, life-span curves provide only a reference point to begin understanding individual differences and the unique trajectories of persons with mental retardation.

When approaching developmental research, there may be additional ways of construing the issue of the nature of the changes investigated across the life span, moving beyond the notions of change in level and form and consideration of both the developmental function and individual differences (McCall, 1981). Adequate accounts of development in any domain often require the integration of information regarding changes in all of these aspects of behavior. However, there is a basic core set of issues that are of great interest to the developmentalist. These include (a) determining the nature of the behavioral constructs to be studied, such as investigating the structure of the ability dimensions comprising the domain, (b) investigating age-related changes in the behaviors under study, such as differential age trends for various ability dimensions; and (c) studying the developmental antecedents and consequents of behaviors as they develop, such as the developmental precursors of developmental advances in particular areas of mental skill and differential relations of these skills to other forms of behavior, such as school achievement (Baltes & Nesselroade, 1979).

Applied implications. Much research in developmental psychology is basic in nature, investigating theoretical propositions with little obvious attention to the applications of the results obtained. But, the results of developmental studies often have applied implications that are not difficult to discern. For example, the domain of intelligence has been the object of concerted investigation for over 100 years (Galton, 1869). At the present time, there are several generalizations that are clearly justified. One conclusion is that there are marked differences in performance on many dimensions of ability during middle adulthood and, especially, during aging. These age-related changes are most marked on dimensions of fluid intelligence and speed, but differences occur on other dimensions as well (Horn, 1988, 1989). A second conclusion is that tasks that require crystallized abilities, such as verbal comprehension or access to long-term memories, in an unspeeded format often exhibit either stability or improvements in performance until rather late in life (Horn, 1988). Findings such as these have implications for the design of a wide array of objects with which people must interact. For example, the highly sophisticated nature of state-of-the-art electronics, including televisions and telephones, may be impressive. But, the lack of familiarity with such devices may mean that older persons are effectively denied access to commonly used modes of communication due to difficulty in adapting to the new forms of technology.

Developmental Issues in the Study of Mental Retardation

In studying persons with mental retardation, the distinction between basic questions and more applied goals of investigations may once again be raised. These differing aims of research will be discussed in turn.

Basic questions. Certain questions of a basic, research nature concern the similarities of the life-span trends for the development of several types of adaptive behaviors. Similarities in the life-span trends may suggest that there are common bases for those behaviors that exhibit similar trends. More confidently, different bases, whether physiological or behavioral, are likely to underlie adaptive behaviors that exhibit markedly different age-related developmental trends. Whatever the outcome, the charting of life-span developmental curves for the several dimensions that comprise the domain of adaptive behaviors will provide some indications regarding the likely presence of multiple bases for the development and aging of different forms of adaptive behavior.

A second type of basic research question involves the extent to which a person's other characteristics moderate the development of adaptive behaviors. In the eighth edition of the classification manual of the American Association on Mental Retardation (AAMR) (Grossman, 1983), the person's level of impairment was categorized into one of four levels, using the terms mild, moderate, severe, and profound. These descriptors have been omitted from the newly adopted AAMR manual, but apparently will be retained in the new Diagnostic and Statistical Manual, Version IV, or DSM-IV, of the American Psychiatric Association (Herbert Grossman, personal communication, May 1993). Under the new, ninth edition of the American Association on Mental Retardation manual (AAMR, 1992), the four levels of mental retardation have given way to an emphasis on describing the person's strengths and weaknesses and assigning a level to the intensity of needed support. Regardless of the changes in definition or nomenclature, however, the person's level of intellectual impairment will likely affect his or her developmental trajectory and the age at which maximal levels of behavior are reached. Moreover, as noted earlier, there are other personal characteristics, such as health conditions or secondary handicapping conditions, that may influence the rate of development of adaptive behaviors (Zigman et al., chapter 5 this volume).

Research should attempt to determine the extent to which such personal characteristics affect the development of adaptive behaviors.

Yet another form of basic research question is the investigation of the operation of factors that may moderate the development of adaptive behaviors. In our research (e.g., see Widaman et al., 1991), we have been studying parental effects on the development of adaptive behaviors. Specifically, we are interested in the ways in which parents, through their childrearing attitudes and behaviors, may either enhance or inhibit the growth or development of certain kinds of adaptive and maladaptive behaviors. But, under a general ecological model (e.g., Bronfenbrenner, 1977), other aspects of the person's environment, such as the extent to which the parent or other caregiver encourages community involvement, should influence outcomes such as adaptive behaviors and social networks (Borthwick-Duffy, Widaman, Little, & Eyman, 1992). Thus, to understand any type of behavior, we must understand how it develops within the contexts within which persons live, including the ways in which these contexts influence the development of the behaviors under study.

Applied implications for care and service. Research on adaptive behaviors is accompanied by clear implications for applied concerns for the care of persons with mental retardation as well as for the service systems for these persons. Life-span curves for adaptive and maladaptive behaviors will provide parents, careproviders, and teachers with projections regarding the behavior of persons for whom they provide care or service. As persons with mental retardation develop, move through middle adulthood, and then age, changes in mean levels of adaptive behaviors occur (Eyman & Widaman, 1987; Widaman et al., 1991). With life-span curves of behavior available, careproviders can plan ahead for the behavioral constellations that are likely to be shown by the persons with mental retardation with whom they interact.

The information provided by life-span developmental curves for the various forms of adaptive behavior should also be of great interest to parents who have children with mental retardation. Having a child with mental retardation leads to a large number of questions on the part of parents, including questions related to the likely developmental outcomes for their offspring. Life-span developmental curves represent average or typical developmental outcomes for children with specific sets of characteristics and provide developmental expectations that can give a realistic indication of the age-related competencies that may be exhibited by the child during his or her life.

Service systems for persons with mental retardation are also influenced by knowledge of the life-span outcomes for persons whom they serve. For example, if persons with mental retardation in a particular program are expected to exhibit higher levels of behavior in years to come, this should influence the types and emphases of future programs that are developed.

Finally, whether living in their own homes or in other placements, persons with mental retardation will exhibit their optimal development under potentially specifiable circumstances. At present, the research base on external influences on development is rather meager; however, the future should see considerable growth in recommended practices, as much work is currently being performed to accomplish this purpose. The key outcome of such work would be sets of recommendations for optimizing the developmental outcomes of persons with mental retardation. These sets of recommendations should contain research-based suggestions for ideal ways of structuring a person's living, work, school, and social environments in order to enhance development as much as possible. At present, some rough guidelines of this sort are available for children and adolescents without mental retardation: children and adolescents without mental retardation appear to show more mature behavioral outcomes if they have been raised by authoritative parents, who provide much structure and control for their children, but also high levels of warmth, nurturance, and information about why certain behaviors lead to given outcomes (Baumrind, 1971, 1991). Children exhibit poorer outcomes, in general, if they are raised by authoritarian parents (high on structure and control, but low on warmth and nurturance) or by permissive parents (high on warmth and nurturance, but low on structure and control) (Baumrind, 1991). Research is currently underway to determine whether these findings generalize to children and adolescents with mental retardation (Widaman, 1992; Widaman & Borthwick-Duffy, 1990; Widaman et al., 1991). Regardless of the degree of generalizability, the findings of this current research on children and adolescents with mental retardation will provide parents with information that should prove useful in providing appropriate experiences for their children.

Designing Life-Span Developmental Studies

When undertaking a life-span developmental study, several issues must be considered at the outset, given the importance of these issues for the generalizability of the results obtained. These issues involve primarily the choice of developmental research design, the manner in which the participants for the study are recruited, and the composition of the battery of measures on which participants are assessed.

Developmental Research Designs

The study of development across the life span typically involves the investigation of behavior (B) as a function of chronological age (A), or $B = f(A)$. Traditionally, two types of developmental design have been used to gather data; these two types of design are cross-sectional and longitudinal designs. More recently, semilongitudinal designs have been proposed that alleviate several of the shortcomings associated with the traditional designs. Each of these types of design will be described briefly, and the problems arising in use of each design will be noted.

Conventional developmental designs. Cross-sectional and longitudinal designs are the conventional, or traditional, forms of developmental study. Using a *cross-sectional design,* samples of participants are chosen so that samples differ systematically in chronological age. For example, participants might be chosen who are 4, 6, 8, 10, or 12 years of age to study the development of behavior during childhood and early adolescence. Samples of participants are then assessed on variables of interest at a single point in time (e.g., a single calendar year). The variables of interest are employed as dependent variables; chronological age is the independent variable. If a dependent variable is related significantly to age, the common attribution is that the variable is a function of age. More specifically, *age differences,* or the differences between the several age groups, are presumed to reflect *age changes,* or the changes that should occur as a function of aging in a single sample.

In a standard *longitudinal design,* on the other hand, a single sample of participants is identified at a given point in time, and an initial assessment of variables of interest is obtained. At the initial time of measurement, the participants comprising the sample are typically of a rather restricted age range. This sample is then assessed at one or more later points in time. Obviously, at the later points in time, the participants differ systematically in chronological age. As with the cross-sectional design, the variables of interest are used as dependent variables, and age serves as the independent variable. But, in the longitudinal design, because a single sample of persons is observed at each of several different ages, the attribution to age of causal status in influencing the dependent variables seems much more direct and reasonable. That is, *age changes* are observed directly using a longitudinal design, so the leap from age differences to age changes need not be made. However, use of a longitudinal design still requires the assumption that observed age changes represent true age-related changes, rather than the effects of one or more alternative explanatory variables.

Problems with conventional developmental designs. A variety of problems are associated with the assumption that differences or changes in behavior across time are age-related changes. We will briefly note several of these problems (cf. Baltes, 1968). First, longitudinal studies usually suffer from selective sampling; typically, participants who agree to participate in a longitudinal study are not representative of the general population of persons. Cross-sectional studies, employing only a single time of measurement for each participant, are less subject to this confound. Selective sampling may well be present in most studies of persons with mental retardation, yet there is little information at present that allows firm, empirical conclusions on this point.

Second, selective survival of persons is likely to occur in developmental research. Persons who live longer almost certainly have different personal characteristics than persons who do not live as long (Damon, 1965; Kuhlen, 1963; Zigman et al., chapter 5 this volume). This presents a problem for both cross-sectional and longitudinal designs, as the two types of design will include differentially representative subgroups of persons across the life span. The importance of selective survival is especially important in research on persons with mental retardation. Current research on mortality in persons with mental retardation (e.g., Eyman & Borthwick-Duffy, chapter 6 this volume) suggests that mortality rates also differ as a function of level of mental retardation. For example, persons with profound mental retardation have much higher mortality rates than do persons with mild or moderate mental retardation, and mortality rates appear to vary as a function of etiology (Eyman, Grossman, Chaney, & Call, 1990; Eyman, Grossman, Tarjan, & Miller, 1987; Thase, 1982). Selective survival as a function of personal characteristics implies that the population of persons with mental retardation varies across the life span in conjunction with survival rates, and this should affect the generalizations to be offered from life-span studies.

Third, selective drop-out often occurs within the context of longitudinal studies, a problem that does not occur in cross-sectional studies. Commonly, participants who drop out of longitudinal studies have less favorable characteristics on an array of psychological variables, leading to limits on the generalizability of the results obtained (e.g., Nesselroade & Baltes, 1974; Zigman et al., chapter 5 this volume). Such effects are likely to occur as well in longitudinal studies of persons with mental retardation, but few (if any) studies of persons with mental retardation have tested for the presence of selective drop-out.

Fourth, there is evidence of "testing effects," or reactivity of measurement, in longitudinal investigations over 1-year spans (e.g., Nesselroade & Baltes, 1974) and even up to over 10-year spans between times of measurement (e.g., Baltes, 1968). Testing effects clearly may influence the results from longitudinal studies, but do not impinge as directly on the results of cross-sectional studies. The presence of testing effects may seem to be less crucial in certain research on persons with mental retardation, especially for research on adaptive behavior, as such measures are typically obtained using the third-party informant method. However, the potential testing effects may surface here if the informant provides data differently as a function of the number of times s/he has been interviewed.

Fifth, "generation" or cohort effects may arise in various ways, and such effects lead to difficulties in comparing results from longitudinal and cross-sectional designs. Cohort effects are the historical and cultural events that accompany development and aging of persons in a given birth cohort (i.e., defined by year of birth). Longitudinal designs typically use participants from a single birth year, so cohort effects usually are not invoked as responsible for observed aging trends because any effects of cohort are held constant by the design of the study. On the other hand, cohort effects are confounded with age effects in the cross-sectional design, so that cohort could always be used as an alternative explanation of results using the latter design.

Semilongitudinal designs. Semilongitudinal designs were proposed to remedy a variety of shortcomings associated with the use of cross-sectional and longitudinal designs. The principal shortcoming of cross-sectional designs was the contention that age differences represent age-related changes, rather than cohort or other effects. That is, the assumption that differences in behavior exhibited by samples differing in age mirror the changes that would occur as a function of age in any single sample is a crucial one, for which there is little solid evidence.

The basic ideas underlying the use of semilongitudinal designs were first articulated by Bell (1953, 1954), who used the term "convergence" to describe the design he proposed. This fundamental idea was that one could study several cohorts of individuals across shorter age spans and then construct a semilongitudinal age trend. Given their membership in different birth cohorts, assessing the different cohorts of persons would result in measures obtained at each of a wide variety of ages. After rearranging the data as a function of chronological age, the developmental trend was the simple average of the age-related changes averaged across cohorts.

These ideas were systematized by Schaie (1965), who noted that behavior could be influenced by age, cohort, or time of measurement. The most widely accepted current view is that behavior of individuals is influenced by a larger number of personal and general contextual factors than chronological age alone. Rather, behavior (B) must be seen as influenced by age (A), birth cohort (C), and by time of measurement (T), or B = f(A,C,T), among a host of other contextual factors. Interestingly, age, cohort, and time of measurement are not independent mathematically; fixing any two of these aspects of a design defines precisely the place of the third variable in the design (Baltes, 1968; Schaie, 1965). For example, designing an Age X Cohort study involves choosing certain birth cohorts and then selecting the ages at which members of those birth cohorts will be observed. Having done this, the times of measurement are thereby fixed. Rather than dwell in detail on the problems arising from this problem, we refer interested readers to Widaman et al. (1991) for a more in-depth presentation of problems and some alternatives for studies of populations of persons with mental retardation.

Semilongitudinal designs have led to important insights in the study of the development of adaptive behaviors (e.g., Eyman & Widaman, 1987; Little & Widaman, 1991; Widaman et al., 1991). In these studies, cross-sectional analyses, based on data from a single year of measurement, provided initial estimates of aging trends, trends that paralleled those from other cross-sectional studies of aging of adaptive behaviors. Such results, however, rest on perilous assumptions regarding the comparability of samples across birth cohorts; differential mortality of persons with mental retardation as a function of various characteristics including level of mental retardation (Eyman & Borthwick-Duffy, chapter 6 this volume) is but one indication that such assumptions may not be valid. Then, estimation of semilongitudinal aging curves, which presumably provide more accurate representations of individual patterns of aging, led to rather different characterizations of growth and development along most dimensions of adaptive behavior for many groups of persons with mental retardation. Details regarding these studies may be found in the references cited above; the "take home" message from these studies is that cross-sectional studies may provide dramatically different, biased representations of aging trends, and that longitudinal or semilongitudinal studies are required to characterize well the growth and aging of adaptive behaviors.

Cohort issues. The influence of cohorts on an array of psychological variables (e.g., Schaie, 1983; Nesselroade & Baltes, 1974) leads to a need to determine the basis of cohort effects (Hogan, 1984). In samples of nonretarded persons, cohort effects on measures of mental ability have been presumed to be related to differential experiences that the cohorts have had, such as the gradual lengthening of mandatory years of schooling (cf. Kuhlen, 1963). Several classic studies of the life-span development of intelligence, studies published before 1950, used cross-sectional designs (e.g., Jones & Conrad, 1933). This resulted in older participants coming from birth cohorts for which the average number of years of formal education was considerably less than for younger participants.

The initial interpretations of such data suggested that the age trends reflected the "true" growth and aging of human intelligence, with many abilities showing dramatic declines after the age of 25 to 30 years. However, such curves could also arise from the systematically differing numbers of years of formal schooling attained by persons from the different cohorts (e.g., Hogan, 1984).

In the study of the life-span development of adaptive behaviors, certain of the variables underlying cohort effects in populations of persons with mental retardation will likely be different than those postulated to underlie cohort effects in nonretarded populations. Perhaps the most obvious influences are those that alter the population of persons with mental retardation. For example, improvements in medical treatment have resulted in much longer life spans for persons with many types of mental retardation. Moreover, genetic screening has and will result in changes in the relative frequencies of births of persons with certain types of mental retardation (Moser, 1992). Further, changes in the definition of mental retardation (e.g., scoring 1 standard deviation or more below the mean on IQ versus scoring 2 standard deviations or more below the mean) can result in the wholesale redefinition of the population of persons with mental retardation within one or a few birth cohorts, making these birth cohorts nonequivalent to birth cohorts that came before or will come after (MacMillan, 1989a, 1989b). Variables such as these will influence the composition of the population of persons with mental retardation, and these variables may then be responsible for cohort differences observed in life-span studies of the development of adaptive behaviors by persons with mental retardation.

Selection of Participants

One crucial aspect of the design of any life-span developmental study is the selection of participants. Selection of participants implies some notion of the population or populations from which participants are selected. The population of persons with mental retardation is a concept that can be difficult to define precisely; this issue is clearly one that goes beyond the confines of the present chapter. In this section, we will discuss issues related to the selection of participants with regard to the positive and negative aspects of each form of selection, as well as the implicit implications each has for the characterization of the population of interest.

Historical influences on population composition. Characteristics of the population of individuals with mental retardation are determined in part by historical factors. For example, Moser (1992) speculated that it will soon be possible to develop DNA markers for all or most of the genetic disorders associated with mental retardation. He stated that "It is likely that not long after the year 2000, it will be possible to define all of the more than 1,000 genetic disorders that are associated with severe mental retardation. It is also likely that early, and often prenatal, diagnosis will become feasible at an affordable cost, with noninvasive procedures" (p. 146). These scientific advancements will impact the accuracy of diagnosis as well as the classification system of etiologies. Although most individuals with newly identified syndromes will have previously been identified as having mental retardation and will have been included in research samples, age-related studies that take etiology into account will be influenced by the identification of new etiologies and the reduction or eradication of others due to genetic and metabolic screening or other preventative measures. Moreover, teratogens that cause mental retardation might differentially affect prevalence rates across different geographic, socioeconomic, and age groups. The exponential growth of mental retardation in children due to HIV-infection, for example, has been shown to be related to each of the above factors (Cohen, 1992).

Changes through the years in medical care and typical modes of behavior within our society may also affect the characteristics of the population of persons with mental retardation. Improved medical care has been shown to have an impact on the life expectancy of certain groups of people with mental retardation, such as individuals with Down syndrome (see Thase, 1982), which in turn affects the numbers of people aging into older groups in life-span studies (Eyman & Borthwick-Duffy, chapter 6 this volume). Types of accidents that may result in mental retardation are also affected by societal habits, such as swimming pool use, improved safety devices for children, seat belt legislation, etc. Finally, the current focus on prevention of mental retardation, including such procedures as early screening methods (chorionic villi sampling, amniocentesis, genetic counseling), education regarding teratogens, and improved prenatal care are likely to impact the prevalence and characteristics of populations and subgroups of individuals whose life-span development is being monitored (Baumeister, Kupstas, & Klindworth, 1990).

Random assignment. Random assignment of participants to conditions is often held up as a sine qua non of the experimental method; likely it is. Random assignment serves a number of functions, one of the most important of which is to ensure that participants in different conditions do not differ systematically on relevant background characteristics. The "equalization" of participants across conditions is the mechanism that allows the stating of the typical null hypothesis, that participants in the different treatment conditions will not differ unless the treatment has an effect on behavior.

Concerns with random assignment lead away from issues regarding the population of potential participants and toward equalizing the samples of participants in the different conditions. Certainly, researchers who employ random assignment are not uninterested in the population of participants, but frequently pay little attention to this issue. But, the issue is an important one, as failures to replicate experimental results may represent different biases in selection from a given population to a greater degree than they reflect variation in substantive results.

The importance of random assignment in experimental studies is so basic and valued that researchers in mental retardation often wish that they could randomly assign participants to conditions in their work. At times this is possible, but random assignment is clearly impossible with regard to some of the conditions that would be most interesting, for example, randomly assigning a child with mental retardation to any of several types of parenting in the natural home. Children are born into families; one may not randomly assign children to families. Similarly, in life-span studies, one cannot randomly assign participants to levels of age or birth cohort; rather, age and birth cohort are characteristics of the person that may affect his or her behavior. With the advent of new statistical techniques, such as structural equation modeling (Jöreskog & Sörbom, 1989), new ways of thinking about causal inferences are being developed. These notions, which do not require random assignment, will mature in the future as we begin to understand their implications. At present, we must be content to pursue causal hypotheses in research situations in which random assignment will never be possible.

Random sampling. Random sampling is another way of obtaining participants for study. Interestingly, random sampling leads automatically to a concern for the implied population; only after the population is specified can true random sampling from that population be performed.

Soon after recognizing this fact, researchers frequently realize that it is extremely difficult, if not impossible, to sample participants randomly from any general population. Random sampling implies that each individual in the sample has a priori an equal probability of being selected; in most cases, this is an unattainable goal. In the study of mental retardation, the researcher must first grapple with the definition of the population of interest, such as all persons with mental retardation, all persons with mental retardation who are identified by an institution (e.g., the school), etc. Once the population is defined, true random sampling will occur only if all persons in the population are equally likely to be selected for study. Falling short of this ideal, researchers often resort to the following option, representative sampling.

Representative sampling. Perhaps the most important goal of systematic sampling is to ensure that the obtained samples are representative of "the population." After defining the population of interest, the investigator may sample with regard to specifiable characteristics of the participants to ensure that the sample obtained is representative of the population. Or, the researcher may obtain a sample of participants in a less systematic manner, but test to determine whether the sample obtained differs significantly from the population of participants with regard to important characteristics, such as age, level of mental retardation, and gender.

Three methods of representative sampling have traditionally been used to describe developmental trends among people with mental retardation. The first method involves the use of nationally representative cross-sectional samples of participants with given characteristics. Developmental expectations then take the form of norms that are obtained through examination of performance by individuals at each age or age group. Such standardization samples for adaptive behavior instruments provide cross-sectional data sets that can characterize development in this way.

Using a second method of selecting participants, Richardson, Koller, and Katz (1985) studied the total population of children born during a five-year period in a British city. Classification of mild retardation was based on placement in special schools, administrative classification, and intelligence test scores. This method of selecting participants has several advantages, especially that of eliminating the risk of selecting a nonrepresentative sample, and is limited only by the degree of generalizability of the population to individuals born outside that particular city.

A more common, and possibly more practical, third method is to use samples defined by service system eligibility criteria. The life-span analyses conducted by Eyman and his associates (Eyman & Arndt, 1982; Eyman & Widaman, 1987), for example, have been based on a longitudinal data base containing adaptive behavior data on all individuals served by the California Department of Developmental Services (approximately

80,000 people). With a data set such as this, it is possible to study very large subgroups of people across the life span and to conduct semilongitudinal, rather than cross-sectional, analyses.

Service system data bases have been referred to as "samples of convenience" because the researcher does not design a systematic sampling procedure and may not be able to influence the quality of data collection. However, samples defined by service systems can provide access to the kinds of sample sizes and longitudinal data required for estimating life-span trends. These trends are generalizable with the following cautions in mind:

1. Service systems do not serve 100% of people with mental retardation. Typically, nearly all people with severe and profound retardation, most people with moderate retardation, but only a biased sample of people with mild retardation are represented in statewide service system data bases. Some individuals with mental retardation, particularly those who are identified as having mild retardation during their school years, do not move into adult service agencies and are thus excluded from data bases as they age. In addition, there is evidence of differential use of services by different cultural groups (Meyers, Borthwick, & Eyman, 1985). Other people with mental retardation can be served by an agency that is not part of the data base being used. Individuals with a dual diagnosis of mental illness and mental retardation, for example, can be served by mental health or mental retardation systems, or they can "slip between the cracks" and not be served at all (Borthwick-Duffy, in press; Borthwick-Duffy & Eyman, 1990). The ideal sampling procedure, which may be virtually impossible to implement in practice, would be one that utilizes data from all potential service providing agencies in order to locate all people being served.

2. Service system eligibility criteria might not conform to professionally accepted definitions. States serve some individuals whose behavioral and physical needs are best met by an agency for people who are developmentally disabled but whose disabilities appeared first after the age of 18 (the definition of mental retardation requires onset before age 18). Accident victims, for example, represent a growing number of people who have brain injury. In California, 3% of the people in the Department of Developmental Services data base are reported to be accident victims. Near-drowning cases, 50% of which occur before the age of 10, meet the mental retardation definitional criteria. However, people whose disabilities were caused by vehicular or other accidents after the age of 18 may also be served by such an agency because the types of services provided by the agency are appropriate to their needs. These adult accident victims, then, would be considered functionally retarded but would not meet the definitional criteria that specifies onset before the age of 18 years, which is a rough indicator of adulthood (AAMR, 1992).

3. *Individuals enter and exit service systems according to eligibility, needs for services available, and other factors that might be age-related.* The President's Committee on Mental Retardation used the phrase "Six-Hour Retarded Child" to refer to students who were identified by schools as having mental retardation, but whose adaptive skills allowed them to function as nonhandicapped individuals outside the academic and social demands of the classroom. It follows, then, that many of these and other individuals who are identified as having mild retardation during their years in school do not receive any kind of service during post-school years and do not appear in service system data bases. Richardson, Koller, and Katz (1988) reported that 71% of the people in their longitudinal sample with IQs above 50 did not receive services after leaving school, whereas none of those with IQs below 50 disappeared from the service system. Individuals younger than 3 years of age represent another group whose membership in a data base is tenuous. Whereas severe, profound, and even moderate retardation are usually identified reliably in the first year of life, people with less severe forms of retardation are better described as "at risk" until the developmental disability is clearly evident. Finally, initial requests for service have been

shown to be age-related and dependent on the types of service needed and available at different points in the life span (Meyers et al., 1985).

4. *Administrative classifications in schools yield a different participant pool than other selection methods.* Although the focus of this volume is on individuals in the latter stages of the life span, issues related to entry into and exit from service systems at all ages, including educational systems, are relevant to life-span studies. If data from studies of school-based samples (e.g., ages 3–21 years) are viewed in a life-span context, the factors that influence identification in schools may impact the interpretations given to developmental trends. Richardson, Katz, and Koller (1986) referred to sampling based on educational placement as administrative classification and concluded that this epidemiological approach would identify different people, and could therefore produce different findings, than if participants were selected on the basis of intelligence quotients or other characteristics without regard to placement. In their review studies, Richardson et al., for example, found that in samples identified by psychometric methods there were no gender differences, whereas samples defined by "educational retardation" showed greater frequencies among boys than girls. In the United States, educational classifications are also subject to federal, state, and local guidelines and are frequently based on programmatic needs (MacMillan, 1989b). Forness (1985), Polloway and Smith (1983), and MacMillan (e.g., MacMillan, 1989a, 1989b; MacMillan, Meyers, & Morrison, 1980) have written extensively on the arbitrariness of educational classifications and on the effects of different operational definitions of mental retardation, learning disabilities, and behavior disorders, on estimates of the prevalence in each category. MacMillan (1989a, 1989b), for example, referred to the steady decline in the prevalence of mild retardation as "disappearing EMRs" and attributed this decline, in part, to methods of classification. These classification issues have implications for the study of age-related trends if an educationally-defined population or sample is used.

Moreover, because a large proportion of persons who are identified as having mild retardation during their school-age years do not "transfer" to other service systems upon exit from school, the question of whether it is meaningful to include these persons in life-span studies is crucial, but has not yet been resolved.

Despite these shortcomings or caveats, samples derived from service system data bases constitute subgroups of persons from specifiable populations, i.e., persons receiving services from a given agency. This is a strength of this type of sampling in several ways, including the definition of the population to which results should be generalized. That is, results based on samples from service system data bases may not generalize to the population of "all persons with mental retardation," as many persons in this latter population never receive services of any kind. But, samples from service system data bases are samples from a subpopulation of "all persons with mental retardation," a subsample that is likely to be, on average, more impaired and therefore more in need of services. Moreover, the samples of persons obtained from this subpopulation can be compared to the entire subpopulation in the data base to determine whether the sample is representative of the subpopulation of persons. This testability is yet another strength of the use of service system data bases for obtaining representative samples from specifiable populations.

Selecting Measures for Life-Span Studies

When selecting measures for life-span studies, special care must be exercised to ensure that the measures are appropriate for all of the differently aged participants in the study. A consideration of the appropriateness of measures should focus on the structure of the measures, the invariance of the structure across age levels, and the comparability of the measurement scales across age levels.

The structure of behavioral domains. Investigating the structure of the measures within any domain is a central topic of inquiry.

Clearly, one must first identify the behavioral constructs of interest before life-span development of these constructs is charted. The first task here is to circumscribe the set of behaviors that fall within the domain. For example, consider the domain of adaptive behavior. The authoritative review by Meyers, Nihira, and Zetlin (1979) of the measurement of adaptive behavior was a major contribution, as Meyers et al. provided a catalog of the types of behavior assessed by extant measures. They concluded that seven subdomains of adaptive skills and competence could be distinguished—Self-Help Skills, Physical Development, Communication Skills, Cognitive Functioning, Domestic and Occupational Activities, Self-Direction and Responsibility, and Socialization. The characterization of maladaptive behaviors was less systematic, but several investigators argued that a division is useful into Social (or Extrapunitive) Maladaption and Personal (or Intrapunitive) Maladaption (Lambert & Nicholl, 1976; Nihira, 1976; Widaman, Gibbs, & Geary, 1987).

Once these forms of behavior are listed, providing a delineation of the domain of adaptive behavior, research may be undertaken to determine whether there is empirical support for the theoretically derived subdomains of adaptive behavior. The typical analytic tool used in such investigations is factor analysis. Over the years, many factor analyses of measures of adaptive behavior scales have been reported, with rather mixed results. Certain of these studies have been limited by a rather narrow coverage of the domain of adaptive behavior; others have been limited by the use of restricted samples. For these as well as other reasons (see Widaman et al., 1987), straightforward replication of factors across studies and instruments has, not surprisingly, been the exception, rather than the rule.

More recently, greater attention has been paid to the need to analyze more complete collections of adaptive behaviors gathered on larger and more representative samples of persons. However, even after following these reasonable guidelines, some notable differences across studies have arisen. For example, Widaman et al. (1987) investigated the structure of adaptive behaviors across 14 samples of children, adolescents, and adults with mild, moderate, or severe mental retardation. Rather than assuming similar factorial structures across the life span, Widaman et al. studied this issue empirically. In each sample, six factors emerged, reflecting four dimensions of adaptive skills and competence—Motor Competence, Independent Living Skills, Cognitive Competence, and Social Competence —and two dimensions of maladaptive behavior—Social Maladaption and Personal Maladaption. The factorial structure replicated very clearly across the samples regardless of age category. Similar results were found in a follow-up study (Widaman, Geary, & Gibbs, 1993) based on six samples of children, adolescents, and adults with profound mental retardation.

However, replication across samples of a differentiated factorial pattern for adaptive behavior has not been reported in all recent studies. For example, Bruininks, McGrew, and Maruyama (1988) analyzed responses to the Scales of Independent Behavior across seven samples of children, adolescents, and adults, including persons with and without mental retardation. Rather than finding a highly differentiated, replicable structure, Bruininks et al. reported inconsistent results across samples, usually finding a single, general factor, but at times obtaining a two- or three-factor structure for the behaviors. Further research on life-span development of adaptive behaviors could provide useful information, such as determining whether different life-span trends are obtained for different forms of adaptive behavior; such information would have implications for choice between a model with a differentiated structure of adaptive behavior and one propounding a single, general dimension of adaptive competence (cf. Bruininks et al., 1988; Widaman et al., 1991).

Measurement invariance across the life span. The applicability of measures across the life span is an important prerequisite for measures used in such studies. Some measures exhibit substantial variance in samples of young persons but less variance as age increases due to ceiling effects in the score distributions. Other, more difficult measures show little variance at younger ages due to floor effects, but variance on the measures increases with increases in the behavioral competencies that accompany increasing age.

The issue of measurement invariance concerns the comparability of the measurement scales at different points in the life span. Recently, Reise, Widaman, and Pugh (in press) compared and contrasted two different approaches to verifying measurement invariance, confirmatory factor analysis (Jöreskog & Sörbom, 1989) and item response theory (Lord, 1980). The technical literature on both confirmatory factor analysis and item response theory can be challenging to the reader who is not highly trained in quantitative matters, but, at base, the techniques have been developed to ensure that measurement scales provide comparable units across age groups, gender groups, etc. That is, these statistical techniques allow one to verify that "one inch" is "one inch" at different points along a continuum. Introducing the use of advanced measurement techniques, such as confirmatory factor analysis and item response theory, into research in mental retardation will allow stronger conclusions to be drawn about the form of age-related curves for the development and aging of adaptive behaviors.

Analyzing Data from Life-Span Studies

Nature of Behavioral Changes Studied

Developmental changes of various kinds may be the object of study in any life-span investigation. In a preceding section, the several ways of construing the question of developmental change were recounted. To provide a context for discussing statistical methods for life-span studies, we briefly recap the types of behavioral changes that can be investigated.

Changes in mean level. One of the more common questions arising in the study of developmental changes is that regarding the presence of changes in mean level of performance and the relation of such changes to chronological age.

Stability of individual differences. Another question of importance is the stability of individual differences about the mean developmental trend. The mean developmental trend tells a story about the development of the "person in general," the average person. If individual differences about this developmental trend are quite stable, then similar age-related trends will hold for each individual, although there will be deviations upward or downward from the mean developmental trend. On the other hand, if individuals exhibit little stability across age, then the mean developmental trend may be a very inaccurate indication of the manner in which any individual develops across the life span.

Statistical Methodology

One of the burgeoning areas of work on statistical methodology is work on the measurement and representation of change. The present section is to introduce, rather than provide an in-depth consideration or presentation, recently proposed procedures. We will discuss several issues in statistical methods for change and then review the types of solutions that have been developed to deal with these issues. That is, our goal is to provide some pointers into relevant literature on recent methodological work. We hope that interested readers follow our leads by investigating these new approaches in more detail and then using these new techniques in their own research on mental retardation.

Issues in analyzing data representing developmental change. At least two general issues can be distinguished that have contributed to statistical methods for the study of change. The first of these issues is the notion of *analyzing versus modeling data.* Data analysis is the term often applied to the statistical analysis of data, as if the analysis of data were a monotonous, cut-and-dried issue. The typical research project attempts to frame a substantively interesting problem, leading to the collection of relevant data. Then, a data analyst is sought who is expected to apply some generally applicable statistical techniques to the data in order to determine the patterns of statistical significance obtained. This was a common scenario over the course of the present century, during which data analysis consisted largely of the testing of null hypotheses, which are ubiquitous, despite their lack of definitive substantive utility (Meehl, 1967, 1978).

In contrast to data analysis, the notion of the modeling of data has grown over the past 10 to 15 years. Rather than testing null hypotheses, the modeling of data begins with the predictions made by a substantive model, leading to the stating of some type of nonnull hypothesis (examples will be noted briefly below). The task of the quantitative methodologist (or data analyst) is to help the substantive researcher to provide as explicit as possible a statement of the nonnull hypotheses guiding the research and then to recommend or perform appropriate tests of these hypotheses. Modeling approaches are in a state of infancy relative to null hypothesis testing, but the greater utility for theory testing that accompanies modeling as opposed to null hypothesis testing will lead to much increased use of modeling methods in the future.

A second issue in the study of developmental change is that of *constructing age-related curves.* In early contributions, age-related, life-span curves were constructed in an "after the fact" manner, piecing together partially overlapping sections of curves (e.g., Schaie & Strother, 1968). During the past 10 years, a large number of contributions have been made to modeling age-related curves (e.g., Meredith & Tisak, 1984; Meredith & Tisak, 1990). The new wave of methods for such problems allows the simultaneous estimation of the life-span growth curves in the same context as the estimation of other parameters reflecting other effects, such as gender or cohort effects. Thus, rather than piecing trends together in a post hoc fashion, the newer methods enable the estimation of the growth curve within a comprehensive model for life-span development of the behavior in question. With these two general issues outlined, we turn to specific statistical approaches that have been used in life-span developmental research.

Analysis of variance approaches. One clear question in developmental research is the relation between age and mean performance on a behavioral variable of interest. In developmental research, analysis of variance (or ANOVA) techniques have frequently been proposed to study age-related differences in performance. Here, age is a factor in an ANOVA design, and the standard main effect of age in such a design provides a test of the statistical significance of change in mean performance with age.

In initial studies using semilongitudinal designs, one or another form of ANOVA design was used to estimate and test the effects of age, cohort, and time of measurement (e.g., Nesselroade & Baltes, 1974; Schaie & Strother, 1968). Indeed, several of the early contributions to the methodological literature on this topic (e.g., Schaie, 1977) consisted of descriptions of the different ANOVA designs that could be formulated, the main and interaction effects specified in each design, and the statistical tests associated with these effects. The ANOVA approach to analyses is a useful one, yet at least two problems are associated with its use. First, the statistical model underlying ANOVA is a "group difference" model, with little obvious way to incorporate individual differences into the typical analysis. As a result, the ANOVA model reinforces theory with regard to aging that is monolithic or nomothetic, implying that aging generally follows the mean trend; demonstrating the differential development by individuals is difficult within the context of the ANOVA model. Second, the statistical test of the main effect of age can be problematic. In general, increasing the number of age groups in an aging design (e.g., from two groups [young versus old] to three or more groups) is preferred, as this allows initial estimation of the form of the developmental trend, such as whether the trend departs from linearity. But, the main effect of age in an ANOVA design is progressively more negatively biased, leading to fewer failures to reject

the null hypothesis as more age groups are included in the design (e.g., Hale, 1977). There are ways to circumvent these problems, but researchers must first be aware that the problems exist.

Correlation/regression approaches. Another approach to the testing of hypotheses concerning age-related trends is the use of correlational or regression techniques. The linear models underlying both ANOVA and correlation/regression are basically alternate versions of the same model, a fact widely known for at least 25 years (Cohen, 1968; Darlington, 1968). However, the regression approach to specifying models and testing effects leads more directly to representing and testing individual difference models than does the ANOVA approach, despite the similarity of the underlying statistical models.

One example of the use of regression modeling to ask questions regarding age effects during middle adulthood and aging is that of Horn (1989). According to theory, the fluid (Gf) and crystallized (Gc) forms of intelligence should evince different aging trends, with a relatively sharp drop in Gf throughout the middle adult years and beyond, but a maintenance of Gc until old age (Horn, 1989). In addition to the differential aging trends, changes in certain basic processes (e.g., mental speed) have been implicated as responsible for the aging decline in tests of Gf. To test the different proposed mediators of aging decline in Gf, Horn included each purported mediator, singly and in combination with others, in a regression equation predicting Gf scores from age. If the set of proposed mediators explained completely (i.e., truly mediated) aging declines in Gf, then the regression weight for predicting Gf from age should be reduced to zero. Such a result never occurred, but a substantial decrease in the regression weight for age accompanied the introduction into the equation of measures of short-term acquisition and retrieval and encoding organization. These findings are consistent with the hypothesis that much of the aging decline in measures of Gf is accounted for by processes underlying the immediate encoding and retention of information. The Horn (1989) strategy would be a good model for researchers in mental retardation who wish to investigate the processes underlying life-span development in their areas of research interest.

Structural modeling approaches. With the advent of structural equation modeling during the past 15 years or so, the incorporation of information regarding both the mean trend and individual differences about the mean trend became possible. As a result, static, exploratory ANOVA designs are being used less frequently in favor of regression or structural equation models that provide some a priori structure to the analysis. These newer developments (see, e.g., McArdle, 1988; McArdle & Epstein, 1987) provide generalizable procedures for testing out the hypothesized variables accounting for age, cohort, or time of measurement effects. Initial attempts in the use of these models for analyzing data from persons with mental retardation have been undertaken (e.g., Little & Widaman, 1991) and should be followed up in the future.

A second, recent development is the use of hierarchical linear model techniques (Bryk & Raudenbush, 1992). Perhaps the most direct application of hierarchical linear modeling to developmental research is the analysis of growth curves from longitudinal studies. Using this approach, a linear model is specified that should account for developmental change for each individual; such a model might include an intercept, or initial level, parameter and a single growth rate parameter for a domain in which growth should be largely linear. Then, the researcher may attempt to explain variability in the intercept or growth rate parameters in terms of other explanatory variables. The applications of these ideas in life-span research on persons with mental retardation should be clear. Initial level may be related to a person's level of mental retardation, and several studies have provided evidence that growth rate varies as a function of level of mental retardation (Eyman & Widaman, 1987; Little & Widaman, 1991; Widaman et al., 1991). Be-cause hierarchical linear modeling has been developed so recently, no study of persons with mental retardation of which we are aware has yet used the method. But, given the good fit with past research and theory on mental retardation, hierarchical linear modeling will likely be used widely in our field in the future.

Special Problems Accompanying Life-Span Studies

Measurement problems. As we mentioned above, measurement problems are of great importance in life-span studies. Although several measurement problems may be distinguished, perhaps the most important issue is the comparability of measurement scales at different points in the age continuum. Testing alternative hypotheses concerning the form of the developmental function (e.g., whether it is linear or a particular nonlinear form) is possible only if measurement scales are invariant across age levels. If measurement invariance does not hold, then permissible rescalings may change the developmental function in important ways. Interested readers are referred to Reise et al. (in press) for a detailed discussion of these issues and the appropriate statistical techniques.

Problems of attrition. Attrition involves the loss of participants during the span of a longitudinal study. If attrition is random, no problems arise when generalizing results of a longitudinal study. However, if attrition is nonrandom, then generalizations must be made more carefully, considering the potential biases arising from the nonrandom processes leading to the final study sample. For the past 25 years, researchers have typically performed core analyses only on persons who remained in a longitudinal study throughout its span, and then performed supplementary analyses to determine whether attrition was random. Usually, attrition is found to be nonrandom (e.g., Nesselroade & Baltes, 1974). This leads to limited generalizations, especially those concerning the form of the developmental function, which may have been different if all participants had remained in the study. Given nonrandom attrition (e.g., mortality) among persons with mental retardation, this is of particular importance to life-span studies of persons with mental retardation.

Recently, McArdle and Hamagami (1992) proposed that data on all participants be used in a single analysis. By proper specification of models, inclusion of all participants, even those who dropped out of the study at some time prior to its completion, can lead to unbiased estimates of many parameters from longitudinal data, including the form of the developmental function. At present, these techniques have been investigated in only a small number of situations, and further research must be done to determine how well the methods work in general. Thus, further research must be done to determine whether these methods lead to less biased results than traditional ways of dealing with attrition in typical situations faced in longitudinal research. At the least, these methods offer ways of estimating and testing more viable and generalizable models of life-span development. These methods are rather difficult to use at the present time, but it is likely that these techniques will be more widely used in the future as they become easier to use.

Problems of missing data. At times, participants are lost to a longitudinal study; at other times, a participant may remain in a study, but some data from the participant are lost due to nonresponse, recording errors, etc. Many computer packages either simply delete participants with any missing data from all analyses or delete only those participants with some missing data for a particular analysis. Either way, the deletion of participants with missing data leads to interpretive problems due to the shifting nature of the samples of participants in analyses.

Over the past 10 years, several new approaches to dealing with this problem have been developed. Perhaps the most important is work by Rubin (1987) on multiple imputation of missing values. Imputation involves estimation of missing values based on reasonable models for how the data arise; imputation methods are simplest and most accurate if data are missing at random. However, data missing within life-span and longitudinal studies are likely to be missing for nonrandom reasons, leading to special problems. In-depth consideration of these issues is beyond the scope of the present chapter (see Rubin, 1987). But, work is continuing apace on imputation methods for missing data that will improve the ways with which missing data problems are handled in life-span studies.

Interpreting and Evaluating Outcomes of Life-Span Studies

The results of life-span studies are of considerable import for research and theory in mental retardation, but have distinct, important implications for practice as well. The practical difficulties associated with life-span studies coupled with the relative dearth of such studies in the field of mental retardation should not deter investigators from conducting life-span research. Instead, these conditions should serve as signals that much important research remains to be done and that the special problems associated with this kind of study are merely a series of hurdles that must be surmounted in this important endeavor.

Implications for Research and Theory

Life-span developmental research, especially with a longitudinal component, has a wide array of implications for research and theory in mental retardation. Due to space limitations, we discuss here only two of the most important— improving our models of development and understanding the effects of cohort and historical change—while admitting that life-span research should enrich our understanding of human development in many other ways as well.

Developing more inclusive and adequate models. The first and most obvious benefit of life-span research on persons with mental retardation is the development of more inclusive and adequate models and theories for the developmental phenomena under study. The typical study on mental retardation has a fairly narrow focus, perhaps by necessity. Rather restricted hypotheses are offered; the results may speak directly to the hypotheses framed, yet the generalizations remain restricted by the scope of the models investigated.

Considering the scope of adequate life-span theories for development by persons with mental retardation can be daunting indeed. Once the life span is invoked as a frame of reference, the limitations embodied in typical research questions are brought to the fore. If an investigator is interested in the relationship between constructs X and Y, the life-span perspective requires one to ask whether the X–Y relationship changes over the life span, whether the change in the relationship interacts with other features of the person's ecology (e.g., family relationships, living situation), and so forth. The resulting challenge, despite its enormity, should lead to at least two improvements in research: (a) goading researchers to frame more careful generalizations, placing their restricted research studies within a broader theoretical context; and (b) encouraging investigators to ask larger questions, designing more adequate, life-span studies of issues important to the lives of persons with mental retardation.

Understanding the effects of cohort and historical change. In life-span research on persons without mental retardation, cohort effects are a central concern to researchers (e.g., Hogan, 1984; Schaie, 1983). Persons in different birth cohorts experience different historical events at different points in their lives than do persons in cohorts that come before or after, and this may influence development. For example, Elder (1974; Elder & Caspi, 1990) found that the American Depression of the 1930s had differential effects on children as a function of their age at the height of the Depression, with persons who were adolescents during the height of the Depression displaying more positive outcomes than did those who were children during the 1930s.

Moreover, historical trends have been documented that reflect systematic change for birth cohorts over the past 100 years or longer in mental abilities and in indices of physical stature or functioning. For example, there has been a trend over the past 100 years for children to be larger at given ages (e.g., children born in more recent cohorts tend to be taller at ages between 8 and 18 years). In addition, females are reaching menarche at earlier chronological ages today than they did 150 years ago (i.e., as much as 3 to 3.5 years earlier; Tanner, 1970). Associated historical trends, such as increased average educational attainment and improved nutrition, are frequently invoked as potential explanations of cohort differences in mental abilities and indices of physical stature or functioning, respectively. These findings underscore the difficulties as well as the importance of attempting to understand the basis for cohort effects (Hogan, 1984).

Implications for Care and Programming

In addition to implications for basic research and theory, life-span investigations of persons with mental retardation have notable implications of a more practical and applied nature. These issues include programming projections for persons with mental retardation and the effects that cohort and historical change may have on these projections.

Projecting needed programs for persons with mental retardation. A number of concerns arise when the results of life-span studies are used to project future programmatic service needs for persons with mental retardation. One issue involves who the persons will be who will be receiving services. Research on differential mortality as a function of level of mental retardation and age (see Eyman & Borthwick-Duffy, chapter 6 this volume) is a key ingredient for determining who is likely to survive to a given age and require particular forms of service. For example, research has shown that persons with profound mental retardation have a much greater risk of dying at a young age than do persons with less severe forms of mental retardation. As a result, services for persons with profound mental retardation are likely to be needed less as a given birth cohortages, given the differential survival of persons with profound retardation.

Other issues may have an impact on the planning of programs for persons with mental retardation. One issue arises in connection with life-span curves for growth, maintenance, and aging of adaptive behaviors (Eyman & Widaman, 1987; Little & Widaman, 1991; Widaman et al., 1991; Zigman et al., chapter 5 this volume). Patterns of typical mean growth and aging of adaptive behaviors can provide initial estimates of the general levels of services required by persons with mental retardation at various points in the life span. These estimates may be moderated in important ways by level of mental retardation (Little & Widaman, 1991; Widaman et al., 1991) or by etiology (e.g., differential aging of persons with Down syndrome, Zigman et al., chapter 5 this volume). Of at least equal importance are age-related changes in the variance on dimensions of adaptive behavior. In research on fluid and crystallized intelligence, fluid intelligence shows large and consistent declines during adulthood, but few changes in variability about the mean; in contrast, crystallized intelligence shows small increases through middle adulthood and some small drops during aging, but variability about mean levels increases dramatically with age (Horn, 1988). If similar findings arise with dimensions of adaptive behavior, then mean trends will have much less importance for projections for needed services on dimensions that exhibit greater variability about the mean during the aging period. On such dimensions, projections must be moderated by the wide range of capabilities of the persons with mental retardation, with services dictated more by individual differences than by nomothetic developmental expectations.

Importance of effects of cohort and historical changes. When we attempt to project the future service needs for persons with mental retardation, the likelihood of cohort and historical trends attains crucial importance. To be sure, the relative scarcity of life-span studies of persons with mental retardation leaves the precise nature of potential cohort and historical effects yet to be determined with any certainty. However, attention to the probable presence of such effects will be of increasing importance in the years to come.

Cohort effects may take any of a number of forms. Some cohort effects will arise due to differential mortality of persons with mental retardation as a function of level of retardation or other characteristics (Eyman & Borthwick-Duffy, chapter 6 this volume). The basis of other cohort effects may include legislation guaranteeing educational opportunities for all children with mental retardation, improvements in prosthetic devices, increased work opportunities, and increased emphasis on integration with nonhandicapped persons. Other cohort effects could be portrayed alternatively as changes associated with historical trends. Chief among these may be the changes in the population that may occur as a function of changes and improvements in prenatal screening and other biomedical advances (Moser, 1992). These and other cohort effects and historical trends will also contribute to projections of service patterns in the future. These cohort and historical trends underscore the need to engage in life-span studies to ensure that our projections for the future are based on our best current estimates of the evolving population of persons with mental retardation and its composition and capabilities in the future.

Summary

Researchers who study the development of persons with mental retardation must deal with the same methodological challenges as those who focus on normal development. One purpose of this chapter has been to review these issues that are related to the design, analysis, and interpretation of life-span data. In addition, a number of challenges are unique to the study of development of persons with mental retardation. We have described external factors, such as the identification of persons with mental retardation and early mortality, that affect sampling designs, and internal factors, such as severity or etiology of mental retardation, that directly influence the developmental trajectories that are produced in life-span studies. Thus, it is our view that both producers and consumers of this research must be aware of these issues that may affect the utility of life-span data and the generalizability of findings.

This chapter may be viewed in some ways as overly broad. Whereas a major focus of this volume is on issues that pertain to persons with mental retardation who are older adults, this chapter has addressed a number of issues that appear to be more relevant during childhood and early adulthood. Early in the chapter, however, the importance of conducting "life-span research," rather than piecing together the research of age-graded subdisciplines, was discussed. In our view, regardless of the research design being used (i.e., cross-sectional, semilongitudinal, longitudinal), issues of sampling, attrition, the nature of behavioral constructs, and influences on development at all ages are methodological challenges that will impact the interpretation of findings of life-span research in relation to any particular age group, including older adults. On the other hand, this chapter may also be viewed as narrow, because most illustrations of methodological challenges have been based on research on the development of adaptive behaviors of persons with mental retardation. Adaptive behavior was selected as the primary behavioral domain for examples because of (a) its central role in the definition of mental retardation, (b) the significance of these behaviors to the development of independence among persons with mental retardation, (c) a growing body of research that includes life-span developmental studies, (d) our own research in this area. Because the chapter focuses on methodology, numerous other domains of behavior might have been used as examples. There is no question that life-span development studies of persons with mental retardation should extend beyond adaptive behavior and address other issues such as health, family-related constructs, service utilization, and community involvement.

In this chapter, we have considered applications of life-span research in terms of both the developmental function and individual differences. In an effort to move beyond historical notions of change in level or form of behavior, we have encouraged the use of designs that allow the integration of information regarding changes of level or form and individual differences in change or form. Moreover, current issues regarding the statistical analysis of developmental change have been presented. The limitations of traditional approaches to the study of life-span development as well as the advantages of newer modeling approaches have been discussed with the hope that research conducted on persons with mental retardation will incorporate state-of-the-art methodology, leading to more accurate and meaningful explanations of development within the behavioral domains of interest. We trust that the present chapter will be an impetus in this direction.

References

American Association on Mental Retardation. (1992). *Mental retardation: Definition, classification, and systems of supports* (9th ed.). Washington, DC: Author.

Baltes, P. B. (1968). Longitudinal and cross-sectional sequences in the study of age and generation effects. *Human Development, 11,* 145–171.

Baltes, P. B., & Nesselroade, J. R. (1979). History and rationale of longitudinal research. In J. R. Nesselroade & P. B. Baltes (Eds.), *Longitudinal research in the study of behavior and development* (pp. 1–39). New York: Academic.

Baumeister, A. A., Kupstas, F., & Klindworth, L. M. (1990). New morbidity: Implications for prevention of children's disabilities. *Exceptionality, 1,* 1–16.

Baumrind, D. (1971). Current patterns of parental authority. *Developmental Psychology Monographs, 4* (1, Pt. 2).

Baumrind, D. (1991). The influence of parenting style on adolescent competence and substance use. *Journal of Early Adolescence, 11,* 56–95.

Bell, R. Q. (1953). Convergence: An accelerated longitudinal approach. *Child Development, 24,* 145–152.

Bell, R. Q. (1954). An experimental test of the accelerated longitudinal approach. *Child Development, 25,* 281–286.

Blacher, J., & Meyers, C. E. (1983). A review of attachment formation and disorder of handicapped children. *American Journal of Mental Deficiency, 87,* 359–371.

Borthwick–Duffy, S. A. (in press). Epidemiology and prevalence of psychopathology in persons with mental retardation. *Journal of Consulting and Clinical Psychology.*

Borthwick-Duffy, S. A., & Eyman, R. K. (1990). Who are the dually diagnosed? *American Journal on Mental Retardation, 94,* 586–595.

Borthwick-Duffy, S. A., Widaman, K. F., Little, T. D., & Eyman, R. K. (1992). *Foster family care for persons with mental retardation.* (Monograph No. 17). Washington, DC: American Association on Mental Retardation.

Bronfenbrenner, U. (1977). Toward an experimental ecology of human development. *American Psychologist, 32,* 513–531.

Bruininks, R., McGrew, K., & Maruyama, G. (1988). Structure of adaptive behavior in samples with and without mental retardation. *American Journal on Mental Retardation, 93,* 265–272.

Bryk, A. S., & Raudenbush, S. W. (1992). *Hierarchical linear models: Applications and data analysis methods.* Newbury Park, CA: Sage.

Cicchetti, D., & Ganiban, J. (1990). The organization and coherence of developmental processes in infants and children with Down syndrome. In R. M. Hodapp, J. A. Burack, & E. Zigler (Eds.), *Issues in the developmental approach to mental retardation* (pp. 169–225). New York: Cambridge University Press.

Cohen, H. J. (1992). HIV infection and mental retardation. In L. Rowitz (Ed.), *Mental retardation in the year 2000* (pp. 131–139). New York: Springer.

Cohen, J. (1968). Multiple regression as a general data-analytic system. *Psychological Bulletin, 70,* 426–443.

Dalton, A. J., & Wisniewski, H. M. (1990). Down's syndrome and the dementia of Alzheimer disease. *International Review of Psychiatry, 2,* 43–52.

Damon, A. (1965). Discrepancies between findings of longitudinal and cross-sectional studies in adult life: Physique and physiology. *Human Development, 8,* 16–22.

Darlington, R. B. (1968). Multiple regression in psychological research and practice. *Psychological Bulletin, 69,* 161–182.

Elder, G. H., Jr. (1974). *Children of the Great Depression: Social change in life experience.* Chicago: University of Chicago Press.

Elder, G. H., & Caspi, A. (1990). Studying lives in a changing society: Sociological and personological explorations. In R. A. Zucker, A. I. Rabin, & S. J. Frank (Eds.), *Personality structure in the life course: Essays on personology in the Murray Tradition* (pp. 276–322). New York: Springer.

Eyman, R. K., & Arndt, S. (1982). Life-span development of institutionalized and community-based mentally retarded residents. *American Journal of Mental Deficiency, 86,* 342–350.

Eyman, R. K., & Borthwick-Duffy, S. A. (1994). Trends in mortality rates and predictors of mortality. In M. M. Seltzer, M. W. Krauss, & M. P. Janicki (Eds.), *Life course perspectives on adulthood and old age* (pp. 93-105). Washington, DC: American Association on Mental Retardation.

Eyman, R. K., Grossman, H. J., Chaney, R. H., & Call, T. L. (1990). The life expectancy of profoundly handicapped people with mental retardation. *New England Journal of Medicine, 323,* 584–589.

Eyman, R. K., Grossman, H. J., Tarjan, G., & Miller, C. R. (1987). *Life expectancy and mental retardation* (Monograph No. 7). Washington, DC: American Association on Mental Deficiency.

Eyman, R. K., & Widaman, K. F. (1987). Life-span development of institutionalized and community-based mentally retarded persons, revisited. *American Journal of Mental Deficiency, 91,* 559–569.

Forness, S. R. (1985). Effects of public policy at the state level: California's impact on MR,

LD, and ED categories. *Remedial and Special Education, 6*(3), 36–43.

Galton, F. (1869). *Hereditary genius: An inquiry into its laws and consequences.* New York: Appleton.

Goulet, L. R., & Baltes, P. B. (Eds.). (1970). *Life-span developmental psychology: Research and theory.* New York: Academic.

Grossman, H. J. (Ed.). (1983). *Classification in mental retardation.* Washington, DC: American Association on Mental Deficiency.

Hale, G. A. (1977). On use of ANOVA in developmental research. *Child Development, 48,* 1101–1106.

Hodapp, R. M., Leckman, J. F., Dykens, E. M., Sparrow, S. S., Zelinsky, D. G., & Ort, S. I. (1992). K-ABC profiles in children with Fragile X syndrome, Down syndrome, and nonspecific mental retardation. *American Journal on Mental Retardation, 97,* 39–46.

Hogan, D. P. (1984). Cohort comparisons in the timing of life events. *Developmental Review, 4,* 289–310.

Horn, J. L. (1988). Thinking about human abilities. In J. R. Nesselroade & R. B. Cattell (Eds.), *Handbook of multivariate experimental psychology* (2nd ed., pp. 645–685). New York: Plenum.

Horn, J. L. (1989). Models of intelligence. In R. L. Linn (Ed.), *Intelligence: Measurement, theory, and public policy* (pp. 29–73). Urbana: University of Illinois Press.

Jones, J. E., & Conrad, J. S. (1933). The growth and decline of intelligence. *Genetic Psychology Monographs, 13,* 223–298.

Jöreskog, K. G., & Sörbom, D. (1989). *LISREL 7: A guide to the program and applications* (2nd ed.). Chicago: SPSS.

Kuhlen, R. G. (1963). Age and intelligence: The significance of cultural change in longitudinal vs. cross-sectional findings. *Vita Humana, 6,* 113–124.

Lambert, N. M., & Nicholl, R. C. (1976). Dimensions of adaptive behavior of retarded and nonretarded public-school children. *American Journal of Mental Deficiency, 81,* 135–146.

Little, T. D., & Widaman, K. F. (1991). *Semi-longitudinal modeling of life-span trends for six adaptive behavior factors in 18 cohorts of persons with mild, moderate, severe, and profound levels of mental retardation* (Report No. LS001). Riverside: University of California, Department of Psychology.

Lord, F. M. (1980). *Applications of item response theory to practical testing problems.* Hillsdale, NJ: Erlbaum.

MacMillan, D. L. (1989a). Equality, excellence, and the EMR populations: 1970–1989. *Psychology in mental retardation and developmental disabilities.* American Psychological Association, Division 33 Newsletter, Vol. 15, No. 2.

MacMillan, D. L. (1989b). Mild mental retardation: Emerging issues. In G. A. Robinson, J. R. Patton, E. A. Polloway, & L. R. Sargent (Eds.), *Best practices in mild mental disabilities* (pp. 3–20). Reston, VA: Council for Exceptional Children.

MacMillan, D. L., Meyers, C. E., & Morrison, G. M. (1980). System-identification of mildly mentally retarded children: Implications for interpreting and conducting research. *American Journal of Mental Deficiency, 85,* 108–115.

McArdle, J. J. (1988). Dynamic but structural equation modeling of repeated measures data. In J. R. Nesselroade & R. B. Cattell (Eds.), *Handbook of multivariate experimental psychology* (2nd ed., pp. 561–614). New York: Plenum.

McArdle, J. J., & Epstein, D. (1987). Latent growth curves within developmental structural equation models. *Child Development, 58,* 110–133.

McArdle, J. J., & Hamagami, F. (1992). Modeling incomplete longitudinal and cross-sectional data using latent growth structural models. *Experimental Aging Research, 18,* 145–166.

McCall, R. B. (1981). Nature-nurture and the two realms of development: A proposed integration with respect to mental development. *Child Development, 52,* 1–12.

Meehl, P. E. (1967). Theory-testing in psychology and physics: A methodological paradox. *Philosophy of Science, 34,* 103–115.

Meehl, P. E. (1978). Theoretical risks and tabular asterisks: Sir Karl, Sir Ronald, and the slow progress of soft psychology. *Journal of Consulting and Clinical Psychology, 46,* 806–834.

Meredith, W., & Tisak, J. (1984, June). *Tuckerizing curves.* Paper presented at the Annual Meeting of the Psychometric Society, Santa Barbara, CA.

Meredith, W., & Tisak, J. (1990). Latent curve analysis. *Psychometrika, 55,* 107–122.

Meyers, C. E., Borthwick, S. A., & Eyman, R. K. (1985). Place of residence by age, ethnicity, and level of mental retardation of the mentally retarded/developmentally disabled population of California. *American Journal of Mental Deficiency, 90,* 266–270.

Meyers, C. E., Nihira, K., & Zetlin, A. (1979). The measurement of adaptive behavior. In N. R. Ellis (Ed.), *Handbook of mental deficiency: Psychological theory and research* (2nd ed., pp. 431–481). Hillsdale, NJ: Erlbaum.

Moser, H. (1992). Prevention of mental retardation (Genetics). In L. Rowitz (Ed.), *Mental retardation in the year 2000* (pp. 140–148). New York: Springer.

Nesselroade, J. R., & Baltes, P. B. (1974). Adolescent personality development and historical change: 1970–1972. *Monographs of the Society for Research in Child Development, 39* (1, Serial No. 154).

Nihira, K. (1976). Dimensions of adaptive behavior in institutionalized mentally retarded children and adults: Developmental perspective. *American Journal of Mental Deficiency, 81,* 215–226.

Piaget, J. (1970). Piaget's theory. In P. H. Mussen (Ed.), *Carmichael's manual of child psychology* (pp. 703–732). New York: Wiley.

Polloway, E. A., & Smith, J. D. (1983). Changes in mild mental retardation: Population, programs, and perspectives. *Exceptional Children, 50,* 149–159.

Reise, S. P., Widaman, K. F., & Pugh, R. H. (in press). Confirmatory factor analysis and item response theory: Two approaches for exploring measurement invariance. *Psychological Bulletin.*

Richardson, S. A., Katz, M., & Koller, H. (1986). Sex differences in number of children administratively classified as mildly mentally retarded: An epidemiological review. *American Journal of Mental Deficiency, 91,* 250–256.

Richardson, S. A., Koller, H., & Katz, M. (1985). Relationship of upbringing to later behavior disturbance of mildly mentally retarded young people. *American Journal of Mental Deficiency, 90,* 1–8.

Richardson, S. A., Koller, H., & Katz, M. (1988). Job histories in open employment of a population of young adults with mental retardation: I. *American Journal on Mental Retardation, 92,* 483–491.

Rubin, D. B. (1987). *Multiple imputation for nonresponse in surveys.* New York: Wiley.

Schaie, K. W. (1965). A general model for the study of developmental problems. *Psychological Bulletin, 64,* 92–107.

Schaie, K. W. (1977). Quasi-experimental research designs in the psychology of aging. In J. E. Birren & K. W. Schaie (Eds.), *Handbook of the psychology of aging* (pp. 39–58). New York: Van Nostrand Reinhold.

Schaie, K. W. (Ed.). (1983). *Longitudinal studies of adult psychological development.* New York: Guilford.

Schaie, K. W., & Strother, C. R. (1968). The cross-sequential study of age changes in cognitive behavior. *Psychological Bulletin, 70,* 671–680.

Silverstein, A. B., Herbs, D., Miller, T. J., Nasuta, R., & Williams, D. L. (1988). Effects of age on the adaptive behavior of institutionalized and noninstitutionalized individuals with Down syndrome. *American Journal on Mental Retardation, 92,* 455–460.

Silverstein, A. B., Herbs, D., Nasuta, R., & White, J. F. (1986). Effects of age on the adaptive behavior of institutionalized individuals with Down's syndrome. *American Journal of Mental Deficiency, 90*, 659–662.

Smith, B., & Phillips, C. J. (1992). Attainments of severely mentally retarded adolescents by etiology. *Journal of Child Psychology and Psychiatry and Allied Disciplines, 33*, 1039–1058.

Tanner, J. M. (1970). Physical growth. In P. H. Mussen (Ed.), *Carmichael's manual of child psychology* (pp. 77–156). New York: Wiley.

Thase, M. E. (1982). Longevity and mortality in Down's syndrome. *Journal of Mental Deficiency Research, 26*, 177–192.

Widaman, K. F. (1991). Qualitative transitions amid quantitative development: A challenge for measuring and representing change. In L. M. Collins & J. L. Horn (Eds.), *Best methods for the analysis of change: Recent advances, unanswered questions, future directions* (pp. 204–217). Washington, DC: American Psychological Association.

Widaman, K. F. (1992, April). *Toward a unifying theory of bi-directional influences between parents and their children with mental retardation.* Paper presented at the meeting of the Gatlinburg Conference on Research and Theory in Mental Retardation and Developmental Disabilities, Gatlinburg, TN.

Widaman, K. F., & Borthwick-Duffy, S. A. (1990, April). *Parental influences on the development of adaptive behaviors.* Paper presented at the meeting of the Gatlinburg Conference on Research and Theory in Mental Retardation and Developmental Disabilities, Gatlinburg, TN.

Widaman, K. F., Borthwick-Duffy, S. A., & Little, T. D. (1991). The structure and development of adaptive behaviors. In N. W. Bray (Ed.), *International review of research in mental retardation* (Vol. 17, pp. 1–54). New York: Academic.

Widaman, K. F., Geary, D. C., & Gibbs, K. W. (1993). *Structure of adaptive behavior: II. Replication across six samples of profoundly mentally retarded people.* Manuscript submitted for publication.

Widaman, K. F., Gibbs, K. W., & Geary, D. C. (1987). Structure of adaptive behavior: I. Replication across fourteen samples of nonprofoundly mentally retarded people. *American Journal of Mental Deficiency, 91*, 348–360.

Wohlwill, J. F. (1973). *The study of behavioral development.* New York: Academic Press.

Zigler, E. (1969). Developmental versus difference theories of mental retardation and the problem of motivation. *American Journal of Mental Deficiency, 73*, 536–556.

Zigler, E., & Hodapp, R. M. (1986). *Understanding mental retardation.* Cambridge: Cambridge University Press.

Zigman, W. B., Seltzer, G. B., & Silverman, W. P. (1994). Behavioral and mental health changes associated with aging in adults with mental retardation. In M. M. Seltzer, M. W. Krauss, & M. P. Janicki (Eds.), *Life course perspectives on adulthood and old age* (pp. 67-91). Washington, DC: American Association on Mental Retardation.

The present work was supported in part by Grants HD-21056 and HD-22953 from the National Institute of Child Health and Human Development, and by Grants G008530208 and H023C80072 to Donald L. MacMillan from the U.S. Office of Education. We would like to thank Mike Begab and the editors, Marsha Seltzer, Marty Krauss, and Matt Janicki, for their valuable comments on a previous draft of this chapter, and Karen Fleck for her help in producing the manuscript.

Chapter 11

Taking Stock: Expected Gains From A Life-Span Perspective on Mental Retardation

Marty Wyngaarden Krauss, Brandeis University
Marsha Mailick Seltzer, University of Wisconsin–Madison

Research on the effects of mental retardation on individuals, their families, and the service systems charged with their support increasingly bears the imprint of the life-span perspective. Such a perspective invites a focus on individual development over time and recognizes that mental retardation extends throughout an affected person's lifetime and that of his or her family. It also supports inquiry into the antecedents and consequences of developmental phenomena, thereby casting a wider lens on the meaning and sources of different developmental trajectories. We view the increased emphasis on the life span of individuals with mental retardation as a healthy and necessary perspective, for it challenges researchers, service providers, and policymakers to be less impressed with the current "status" of an individual with mental retardation and more concerned about the implications of having mental retardation for future development.

The chapters in this volume are focused primarily on the adult and elder years of persons with mental retardation. This focus is appropriate and necessary, as these stages of the life course have been less well researched and less frequently discussed than earlier stages and therefore constitute essentially uncharted territory ripe for intense, varied, and multidisciplinary investigation. Nevertheless, there is recognition throughout the volume that adult development is firmly rooted in childhood and adolescence, with continuity as well as change characteristic of the transition from one stage to the next.

Some of the research summarized in this volume is descriptive, portraying the "average" or "typical" characteristics of persons with retardation during their adult years, their families, and the services they receive. Examples include the Janicki and the Smith, Fullmer, and Tobin chapters. These studies are critically important, for they establish the basic boundaries of scientific interest and provide the landscape in which other studies are set. The volume also contains comparative research, drawing important distinctions between one stage of the life course and another with respect to specific issues. Examples include the Zigman, G. Seltzer, and Silverman and the G. Seltzer and Luchterhand chapters. These studies are instructive in highlighting differences that warrant longitudinal investigation. Yet other chapters focus on specific events that typically occur during the adult and elder years of persons with mental retardation, such as the need to establish plans for their long term care (see Freedman & Freedman), the conditions under which transitions from one setting to another can proceed more smoothly (see Heller & Factor), and the challenge of establishing relationships between formal service providers and informal caregivers who have resisted outside assistance (see Smith, Fullmer, & Tobin).

The purpose of this final chapter is to review what has been learned about the adult and elder years of persons with mental retardation, their families, and the service systems that sustain them. Rather than present new data or arguments, the chapter draws from the results of the chapters in this volume. Our goal is to integrate the various issues and findings presented in these instructive chapters and to articulate the range of research, service, and policy challenges that await us in the 21st century.

Five important themes can be extracted from the chapters in this volume. These themes illustrate the range of new basic and applied knowledge that has been generated over the last decade regarding the adult and elder years of persons with mental retardation and their families. They include increased life expectancy, patterns of age-related changes, factors affecting quality of life, an awareness of later-life family impacts, and the value of an extended lens in basic and applied research.

Changes in Life Expectancy

There is, arguably, no more succinct indicator of the effects of improved health, educational, and social services for persons with mental retardation than the dramatic increase in life expectancy witnessed by the majority of this population during this century. For persons with mild mental retardation, life expectancy now mirrors that of the general population. Although the life expectancy of persons with Down syndrome is still shorter than average, it has increased by more than 30 years, as reported by Eyman and Borthwick-Duffy.

These impressive gains do not extend, however, to all persons with mental retardation. The research reported by Eyman and Borthwick-Duffy illustrated the importance of distinguishing among subgroups of the population with mental retardation for whom significant risk factors compromise life expectancy. Specifically, nonambulatory persons with profound retardation are now known to be at high risk for early death from respiratory infections. Persons who do not acquire the basic skills of ambulation, toilet training, and feeding bear a notably higher risk of mortality. Eyman and Borthwick-Duffy also reported that persons living in institutional settings have a shorter life expectancy than those living in community residences or with their families. This finding is complicated by the selection factors that contribute to institutionalization, particularly the influence of chronic medical conditions and compromised self-help skills. The same factors associated with institutionalization are also associated with shorter life expectancies.

These findings are critical to life-span studies, which must first have some estimate of how long the expected length of life is for different groups of persons with mental retardation. Understanding the specific risk factors that explain differences in life expectancy—such as self-help skills, etiology of retardation, residential arrangements, and lifestyle factors—is important for both prevention of untimely death and for service and policy initiatives that can ameliorate such risk factors. The findings are also a bold reminder of the effects of environmental variables on the health of individuals with mental retardation. For many persons with mental retardation, the reward of having access to a system of care with standards of quality similar to that of the general population is an increase in their life expectancy. This accomplishment should reinforce ongoing efforts to raise the level of service in all communities to persons with mental retardation and their families.

Patterns of Age-Related Changes

A basic developmental question concerns the extent to which there is stability or change over the life course in various dimensions of individual functioning. For persons with mental retardation, the "front line" dimensions are adaptive behavior and cognitive skills. Although it can be argued that these dimensions are insufficient to describe the full range of important life functions, they are central to the study of mental retardation because of their prominence in the definition of the condition and because of the comparative sophistication of their measurement, as described by Widaman, Borthwick-Duffy, and Powell.

One of the most important findings from research is that, due to the heterogeneity of the population with mental retardation, there is no "typical" age-related trajectory in adaptive behavior or cognitive skills. Rather, age-related changes in these areas are conditioned by many preexisting and concurrent characteristics, particularly etiology, level of retardation, and lifestyle. Edgerton, for example, provided dramatic evidence regarding the capacity of change in life circumstances, along with age, to provoke or support remarkable growth in personal adaptive competence. He noted that persons with mild mental retardation who have lived independently from the formal service system tend to seem more "normative" in older age in comparison to their age peers without mental retardation than they did when they were younger. He noted that advancing age may bring relative increases in social competence, life satisfaction, and the ability to give meaningful support to others. In this vein, Edgerton asserted that many persons with mental retardation are "very good at being old, better, in fact, than they were at being young" (p. 53). His research illustrates that advancing years often bring a newfound stability and generativity for persons whose early adult lives were marked by precipitous highs and lows in personal functioning. His research is particularly powerful because he has followed a cohort of individuals for several decades, providing him with an enviable period of time over which to observe and record *individual* changes in adaptive behavior and social competence.

Edgerton's ethnographic studies have yielded vivid portrayals of adaptations and experiences of persons with mild mental retardation who do not receive formal mental retardation services. In contrast, Zigman, G. Seltzer, and Silverman's review of research on age-related changes examined trends in development in individuals who receive formal services. The large samples used in the research they summarized are characterized by heterogeneity with respect to levels of retardation, etiology of retardation, and current and historical residential settings. In contrast with the findings reported by Edgerton, a less optimistic portrayal of lifespan development emerges from these studies.

Zigman, G. Seltzer, and Silverman noted that patterns of aging differ depending upon the etiology of the retardation. For example, adults with Down syndrome over the age of 50 evidence age-associated deficits in adaptive skills in comparison to matched controls

and have an increased risk for dementia. Similarly, G. Seltzer and Luchterhand noted that persons with cerebral palsy experience substantial age-related changes in their musculoskeletal system, rendering them at risk for more severe ambulation difficulties and fractures. The research summarized by Zigman, G. Seltzer, and Silverman also confirms that intellectual capacity, as measured by standardized intelligence tests, remains relatively stable in persons without Down syndrome until about age 65. For persons with Down syndrome, however, intellectual capacity is relatively stable only until about age 45 to 50.

There is a strong need to describe and understand the difference between changes in functioning associated with *age* and changes in functioning associated with the *progressive expression of the underlying cause of retardation*. Results from this research will have special meaning for families of individuals with mental retardation (who provide the bulk of their care and support), for service providers (who must adjust programs and supports to the changing needs of the individuals they serve), and for policymakers (who must wrestle with the conflicting goals of ensuring high quality programs with expected standards of performance and allowing meaningful and sensitive adaptations of programs in light of the changing needs of participants). Until there is a stronger track record of experience and research on the extent to which age, *per se*, is responsible for specific adaptive, cognitive, social, and behavioral changes, it is vitally important that the progressive influence of the underlying disability, as well as the progressive impact of advancing age, be recognized as potentially *joint* contributors to observed changes in persons with mental retardation.

Factors Affecting Quality of Life

Scholarly and programmatic interest in the adult and elderly population with retardation has focused on factors associated with their quality of life. The issues that seem to define quality of life at this stage of the life course revolve around the maintenance of functional independence, the comfort that derives from a sensitive and responsive support network, the security of having a familiar and decent place to live, and the development of personally meaningful activities that replace or supplement traditional day or employment programs.

Several chapters in this volume (Freedman & Freedman; Heller & Factor; Smith, Fullmer, & Tobin) noted the importance of planning as a determinant of the *future* quality of life of persons with retardation who will likely survive their primary caretakers. Many older families have avoided or postponed the task of making residential, guardianship, and financial plans for their adult child with retardation. The reasons for avoidance of long-term planning are complex and go well beyond basic demographic factors such as ethnicity and socioeconomic status. The result, however, can be a precarious uncertainty about the future quality of life for adults with retardation.

Edgerton hypothesized that personality characteristics such as perseverance, optimism, self-esteem, sociability, and emotional equanimity shape the course and quality of life, especially for persons with mild retardation who do not receive formal services. However, once service providers are involved, according to Edgerton, many basic lifestyle choices are beyond the personal control of the individual with mental retardation because of the pervasive practice of substitute decision-making by professionals and family members. In such instances, the quality of life of persons with mental retardation is largely a function of the decisions made by others on behalf of such persons. The need to ask and act on the individual desires of persons with mental retardation is clearly a difficult challenge for service providers and families, as noted by Heller and Factor, but is required by law in many instances (see Freedman & Freedman).

A critical ingredient to maintaining a high quality of life is the availability of appropriate services. G. Seltzer and Luchterhand presented a rich description of a specially designed clinic that addresses a variety of issues facing older persons with mental re-

tardation. Although exemplary services such as the program at the University of Wisconsin may be the exception rather than the rule, it is important that the structure, operations, and goals of such programs be carefully documented and disseminated to other professionals and policymakers. The ability to replicate and adapt innovative service models is one measure of the strength of a service system. It is clear that innovative service models are not created easily—they require a talented cadre of dedicated professionals who share fundamental beliefs in the power of interdisciplinary models. Such models offer a degree of flexibility to older persons with mental retardation and their families, whose full range of strengths and needs may become evident after the intensive and extensive review that such inter-disciplinary clinics provide. Continued research on the important ingredients of such clinics will facilitate their replication in locations without the ready pool of talent that is typically available in university settings. As exemplified in the G. Seltzer and Luchterhand chapter, the field must continue to distill those elements of "best" programs that can be replicated in a much more diverse universe of service environments.

Janicki also highlighted the role of innovative service options for older persons with mental retardation. His focus, however, is on the role of public policies and of generic aging services for this population. Spurred by critical changes in federal legislation, the community service system should be much more receptive and integrative for older persons with mental retardation and their families in the future. Janicki's emphasis on capacity building within the service system and on the creative use of a wide array of service options that were not initially designed for persons with lifelong impairments illustrates the growing trend towards full inclusion models of services.

The Centrality of the Family

To a far greater extent than is typically acknowledged, the families of persons with mental retardation represent the most powerful and enduring component of their lives. As we noted in chapter 1, the vast majority of persons with mental retardation live with or under the supervision of their families throughout their lives. Three critical findings from the research presented on family care warrant emphasis. First, there is accumulating empirical evidence that family-based care brings its share of psychological and emotional rewards to parents and siblings of persons with mental retardation, as well as stresses and burdens. As we observed, the adaptational hypothesis of the impact of family-based care has engendered considerable support. Specifically, it seems that over time, most families accommodate to the extra requirements of rearing a member with retardation. Although there are undeniable stresses, parental health and psychological well-being are not unduly compromised in most families, and sibling relationships are often effectively maintained with a strong emotional base throughout the life span.

These findings suggest that professional predictions about lifelong family-based care, often reported by parents to have been discouraging and pessimistic, have not been borne out, as parents often perceive their son or daughter with retardation to have greater abilities and a better quality of life than they were initially led to expect. Therefore, there may be grounds to reappraise the content and context of long-term family caregiving. Further, the salutary effects experienced by some parents of a continued purpose and role in later life, the notion that the caregiving history of these mothers provides them with a "career" from which they have yet to retire, and the general resolve of many parents to maintain this role into the future, constitute important lessons for service providers, policymakers, and researchers.

The second important result from research on older families is that parental care does not guarantee future residential and financial security for adults with retardation. The difficulties that parents experience in establishing detailed and legally binding plans for their child with retardation have been reported consistently (see Heller & Factor;

Freedman & Freedman). Other family members (most notably, siblings) may well be willing and available to assume responsibility for the security of their relative with retardation when the parents are no longer able (see Heller & Factor; M. Seltzer & Krauss). However, the evidence suggests that parents of persons with retardation are no more likely to engage in long-term planning than are other adults in this country who resist the establishment of wills and financial plans.

The third important result from research on families is that some are estranged from the formal service system and therefore are not deriving the benefits for themselves or their child with retardation that the system is intended to provide (see Smith, Fullmer, & Tobin). There is a curious tension for policymakers and service planners in reconciling the national estimates that more than 63,000 individuals with mental retardation are waiting for residential services (Heller & Factor) with the unknown, but presumably large, number of families who resist or distrust the service system. As Edgerton noted, there are also many adults with retardation who live with virtually no safety net cast by families or service providers.

The factors that induce families and individuals to seek services, particularly as the families and individuals enter their older years, have not yet been identified. One intriguing hypothesis is offered by Heller and Factor, who observed that services are more likely to be sought by families who have specific risk characteristics, such as having a son or daughter with behavior problems, poor parental health, or less parental gratification with the caregiving role. It may be that as long as the adaptive capacities of families are intact and not severely strained, parents may view the service system with suspicion for its ability to supplant their own caregiving. The view of services as a helpful supporter of family caregiving may be achieved only when the need for support is more strongly experienced.

As Smith, Fuller, and Tobin discussed, it has been extremely difficult for service providers to discover effective mechanisms to reach out to older caregiving families who have resisted a major involvement with the service system. This suggests that the felt needs of older families may differ sharply from those of younger generations of parents, for whom support services have been more widely available. In part, the difficulties in providing supportive services to older families may rest on the struggle with control that often emerges between *families* and *professionals*. As our research illustrated (M. Seltzer & Krauss), most older parents are pleased and proud of their caregiving efforts and intend to maintain their roles as primary caregivers for as long as they are able. It is also the case, however, that professionals and service systems may view later-life family caregiving as a somewhat precarious or overly restrictive residential setting for adults with mental retardation. Efforts to assist families in advancing alternative plans may meet with strong resistance from families, which in turn generates frustrations among service providers.

The chapters by Heller and Factor and Freedman and Freedman took up the issue of long-term planning during this stage of life. What is clear is that there are multiple life trajectories that are being negotiated—those of the parents, those of the adults with mental retardation, and those of the siblings in the family—and each of these individuals may have important differences in expectations and preferences. The growing awareness among policymakers, service providers, and families of the complexity of long-term planning underscores the need for continued research on the factors that facilitate planning, the appropriate timing of such endeavors, and the constellation of individuals whose views on specific plans need to be incorporated.

The Long Lens

Throughout this volume, the value of longitudinal methods and a life-span perspective are acknowledged repeatedly. Many intriguing questions of human development can only be answered with prospective longitudinal research. Other questions addressing the antecedents of particular outcomes can only be answered by retrospective inquiry. Theoretical models of human development based on causal linkages between key events and outcomes are being challenged by new models that are less linear and more interactive with respect to describing and understanding the unfolding of human lives. Until recently, there was a virtual vacuum in our understanding of what happens to persons with mental retardation in their adult and elder years—with respect to cognitive development, adaptive behavior skills, mental health, social competence, life aspirations, the role of the environment as a facilitator or thwarter of growth, the effect of services on family and adult child well-being, etc.

This volume contains a number of illustrations of the value of the long lens. For example, Edgerton eloquently noted that individual trajectories change dramatically over time, with improvements in social competence and social expectations of behavior manifested at the later stages of the life course. Many of the very qualities that suggest social incompetence at one stage of life are tolerated or expected at another stage.

However, as clarified by Widaman, Borthwick-Duffy, and Powell, the study of how the lives of persons with mental retardation unfold is fraught with challenges. Some of these methodological challenges are common to developmental research in general (e.g., aging versus cohort effects, problems with attrition, comparability of measures across the life span), and some are specific to the developmental study of persons with mental retardation (e.g., early mortality, entry and exit from service system data bases, different developmental trajectories for different subgroups of the population with mental retardation). In addition, the issues presented in this chapter suggest the vulnerability or sensitivity of persons with mental retardation and their families to changes in legislation, social attitudes, and opportunities for inclusion, magnifying the risks of generalizing from one generation to another.

These challenges, however, should not dissuade investigators from embarking upon longitudinal, developmentally-oriented research. Rather, the articulation and discussion of these challenges should result in a growing literature on methods that addresses these issues in order to produce useful and defensible information on the development over time of individuals with mental retardation and their families.

The "long lens" of life course research extends not only to individuals with mental retardation and their families, but also to the service system that must adapt to different needs of individuals at different points in time. As Janicki noted, current thinking about service system supports incorporates the utilization of *a variety of sectors* within the full range of community-based programs. He noted the wide range of programs available to older persons in this country (without regard to individual disabilities) and the appropriateness of utilization of these services by and for persons with mental retardation. The emphasis on *inclusion* that is prevalent within the educational system for young persons with developmental disabilities is quite present within the service system for adults and elders as well. The emergence of new opportunities within the formal service system for persons with mental retardation will affect studies of the relation between environmental supports and individual development. The need for increased research activity to evaluate the effects of different environments and to identify subgroups for whom specific services or supports are most beneficial and cost-effective constitutes an obvious arena for invigorated investigation.

In the future, the lens we use in our research could fruitfully be broadened to include a wider variety of types of research—population-based studies (exemplified by the work of Eyman & Borthwick-Duffy), clinical investigations (as presented by G. Seltzer & Luchterhand), ethnographic studies (illustrated by Edgerton's research), quantitative analyses (as described by Widaman, Borthwick-Duffy, & Powell)—in order to develop a more complete understanding of the life experiences of persons with mental retardation and their families. That there are excellent examples within this volume of different research methods focused on a particular stage of development within the population with mental retardation attests to the growing strength of this area of research. That these diverse investigations have yielded a complex and differentiated portrait of the adult and elder years of persons with mental retardation, the challenges faced by their families, and the expansion of the service options available to them, attests to the value of systematic inquiry and observation within the human services arena. That there is much yet to be learned about this stage in the life course is also evident.

At this stage, the *questions* we ask about human development may be more important than the tentative *answers* we can give. Over the last few decades, discerning questions have been posed about the full life span of persons with mental retardation. The evidence that individual development continues throughout the life-span challenges the field to unravel the mysteries of that development, to seek new strategies for facilitating optimal development, to reach a new understanding of the meaning of lifelong development for the families and service systems that provide the basic support for such individuals, and to advance the practice of research in order to take stock of these important issues. The chapters in this volume illustrate the dividends that can accrue from careful investigation, diligent observation, and rigorous thinking about the meaning of development over the life course and the responses of families, professionals, and society to the challenge of mental retardation.

Contributors

Sharon A. Borthwick-Duffy, Ph.D.
School of Education
University of California at Riverside
Riverside, CA 92521

Robert B. Edgerton, Ph.D.
Department of Psychiatry and
    Biobehavioral Sciences
UCLA School of Medicine
740 Westwood Plaza
Los Angeles, CA 90024-1759

Richard K. Eyman, Ph.D.
School of Education
University of California at Riverside
Riverside, CA 92521

Alan Factor, Ph.D.
Illinois University Affiliated Program
    in Developmental Disabilities
University of Illinois at Chicago
1640 West Roosevelt Road
Chicago, IL 60608

Donald N. Freedman, J.D.
Concannon, Rosenberg, Freedman,
    Goldstein & Magence
246 Walnut Street
Newton, MA 02160

Ruth I. Freedman, Ph.D.
Boston University School of Social Work
264 Bay State Road
Boston, MA 02215

Elise M. Fullmer, Ph.D.
Department of Sociology, Anthropology,
    and Social Work
University of North Carolina, Charlotte
Charlotte, NC 28223

Tamar Heller, Ph.D.
Illinois University Affiliated Program
    in Developmental Disabilities
University of Illinois at Chicago
1640 West Roosevelt Road
Chicago IL 60608

Matthew P. Janicki, Ph.D.
New York State Office of Mental
Retardation and Developmental
    Disabilities
44 Holland Avenue
Albany, NY 12229

Marty Wyngaarden Krauss, Ph.D.
Heller School
Brandeis University
P. O. Box 9110
Waltham, MA 02254-9110

Charlene Luchterhand, M.S.S.W.
University of Wisconsin-Madison
Waisman Center
1500 Highland Avenue
Madison, WI 53705

Justina C. Powers
Department of Psychology
University of California at Riverside
Riverside, CA 92521

Craig Ramey, Ph.D.
Civitan International Research Center
University of Alabama at Birminghamn
1720 Seventh Avenue South
Birmingham, AL 35233

Sharon Landesman Ramey, Ph.D.
Civitan International Research Center
University of Alabama at Birmingham
1720 Seventh Avenue South
Birmingham, AL 35233

Gary B. Seltzer, Ph.D.
University of Wisconsin–Madison
Waisman Center and School of Social Work
1500 Highland Avenue
Madison, WI 53705

Marsha Mailick Seltzer, Ph.D.
University of Wisconsin–Madison
Waisman Center and School of Social Work
1500 Highland Avenue
Madison, WI 53705

Wayne P. Silverman, Ph.D.
New York State Institute for Basic Research
   in Developmental Disabilities
1050 Forest Road
Staten Island, NY 10314

Gregory C. Smith, Ed.D.
Department of Human Development
3304 Benjamin Building
University of Maryland
College Park, MD 20742

Sheldon S. Tobin, Ph.D.
Ringel Institute of Gerontology
School of Social Welfare
State University of New York at Albany
Albany, NY 12222

Keith F. Widaman, Ph.D.
Department of Pyschology
University of California at Riverside
Riverside, CA 92521

Warren B. Zigman, Ph.D.
New York State Institute for Basic Research
   in Developmental Disabilities
1050 Forest Hill Road
Staten Island, NY 10314

Index

Heart disease, 94, 96, 98, 118 (*see also* cardiovascular)
Hepatitis, 96, 111
HIV infection, 195
Home equity conversion, 158
Hospice care, 127-130
Housing (*see also* out-of-home placement)
    aging network, 145
    options, 157-158
    plans, 42
    quality of life, 116
Hydrocephalus, 96
Hypertension, 118
Hypothyroidism, 119, 125

I

Immobility, 95, 97, 121
Immune system, 133
Immunologic deficiencies, 120
Incompetency, 180 (*see also* competence)
Incontinence, 95, 96, 121
Independent living skills, 200
Infection
    chronic, 95
    gastrointestinal, 96
    hepatitis, 96
    HIV, 195
    respiratory, 94, 96, 97, 214
    sleep apnea, 119
    urinary tract, 121
Institutionalization, 70, 173 (*see also* out-of-home placement)
Intellectual ability, 75
Intellectual functioning, 174 (*see also* cognitive functioning)
IQ, 76-78, 78-80, 98, 198
Intelligence, 188, 190

L

Learning disabilities, 198
Legal majority, 170
Legal planning, 35, 41, 167-182
Legal rights, 134, 168, 169, 173
Leisure, 5, 130-132, 136, 173
Life expectancy (*see also* longevity, mortality)
    cohort effects, 70
    defined, 94
    increases, 4, 5, 67, 148, 214
    life-span studies, 195
    methods of determining, 94-95
    normal, 94
    predictors, 93, 95-98
    terminology, 96-97
    trends, 93-103
Life satisfaction, 30, 116
Life tables, 97
Longevity (*see also* life expectancy, mortality)
    general population, 98
    premature aging, 148
    service demands, 144
    severity of retardation, 93
    social support, 133

M

Maladaptive behavior(s)
    age-related change, 82
    diagnostic issues, 80, 84
    domains, 199, 200
    family support needs, 45
    life-span curves, 191
    out-of-home placements, 11, 43
    psychoactive medication, 81
Maternal well-being, 6-8, 30-31
Medi-Cal, 63
Medicaid
    financial planning, 170, 178, 180
    health care access, 25, 63, 114, 136,
Medicare, 63, 64, 114
Medication review, 123
Medication(s)
    adverse reactions, 83, 123
    antipsychotic, 123
    interactions, 64, 123
    overprescribing, 63, 64
    psychoactive, 81, 83, 123
    psychotropic, 83, 85, 123, 173
    repetitive behaviors, 127
    review, 123
    seizure, 121, 123
    side effects, 121, 123, 125
Memory, 71, 78, 79, 126
Mental health
    age-related change, 67-86
    assessment, 126-128
    service system data base, 197
Mental health problems, 80-84, 100
Mental illness, 56, 80, 81, 83, 197
Mental retardation
    borderline, 5, 77, 94
    cerebral palsy, 96
    definition, 118 n, 174, 188, 190, 195, 198
    level and differential mortality, 95, 96, 193, 194, 206
    poverty, 59
    prevalence, 195-196
    prevention, 196
Mental retardation service system, 34, 197
Mental status assessment, 126
Methodological issues (*see* research issues)
Mobility, 68, 95-98, 102
Mortality rates, 23, 67, 93-103, 193, 206
Mortality predictors, 93, 95-98
Motor integration skills, 117
Multiple sclerosis, 120
Muscle loss, 118
Musculoskeletal changes, 113, 118, 119, 214
Musculoskeletal impairments, 113
Myocardial infarction, 96

N

National policies, 143-148
Neuromuscular components of performance, 117
Neuropsychological measures of aging, 78-80
Neuropsychological test(s) 78-80, 125-126

interns, 118
job, 155
parents, 27
preretirement, 154
service providers, 181
sexuality, 130
skills, 101-102, 130
staff, 85, 113-114, 148, 150, 152
Training guides, 118 n
Transfer trauma, 44, 168-169
Transitions, guidelines for facilitating, 46
Transportation services
program access, 63, 134, 155, 156
utilization, 25, 26
Trust(s), 28, 41, 176, 179-181

Trustee(s), 176-177, 179-180, 181
Tube feeding, 97, 98, 99, 100, 103

U
Urinary tract infections, 121

V
Vision, 111, 118, 121, 122-123, 126, 150
Volunteering, 154-155

W
Will(s), 28, 170 (*see also* trust, estate)
Work (*see* employment)
Work and Retirement Planning Curriculum, 131